Scandinavian Design

Scandinavian Design

Alternative Histories

Edited by Kjetil Fallan

BERG
London · New York

English edition
First published in 2012 by
Berg
Editorial offices:
50 Bedford Square, London W1CB 3DP, UK
175 Fifth Avenue, New York, NY 10010, USA

Berg is an imprint of Bloomsbury Publishing Plc.

Library of Congress Cataloging-in-Publication Data

A catalogue record for this book is available from the Library of Congress.

British Library Cataloguing-in-Publication Data

A catalogue record for this book is available from the British Library.

ISBN 978 184788 912 6 (Cloth)
978 184788 911 9 (Paper)
e-ISBN 978 085785 218 2 (individual)

Typeset by Apex Publishing, LLC, Madison, WI, USA
Printed in the UK by the MPG Books Group

www.bergpublishers.com

Contents

Illustrations

About the Authors

MALENE BREUNIG is Associate Professor of Cross-Aesthetic Studies in the Department of Literature, Media and Cultural Studies at the University of Southern Denmark. She holds a PhD in cross-aesthetic studies from the University of Southern Denmark and is the author of *Tolkninger af det intime* (2007), on the notion of the intimate within literature and art, and the co-author of *Vilkår og tolkninger: Billeder af dansk kulturhistorie 1700–2000* (2010), on the development of modern culture in Denmark interpreted through different aesthetic modes of expression. Dr Breunig has also published articles on Poul Henningsen's lighting design and on the modernist standards of 'good taste' as practiced by the Louisiana Museum of Modern Art.

KJETIL FALLAN is Associate Professor of Design History in the Department of Philosophy, Classics, History of Art and Ideas at the University of Oslo. He has studied engineering design, sociology and history and holds a PhD in cultural history from the Norwegian University of Science and Technology. He is the author of *Design History: Understanding Theory and Method* (Berg, 2010) and a number of articles on various aspects of design history published in journals like *Design Issues*, *Journal of Design History*, *Enterprise and Society* and *History and Technology*. Dr Fallan also serves on the Editorial Board of the *Journal of Design History*.

HANS-CHRISTIAN JENSEN is Associate Professor of Design History in the Department of Literature, Media and Cultural Studies at the University of Southern Denmark, where he also earned his PhD. He was actively involved in the research project (2006–9) investigating the cultural criticism of Poul Henningsen as co-editor (with Carl-Erik Bay) of *Tradition og modernisme: Indfaldsvinkler til PH* (Syddansk Universitetsforlag, 2008) and contributing author to another anthology resulting from the same project, *Kulturmoderniseringens paradokser* (Syddansk Universitetsforlag, 2010).

ESPEN JOHNSEN is Associate Professor of Architectural and Design History in the Department of Philosophy, Classics, History of Art and Ideas at the University of Oslo. He holds a PhD in art history from the University of Oslo and was previously Senior Curator and Research Coordinator at the Norwegian Museum of Cultural History (Norsk Folkemuseum). Dr Johnsen has written extensively on early-twentieth-century interior design, mid-twentieth-century architecture and contemporary design. Recent research projects include co-curating and editing the catalogue for the exhibition Discords: Norwegian Architecture 1945–65, shown at the National Museum of Art, Architecture and Design in 2010–11.

FINN ARNE JØRGENSEN is Associate Senior Lecturer in the History of Technology and Environment at Umeå University, Sweden. He holds a PhD in science and technology studies from the Norwegian University of Science and Technology and is the author of *Making a Green Machine: The Infrastructure of Beverage Container Recycling* (Rutgers University Press, 2011). His current research includes a project on Scandinavian leisure cabin culture.

PEKKA KORVENMAA is Professor of Design and Culture at and Vice Dean of the Aalto University School of Art and Design, Helsinki. He holds a PhD in art history from the University of Helsinki, specializing in the history of architecture. From 1991 he has worked at his present institution, first as Research Director and from 2000 as Professor. He was also deeply involved in generating a national design policy program for Finland in the late 1990s and has since acted as a design policy consultant to foreign governments as well. Professor Korvenmaa has published extensively on Finnish architectural and design history. His latest book is *Finnish Design: A Concise History* (University of Art and Design Books, 2009).

SARA KRISTOFFERSSON is Guest Professor of Design History and Theory at Konstfack University College of Arts, Crafts and Design in Stockholm and a critic writing in *Svenska Dagbladet*, one of Sweden's major morning newspapers. She holds a PhD in art history and visual studies from the University of Gothenburg. Dr Kristoffersson has published a number of articles on various aspects of design, fashion, art and architecture and lectures widely on these topics at museums and universities. She is currently working on a research project about IKEA.

STIG KVAAL is Associate Professor of Science and Technology Studies at the Norwegian University of Science and Technology, Department of Interdisciplinary Studies of Culture, Centre for Technology and Society. He holds a PhD in history from the Norwegian University of Science and Technology. His main research interests are the cultural history of food and kitchen technologies, consumption and science policy. Dr Kvaal has also published widely in the field of business history and the history of research and higher educational institutions.

HELENA MATTSSON is Associate Professor of History and Theory of Architecture at the Royal Institute of Technology in Stockholm. Her doctoral thesis was published in 2004 as *Arkitektur och konsumtion: Reyner Banham och utbytbarhetens estetik* ('Architecture and consumption: Reyner Banham and the aesthetic of expendability'). She has written extensively on architecture, art and culture and is the co-editor (with Sven-Olov Wallenstein) of *Swedish Modernism: Architecture, Consumption and the Welfare State* (London: Black Dog, 2010). Mattsson headed a research project at the Museum of Architecture in Stockholm, Architecture and Consumption in Sweden 1930–1970 (from 2005 to 2007), and is a member of the Editorial Board of the journal *SITE*.

ANDERS V. MUNCH is Associate Professor of Design History in the Department of Literature, Media and Cultural Studies at the University of Southern Denmark and Adjunct Professor at the Oslo School of Architecture and Design. He has studied the history of ideas and art history, and his PhD thesis from the University of Aarhus has been translated into German and published as *Der stillose Stil: Adolf Loos* (Fink, 2005). His writings on design history include the articles 'Design as Gesamtkunstwerk' and 'Throughout Any Scale', both published in the *Scandinavian Journal of Design History* (2001, 2004).

PER ØSTBY is Professor of the History of Technology at the Norwegian University of Science and Technology, Department of Interdisciplinary Studies of Culture, Centre for Technology and Society. He holds a PhD in history from the Norwegian University of Science and Technology. His research focuses on the cultural integration of science and technology, especially within medicine, biotechnology, environmental issues but also examines the cultural implications of design and innovation, as well as the history of the environment and of mass motorization and transport. Professor Østby has participated in or directed several national and international research projects within these fields.

MINNA SARANTOLA-WEISS is Head of Research at Helsinki City Museum. She holds a PhD in history from the University of Helsinki, and her research interests include the history of interiors, the furniture industry and design, as well as history of the postwar consumer society. Amongst her publications are the monographs *Sohvaryhmän läpimurto: Kulutuskulttuurin tulo suomalaisiin olohuoneisiin* on Finnish consumer culture and domestic interiors (Finnish Literature Society, 2003) and *Reilusti ruskeaa: 1970-luvun arkea* (WSOY, 2008) on everyday life and consumption in the 1970s Finland.

LEENA SVINHUFVUD is Curator of Education at Design Museum Helsinki. She has curated several museum exhibitions on textiles and craft, for example the exhibition Ryijy! The Finnish Ryijy-Rug in 2009, for which she also edited the catalogue. She holds a PhD in art history from the University of Helsinki and has published widely on Finnish textile art and design. Dr Svinhufvud is currently engaged in a research project on hand weaving as a medium of woman designers.

STINA TEILMANN-LOCK is a Postdoctoral Research Fellow at the Faculty of Law, University of Copenhagen. She has studied comparative literature, rhetoric and political science at the University of Copenhagen and holds a PhD in comparative literature from the University of Southern Denmark. She is the author of *British and French Copyright: A Historical Account of Aesthetic Implications* (DJØF Publishing, 2009) and co-editor of *Art and Law: The Copyright Debate* (DJØF Publishing, 2005) and has published numerous articles on copyright and intellectual property. She has worked as a patent administrator and has held a Carlsberg research fellowship at the Danish Design School.

JEFF WERNER is Professor of Art History at Stockholm University. Previously he has been Director of Research at Göteborg Museum of Art and Professor of Art History and Visual Culture at Gotland University. He holds a PhD in art history from the University of Gothenburg. His 2008 two-volume publication *Medelvägens estetik* discusses relations between the production of country images and Swedish visual culture in the USA. Together with Kristoffer Arvidsson he is the editor of the scholarly publication series Skiascope. In addition to his work on design history, Professor Werner has published a number of articles and books about museums and collections and historiography, as well as modern and contemporary art.

CHRISTINA ZETTERLUND is Senior Lecturer in the History of Craft and Design at Konstfack University College of Arts, Crafts and Design in Stockholm and a freelance curator. She holds a PhD in art history from Uppsala University and has previously worked as a curator at the Röhsska Museum in Gothenburg and as a special advisor in design matters at the Ministry of Industry. Dr Zetterlund has been involved in several research projects, including Design History in Sweden, which analysed the history writing of the Swedish applied art museums, and Forms of Sustainability, examining critical perspectives in history writing as well as in current design practice.

Introduction

Kjetil Fallan

Scandinavian design is not all it is cracked up to be—but then again, it is also so much more. The straightjacket of mythologies meticulously woven around design from the Nordic countries by marketers, promoters and historians alike has resulted in a strong but severely distorted image of what Scandinavian design is. Particularly the international and popular reception of this cleverly crafted concept has led to a disturbingly narrow understanding of Nordic design culture. There are countless cases that run counter to the master narratives; that elude canonization or otherwise represent an 'otherness' and thus make up alternative histories. Through different views on and approaches to our common topic the alternative histories presented in this book offer a corrective to the persistent mythologies and pervasive reductive accounts of Scandinavian design.

The image on the front cover shows the tablecloth Underfull by Norwegian designer Kristine Bjaadal (prototype, 2009). At first glance this tablecloth appears to be a traditional white floral damask, but it contains the most wonderful secret: a hidden pattern that is revealed only when wet—turning spilling into poetry. An everyday negative situation is turned into a positive experience by the tablecloth becoming a conversation piece, generating stories. In the prototype, butterflies spread out over the woven floral pattern, creating a layered image. The concept allows a collection of different patterns, making for different stories. Both through its layering of imagery and through its facilitation of alternative narratives, the Underfull tablecloth provides an excellent illustration of what the present publication seeks to achieve.

The English-language literature on Scandinavian design is sparse. What little there is largely falls into two categories: general survey histories and singular accounts of individual designers, companies and the like. Much of it is also rather celebratory—explicitly or implicitly—in nature. Based on twelve case studies forming alternative histories of Scandinavian design, this book proposes a different format and approach, allowing critical, in-depth analysis of the material while also providing a scope beyond the individual cases.

The book highlights examples of design culture that are marginalized in existing accounts of Scandinavian design. Alternative histories are drawn from underrepresented fields such as transport design, engineering design, packaging and corporate identity, and the cases focus on unconventional topics like anonymous design, systems design, design photography and design legislation. Each is approached from different perspectives, focusing variously on production, mediation and consumption—or a combination thereof. The cases also represent different nations/regions, different industries, different time periods and different theoretical perspectives and methodological approaches.

Any volume with the term 'Scandinavian Design' in the title must include a clarification of that term, as its meaning is far from given. First of all, we need to bear in mind the crucial distinction between the concept 'Scandinavian Design' (often signified with a capital *D*) as an actor's category and the term 'Scandinavian design' (with a lower-case *d*) as an analytical category. As an actor's category the definition of the term and the meanings ascribed to it are that of historical actors, based on their sociocultural context and their motives and agendas. As an analytical category, on the other hand, the term becomes a tool with which historians describe and categorize historical phenomena. It should be fairly obvious that significant discrepancies may occur between the two, and it is essential to distinguish between them—especially since any historical study of Scandinavian design will have to manage both.

The geographical component of the term 'Scandinavian design' may seem to be quite straightforward, but even this needs some deliberation. Strictly speaking, the geographical definition of Scandinavia is limited to the three countries Denmark, Norway and Sweden, whereby the latter two comprise the Scandinavian Peninsula. In other words: Finland is not part of Scandinavia by such a geographical definition. Finland is, however—alongside Iceland and the Scandinavian nations—a Nordic country. But geography is complicated by politics. Finland was part of the Swedish kingdom for centuries until it was ceded to Russia in 1908. An independent republic since 1919, it nevertheless harbours a Swedish-language minority to this day. Iceland was populated by Norwegians in the ninth century and joined when the union of Norway and Denmark was established in 1380—a union which for an extended fifteenth century also included Sweden. Whereas Iceland remained under Danish rule until independence was declared in 1944, in 1814 Denmark lost its dominion over Norway, whose subsequent union with Sweden lasted until full independence was won in 1905. Thus, in a historical geopolitical perspective, the divide between the Nordic and the Scandinavian is not at all clear-cut, and these countries' common history has resulted in a significant cultural unity—although by no means eradicating national differences. Also, when from the early nineteenth century on nationalist movements made their mark all over Europe, in Scandinavia they were paralleled by an ideological and political Scandinavianism conceived as a convenient meso sphere, or buffer, between these small nations and the world at large.[1]

But why, then, is Finland included in most understandings of and publications on Scandinavian design, whereas Iceland (mostly) is not? This is where the significance of 'Scandinavian Design' as an actor's category becomes so manifest: when that phrase was coined as a specific concept in the mid-twentieth century, the actors involved in its construction chose to include Finland in their definition of the concept and the events that underpinned it. Their habitual exclusion of Iceland may be largely due to a relative lack of corresponding infrastructures but perhaps partly also to that country's relative remoteness, minute size and late independence.

The term 'Scandinavian Design' also has a temporal component requiring clarification. It was coined in a specific historical context in connection with exhibitions showcasing contemporary design from Denmark, Finland, Norway and Sweden in Britain and North America in the 1950s. As an actor's category, then, it has a severely restricted use and meaning as it pertains to a narrow definition of design made and presented during a distinct and limited period in time. To apply the term to older and more recent design, then, implies a shift in the understanding of the concept from actor's category to analytical category.

In addition to these geographical and temporal dimensions the concept Scandinavian Design is delineated by a material aspect as well: far from representing a cross section of Nordic design culture, the products promoted under the catchphrase—or brand—'Scandinavian Design' formed a particular and carefully orchestrated blend of gourmet objects selected from a very narrow segment of the region's design practice. This clearly is to be understood in light of the concept's origin as a promotional tool, and it is only to be expected that exhibitions of the kind through which the term 'Scandinavian Design' gained currency for strategic reasons displayed almost exclusively objects for the home conforming to a modernist notion of aesthetic quality. What is worrying, though, is that this conception of Scandinavian Design, through a seemingly unreflexive blurring of actor's category and analytical category, to a large degree has been perpetuated, creating a homogenizing effect resulting in narrow design historical accounts that push the rest of the highly varied design production in Scandinavia out of sight.

Because of the currency attached to Scandinavian Design as a shorthand signifier, the term has been chosen as the title of this book. This does not mean that the subject matter of the book and the understanding of design it conveys are restricted to that described in the preceding as the actor's-category version of the term. Although—coherent with the actor's category—the present study includes Finland and excludes Iceland from its purview, Scandinavian design is here intended as an analytical category. This is reflected in how the book covers a time period that far exceeds that normally associated with the designation-cum-title and treats an array of design culture that pushes far beyond what is conventionally considered under the heading of Scandinavian Design. As an analytical category, the term is disconnected from the restricted use and meaning assigned to it by its conceptual architects and may be appropriated as a category simply denoting design from Denmark, Finland, Norway and Sweden.

What, then, is Scandinavian about Scandinavian design? Is there anything specifically Scandinavian about Carlsberg, Nokia, Helly Hansen and IKEA—or Scandinavian Airlines for that matter? The notoriously difficult question of national and regional design styles has long haunted design history and has taken on renewed importance in the wake of the massive increase in international trade and global production and consumption networks over the last several decades. Far from unproblematic in the many studies of the role of design in late-nineteenth-century nationalism—particularly prevalent in then-emerging nation states like Finland and Norway—and in studies of design as an economic and cultural catalyst in countries that—like Greece, Portugal and Spain—made the leap from dictatorships to European Union membership in the 1970s and 1980s, the question becomes even more convoluted in the age of globalization. No matter the historical context, pinning down 'national characteristics' is a futile task normally resulting in a list of adjectives that are superficial and stereotypical at best, outright demeaning and petty caricature at worst. Equally reductive are the merely stylistic pigeonholes whereby a whole nation's or region's design output is summarized in a few idiosyncrasies.

Scandinavian design has had more than its share of such simplistic characterization, especially in design journalism and popular history accounts, which tend to be littered with words like 'humane', 'democratic', 'organic' and 'blond'. Whatever its shapes and guises, the question of national and regional design styles is also fed back into promotional processes. What does it mean when a company like Muuto adopts as its slogan 'New Nordic'? Viviana Narotzky considers this practice a vulgarization of the issue of design and regional and national identity: 'The distancing of nationalism and ideology, and the former's reduction to commodity-led, business-oriented formalism, became the cornerstone of approaches to design and national identity . . . throughout the late twentieth century.'[2] Although not a study that reclaims the notion of national style from the realm of commerce and promotion, this book refrains from all essentialist definitions of national and regional traits in products and people alike.

While this volume does have a regional framework, it does not make a case for a particular 'regional style' of Scandinavian design; on the contrary, one of its ambitions is to challenge and nuance the image of Scandinavian design. Regions and nations are complex and contested units but nonetheless make viable arenas for studying design history. The mesh of cultural, social, political and economic configurations and codes that makes up our society clearly contributes to maintaining the regional and the national as valid categories of demarcation and identity. It is thus both possible and meaningful to discuss Scandinavian design in its own right and on its own terms, without striving to find some innate 'Scandinavian-ness' in its form.[3]

As announced, this book presents alternative histories: a set of cases that run counter to the master narratives and complement established histories. While such re-evaluation and supplementation are the mark of healthy scholarship in history at large, it seems particularly appropriate in the history of Scandinavian design. At least since Jean-Francois Lyotard pronounced the demise of the master narratives—*grands récits*—more than thirty years ago, and with it the fragmentation of history,[4] we have witnessed a growing awareness of the relativity and plurality of historical accounts—a development catalysed by the work of scholars like Hayden White and Dominick LaCapra on the literary and rhetorical nature of historical writing.[5] In this sense, the postmodern challenge to history implies a crisis in the narratives' abilities to compel consensus—and thus become master narratives.

From an early stage many design historians have acknowledged this requirement for histories in the plural as a response to the discipline's monistic tendencies, such as its modernist hegemony and class and gender bias. Fran Hannah and Tim Putnam, for example, argued in 1980 that 'the meaning of design is continually being re-constituted' and that 'therefore there must be multiple *histories* of design'.[6] Similarly, in 1989 John Walker reminded us that 'there are always multiple histories, various histories of design'.[7]

When the history of Scandinavian design, at least in its popular and international reception, seems to have cultivated rather than challenged lingering master narratives, it is pertinent to question whether its research literature is too conformist and homogeneous—in other words: whether it has taken on the challenge posed by recent historiography and by theoretical discourses in international design history. In Scandinavia, design history remained for a long time relatively conventional in its subject matter, disciplinary framework, theoretical underpinnings and methodological approaches. This is not to detract from the quality or significance of research carried out in this context; surely, much fine work on important topics has been produced under this traditional paradigm. But at the same time it should be clear that such a setting is not ideal for challenging conformity—a key ambition in recent historiography.

The situation has changed significantly over the last decade or two, however, with a considerable expansion of the scholarly community, a broadening of the empirical horizon and increased interdisciplinarity. The result has been a marked growth in output, much of which is characterized precisely by an invigorating multiplicity, heterogeneity and criticism. Unfortunately, most of this work has received only a limited readership due to language barriers and publishing venues with less than optimal distribution. This volume is a modest effort to improve this situation, by drawing on current research that in various ways challenges the orthodoxies of established design history in Scandinavia and presenting it in an accessible form as a coherent selection of alternative histories of Scandinavian design.

The histories offered here represent alternatives in that they both enrich and disrupt established historical narratives. It is paramount, though, to emphasize that the ambition of the book is not merely to fill in a few blank spots in the canonical accounts. The poverty of such an enterprise was made evident by one strand of early feminist art and design history, whose desire to recover (great) women artists and designers amounted to little more than a (slight) expansion of the orthodox canonical system.[8] New empirical material—whether it concerns female practitioners or other less explored areas on the design historical map—should move beyond the additive aspect and be employed also in raising new questions contributing to the historiographic discourse. The work gathered here seeks to do so in a number of ways, with the common aim to invite new perspectives on design culture.

Although design history is just as much history *from* things as it is history *of* things, a history of ideas as much as a history of artefacts, material objects remain key to our endeavour. In its engagement with artefacts, this volume is dominated by everyday objects, quotidian things. Despite the prominence awarded to exclusive objects in much design history, considering more mundane objects is nothing new. But when everyday objects have been included in design historical writing, they have often been aestheticized and mythologized and thus effectively lifted out of their quotidian context. Particularly common in museums, this is also what led Theodor Adorno to declare that 'museum and mausoleum are connected by more than phonetic association'.[9] The Museum of Modern Art in New York has perfected this approach, from the Machine Art exhibition in 1934 to the Humble Masterpieces show in 2004.[10] In contrast, this book strives to understand everyday objects primarily in terms of the many and varied relations they form part of. When exclusive objects do feature, they are subjected to analyses that constitute critiques of the very processes of aestheticization and mythologization already mentioned, thus joining rank with their more modest brethren under the banner of counter-history.[11]

For the notion of alternative histories to make sense, an understanding of established histories is required. Recognizing the scarcity of English-language academic publications on Scandinavian design, this volume starts off with a chapter outlining the historiography of design in the region. The chapter is divided into five sections: one discussing literature with a pan-Scandinavian or pan-Nordic scope, followed by four sections discussing the national literatures of Denmark, Finland, Norway and Sweden respectively. Most of the design history literature from the Nordic countries is published in native languages only, and since hardly anyone outside the region speaks our languages, these considerable resources are thus not accessible to the rest of the world. By offering an English-language historiographic survey we hope that this book may provide non-Nordic students and scholars with a fuller knowledge of the region's design history literature, past and present. Such a survey could surely merit a volume in its own right. Therefore, given the restricted space available in the present context, the historiography presented here will have to be compendious. Necessarily more descriptive than analytical in character, its chief ambition is to offer an overview of the existing literature and its subject matters, themes and approaches. As far as the format allows, however, the literature surveyed is discussed in a critical manner, thus affording a more informed reading.

Following the historiographic survey, the book is structured in three parts: *Networks, Appropriations* and *Mediations*. This structure reflects the theoretical ambitions and thematic approaches of the individual chapters but also serves as a pedagogical device clarifying the book's contribution to contemporary developments in design history's theory and method. Any organizing principle necessarily entails a certain rigidity and risk of simplistic categorization. Several of the texts included here touch upon issues that are pertinent to more than one of the three subheadings. Despite its 'impurity', it is hoped that the thematic grouping will help improve coherence in an otherwise heterogeneous collection of texts and show that their value as a whole is greater than the sum of the parts.

Contrary to the popular myth of the genius individual and disinterested experience, design is by no means an autonomous phenomenon. Far from it; design is fundamentally embedded in the societal texture. Consequently, what Hazel Conway has dubbed 'the heroic approach' is ill suited in understanding design culture.[12] In acknowledgement of this, design historians are taking a greater interest in how design is enmeshed in systems and networks and are studying how these are constructed and how they function. Although true of all types of design, everywhere and at all times, the cooperative and relational nature of design emphasized by a systems or networks perspective is perhaps particularly evident in design for industrial manufacture.

The systemic and networked nature of design was made abundantly clear already in the early stages of the Industrial Revolution, when Adam Smith used the example of the labourer's coat to demonstrate the virtually endless number of connections that can be made in tracing the network underpinning the manufacture of this unassuming product.[13] More recently, Vilém Flusser has remarked how 'industrial production, including design, has developed into a complex network . . . Consequently, it has become necessary to act in teams combining human and artificial components'.[14] What is especially interesting about these two descriptions, written more than 200 years apart, is the prominence given to the non-human inhabitants of the networks. How material matters has been subject to much attention both in design history and in several other neighbouring fields, but the explicit elaboration of how non-humans and humans are integrated in socio-technical systems is probably articulated most radically under the auspices of actor-network theory (ANT), an approach which—along with other, related theoretical frameworks developed in science and technology studies (STS)—has been met with considerable interest in design studies.[15] One specifically rewarding feature of these approaches is that they circumvent the conventional production–consumption dichotomy that long proved so tenacious in the histories of design and technology alike.

The first part of this book explores the systemic and networked nature of design in a variety of ways. Through a case study basking in a decidedly underexploited reservoir—design's legislative framework—Stina Teilmann-Lock uncovers the intricate systems constructed to regulate and enforce legal protection of design in Denmark. Investigating how Danish courts have interpreted copyright law from its 1908 revision to include applied art until today, Teilmann-Lock traces a network crucial to the power relations of design in terms of economics, ethics and aesthetics.

Leena Svinhufvud's contribution maps out networks of design in at least two distinct, but related, conceptions. Taking a closer look at Finnish textiles sold by the yard from the interwar period, she effectively problematizes some stubborn assumptions regarding manufacturing systems, disrupting demarcations between artistic creativity, craft skills and industrial technology. At the same time, the case chosen shows how the textiles in question played a central but subdued role in broader portrayals of modern design, thus critiquing discriminatory practices administered through professional and promotional networks.

A different take on the systemic approach to design is represented by Helena Mattsson's study of the Swedish Cooperative Union's grand effort at configuring its consumers through the introduction of a new corporate policy around 1970. This organization, with official and highly developed links to the spheres of manufacture, distribution and retailing as well as to governmental bodies and political agencies, was in a unique position to forge elaborate networks and establish a comprehensive design strategy and a carefully orchestrated design practice. Despite this favourable setting, Mattsson argues, the concerted attempts at designing the eternal consumer would prove a far less predictable and more arduous task than designing products.

Just how heterogeneous, complex and significant networks of design can be is revealed in Finn Arne Jørgensen's analysis of the reverse vending machines (RVMs) for beverage container recycling manufactured by the Norwegian company Tomra Systems. The remarkably inconspicuous design of these objects, which are little more than holes in supermarket walls, belies the density of meaning permeating the socio-technical system through which they work. Designing a hole in the wall is no easy feat but rather a constellation of forces ranging from technological development and international business management to governmental policymaking and the onset of environmental concerns.

Part 2 of this book explores appropriations. It follows from the understanding of design as something fundamentally systemic and networked that both the making and meaning of design more often than not are conditioned by existing experiences. One way of making sense of this acknowledgement is to ask how ideas about design move through time, society and space and are appropriated, translated and converted into new entities of mind and matter. The notion of appropriations applied here is drawn from the work of Mikael Hård and Andrew Jamison, whose studies of intellectual and cultural appropriations of technology have proved the value of the concept.[16] A key feature is that the visions and ideas in question are always negotiated and that they are adapted to the cultural settings in which they are introduced while the appropriators simultaneously also adjust to what is being appropriated. Hård and Jamison define appropriation as the process whereby people seek to make sense of new products and concepts, but, clearly, historical artefacts and ideas are also subject to appropriations—as evidenced, for example, by Elisabeth Guffey's investigation of retro culture.[17] Although empirically dissimilar, the texts making up this second part of the book all engage with such processes of appropriation where design culture—new and old—is negotiated and transformed.

In her contribution, Christina Zetterlund questions the contemporary use of the Swedish design 'heritage', tracing central features of the particular and partial picture thus created of a much more diverse historical reality to the marginalization of the decorative in early-twentieth-century Swedish design ideology. Zetterlund thus construes canonization as the appropriation of select designs meeting specific criteria laid down by a professional and cultural elite along distinct ideological and political guidelines, whilst at the same time also revealing the selective appropriation of Swedish design history by governmental bodies for promotional purposes and by commercial businesses for marketing purposes.

Shifting focus from the usage of domestic heritage to the international flow of ideas and local interpretations of a design paradigm normally considered foreign to Scandinavia, my own chapter investigates the curious case of Oslo's streamlined aluminium trams. The Norwegian appropriation of streamlining, which is primarily associated with the USA, provides a favourable opportunity to explore the centre-periphery model featured in recent discourse on design history's geographical biases and to critique its implicit hierarchies of significance.[18] In another sense, the monocoque aluminium tram under scrutiny also illustrates how design constitutes an appropriation of new technology, as design is the interface through which technological artefacts acquire and articulate meaning.

In a study which portrays the non-appropriation of 'good design' as the mirror image of the appropriation of comfortable furniture, Minna Sarantola-Weiss charts the massive popularity of the upholstered sofa group in Finland in the 1970s and 1980s as a physical manifestation of the onset of what she terms a hedonistic consumer culture. Part of a design culture completely at odds with the ascetic ideals of modernist Finnish design, this type of furniture, in all its ubiquity, represents a sobering reminder of the limited success of the 'good design' movement and comprises solid testimony of consumers' resistance to missionaries of taste.

Processes of appropriation work on many levels. This becomes particularly evident in the fourth and last chapter of part 2, Hans-Christian Jensen's critical analysis of a contemporary Danish 'lifestyle' kitchen—the Lifa kitchen designed by the consultancy Jacob Jensen Design. This case study simultaneously depicts the appropriation of the personal 'aura' of a famed designer to promote the services of a company and peddle its eponymous product line and the appropriation of a signature formal language developed through the consultancy's collaboration with Bang & Olufsen from the 1960s onwards to (ever) new settings and products. Jensen even proposes a third conception whereby the meticulous management of meaning in the design and mediation of the Lifa kitchen can be seen as a pre-appropriation of it on behalf of the consumer. Personality cults and branding strategies are core issues in this much-needed critique of the way design and 'designer goods' tend to be portrayed in the media and the public realm.

The third and final part of the book discusses mediations: the sites, processes and agents involved in the mediation of and by design. Mediation is a process where information is communicated, but mediators are never neutral conveyers; they inevitably affect and transform the message.[19] Mediations can thus be seen as translations. And as surely as meaning can be lost in translation, meaning can also be gained in translation. As fluid, relational spaces in which the meanings of things are formed, mediations are increasingly acknowledged as a particularly fertile ground for understanding design culture, both by design history and by related fields such as the history and sociology of technology.[20] Although thirty years have passed since Dick Hebdige pointed to mediation as one of three 'moments' in the design cultural continuum alongside production and consumption,[21] it is only in more recent years that the amount of research into this sphere can be said to have reached critical mass, making mediation a central concern in design history. Following a long-standing tradition of focusing on the production side of design, and the later interest in the consumption of design, mediation has recently been identified as, in the words of Grace Lees-Maffei, 'a third stream in design history, with three currents': studying how design is mediated through various communication channels, studying the design of these channels/platforms and studying designed objects as mediators of meaning.[22] The first of these streams is probably the strongest as of now and has resulted in a strand of studies on how design is mediated in, for example, retailing, television, film, magazines, museums, and exhibitions.[23] This conception of mediation is represented in the texts included here as well, but these also provide a broader understanding of the concept, spanning from corporate branding practices to national design policies. Moreover, the notion of designed objects *as* mediators appears in at least two of the case studies in this section.

Through a case study venturing into areas of design practice that normally fly under the radar of design history—foodstuffs and packaging—Stig Kvaal and Per Østby follow the Norwegian chocolate bar Stratos through hardship and mutations since its inception in 1936, focusing on a massive rebranding campaign in the 1980s. Providing a fascinating picture of how product design, packaging design and advertising design combine to form a dynamic force in mediating the product, Kvaal and Østby demonstrate how, on the one hand, design is a crucial component in the mediation of the product, while, on the other hand, the designed product itself also becomes a mediator in the sense that it co-shapes human experience.[24]

Photography is one of the most manifest modes of mediating design, but it remains all the same little explored in design history. In what might seem fairly objective representations, objects of high modernism are typically portrayed in white spaces with few distracting elements. Yet such framing of design creates aesthetic, historical and ideological meanings that are far from neutral. Through an analysis of photographer Keld Helmer-Petersen's portrayal of Poul Kjærholm's furniture design, Malene Breunig argues that iconic products do not derive their status primarily from their intrinsic properties but that their meaning to a large extent is constructed by how they are mediated in images.

Branching out from the very literal understanding of image as photographic representation to a figurative conception of image as constructed meaning, Jeff Werner challenges the geography of identity, meaning and design in his case study of how Volvo cars have been portrayed and perceived in the USA. As the car industry has become fundamentally international, national imagery persists in its mediation practices. This essay examines the design, promotion and reception of Volvo in the USA, probing its mediated 'Swedish-ness' and investigating the relationship between image, brand and design.

Expanding the scope from the corporate to the political scene, Pekka Korvenmaa demonstrates the broad range and rich texture of the mediation concept through an analysis of Finnish national design-promotion strategies. Here, mediation takes the form of professional, public and political design discourse. Tracing how central institutions revised their views on the role of design in response to the drastic changes in international trade, business structures, manufacturing systems, design practice, consumption patterns and political ideologies in the 1960s and 1970s, Korvenmaa demonstrates how design policies became politics.

The three themes outlined here do not cover the theoretical ground of the recent historiography of design any more than the twelve cases presented provide a survey of Scandinavian design history. There are, of course, many issues and approaches which could be valuable in a reappraisal of the topic at hand that are not explored here, but these will have to wait for future publications presenting further alternative histories. Nevertheless, the ambition of this book is to highlight some of the more current concerns in design history—in Scandinavia and elsewhere—through a selection of case studies that, although by no means exhaustive, represent alternative histories of Scandinavian design and also go some way in providing a representative image of the current state of design historical scholarship in Scandinavia.

–1–

A Historiography of Scandinavian Design

Kjetil Fallan, Anders V. Munch, Pekka Korvenmaa, Espen Johnsen, Sara Kristoffersson and Christina Zetterlund

PAN-SCANDINAVIAN LITERATURE

In contrast to the common currency awarded to Scandinavian design as a terminological concept, there is actually relatively little design history writing that has a pan-Scandinavian or pan-Nordic scope, that is literature covering design history in Scandinavia as a whole. A partial exception is the segment known as coffee table books, which exist in abundance on Scandinavian design: lavishly illustrated, extravagantly designed, generous in format, hagiographic and mythopoeic in style. Coffee table books are significant in the sense that they perhaps more than anything have helped perpetuate the myths, personality cult and fetishism permeating the popular image of Scandinavian design. However, as the scholarly value of such publications is minimal, they will be omitted from the current discussion.

Beyond the coffee table book segment (which also includes so-called sourcebooks), one category of publications seems to dominate the pan-Scandinavian literature: exhibition catalogues. Some of these, like those accompanying the Design in Scandinavia exhibition that toured North America from 1954 to 1957 and the identically titled show sent to Australia in 1968–9, although they do contain (cursory) historical essays, are of interest first and foremost as primary sources elucidating the role of design in the cultural diplomacy and the construction of Scandinavian Design as a brand.[1] Other exhibition catalogues contain more substantial texts and may therefore be considered contributions to the academic literature, albeit with the constraints and conventions that follow from the exhibition catalogue format. Although the later, more scholarly ambitious publications that have done much to historicize the phenomenon are less overtly promotional in character than the texts produced as part of the contemporary events co-constructing the concept of Scandinavian Design in the 1950s and 1960s, they by and large retain the endorsing function and celebratory tone of their predecessors. In principle, exhibitions may of course be critical in character. But due to their official status, the structure of their funding and the purpose they serve as generators of goodwill, exhibitions on Scandinavian design—and the accompanying publications—rarely, if ever, surpass the promotional rhetoric and rationale.

In the aftermath of what is often perceived as the 'golden days' of Scandinavian design—the 1950s and early 1960s—the desire to recapture past pride and resuscitate the international recognition of the brand spurred new exhibitions and publications. The most ambitious events of a pan-Scandinavian character have generally been played at away ground, targeting foreign audiences, but the rescue mission was taken to the home front as well. While a show called Exposicao de desenho industrial da Escandinàvia toured Brazil, in 1971 the Röhsska Museum of Decorative Arts in Gothenburg staged an exhibition of Nordic industrial design conceived as a continuation of an established tradition of Nordic collaboration in the field of design cultural diplomacy. A similar event took place five years later, when on the occasion of the centennial of Oslo's Museum of Decorative Arts and Design in 1976, its direction argued that 'such information on where Nordic industrial design stands today is at least as important at home in the Nordic region as it is abroad', and organized a touring exhibition with the hope that it would not only improve the understanding of design culture amongst the home public 'but also stimulate the industrial designers themselves, so that Nordic industrial design will be able to retain its reputation in a global context'.[2] In its campaigning for the industrial design profession, Alf Bøe's catalogue essay is coloured by his background as Director of the Norwegian Design Centre, but it is interesting how he seeks to inscribe industrial design into a history of Scandinavian design hitherto dominated by the decorative arts.[3] To Bøe, who also wrote the catalogue essay for the 1971 exhibition at the Röhsska Museum, the increasingly prominent role played by industrial design since the 1960s represented a new twist on the trope of social responsibility so carefully constructed in the prevalent historical narratives of Scandinavian design.[4]

One of the first exhibitions that can be said to have a commemorative function and that featured a more substantial publication was the Form og Funktion show at Sophienholm in Lyngby, Denmark, in 1980—an event explicitly intended as a celebration of the fiftieth anniversary of the 1930 Stockholm Exhibition. The catalogue includes reprints of programmatic texts by Gregor Paulsson and Poul Henningsen as well as historical and critical essays by contemporary scholars.[5] A smaller exhibition of Nordic craft and design took place at Maihaugen in Lillehammer, Norway, in 1981, accompanied by a catalogue including an essay by Fredrik Wildhagen in which he emphasizes the role of the national design organizations' intra-Nordic collaboration in postwar Scandinavian design.[6] Focusing on a single but central institution in the 'golden age' of Scandinavian design, the Lunning Prize, awarded to Nordic designers from 1951 to 1970, Stockholm's Nationalmuseum celebrated the award's twenty-fifth anniversary in 1986 with an exhibition and bilingual catalogue containing retrospective essays deliberating Scandinavian Design as an idea and an epoch, as well as presentations of the forty designers honoured over the two decades.[7]

The first large-scale retrospective exhibition on Scandinavian Design outside Scandinavia took place in 1982 when the Cooper-Hewitt Museum in New York organized Scandinavian Modern: 1880–1980, accompanied by a large and lavishly designed catalogue.[8] To date, this remains one of the most comprehensive and conscientious surveys of Scandinavian design history available in English, although its commemorative tone and connoisseurial approach appear somewhat outmoded thirty years down the road. Another major museum in the sector has also contributed to the international literature on Scandinavian design: in 1989 the Victoria & Albert Museum in London made use of its own collection to produce the exhibition and catalogue *Scandinavia: Ceramics and Glass in the Twentieth Century*.[9] Highly conventional in its subject matter and in its analytical perspective, this publication is probably more a contribution to the history of decorative art in ceramics and glass than to the history of Scandinavian design.

The most recent contribution to this strand of publications is *Scandinavian Design beyond the Myth*, the textual companion to a travelling exhibition that toured European cities from 2003 to 2007.[10] Despite the ambitions of the project and the merits of the individual essays, this publication is problematic in several respects. First of all, like most exhibition catalogues it does not work well on its own. More concerning, though, is that its title is misleading, as the book is a parade of 'great' designs and 'great' designers and thus contributes to the perpetuation rather than the challenging of myths. The 'beyond' of the title, then, implies continuance rather than disclosure—the catalogue includes contemporary design portrayed as a projection of that of the 'golden age', giving the project a decisively promotional character. But, then, this is hardly surprising given that the exhibition was commissioned by the Nordic Council of Ministers.

A celebratory and promotional character is not restricted to exhibition catalogues. In fact, the majority of publications with a pan-Scandinavian scope seem to have been conceived of primarily to generate goodwill for the region's design culture. Prime examples are a couple of books from the early 1960s by Ulf Hård af Segerstad: one on Nordic decorative art and one on modern Scandinavian furniture design.[11] In these texts, history is present but is consistently treated as an explanation for the character of contemporary practice, rather than being studied for its own sake—an instrumental and legitimizing outlook prevalent in much of this type of literature. Although less blatant in style, this is true also of the most comprehensive work in this category, a 1961 volume whose US edition is entitled *A Treasury of Scandinavian Design*, edited by Erik Zahle.[12] Nevertheless, this book has for half a century proved a valuable resource for those—particularly non-Scandinavians—seeking an introduction to Scandinavian design history. More polemical than promotional, Viggo Sten Møller's 1978 book on functionalism and applied art in Scandinavia reflects the ageing modernist author's oscillations between resignation and zest but still comprises a compendious but not uncritical historical account, including historiographic remarks.[13]

Of all the eulogies pronounced on Scandinavian design, none is more flagrant than Eileene H. Beer's *Scandinavian Design: Objects of a Life Style*. Rather than arising from academic ambitions, this book was conceived *con amore*, and through the most romanticizing wordings we learn, for example, that 'Scandinavians have instinctively been aware that one cannot create something pretty in the hope that it might also be useful, but an object made to perform a function can always be pleasing in form'.[14] This form of stereotyping of character and naturalizing of modernist design ideology is disturbing on many levels and goes to show how being flattered by others can be as awkward and unseemly as self-flattery.

Literature on Scandinavian design with higher academic ambitions has tended to be more national than pan-Scandinavian in scope. However, the establishment of the Nordic Forum for Design History in 1982 provided a network for scholars in the field and a platform for publications. A few conference proceedings were produced, on topics like Nordic functionalism and the still very current issue of the place of industrial design in museums.[15] More important, this community also formed the basis for the *Scandinavian Journal of Design History*, published as an annual from 1991 to 2005. Individual articles in the journal were normally not pan-Scandinavian in scope,[16] but taken as a whole this project is perhaps the most comprehensive publication on design history in Scandinavia.

Amongst the few English-language survey texts that largely eschew the celebratory tone, the chapters on the Scandinavian countries in the three-volume *History of Industrial Design* edited by Carlo Pirovano stand out. Spanning the period 1750 to 1990 in a mere forty-five pages combined, Christine Stevenson, Lars Dybdahl and Fredrik Wildhagen do a good job of presenting design from Scandinavia in a fairly balanced manner.[17] On the whole there are very few scholarly monographs taking a regional perspective, at least of a more recent date. One rare exception is Ingeborg Glambek's book on the foreign reception of a 'Nordic' identity in architecture and design.[18] Although reception history is an established approach in art history, it has been little applied to design history—at least in Scandinavia—and the book therefore represents a refreshing perspective. Leaving the relatively sparse pan-Scandinavian literature behind, we now move on to surveys of design history literature in Denmark, Finland, Norway and Sweden, which combined will complement this outline for a historiography of Scandinavian design.

DENMARK

Not much has been published internationally on the history of Danish design beyond the illustrated presentations of the most famous designers and most worshipped objects of Danish design. You can find vast amounts of stories and even quite detailed historical facts on Danish designers and especially on the 'furniture classics' on the Internet, but such accounts tend to have too many heroes, and these protagonists are in fact often too obscure for an interesting historical narrative to emerge.

In the more scholarly literature, the international contextualization of Danish design has been a prevailing topic. For instance, the single most celebrated Danish designer in recent years, Arne Jacobsen, is predominantly acknowledged for his appropriation of American postwar impulses. Still, most discussions of the historical development are inwardly focused on the roles of the same persons, exhibitions and a few companies, and it seems that 'usual suspects' such as Kaare Klint and Poul Henningsen are considered difficult to present in an international context. The latter is of course known internationally for his lamps, but his critical writings on design and culture had a far wider importance.[19] The conventional understanding of the national character of Danish applied art that was established early on, especially in the wake of the World's Fairs of 1893 and 1900, was that the Danes were not influenced by any international styles; their work was resistant to style as such, it was claimed.[20] This attitude has been rehearsed time and again at later points in the history of Danish design, for example in the case of functionalism, the Danish adaptation of which is habitually presented as the reawakening of age-old traditions in handicraft and architecture—often evidenced through historicist examples, no less. These rather restricted notions of the nation's design history stem, of course, from the ideological and political fights of the design professions and institutions, but they nevertheless have had a strong impact on the subject material even for later design historians, partly as ready templates for use in the presentation of familiar narratives, partly as mythological constructs to be challenged.

In Denmark, as in many other countries, architects played a dominant role in establishing design as a profession, discourse and institution. Critics, teachers and directors of design schools were usually the more theoretically trained architects. But on top of that Denmark has had its core of 'furniture architects' fighting over the power to control the legacy of the so-called Klint School and thereby the right to define the 'timeless' qualities of the genuine classics of the golden age of Danish furniture design. In this outline of literature on Danish design I include key books on furniture, because this dominant topic has provoked some of the most advanced questions about the development of design in the contexts of society, economics, culture and media. There are many fine studies, especially from the Design Museum Denmark, of other special fields such as posters, textiles, silver and ceramics that are relevant to the historiography of Danish design, but they are omitted in this short presentation. As argued in the first section of this chapter, international exhibitions of Scandinavian design since the mid-twentieth century have often had a Scandinavian rather than national scope. With rare exceptions like A Century of Danish Design, which toured the United Kingdom in 1968, and Dansk design 1910–1945, shown at the Danish Museum of Art and Design in 1997, the history of Danish design has seldom been the subject of designated exhibitions.

Viggo Sten Møller's two-volume survey history *Dansk kunstindustri*, published in 1970, forms the entry point to this historiography, because it represents the characteristic selection of cases and persons, and Møller himself was part of the personal network and institutional initiatives he describes.[21] Trained as an architect, he had worked at the offices of figures such as Anton Rosen and Knud V. Engelhardt, who are presented as pioneers in his book. Later, Møller became the Editor of the leading Danish design magazine, *Nyt Tidskrift for Kunstindustri*, and Director of the School of Arts and Crafts (now part of the Danish Design School). In his historical presentation, he adapts the art historical scheme of styles and the traditional fields of decorative arts: furniture, ceramics, glass, silver, textiles and books. The second volume, covering 1900–50, presents the building, furnishing and decorating of the Copenhagen Town Hall as the calling for leading figures in the fields of arts and crafts and follows how these fields later develop and approach industrial production. He adds 'intermezzi' where he wants to highlight individuals who do not fit the scheme but nevertheless represent moral ideals to be followed. In sum, this publication may not have any academic pretensions, but it remains an important historical source with a wide curriculum that later histories refer to. For instance, the histories of Danish design written by Møller's own son, Henrik Sten Møller, in 1975 and by Svend Erik Møller (not related) in 1974, both published in English, follow his line.[22]

The art historical focus on styles is examined in Mirjam Gelfer-Jørgensen's *Dansk kunsthåndværk fra 1850 til vor tid* from 1982.[23] She follows formal motifs as special national paths through the very complex scheme of stylistic development that international impulses introduced. The national character has been read into more individualistic styles such as national romanticism and *skønvirke* (as a national derivate of art nouveau) and, more paradoxically, neo-Empire or the second neoclassicism. The strict account of national stylistic variations gets close to a caricature on the threshold to the modern idiom, but this is partly the point and leads to the more critical discussion of functionalism as style. Gelfer-Jørgensen wants to go beyond 'looking through the glasses of the functionalists on functionalism'.[24] This leads to a nuanced picture of the more continuous developments from Empire, historicism and neoclassicism—which is the author's primary field of expertise[25]—to modernism, although her understanding of national motifs resisting international tendencies, exemplified by the belated appreciation of the Bauhaus in Denmark, is not far from the conventional narratives of modernism she aspires to transcend. The focus on styles seems to favour constantly reoccurring classicisms and is of little help beyond the period of functionalism. The question raised in the final chapter, 'In which style do we live?' has not been answered in the thirty years that have passed, as recent historiography has been less preoccupied with style—although now the cult of classics and retro manoeuvres in current design practice could perhaps provide a partial answer.

In the exhibition Dansk design 1910–1945: Art déco og funktionalisme, shown at the Danish Museum of Art and Design in 1997, curator Lars Dybdahl proposed an alternative to the understanding of the healthy, Danish design as 'style-resistant' by using art deco in presenting the period and admitting more fashionable developments and international flavour.[26] Dybdahl's catalogue text shows a coherent picture of the broad, formal development of the functionalist idiom in Denmark, though with very few international parallels. He repeats the traditional scheme of decorative arts and leading figures but adds new material such as the design of posters, lamps, domestic devices, radios and trains and widens the scope with more common consumer objects. The text lacks references and mostly adds to the roster of heroic figures and design icons, albeit drawn from a broader industrial segment, but the essay can be seen as an appetizer to Dybdahl's later thorough survey history, *Dansk design 1945–1975*, published in 2006.[27] Here he addresses a wide spectrum of relevant historical factors in the nascent professions of industrial and graphic designers, and the development of trades based on new materials such as aluminium and plastics, all placed in the context of international references and connections. The traditional scheme is here transformed into innumerable categories of industrial objects and becomes a valuable source of microhistorical cases, leaving virtually nothing behind. Dybdahl's curatorial activities with collections and exhibitions form the basis for this much-needed and -appreciated expansion of Danish design history's subject matter—the downside to which is an even longer list of objects to worship.[28] Dybdahl's presentation is pleasantly independent of dominant agendas of functionalism but does return to the big questions of national identity and ideals in a brief, schematic conclusion and a manifest on humanistic design studies.

Recent years have seen a surge in the publication of monographs on individual designers, as exemplified by the series on Danish designers published by Aschehoug in cooperation with the Louisiana Museum of Modern Art.[29] These easily accessible but disturbingly hagiographic books are accompanied by other popular historical accounts like the architect and designer Thomas Dickson's *Dansk design* from 2006 (English edition published in 2008), which is basically an updated version of the format established by Viggo Sten Møller but expanded to include a very broad range of categories (much as Dybdahl did) and adhering to an expanded notion of design seen earlier—albeit using international examples—in Ida Engholm and Anders Michelsen's *Designmaskinen.*[30] What would be next in more academic investigations of the history of Danish design are discussions on the role of professions, businesses and media as well as more critical studies of institutions like design schools and periodicals.[31] In the field of furniture history, more detailed studies have emerged on the many different actor groups and factors producing the international success: furniture architects, cabinetmakers, industrialists, exhibitions, distributors, periodicals, critics, books on home decoration, furniture shops and many others.

Just as Viggo Sten Møller summarized the heritage of functionalism in the art industry in his two-volume publication from 1970, Arne Karlsen has done the same for Danish furniture in his *Dansk møbelkunst i det 20. århundrede* from 1991.[32] Karlsen formed part of the dominant Klint School as Professor of Furniture Design at the Aarhus School of Architecture. His account is based on the thesis of the special Danish sense of crafts and function combined with the ideal of high-quality furniture in mass production that is within everyone's economic reach. And this becomes a very long story with circumstantial detours because neither Kaare Klint, as founding father in this tradition, nor the first alliances of architects and cabinetmakers, engaged in industrial manufacture. In Karlsen's gloss, this story is presented as a hard fight for artistic skills and ideals against commercialism, and only a chosen few get through the transformation from furniture architect to industrial designer with their artistic and moral integrity intact. In this way this kind of history becomes based on the character and habitus of the persons presented, and it is told in the context of education at the schools of architecture and design.

Danish design has been, and still is, a field of heated discussions, where professional ethics, individual habitus, the status of furniture classics and economic interests are at stake. This has drawn scholars from other disciplines to join the discussions and investigate the context. The ethnologist Birgit Kaiser in *Den ideologiske funktionalisme* in 1992 partly reproduced the ideals and arguments of the furniture architects and then tried to test their impact on public taste, in political discourse and in marketing.[33] This, of course, shows a discrepancy between the dream of a democratic style beyond class on the one hand and the elitism associated with 'good design' on the other and has called for further studies of the furniture industry and marketing. The British design historian Kevin Davies has written on the marketing of Danish furniture in the United Kingdom, and the international reception is a very important aspect in understanding the success of Danish Modern.[34]

The most comprehensive and critical study of this kind, though, is business historian Per H. Hansen's *Da danske møbler blev moderne* from 2006, in which he questions the role of the craft tradition and looks for what it takes to make an international success in industrialization, consumption and marketing.[35] It becomes another history with other actors and other discourses going beyond the hagiography of the Klint School. This study is based on quite different historical theories drawn from economic history, that is path dependency, storytelling and the necessity of 'creative destructions' to open new opportunities. From this perspective the story of the Klint School, of the alliance of architects and cabinetmakers, is seen as an effective branding of Danish modern furniture, so that even quite undistinguished, mass-produced chairs are connected to idealistic values, artistic genius, craftsmanship, educated taste and culture. According to Hansen, this story was too good to last or fulfilled a purpose only in the first postwar decades. This phenomenon is difficult to control and rebrand in new commercial adventures, although it is constantly subjected to re-mediation in the marketing of furniture classics, reissued products, 'neoclassics' and other retro-style products such as Normann Copenhagen's 'New Danish Modern' across the range of new media from lifestyle magazines to web auctions. There is plenty of room for alternative stories to be told beyond the version first established by the furniture architects, and the most productive task will be to explain them internationally and contextualize the Danish success beyond the conventional hagiography.

FINLAND

Historical scholarly inquiries into Finnish design are quite recent, despite the long-standing domestic importance and international fame of this field. The following section outlines the main sources of knowledge production in this area and the varied subject matter and methodological approaches in question.

Writings on the history of Finnish crafts naturally have a long history, stemming mainly from the curatorial activities of museums and starting in the late nineteenth century. Due to the late industrialization of the country, however, we can speak of design in the present meaning of the word—that is intentionally and professionally designed, predominantly serially produced goods—only from the late 1920s onwards. With the advent of what can be called modern/modernist, design writings on the topic also began to appear, often with a historical backdrop mainly citing domestic craft traditions—a way of presenting current Finnish design that prevailed into the 1990s.[36] Such works may not be classified as historical scholarship; instead, they used a meticulously reduced and reworked past to attach modern items to a genealogy of simple, utilitarian objects, thus creating a continuum of 'Finnishness' stretching from the age-old agrarian way of life to the present day. It was also already in the late 1930s that foreign writers began their still-continuing interest in Finnish design and related writing—very often seeking its background in a simple agrarian past and the supposedly intimate relationship with nature that resulted from it.

Thus, along with Finnish design's international fame and even commercial success from the early 1950s to the 1970s, a bulk of writing was produced both domestically and internationally in which history served as a teleologically predestining gateway to the present. One of the key works of this kind—and actually the first more comprehensive presentation of Finnish design—came from abroad, written by the Swedish art historian and critic Ulf Hård af Segerstad.[37] Rigorous scholarship, however, remained absent for a long while. One reason was that the Finnish Museum of Applied Arts (now called the Design Museum), founded in 1873, was hibernating for several decades, unstaffed and its holdings packed in a warehouse; it reopened only in 1979. Although it obtained university status in 1973, the University of Industrial Arts (now the Aalto University School of Art and Design)—the only major design school in the country—had neither the capacity nor the structure for scholarly research before the 1990s.

The first comprehensive history of Finnish art, published in 1945, included a couple of pages on the 'decorative arts since 1900', and the next volume of similar scope slightly more.[38] The approach had changed dramatically when a comprehensive, multi-authored, six-volume work on the history of the arts in Finland appeared in 1990.[39] Here, design from the 1870s to the 1990s was given a voluminous, well-studied presentation by Leena Maunula. A change in the hierarchy of the arts was apparent: craft and design, long marginalized in art history as 'lesser arts', were now given serious attention as part of the widening scope of the field. Doctoral candidates were now increasingly choosing design as their topic, and the fruits of this research began to appear in the mid-1990s.

Despite the dominance of art history, design history has many disciplinary bases—even in Finland. Cultural history, which began to emerge as an independent discipline in the 1970s at the University of Turku, includes a strand on the history of design. As early as 1982, a chapter on design was included in a three-volume work on the cultural history of Finland.[40] When a new work on the same topic appeared in 2004, design was included but only fragmentarily—probably because of the growing specialized literature on design history.[41]

In spite of all these new efforts and inquiries into the heritage of Finnish design, there was still no comprehensive survey history by a sole author. This situation was amended in 1989 when Erik Kruskopf, an art historian and critic, published his study on crafts and design from the 1870s to the 1970s.[42] The book is a balanced, well-studied work with much greater focus than in earlier accounts on issues such as education, technology, the development of professions and promotion. The book was of high value to the Finnish and Nordic context—but, like all previous studies, it was not translated into

English. The non-Nordic audience still had to rely on texts of lesser ambition and rigour.

It was obvious that by around 1990 design history had both gained visibility and become a distinct scholarly field. The authors came almost solely from art history but with careers not only in academia but also as critics and museum curators. The re-establishment of the Museum of Applied Arts in 1979 soon led to a modest series of monographs accompanying exhibitions. Before long, both the scope and depth of the publications grew. These have mostly focused on designers, such as a comprehensive work on Tapio Wirkkala, or on design-intensive enterprises, such as Marimekko and Arabia.[43] For works such as these, the museum has always recruited external authors, thus providing others with an opportunity for scholarly publishing as well. Other museums, such as the Finnish Glass Museum, established in 1981, have also provided space for scholarly publications in their respective fields, as demonstrated by Kaisa Koivisto's doctoral thesis on postwar Finnish glass design.[44]

By the early 1990s, a new locus for producing design historical knowledge appeared alongside museums and traditional universities: the University of Art and Design, which at this point was building its research infrastructure and system of doctoral education. From the outset, historical inquiry was here regarded as pertinent for answering questions on the origin and position of the design professions and their educational background. Doctoral theses such as Marjo Wiberg's on the development of the textile designer profession and related educational institutions and Anna Valtonen's on recent professional changes in industrial design proved relevant not only to the design history community but also to the professions themselves.[45] What made this history writing different from work at traditional universities was that these researchers had a background in design education and practice—and hence the research questions stem from that realm.

The recent consolidation of the field has also implied a methodological versatility and a rich array of approaches in comparison with the previously predominant empirical and positivist narratives. Discourse analysis, post-structuralism, gender studies and Foucauldian thinking all enriched the way in which the now empirically familiar individuals, works and processes were analysed and presented. Also, following the rule of thumb that there must be one generation or forty years between the object and the researching subject, the 'golden age of Finnish design', the 1950s, has come under scrutiny. The seminal work in this respect was Harri Kalha's doctoral thesis from 1997, which used discourse analysis to open up the period and its main actors.[46] Now, the University of Art and Design also became an object of historical investigation. For its 130th anniversary, it published a significant, multi-authored volume of its history with essays that also portray the more general development of design in Finland.[47] At the same time, the historian Ilkka Huovio conducted a thorough institutional and pedagogical analysis of the same school.[48] Also, design professions and their organizations—first interior architects and later industrial designers—have commissioned studies of their own historical development.[49]

As mentioned, there has been continuous foreign interest in writing and publishing on Finnish design. In the 1990s this turned into research-based historical inquiry. There are two categories of foreign input: work by foreign scholars and publications produced outside Finland with both foreign and Finnish authors. The first category includes, for example, Kevin Davies's work on the reception of Finnish furniture design in Great Britain, Gay McDonald's on the American Home 1953 exhibition in Helsinki, Charlotte Ashby's on late-nineteenth-century nationalism and Asdis Olafsdottir's on the international distribution of Aalto furniture.[50] Among the publications produced outside Finland with both foreign and Finnish authors, one could mention Marianne Aav and Nina Stritzler-Levine's edited volume *Finnish Modern Design.*[51]

It is obvious that the 1990s marked a coming of age for Finnish design history. Since then, the institutional structure has remained quite stable. There are no specific chairs in design history, but it is practised in several institutions and within many disciplines. Design research bordering on history has even become topical in consumer studies and economic history. The continued existence of lacunae in both knowledge and methodological approaches is demonstrated by two recent doctoral theses, both expanding our understanding of the phenomena in question and the ways to penetrate it: Leena Svinhufvud's work on textile art in the interwar period and Susanna Aaltonen's study of the birth of the interior architect profession in Finland.[52] Both are by women researchers, and both combine a gender perspective with thoroughly researched empirical evidence.

Despite significant expansion and deepening of the knowledge of Finnish design history since Kruskopf's survey from 1989—or perhaps precisely because of the large body of recent research available—a new survey history has appeared only recently: Pekka Korvenmaa's *Finnish Design: A Concise History* from 2009. In its bibliography, the reader can find a more detailed list of resources.[53]

NORWAY

Like that of many other nations, the historiography of Norwegian applied art and design remains poorly investigated. Over the years, the history of Norwegian design has been dominated by a modernistic perspective and has only to a very limited degree responded to postmodernist critique. This does not necessarily mean that what has been written is of a low scientific standard. In general, this type of design history is derived from the conventions of art history, with an emphasis on individual designers, issues of style and aesthetic discussions of form and material. However, most studies fall short when it comes to methodological self-reflection. Even the use of terminology has historically been confusing. Central concepts such as *kunstindustri* (industrial art), *brukskunst* (applied art), *kunsthåndverk* (handicrafts), *industridesign* (industrial design), *formgivning* (design) and *design* have been used with varying degrees of accuracy and different interpretations.

An early awareness among Norwegian art historians of an emerging field of design history can be traced to personal networks connected to certain academic communities in Britain during the 1950s. Instrumental in this were Stephan Tschudi-Madsen's *Sources of Art Nouveau*, based on his doctoral thesis, which was partly conceived in London, and Alf Bøe's *From Gothic Revival to Functional Form*, based on his MPhil thesis from the University of Oxford.[54] These works marked an early interest among Norwegian researchers in central issues in international design history.

Although Norway was only a modestly industrialized nation in the nineteenth century, no fewer than three museums of applied art were established: in Oslo (1876), Bergen (1887) and Trondheim (1893). The background for and establishment of these important institutions is the subject of Ingeborg Glambek's doctoral thesis *Kunsten, nytten og moralen* ('Art, utility and morale').[55] Conceived to improve manufacture and taste, the museums gradually gained more freedom to evolve into scholarly institutions in the twentieth century.[56] Much of the research produced by the museums has focused on stylistic issues, individual designers or specific materials. This has resulted in a number of fine studies of designers who have gained distinction for their work in, for example, enamel, glass, ceramics and textiles.[57] The Museum of Decorative Arts and Design in Oslo (since 2003 part of the National Museum of Art, Architecture and Design) has played a particularly important role in promoting central Norwegian female designers through exhibitions and publications.[58] However, a notable lack of critical (historical) distance to both work and designer can be discerned, particularly when contemporary designers are portrayed. Also, it appears that the close interaction among the Norwegian museums of applied art has given rise to a certain consensus on the subject matter of and approach to design history.

Surveys of Norwegian design history are even fewer and further between than in the other Scandinavian countries. Themes relating to differences between European styles and national character have been a recurring issue in the Norwegian literature, especially in older work. One early attempt to discuss these themes can be found in Thor Kielland's chapter on modern applied art in *Norsk kunsthistorie* (1927).[59] Kielland structured his survey according to materials—a categorization which proved normative for a long period of time.

Half a century would pass until the next major survey, also published as part of a multivolume publication: *Norges kunsthistorie* from the early 1980s. The chapters on decorative art and design in volumes 5, 6 and 7 remain the most thorough survey of the field from an art historical perspective. In volume 5, Bøe describes the period 1870–1914 as a national reformation, dominated by applied art museums, the advance of handicrafts and the dragon style.[60] In the 1970s, interwar design was the subject of a number of art historical studies, including Randi Gaustad's work on the Norwegian Applied Art Association (Foreningen Brukskunst),[61] and this is reflected in Bøe's contribution to volume 6, covering the period 1914–40. Here, Bøe sustains the modernistic perspective by accentuating the work of organizations such as the Norwegian Applied Art Association in light of influence from the Deutscher Werkbund and the Swedish Society of Crafts and Design.[62] Bøe also maintains Kielland's approach, focusing on style, form and materials and concentrating on elite products, especially furniture, tapestry, precious metals, ceramics and glass.

The postwar period receives a more tentative review by two authors in volume 7. The problematic conceptual uses of *brukskunst* (applied art), *kunsthåndverk* (handicrafts) and industrial design come to the fore, particularly in Anniken Thue's use of the term *kunsthåndverk*.[63] Thue distinguishes between handicrafts in the years from 1940 to 1970, defined as 'made by hand in conventional workshops', and the new interpretation emphasizing the craftsperson's control of the entire process, from initial concept to finished product. However, the delineation between this and applied art, or *brukskunst*, becomes unclear, and it is evident that the text was written during the period when handicrafts were undergoing radical changes. Bøe wrote a parallel chapter entitled 'Kunstindustri og industridesign etter 1940' ('Applied art and industrial design after 1940'), in which he continued his dialogue on organizations and material groups within applied art.[64] In his former positions as Director of the Norwegian Design Centre and Curator at the Museum of Decorative Arts and Design in Oslo, Bøe was an eager promoter of industrial design, so it is not surprising to find that he pays a lot of attention to the concept of industrial design in his writings—but it is noteworthy that his role as an actor in the field is not mentioned in the text.

However, Bøe was also able to identify weak points in his own interpretation. When discussing the interwar period, he points out that the history of design often disregards both lavishly ornate objects deemed vulgar by modernist critics and products designed by engineers and technicians. Bøe's views relate to the contemporary postmodern criticism of dichotomies such as innovation versus tradition, centre versus periphery, high versus low culture, as well as to the call for accounts moving beyond elite products and the heroic designer, a call that was emerging in international design history at the time.

Fredrik Wildhagen addresses a number of these issues in an attempt to provide a more comprehensive presentation of Norwegian design history in his book *Norge i form* (1988).[65] Wildhagen breaks away from the typical features of art history to focus instead on the relationships between handicrafts and design, between designers and industry. This issue runs through

Wildhagen's book as a recurrent theme, and he provides in-depth discussions on the design process and aspects such as concept development, technological affordances and the role of the manufacturer. Although Wildhagen's book represents a much more progressive approach to design history that is more conversant with developments in the field internationally, it is interesting to note that international reviewers requested more on design culture unique to Norway.[66] Unfortunately, Wildhagen's book lacks a clear methodical grasp and does not adhere to academic conventions in terms of references. The author's active engagement in the international design history community undoubtedly made him an important figure mediating new perspectives to Scandinavian colleagues—although the impact of his effort in this respect seems to have been limited and belated.

The only recent attempt to write a survey history of Norwegian design is aimed entirely at a non-academic audience and has no scholarly merit; it is therefore of minor interest in this context.[67] This can be seen as symptomatic of design history's poor standing in Norway as a distinct field of study, dominated by conventional art historical approaches and the position of the museums of applied art. The University of Oslo, and to a lesser degree other universities, has fostered a number of postgraduate theses on various issues in modern design history, but very few of the graduates have gone on to pursue careers in research. From the 1990s onwards, an increase in attention to theory and history at architectural and design schools, coinciding with increased support to institutions such as the Foundation for Design and Architecture in Norway (Norsk Form) and the Norwegian Design Council, has contributed to an escalation in interdisciplinary perspectives within this field, even though their publications can seldom be characterized as research into the history of design. One of the exceptions is Trygve Ask's doctoral thesis from the Oslo School of Architecture and Design (2004) on the constitution of industrial design as a profession in Norway, which presents a number of new perspectives on educational and organizational issues.

New actors and perspectives have emerged from other sectors as well: the recent research collaboration between various museums of cultural history and museums of applied art has resulted in interesting work with a more multifaceted outlook. One such example is the research project Plastics in Modern Norway.[68] Yet another is the Norwegian Museum of Cultural History's research into home and living environments, based partly on ethnological approaches, which attempts to identify a broader base of perspectives relating to social and cultural history for the interior decor and furniture design prevalent in the interwar period.[69] To these contributions from congruent fields can be added the interdisciplinary informed work of historian Kjetil Fallan on twentieth-century industrial design.[70] Also, at the other extreme of the practices studied by design history, handicrafts, there is a growing literature with an international orientation, best exemplified by the work of Jorunn Veiteberg.[71]

In general, however, Norwegian design history remains underdeveloped, maintained by a small number of scholars producing only a very modest volume of research which interacts with the international community and reflects current theoretical perspectives.

SWEDEN

Swedish design has long been characterized by consensus, perhaps because the Swedish design community has been and still is relatively small. In other words, a limited group of people have alternated between different key roles, which has had an impact on the shaping of the content of Swedish design history. These key roles include university positions as well as those at applied art museums such as the Röhsska Museum in Gothenburg and the National Museum in Stockholm. Another influential institution in this context is the Swedish Society of Crafts and Design (Svenska slöjdföreningen until 1976, then Svensk Form).

In Swedish design history literature, the Society of Crafts and Design's view on design permeates the definition of the design historical object. In addition, the spotlight has constantly been placed on the society's activities, with repeated references to certain indisputable milestones, as is amply demonstrated in Kerstin Wickman's edited volume *Formens rörelse: Svensk form genom 150 år*, a book published on the occasion of the society's 150th anniversary in 1995.[72] Wickman, one of the more influential Swedish design historians in the last decades of the twentieth century, started to work for the society's journal, *Form*, in 1966 and has been active in the organization ever since. In addition, she taught the history of design and crafts at Stockholm's Konstfack University College of Arts, Crafts and Design from 1970 to 2006.

Formens rörelse is a chronological anthology outlining the history of the Society of Crafts and Design, with texts by prominent historians in the areas of crafts, design and architecture. The title of the book is intentionally ambiguous. There is an underlying claim not only to write the society's history but also to provide a survey of Swedish design history: how design has been shaped and changed, and why. Still, the anthology remains a design history centred on the organization and its achievements. In other words, the impression is that the society's history is synonymous with Swedish design history. Even if the society, for obvious reasons, is not given an equally prominent place in other books, it is a constantly recurring point of reference.

The formulation of modern Swedish design history has been relatively long in the making. No comprehensive survey was published until 1975, but parts of the history were formulated in a number of books in the previous decades. The early historical writing includes *Nutida svensk konstslöjd* (1931) by Nils G. Wollin. The book covers the period 1917–30 and comprises a limited amount of texts and a great number of images divided into materials such as ceramics, furniture, metal, textiles and glass.[73] Ten years later, *Konsthantverk och hemslöjd i Sverige 1930–40* (1941) was published, focusing on the 1930 Stockholm Exhibition and its significance.[74] *Nyttokonst* (1951) by Arthur Hald and Sven Erik Skawonius, who were both active in the Swedish Society of Crafts and Design, may be regarded as a continuation of *Konsthantverk och hemslöjd i Sverige 1930–40.* Just like *Nutida svensk konstslöjd*, it was, in the main, an illustrated work with shorter texts. Hald and Skawonius's work chiefly deals with the 1940s, but the book also contains a short chapter reaching back to 1915 when the society began its struggle for 'the refinement of production' and 'a sound, democratic domestic culture'.[75]

Yet a decade later, in 1961, Skawonius contributed an essay on crafts and applied art in Sweden to the anthology *Konsthantverk och konstindustri i Norden* (the US edition was entitled *A Treasury of Scandinavian Design*).[76] The same year saw the publication of *Svensk Form* by Åke Stavenow and Åke H. Huldt, which, in contrast to previous surveys, included a richly illustrated section on industrial design.[77] These authors were also active in the Swedish Society of Crafts and Design. Stavenow was the society's president from 1936 to 1946 and then became Director of Konstfack. The aim of *Svensk Form* was to describe 'Swedish applied art in the 1950s', but just as with *Formens rörelse*, the perspective is ambiguous. In the early 1970s, several doctoral theses portraying modern design and architecture were published, including Per G. Råberg's on the discourse of early functionalism, Elisabet Stavenow-Hidemark's on early-twentieth-century Swedish villas and Bengt Nyström's on two Swedish applied art pioneers.[78]

Dag Widman's *Konsthantverk, konstindustri, design 1895–1975* (1975) is the first book that takes an integral perspective in a longer survey.[79] The book is part of the multivolume art historical publication *Konsten i Sverige* (1974–81), edited by Sven Sandström. Widman was one of the people who held several important positions both at the National Museum in Stockholm and within the Swedish Society of Crafts and Design. Through his double institutional affiliation, Widman thus formulated the history in writing and institutionalized it at the museum.

Widman's presentation is chronological and begins with a review of the arts and crafts movement's influence in Sweden. In the eyes of the author, it was designers and the Swedish Society of Crafts and Design that propelled the development forward and played important roles. It is evident from Widman's choice of perspective that it is the so-called applied arts that constitute Swedish design. Industrial design is not introduced until the chapter covering the 1950s and then very briefly.

It should be evident from what has been said thus far that Swedish design history writing initially was a rather male affair, that is produced by men—a fact that changed in the 1970s. However, comprehensive surveys continued to be rare. One such publication is Hedvig Hedqvist's *1900–2000: Svensk form: Internationell design* (2002).[80] In comparison to the earlier survey, this one has a more international outlook, as indicated by the title. Here, Swedish design is discussed in a wider context. It also contains other and more different examples of industrial design, but Hedqvist's perspective is largely reminiscent of Widman's.

As already mentioned, there are few surveys of Swedish design history but rather more anthologies. In addition to *Formens rörelse*, one should mention books on specific design media such as furniture, textiles and glass: *Svenska möbler 1890–1990* (1991), edited by Monica Boman; and *Svenska textilier 1890–1990* (1994) and *Svenskt glas* (1991), both edited by Jan Brunius.[81] There are also some larger works in the fields of art history and architectural history that encompass design: both *Signums svenska konsthistoria* (1994–2005) and *Att bygga ett land* (1998) contain important sections on design.[82] There are also a number of publications that have been fully or partly funded by the Swedish Institute, including *Design in Sweden* (1972), by Lennart Lindkvist; *Design in Sweden* (1985), edited by Monica Boman; and *Swedish Design* (2001), by Denise Hagströmer.[83] The Swedish Institute is a governmental agency answering to the Ministry of Foreign Affairs, tasked with boosting Sweden's reputation internationally. Swedish design history has thus been a way of promoting Sweden abroad, and today there are a number of companies that use Swedish design history in their marketing strategies.

Since Widman's book, industrial design has become more present, an advent that, to a degree, has changed the previously dominant applied art perspective. In Stavenow and Huldt's book *Svensk Form* industrial design already enjoyed a relatively prominent position, but it was not until the National Museum's 1978 exhibition Industridesign under 200 år ('200 years of industrial design') that this field was incorporated properly into Swedish design history. The exhibition catalogue was published as an issue of the Swedish Society of Crafts and Design's magazine *Form*, another example of how close-knit the design community has been in Sweden.

However, the decisive breakthrough for an industrial design perspective on Swedish design history came with the anthology *Svensk industridesign: En 1900-talshistoria* (1997), edited by Lasse Brunnström.[84] A former director of the Röhsska Museum, Brunnström is currently Adjunct Professor of Design History at the University of Gothenburg's School of Design and Crafts (Högskolan för Design och Konsthantverk, or HDK). In the survey *Svensk designhistoria* (2010), Brunnström further develops his views on industrial design and also describes other design practices beyond the applied arts. Moreover, the book is the first survey of Swedish design history in which the Society of Crafts and Design does not play a central role. Brunnström critically points to the lack of diversity in the earlier institutionalized form of Swedish design history and claims that it was characterized by 'repetitions of relatively well-known facts and phenomena' and that there are gaps in the knowledge concerning, for example, graphic design, packaging design and service design.[85] Thus, this book represents an altered understanding of the design historical object. It represented a shift in the definition, which was also present in several doctoral theses defended during the last decade, such as Helena Kåberg's study of office buildings as an advertising tool and Johanna Rosenqvist's work on handicrafts and gender.[86]

However, this is not the first or only time a different perspective has been formulated. Already in the 1960s the Swedish Society of Crafts and Design's approach was questioned, and, as in other countries, 'good design' came under attack. In the mid-1990s, this criticism flared up again, leading to a discussion focusing on taste. This critical discourse of the 1990s was expressed in various forms, and the discussion was liveliest among designers, at galleries and in the daily press.

Among other things, the debate centred on power seen in an historical perspective but also touched upon contemporary power positions. A younger generation of craftspeople and designers disassociated themselves from traditional concepts of taste and quality, norms and taboos. One outcome of this debate was the book *Svensk smak* (2005) by the craftsperson Zandra Ahl, now Professor at Konstfack, and the journalist Emma Ohlsson.[87] Another example is Linda Rampell's *Designatlas* (2003).[88]

Today Sweden is a transcultural country in a globalized world in the age of late capitalism. Needless to say, these new conditions affect the definition of 'Swedish' as well as the conditions for writing history, which, most likely, will be increasingly noticeable in how design history will be formulated in Sweden. The mediation of history will probably be marked by a larger number of perspectives and thus more and more varied histories.

NOTE ON AUTHORSHIP

The section 'Pan-Scandinavian Literature' was written by Kjetil Fallan, and the sections on Denmark, Finland, Norway and Sweden were written, respectively, by Anders V. Munch, Pekka Korvenmaa, Espen Johnsen, and Sara Kristoffersson and Christina Zetterlund.

PART 1

NETWORKS

–2–

'What's Worth Copying Is Worth Protecting': Applied Art and the Evolution of Danish Copyright Law

Stina Teilmann-Lock

The law is always an indicator of social and cultural assumptions. Thus a great deal may be learned of the assumptions about Scandinavian design in the twentieth century by studying what has chiefly regulated it during that time: the law of copyright. Particularly, the changing status of the applied arts within copyright law is a reflection of the changing importance of design within larger economic, cultural and social networks.

A Supreme Court decision from 1907 (U.07.619) constitutes the *Ur-Szene* for copyright protection of the applied arts in Denmark.[1] The two parties to the case were Aluminia (the owners of the Royal Porcelain Factory, today known as Royal Copenhagen) and a German porcelain manufacturer, Porzellanfabrik Kalk. The objects of dispute were coffee pots (see fig. 2.1). Aluminia claimed that Kalk had infringed their artistic copyright in a blue fluted china coffee pot designed by Arnold Krog. Krog was not only one of the most eminent designers in the history of the Royal Porcelain Factory; he was also the director of the company for several decades and the originator of many of its classic pieces.

Experts[2] called by the court agreed unequivocally that Krog's shapely coffee pot was a highly original work of art,

> made with such artistic delicacy and insight that the operations within the [Royal Porcelain] Factory could rightly be considered operations of an artistic kind, and thus the manufactured works should be treated as works of art protectable by the Act on Authorial and Artistic Rights.[3]

Moreover, the plaintiff, Aluminia, was able to demonstrate that the designs by Krog were his own 'unique works'; they produced his original drawings in court. It was thus argued that 'shapes such as those of Professor Krog's model had not existed before, and such shapes, insofar as they are found now, must be imitations of it'.[4] The defendant, Porzellanfabrik Kalk, had argued that its

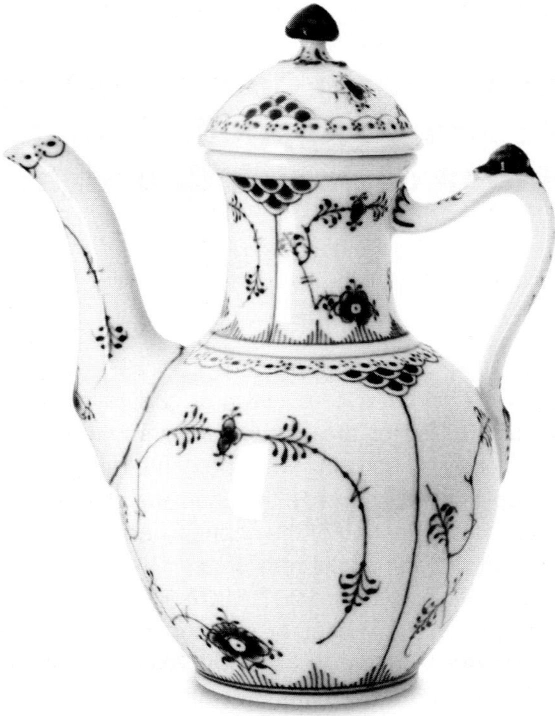

Fig. 2.1 Blue fluted china coffee pot designed by Arnold Krog. Photograph courtesy of Royal Copenhagen.

coffee pot had been designed in conformity with traditional shapes found in eighteenth-century German porcelain. Yet no evidence of such a tradition or shape was produced, and not even the defendant denied that the shape of Kalk's coffee pot bore a very close resemblance to the shape of Aluminia's coffee pot.[5]

However, notwithstanding the originality of Krog's design and the undisputed similarity of the other design—amounting to imitation—the Supreme Court ruled that there had been *no* infringement. The ruling explained that

> the plaintiff's pot, according to its description as ordinary industrial ware, the foremost purpose of which is practical usage, cannot be considered a work of art in the sense wherein this expression is used in the Act of 19 December 1902 § 24.[6]

Krog's design was not a 'work of art' according to the Danish Act of 1902 on artistic copyright.[7] Hence, it was not subject to copyright protection, and there was no basis in the law for preventing rival companies from making imitations.

The crux of the matter—where Krog's work fell short of being a 'work of art'—was in its possession of intrinsic features which did not conform to the *purpose* of 'being a work of art'. As explained by the Supreme Court, Krog had designed a *coffee pot model* with the aim that it be the prototype for the industrial production of coffee pots. That is to say, its purpose was to be multiplied by imitation: Krog had thus created a work of applied art. As such, the artistic properties of its design remained insufficient as grounds for the design to be regarded as a 'work of art' under copyright law.

However, recognizing some sort of inconsistency in such a stance, the Supreme Court included in its ruling a clear message to Danish legislators:

> There being no explicit provision in the Act of 19 December 1902, there are no grounds for classifying industrial goods within its framework, their production—as is the case with the coffeepot that this lawsuit concerns—being undertaken, with however much artistry, for practical use and with the aim of mass production.[8]

The message was quickly heeded.[9] Early in 1908 the Danish copyright law was amended. In the 1902 Act on Authorial and Artistic Rights (as amended by the 1904 law) it had been stated in § 24 that,

> an artist has, according to the restrictions of this Act, the sole right to publish or sell or let be published or put up for sale reproductions of his original work of art or of parts of it. This is so when the reproduction requires mediating artistic work as well as when the reproduction takes place by purely mechanical or chemical means.[10]

In an amendment to the Act on Authorial and Artistic Rights of 28 February 1908, the second sentence of the preceding quotation was replaced by the following passage:

> According to this Act, original artistic works intended to be prototypes for industrial art and handicrafts, as well as the objects created on the basis of such works, are to be considered works of art whether or not these are produced individually or in a larger quantity. The right according to this Act is valid for any type of reproduction, when it requires mediating artistic work as well as when the reproduction takes place by purely mechanical or chemical means, and whether or not the reproduction takes place with a purely artistic purpose or with an industrial purpose or to serve a practical use.[11]

By amending § 24 of the Act, the Danish Parliament ensured that works of applied art were not routinely disqualified from copyright protection. In fact, the securing of copyright protection for works of applied art had been the intention of the 1902 Act. An earlier law of 1864 concerning the reproduction of artworks[12]—which had conferred a ten-year exclusive right on the originator of works to be used as prototypes in the production and decoration of articles for everyday use—had been repealed by the 1902 Act. The implied meaning of allowing the 1864 law to lapse had been that *all* such works should fall under the new copyright law. As recorded in the Official Report of Parliamentary Proceedings 1907–08, the contention that artists were being subjected to 'damaging abuse' of their works (when 'for example their works, without their consent, were reproduced on handkerchiefs and so forth')[13] had been a reason for introducing copyright protection of the applied arts in Denmark. Furthermore, as was also noted in the report, similar developments had been taking place in a European context. Copyright protection of applied art had been introduced in France with the Law of 11 March 1902 and in Germany with the Law of 9 January 1907. In a similar vein, the British Copyright Act 1911 was to include 'works of artistic craftsmanship' as objects of copyright protection. There was thus a general movement in copyright law to allow the applied arts a legal status that had previously been reserved for the fine arts.[14] Without doubt the development in the law was related to the renewed prestige of the applied arts brought about by (most famously) the arts and crafts movement in Britain.[15] And similar trends were making themselves felt in Denmark. Thus the 1908 amendment did what the 1902 Act had failed to do, even though it had been Parliament's intention all along 'to protect any work of art against any kind of reproduction'. Copyright protection of the applied arts in Denmark was then brought 'into accord with the approach of other European countries'.[16]

THE KANTIAN DISTINCTION BETWEEN *KUNST* AND *HANDWERKE*

The division between (fine) art and applied art had effectively excluded the latter from copyright protection and, as we shall see, continued for decades to render problematic the status of the applied arts as the object of copyright protection. This division has its source in Kant's distinctions between 'art' (*Kunst*) and 'craft' (*Handwerke*), and between 'free art' (*freie Kunst*) and 'mercenary art' (*Lohnkunst*).[17] Kant introduces the distinction in his *Kritik der Urteilskraft* of 1790. And the Kantian categories offer an effective means of illuminating the reasoning of the Danish Supreme Court in the case of the coffee pots. This is no coincidence; the philosophy of Kant had been a fundamental influence on the development of continental copyright,[18] and Kant had himself been active in the debate on copyright in the late eighteenth century.[19] Thus the Kantian categories constitute a seldom-acknowledged basis of the conceptual framework of European copyright law.[20]

Art, in Kant's threefold definition, is (1) distinguished from nature: works of art come into being only through 'the power of choice that bases its acts on reason'.[21] (2) Art is a human skill and is distinguished from science in the way a practical ability is distinguished from a theoretical ability. (3) Art is distinguished from craft: 'the first is also called *free art*, the second could also be called *mercenary art*'.[22] Fine art succeeds (is, in Kantian terms, 'purposive') only if it is 'play' and agreeable as an occupation on its own account: though the artist may have an ulterior motive, the work can have no ulterior purpose. Mercenary art, on the other hand, is not an end in itself; it is made as a means to an end, with some usefulness in view.

Kant does not define in advance which professions belong to the category of artists and which to that of craftsmen: 'to judge whether, in a ranking of the guilds, watchmakers should be counted as artists but smiths as craftsmen, we would have to take a viewpoint different from the one adopted here: we would have to compare (proportion) the talents that each of these occupations presupposes'.[23] Instead, Kant's concern with the aesthetic shifts the distinction from the object to the perceiving subject. Moreover, in his analysis of the various classes of fine art, Kant, listing architecture as one of the plastic arts, defines it as an art form that is determined by its usefulness. 'Architecture' has an extended sense for Kant, comprising anything made for a purpose. Architecture is thus to be distinguished from sculpture, whose purposiveness is not in use but in resembling some natural object, notably the human body. Sculpture was in Kant's day pre-eminent among the fine arts and exemplifies their mimetic purpose. By contrast, architecture submits its materials to a particular form for 'a chosen purpose'. In realizing the material in architectural form there may also be aesthetic purposiveness, yet the main concern is the *use* to be made of the object, and this use must limit and condition any aesthetic ideas.[24] Buildings, temples, residences, memorials and so forth are all works of architecture. Yet, Kant continues, 'we may even add to this all household furnishings (such as the work of the cabinet maker and other such things that are meant to be used). For what is essential in a *work of architecture* is the product's adequacy for a certain use.'[25]

On the one hand, Kant excludes crafts from the category of art since such works are made with non-artistic purposes. On the other hand, the fact that the making of a work is conditioned by its being destined for a type of use—that its adequacy as a usable product is a criterion for its success—does not per se deprive it of its place among the fine arts. Rather, fulfilling the chosen purpose of a particular use while doing it with aesthetic purposiveness is the defining feature of the class of fine art that Kant names 'architecture'. In other words, within the Kantian system, a work of applied art may belong to either the category of craft/mercenary art *or* the category of fine art—depending on the *talent* with which it is made. Talent, as a Kantian category, is a quality of Genius: it is 'an innate productive ability of the artist'. And 'fine arts must necessarily be considered arts of genius'.[26] Furthermore, applied art is always characterized by a twofold purpose. First, it has a particular use as its purpose, and this use is instrumental in shaping its aesthetic expression. The second kind of purpose has to do with the destination of the work: the work is either an end in itself (as free art), or it is made for an effect (as mercenary art).

In 1907, the Supreme Court, in its consideration of Krog's coffee pot, implicitly pointed out the twofold purpose of applied art. Krog's work was categorized as an item (1) made for practical usage and (2) aimed for industrial mass production. Within a Kantian framework of thinking it was entirely justified that the Danish Supreme Court should have denied a coffee pot the protection of copyright law. Equally within the spirit of Kant, however, the Danish Supreme Court simultaneously demanded that copyright protection *ought* to be extended to this same coffee pot. As is evident in the argumentation of the court, the design was perceived as an instance of mercenary art. Insofar as Krog was presumed to have created a 'model' or a 'prototype' (which was not an end in itself), his work would necessarily be alien to copyright law, which restricted its protection to works of free art (i.e. ends in themselves).

Offering protection to a coffee pot—albeit one of artistic quality—would in 1907 have been an anomaly in artistic copyright. The notion of a 'work of art' in Danish copyright law had to be reconceptualized. In legal terms: an extension of the scope of copyright was necessary. It required positive regulation from Parliament to reconceptualize the object of copyright law, yet Parliament could only respond because that reconceptualization was already taking place in aesthetic and social debates. By 1908 Parliament had amended the definition of a 'work of art' to ensure that the applied arts had a place in copyright law. The 1912 Act on Authorial and Artistic Rights confirmed the new definition.[27]

DEBATING DEGREES OF ARTFULNESS

It would be too simple to suggest that by the 1912 Act and the 1933 Act (which reaffirmed the 1908 definition of a 'work of art') applied art in Denmark was placed under copyright protection. Rather, the state of affairs was that applied art was not *necessarily* dismissed as falling outside of copyright law. It is hardly surprising that the matter was not resolved by one piece of legislation. Even today the applied arts remain among the most difficult concepts in copyright law (in Denmark and many other countries). Nevertheless, a number of works of applied art were granted copyright protection under the 1912 and 1933 Acts. For example, silver jewellery from the renowned silversmith Georg Jensen, a bottle opener shaped like a seahorse, a lampshade designed by Poul Henningsen and a set of wax mannequins.[28]

In 1926 the new definition of 'artwork' in copyright law passed an important test when the Royal Porcelain Factory was once again involved in a lawsuit over copyright.[29] Royal Porcelain was suing the wholesale dealers Holst

& Knudsen for importing and marketing imitations of Krog's coffee pot along with other pieces from his blue fluted tea and coffee set. Yet again the case went to the Danish Supreme Court. As was to be expected—since Royal Porcelain had occasioned the change in the law—Krog's design was found to be protectable as a work of art under § 24 of the 1912 Act on Authorial and Artistic Rights. The court followed the expert opinion which maintained that the tea and coffee set constituted an 'artistic whole' which had come into being through the 'thorough artistic preparations' carried out by Krog.[30] And to complete the artistic rehabilitation of Krog's porcelain designs, the Supreme Court affirmed that the goods imported by Holst & Knudsen infringed Krog's artistic copyright. Damages were ordered against the defendant, and all the infringing sets of porcelain that remained in Denmark were to be destroyed.[31]

In all cases where a work of applied art was ruled to qualify for copyright protection, the judges relied on expert opinion. Experts had provided statements deeming the work in question to be worthy of protection.[32] The courts, to be sure, are under no obligation to follow the *aesthetic* judgements of the experts (who are laymen with respect to the law); they are to make judgements on a *legal* basis. Yet for judges actually to contradict the evaluation of experts is extraordinary and exceptional. This nevertheless occurred during the first half of the twentieth century when judges were still hesitant about allowing applied art a place in copyright and would challenge the experts' opinion. Remarkably, according to the terms of the judgement, two judges of the Supreme Court in the 1926 Royal Porcelain case had *not* considered Krog's design to be a 'work of art', regardless of the law. They were, in other words, prepared to disregard not only the statement of the experts but also the 1908 amendment. Moreover, the vote in favour of copyright protection for the pot in 1926 carried by the narrowest margin of 5–4.[33]

Kant's categorical thinking offers a means of shedding light on this situation. Why were some judges still prepared to go against the spirit of the amended copyright law? This may well be explained by the inherent uncertainty of the artistic status of applied arts. As we have seen in our reading of Kant's *Critique*, applied art (classified as 'architecture') may belong to the category of fine art *or* to the category of mercenary art, depending on the talent involved in its making. A consequence of this potential of applied art to belong to *either* category is that it becomes susceptible to an evaluation of quality in a way that other classes of fine art are not. The judges, so to speak, are tempted to engage in estimating the artistic merits (or, as Kant says, the invested talent) of a work of applied art in order to find whether it qualifies as a work of 'fine art'. (This was, obviously, the category with which judges in copyright disputes of the time were familiar.) Such an evaluation of artistic merit would be unheard of in a courtroom in relation to the classes of fine art that have belonged to copyright law since its beginning, for example painting. It has been doctrine since the early twentieth century in continental (as well as Anglo-American) copyright law that lawyers are *never* to make aesthetic evaluations of a work.[34]

Yet such evaluations by 'lawyers' of merit in works of applied art took place regularly in Danish copyright law until the 1961 Copyright Act specifically named 'applied art' (*brugskunst*) as an object of protection.[35] Paradoxically, until 1961, because works of applied art would at times be perceived as fine art (ends in themselves), instances of applied art assigned to the category of 'mercenary art' were always at risk of being disqualified as 'works of art'—this notwithstanding the fact that the Danish law of 1908 had spelled out that a prototype for manufacture should be subject to copyright protection. Applied art's 'double life' as either fine art or mercenary art has continued to be a factor destabilizing its protection by copyright.

ARTLESS=WORTHLESS?

The year 1935 saw the most notorious case in the early history of Danish law and the applied arts. The case, U.1935.695H,[36] heard by the Supreme Court, concerned a set of icons of modern design: Thonet-Mundus tubular steel furniture.[37] Parties to the case were Scandinavian Thonet-Mundus, as the original plaintiff, and a Danish manufacturer of steel furniture, Dansk Staalmøbelfabrik, as the defendant and, later, appellant at the Supreme Court. Among the disputed pieces were the cantilevered chairs S 32 and S 64 designed by Marcel Breuer, former director of the carpentry workshop of the Bauhaus design school and one of the most celebrated designers of the modern era. The chairs are still produced and remain classics of the Bauhaus school.[38] In 1932 the Reichsgericht in Germany had found that such tubular steel chairs of the *Freischwinger* type were worthy of copyright protection.[39] Three years later the Danish Supreme Court decided emphatically that they were not.

However, the experts called by the Danish court had been very positive in their estimation of the furniture. About Breuer's chairs it was said that 'such a shape had been achieved as to render them works of art':

> Nowadays the artistic task in designing an article of everyday use such as a steel chair consists in giving it as simple a shape as possible; taking into consideration, on the one hand, the material and its technical utilization and, on the other hand, the most functional shaping of the article. By contrast, the conception of art of former days consisted in putting the chief emphasis on the ornamentation of the article whereby a large amount of slackness and crudity could be concealed. The chairs from the Thonet-Mundus Factory possess by their elegant and seemingly matter-of-course simple lines and the practical positioning of the seat, back, arm rest and so forth precisely such qualities [as first-mentioned] and ought therefore to be regarded as works of art as defined by the law.[40]

While the first court based its judgement on the experts, the Supreme Court went against them in their decision, finding that,

> the pieces of furniture presented by plaintiff were all very simple models and the shapes that they had been given were naturally and technically motivated by the material and the intended use. The attractive form which has been the result does not imply such artistic characteristics as to render the furniture works of industrial art according to § 24, article 3 of the Act on Artistic and Literary Rights.[41]

The Supreme Court was not prepared to consider tubular steel cantilever chairs to be 'original artistic works destined to be prototypes for industrial art',[42] as the object of artistic copyright was defined, disregarding the positive appraisal and the exemplification of modern aesthetic principles presented by the experts. As is clear from the formulation of the judgement, the judges regarded the effort invested in making the chairs not as the artistic accomplishments of an artist. Rather, such effort was viewed as the technical skill of the craftsperson who was familiar with the potentials and the shortcomings of materials for making a chair. The experts attributed the simplicity of the lines and the exploration of new technologies to a chosen style (as intended by their maker): they were characteristic of what we refer to today as functionalism. However, the judges interpreted the same features to be the consequence of working with particular materials; any aesthetic qualities of the furniture were thus considered more or less accidental. In Kantian terms: the judges did not see the chair as an example of fine art—as an aesthetic end in itself—because the chair was perceived only as a means to another end (that of sitting down).

The artistic idiom of functionalism added an extra complexity to the already-problematic relationship between applied art and copyright law. The industrial and de-individualized expression of functionalist furniture, combined with the rhetoric of the modernist movement in architecture and design, made applied art even more problematic as a category of copyright law. If 'form follows function' (as Louis Sullivan had insisted in 1896) and if everything that 'serves no practical purpose' is to be excluded, as runs another axiom of functionalism, little was left of the 'work of art' in copyright law, based as it was on nineteenth-century aesthetics with its Romantic values of individuality, personality, distinctiveness and the aesthetic ingenuity of ornamentation.

Danish works of applied art were also denied copyright protection. In 1954, a rocking chair was judged to be the result of the 'skilled efforts of a craftsman' rather than a 'work of art'.[43] In 1956, a bread cutter designed by the artist Ove Larsen for Raadvad Knivfabriker was turned down by the Supreme Court on the grounds that it was a 'tool' in which the 'artistic design was a matter of secondary importance'.[44] However, in 1960, copyright protection was offered to Hans Wegner's armchairs number 501 (from 1949) and number 503 (from 1950).[45] (See fig. 2.2.) During the trial, the chair—which has become world-famous under the label 'The Chair'—was described by one expert as a 'marked example of what is covered by the law's [category of] "original work of art"'.[46] Another expert, however, declared that he did not think that 'a chair, which is an object of everyday use for lots of people, and which is, in advance, made for such a use, and which can be made by any decent cabinetmaker, and which to a large extent looks like any other chair, could be considered as an original work of art'.[47]

Nevertheless, the plaintiff was able to present ample testimony that 'The Chair' was nothing short of an artistic masterpiece. Thus it was pointed out that the American magazine *Interiors* had praised the chair in several articles in the early 1950s. In 1952, it had been selected by a committee from the Museum of Modern Art in New York and awarded the prestigious 'Good Design' label. 'The Chair' had also been awarded the Grand Prix at the IX Triennale di Milano in 1951. Like Marcel Breuer's, Wegner's chair had been acquired by

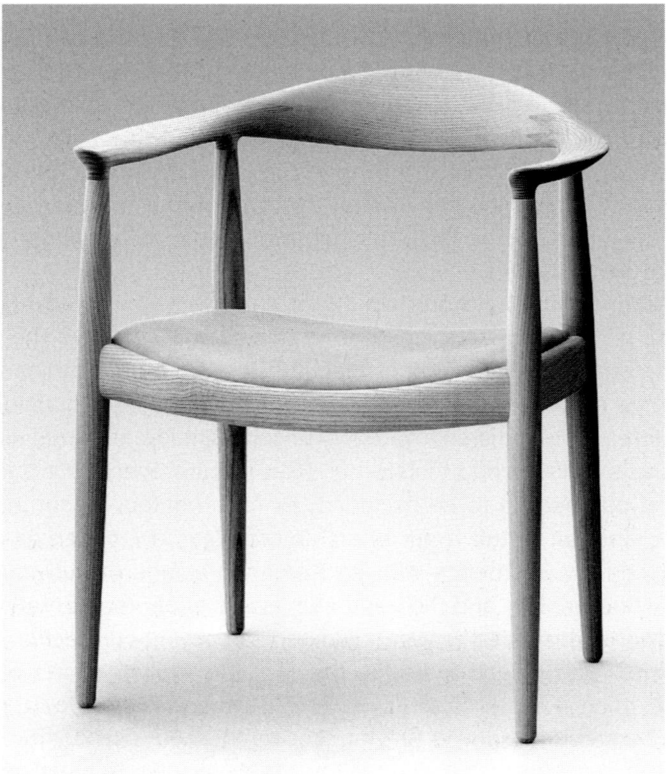

Fig. 2.2 PP503 'The Chair' designed by Hans J. Wegner (1950). Photograph: Jens Mourits Sørensen. Courtesy of PP Møbler.

museums around the world. The plaintiff also emphasized the fact that significant international institutions had bought the chair, such as the NATO and UNESCO headquarters in Paris. Though the chair was purchased for practical use, there was obvious aesthetic value and prestige in the choice of furniture for these international organizations. Furthermore, the plaintiff was able to cite from numerous declarations paying tribute to the artistic expressiveness of the chair; it was generally recognized that Wegner had created a 'classic work of art' remarkable for its 'aesthetic qualities' and that Wegner, himself, was 'an artist'.[48]

The court did not hesitate to affirm the assertion of the first expert cited in the preceding: Wegner's chair was a 'work of art' protectable by § 24 of the Act of 26 April 1933. By the same token, the court acknowledged the worldwide appreciation of the chair's artistic value. It was evident in this case that a work of applied art—a chair, a means for sitting down—was also a work of fine art. Hence it was a mere chair that transformed the understanding of what could be protected by Danish copyright law.

TURNING DESIGN INTO ART

The Danish Copyright Act of 1961 bore evidence of a change in the attitude to copyright protection of design; the Act specifically mentioned applied art (*brugskunst*) as an object of copyright.[49] According to this law, the originator of a literary or artistic work holds the copyright to his or her work whether it manifests itself in writing or speech; as music, drama or film; as a work of visual art, architecture or applied art; or in any other way.

Before the passing of the Act, the drafted bill of 1959–60 had proposed that,

> articles of everyday use within the realm of household furniture and effects, with a form which is not entirely determined by their practical purposes, and with a quality of artistic creation, [are to be] protected as actual works of art.[50]

This formulation was criticized by the Danish Arts and Crafts Association, in particular for the clause 'with a form which is not entirely determined by their practical purposes'. This runs counter to the very heart of the functionalist aesthetic. The sole criterion ought to be whether an article had the quality of an artistic creation. Hence, in a White Paper of 27 April 1961 it was stated that, in the assessment of whether an article of everyday use was to be regarded as protectable by copyright law,

> emphasis ought to be on whether the article is an artistic creation which fulfils the usual requirements for a work as defined by the law. In that case it ought

> to be protected without taking into account its practical purpose even when the consideration of the functionally appropriate design has had a decisive role in the shaping of the article.[51]

By wilfully disregarding the functional element of works of applied art, the 1961 Act had, so to speak, promoted design to the status that 'art' had long enjoyed in copyright law. A decisive effort had been made to reconceptualize the notion of applied art. It was to be seen as a work in itself rather than a prototype, as it had been in the 1902, 1912 and 1933 Acts. The former acts had all contained the formulation 'original artistic works destined to be prototypes for industrial art'.[52] By the 1961 Act, the judiciary was, so to speak, instructed to see works of applied art as ends in themselves.

Since 1961, Danish courts have been given an apparently simple task: to ask only whether a given work of applied art is an 'original work' according to copyright law.[53] This does not imply that the work has to be novel. Rather, it means that it has to 'originate' from the artist who claims the rights in it. It has to be the result of his or her 'personal', 'creative' and 'independent' effort.[54] Likewise, if a work of applied art is denied protection, it must be on the grounds that it is not an 'original work'. That is to say, a work of applied art is not to be disqualified either because a certain relation exists between its aesthetic expression and its function or because the work might look like another work with a similar function.

Needless to say, applied art has not ceased to cause legal difficulties. As identified by Kant, in applied art 'the main concern is what *use* is to be made of the artistic object, and this use is a condition to which the aesthetic ideas are confined'.[55] Thus applied art remains distinct from the various types of fine art (painting, sculpture and so forth) that the law of copyright was initially intended to protect. Inevitably, all the categories of copyright law are destabilized when an anomaly is introduced and remains unresolved.

WHAT IS A COPY?

The 1961 Act brought about a change in the direction of Danish copyright law, notably through a decision concerning a set of cutlery. The decision did not dispute the set's status as a work of art. This status was affirmed by all judges of the first instance and of the Supreme Court, despite general agreement that the ribbed handles that allegedly constituted the distinctiveness of the design were neither unique nor innovative.[56] In a similar vein, a range of other consumer goods (unimaginable in 1907 as objects of copyright) have been granted protection: a coffee grinder, a holder for a dishwashing brush, a pocket-torch and many other products resulting from the 'personal', 'creative' and 'independent' efforts of aspirant copyright holders.[57]

The more liberal granting of copyright protection poses a potential threat to the freedom of competition for producers of industrial art. However, to prevent copyright law from playing too active a role in the creation of monopolies, the court may choose to relax the criterion for infringement. The decision in the cutlery dispute of 1961 is an example of such an approach. It was ruled that the defendant's use of a design very similar to the plaintiff's did not amount to infringement even though the latter's design was protected by copyright. Arguably, the battleground has thus moved from the question: is applied art protectable by copyright law? to the question: what are the criteria for infringement in cases that concern applied arts?[58]

We can echo Justice Peterson's claim from 1916: what's worth copying is worth protecting.[59] But we must add that much still depends on what the court understands as copying.

–3–

Handwoven Fabrics by the Yard: Unveiling the Modern Design Industry of the Interwar Period

Leena Svinhufvud

Textile art has a prominent position in Finnish design, both in its history and in contemporary practice. In the context of Scandinavian design, textile art is very often romanticized as the continuation of an innate crafts tradition, especially in the cases of Finland and Sweden.[1] If examined within the framework of the social and material production systems, however, Finnish textile design might look quite different from this conventional image. Focusing on the modernizing design field of the interwar period, this case study draws attention to a previously disregarded genre of textiles, handwoven fabrics for interior decoration and garments, called *fabrics by the yard*. The expression refers to serial or mass production, the manufacturing of textiles by the yard or by the metre, as opposed to single pieces. Based on evidence from published sources and archives, I outline the scale and commercial significance of such mass production of handcrafted textiles. By investigating the opportunities provided by hand weaving this essay re-evaluates the habitual polarization of industrial production and crafts in much design historical research whilst highlighting the systemic and networked nature of design practice.

TEXTILES AND MODERNISM

Following the lively international exhibition activity after the First World War there were a lot of publications of applied arts and design. Also in Finland new journals and catalogues from this period illustrate the changes in both the ideologies and the practice of the developing designer profession. The national design organizations, the Finnish Society of Crafts and Design (Suomen Taideteollisuusyhdistys, est. 1875) the Finnish Association of Decorative Artists Ornamo (Koristetaiteilijain Liitto Ornamo, est. 1911), promoted the work of Finnish decorative artists in exhibitions and publications both domestically and internationally.

Specialized training in textile art was established in 1929 at the Central School of Arts and Crafts in Helsinki (est. 1871, now the Aalto University School of Art and Design).[2] The title 'textile artist' can be misleading, as, in all the school's programs, the training aimed at teaching design skills. Still, textile students learned weaving by hand, and industrial manufacturing methods were not taught until the early 1950s. The topical nature of the handloom is reflected in publications on applied arts from the interwar period, where textiles often outnumber other products in the images. Woven wall hangings and carpets, embroidered tablecloths and sofa cushions with fashionable motifs and decoration are pictured individually and in their settings of contemporary interiors. In the early 1930s these were accompanied by new kinds of images in the form of carefully constructed photos portraying the structure and quality of woven textiles—much like the furniture photographs analysed in Malene Breunig's contribution to this volume: heaps of cascading fabrics, close-ups of folded and twisted weaves showing the transparency of a curtain fabric and the gloss in the surface of damask, or cropped takes of heavy carpets with rough pile and distinctive material (fig. 3.1). These modern handwoven fabrics are the protagonists of this study.

Judged by the interiors depicted in publications, for example in the catalogue *Innenräume*, showing interiors and furnishings from the Deutscher Werkbund exhibition Die Wohnung in Stuttgart in 1927, woven curtains and furnishing fabrics were from the late 1920s on a distinct feature of international avant-garde architecture.[3] However, the value and meanings of textile design within modernism are complex. In modernist discourses of the 1920s and 1930s—in published projects and writings—textiles were re-evaluated; some were described as ideal and others as unwanted or banned. Textiles were important but were subjected to careful selection and, in some cases, to the powerful gesture of being omitted altogether.[4]

In Finland the modernist ideal of rationalist and functional design for mass production was manifested in the Small Apartment Exhibition (Pienasuntonäyttely) in Helsinki in 1930. Organized in conjunction with the annual applied art exhibition it manifested the repositioning of work in this field. The exhibition was curated by the architect Alvar Aalto, who was active in the networks of European reformist architects. In the exhibition catalogue Aalto and his colleague P. E. Blomstedt insisted on breaking with the decorative arts in order to design for the masses.[5] The kitchen in the interior designed by Aalto and his architect wife, Aino Marsio-Aalto, illustrated the argument (fig. 3.2). This was not the first Finnish design for a modern kitchen but one that particularly emphasized Taylorist ideals, technical innovations and rationalist production methods.[6]

One feature that radically differed from earlier proposals was the absence of textiles. In the reformist kitchen designs of the architect Elna Kiljander from the mid-1920s,[7] she used chequered curtains in the window and a rag

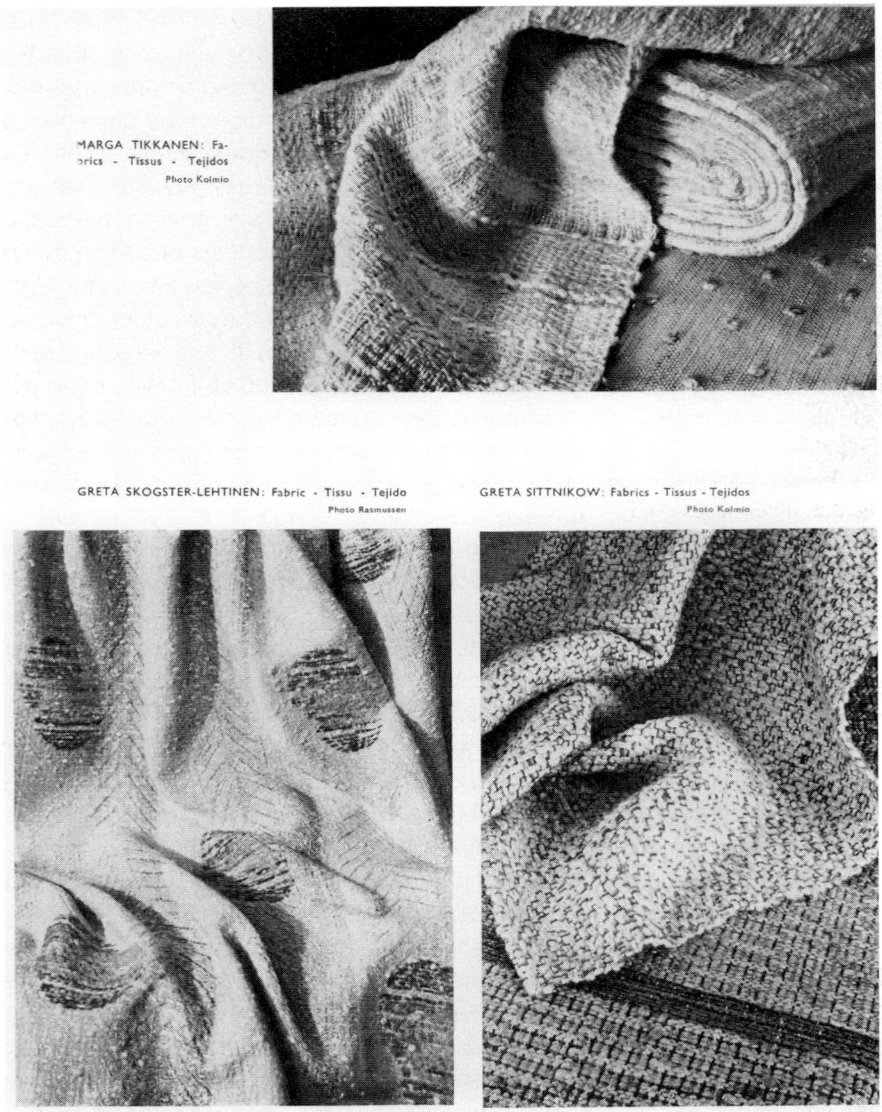

Fig. 3.1 Fabrics by the yard designed by Marga Tikkanen, Greta Skogster-Lehtinen and Greta Sittnikow as featured in the catalogue *Applied Art in Finland* that was published for the New York World's Fair in 1939. Out of copyright.
Source: H. [Harry] Röneholm, W. [Werner] West and W. [Walter] Wahlroos (eds.), *Applied Art in Finland=Les arts appliqués en Finlande=Las artes utiles en Finlandia* (Helsinki: The Finnish Section of New York World's Fair, 1939).

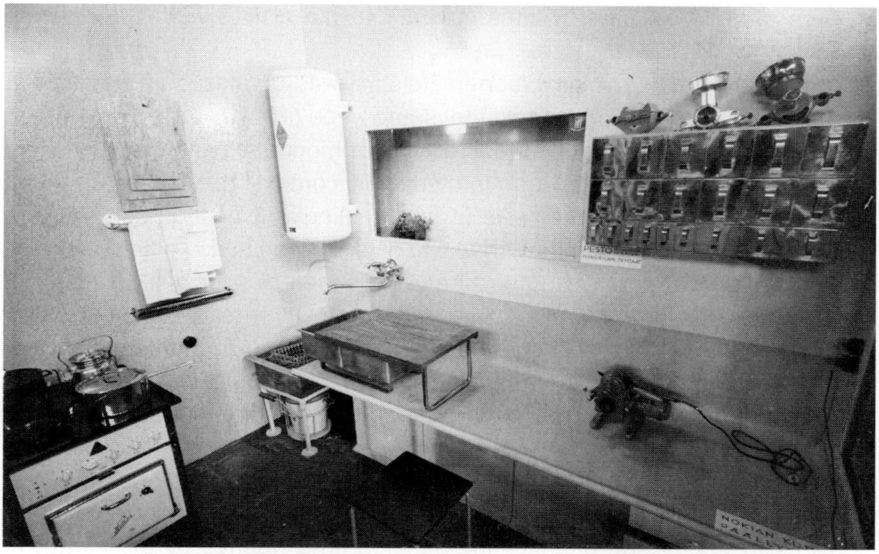

Fig. 3.2 Kitchen designed by Aino Marsio-Aalto and Alvar Aalto and shown at the Small Apartment Exhibition in Helsinki in 1930. Photograph courtesy of Alvar Aalto Museum, Jyväskylä.

rug on the floor, following the idiom of modern homes established in the Swedish context. Just how important textiles were in this idiom can be gauged, for example, from Ellen Key's influential text *Skönhet i hemmen* ('Beauty in the home') from 1899:

> And how cosy and beautiful is an old parlour in a country parsonage, where the furnishings are pearl grey, the floor shines blinding white and beautiful rag rugs create pathways on the floor; where white home made curtains let in the sun on well-tended flower pots, where there is a simple handwoven tablecloth on the table and an old blue-and-white tiled stove in the corner.[8]

The Aaltos chose the opposite strategy, implementing the modernist method of 'mechanical selection',[9] using only industrially produced textiles by anonymous designers in their interiors for the Small Apartment Exhibition. They made a statement by limiting the scope and quality of textiles and thereby also limiting the participation of other designers. Less well-known parts of the same exhibition, such as a living room interior by the architect Erik Bryggman and a hotel room and a domestic bedroom by architects P. E. Blomstedt and Märta Blomstedt, included handwoven and industrially produced fabrics and carpets by the textile artist Greta Skogster (later Skogster-Lehtinen). In these settings the use of textiles was also restricted to a functional one, allowing only curtains and carpets; here, however, the production method of the fabrics was not, it seems, considered an absolute criterion. Moreover, in these modern interiors textiles by contemporary textile artists were an essential feature.

The Small Apartment Exhibition in Helsinki was organized in response to the Stockholm Exhibition earlier the same year (1930). Both can be considered manifestations of the breakthrough of modernism—or functionalism, which became the preferred term in the Nordic context. The manifesto *Acceptera* (1931) published in the wake of the Stockholm Exhibition declared that the world had changed and that art would have to change accordingly. The prevailing artisanal manner of production was condemned for being elitist, and the text attacked, among others, Sweden's most highly regarded organization in textile art, the Association of Friends of Textile Art (Handarbetets Vänner, est. 1874): 'A carpet by the Association of Friends of Textile Art or a Rolls Royce are different yet typical examples of luxury goods.'[10] Here, expensive handwoven carpets were banned. The text nevertheless appreciated handwoven fabrics, the products of *hemslöjd* (i.e. work by anonymous craftspersons) based on hundreds of years of tradition. The modernist manifesto posits the timeless, peaceful and unassuming *metervarorna* (fabrics by the metre) as ideal.[11] One of the authors of *Acceptera*, the art historian and design reformer Gregor Paulsson, suggested in an article published the following year that traditional handwoven fabrics could function as a model for the evolving textile industry.[12] A similar idealizing of traditional homemade utility goods paired with a naturalizing of technology and rationalist thinking was expressed in Finland by the art historian and critic Nils-Gustav Hahl, co-founder and managing director of Artek—the company set up in 1935 to market Alvar Aalto's furniture. Hahl claimed that handwoven textiles could survive alongside industrial production because of their high technical and material quality and their flexibility of manufacture, making it possible to accommodate the requirements of different customer groups.[13] Hahl's conception of the role of handicraft in modern manufacture of textiles may point towards a more nuanced understanding of design history.

MACHINE INDUSTRY VERSUS CRAFTS PRODUCTION

The modernization of design is often perceived as a result of trained designers working for industry. However, the concept of industrial design is problematic with regard to the history of textile production in interwar Finland, because trained designers did not work for the industry on a broader scale until the 1950s. Until the 1920s patterns were imported from Central Europe along with the technology, and even after this the commercial pattern design studios of France and Germany provided a lot of material for the Finnish mills, as they did for the entire European textile industry. Later, some of the Finnish mills founded their own pattern design studios recruiting designers from abroad and training a new workforce. Thus, the textile industry had an established system of organizing the design of products that bypassed the organized design profession.[14]

In a European perspective the economic recessions of the interwar period had a relatively mild effect in Finland. Industrial development was even faster in Finland than in the other Nordic countries, the years of fastest growth being 1924–8 and 1933–7. The textile and fashion industry as a whole was very successful in this period, as the general rise in the standard of living was reflected directly in the growth of consumption.[15] The industry, using new technologies, screen-printed fabrics and tricot, was also the first to hire trained designers in the 1930s and 1940s.[16] The growth of this sector was most visible in the capital region, where the professional designers' activity was also concentrated. Helsinki also constituted a unique market, where the inhabitants' average income was much higher than elsewhere in the country. Specialized small companies and luxury shops flourished in Helsinki during the interwar years.[17]

Compared to the success of craft-based production and smaller-scale industries using new technologies, the times were not as favourable for the traditional textile mills. With a long history starting in the eighteenth century, Finland's cotton and linen industries were Nordic leaders in terms of production volume in the early twentieth century when the markets in Russia provided successful business. This was disrupted by the Russian Revolution and Finland's independence in 1917, leaving the Finnish textile industry to rely on the domestic market until the 1950s. The capacity of mechanized mass production was affected by the availability of foreign raw materials in periods of worldwide recession. Challenges with domestic raw material production restricted mechanization and standardization and, accordingly, opportunities for large-scale manufacturing. In these situations, small companies were more flexible in adapting to changes.

The term *industrial handicraft* has been used to denote organized manufacturing outside the context of large-scale, mechanized industry. Interestingly, in Finland both machine-based industry and craft-based industry experienced growth during the interwar period. In fact, the 1930s represented a peak period for industrial handicraft, and employment in this sector diminished only after the Second World War.[18] Another important concept is that of the cottage industry, or *home-based industry*, which prevailed in agrarian Finland as an extra source of income for quite a long time.[19] A skilled workforce is a requirement for producing woven fabrics on a handicraft basis. The necessary expertise was created in the women's handicraft and weaving schools that were founded in the late nineteenth century. The method of hand weaving at the loom did not change much from the mid-nineteenth century on, but the fact that industrially produced yarns became widely available at the end of the century and the introduction of electric lighting in Finnish homes had a considerable influence on the production capacity. By then, access to industrial fabrics had already diminished the necessity of weaving utility textiles at home. However, the First World War and the Finnish civil war of 1918 hampered industrial production and importation of textiles, and this period of shortages and economic recession provided new structures for the production and processing of raw materials in this field. It also regenerated the tradition of weaving at home and even created new markets for yarns and materials for weaving.[20] Home-based industries (Fin. *kotiteollisuus*, Sw. *hemslöjd*) were institutionalized by the introduction in 1918 of state-appointed inspectors and by the organization of training in this field. The importance of textile production to the organized home-based industries was noted in 1925 in the Finnish magazine *Käsiteollisuus* ('Crafts industries'), where a comparison of crafts organizations' shops in Nordic capitals showed that most of the trade consisted of textiles.[21] The same magazine could also report that the shop run by the Association of Swedish Handicraft (Svensk Hemslöjd) in Stockholm sold almost 7,000 metres of handwoven furnishing fabrics annually.[22] The trade in crafts production was institutionalized in 1929 in the Home-based Industries Federation (Suomen kotiteollisuusliitto), which consisted mostly of textile organizations. Markets were also sought abroad, for example with the aid of a touring exhibition held in the United States in 1935–8.[23]

One of the more successful companies in this sector was the Kotikutomo Helmi Vuorelma Oy of Lahti (the Home Weavery Helmi Vuorelma Ltd, est. 1914). The company made fabrics for interiors and garments—including Finnish national costumes, a very popular nationalistic fashion during the interwar years. In the early 1930s the firm's index of weavers listed 109 names, and this figure grew to almost 300 by the end of the decade. Most of the weavers, all of them women, worked on commission at home. One home-based weaver could specialize in a specific quality or pattern and produce several hundred metres of fabric per year. This was the case for a certain Hilma Kaukonen from the village of Ämmälä, who one year (1939/40) wove almost 300 metres of the fashionable curtain fabric Kaunotar ('Beauty'; fig. 3.3). The pattern for this fabric was probably designed by the Lahti-born Maija Kolsi (later Kolsi-Mäkelä), who had been hired by Vuorelma as a designer in 1935 immediately after she graduated from the textile art department of the Central School of Arts and Crafts.[24]

In the case of the company Vuorelma, the high production volume and high product quality were achieved through systematic organization of the work. The low cost of labour was crucial when counting the price per metre. The production was flexible compared to traditional industrial mills and their mechanized manufacturing systems: hundreds of metres of fabric could be produced with very low set-up costs and with the flexibility of using different materials and changing colours and bindings (structure). The example of Vuorelma shows that trained designers had access to a considerable potential

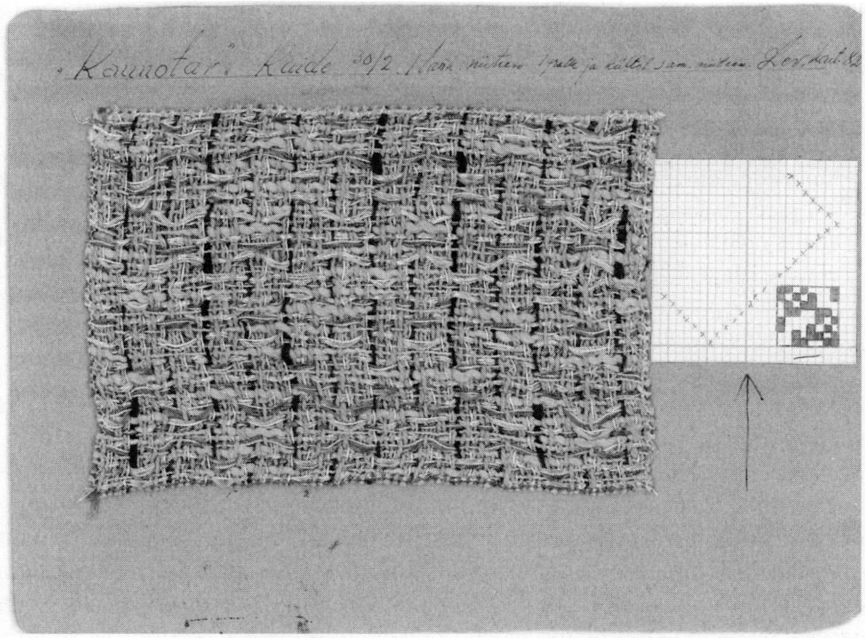

Fig. 3.3 Kaunotar furnishing fabric produced by the Home Weavery Helmi Vuorelma Ltd of Lahti in 1939. Photograph courtesy of the Craft Museum of Finland.

for textile production. However, in the crafts or home-based industries sector, the attribution of an individual fabric pattern to a certain designer is complicated. The name of the designer has not often been considered worth documenting, and there is still very little research on this phenomenon.[25]

WOMEN'S ENTREPRENEURSHIP

In an article on new directions in Finnish textile art published in the *Yearbook of the Finnish Association of Decorative Artists Ornamo* in 1933 textile artist Eva Anttila sketches an image of the new textile artist as a modern professional whose work is based on old traditions and folk art but in a period of changing values when 'the new is emerging from its egg shell at the speed of an express train'. Using modernist rhetoric, Anttila sought to dispel the image of the 'arty' designer. She underlined the mission to serve the urban dwellers: 'Just some years ago the prevailing idea was that applied art products are only for the wealthy, who in their sumptuous homes have a suitably dignified place for an artistic tankard or a laborious wall-hanging. Today a modest young couple will visit the applied arts workshop and equip their standard home of two rooms and a kitchen inexpensively and practically.' According to Anttila, contemporary socioeconomic conditions primarily dictated the nature of the pioneering work carried out by 'researchers' in the laboratories of textile art:

> Knowledge of colours and materials together with the correct sense of style are the most important preconditions for a modern textile product. These considerations predominate even in the simplest objects and the right solutions to them are the result from which a truly modern type is created. Economic conditions, changes in society, and the most recent achievements in interior design affect the manifestations of textile art just as much as the artist's own creative will.[26]

Anttila thus saw textile art as essentially connected to utilitarian aims and commercial practices.

In the Finnish applied art scene of the interwar period there were some twenty 'weaveries', 'design offices', 'studios' and so on run by trained textile artists. Only a few of them were formally registered, and many did not last very long.[27] The extent of activity suggests that it was relatively easy to establish small-scale handicraft production in the textile sector, especially when weaving by hand. Perhaps the largest private enterprise was Greta Skogster's Textile Office, founded by Greta Skogster-Lehtinen in 1929 in Helsinki. A decade later, in 1937, a Finnish newspaper article described the work of her new weaving studio in Enso, East Finland, where the textile artist had moved with her family. There were twenty-three weavers employed, and the studio had bought power looms for producing patterned weaves in large quantities. Textiles for a railroad sleeping car for the Finnish Railways and for a cabin on a passenger ship of the Finnish Steamship Company as well as other utility fabrics were being prepared for the Paris World's Fair of 1937. The newspaper also reported on the studio's commissions for big corporate building projects for industry and the restaurant business.[28]

Greta Skogster's Textile Office also secured significant commissions for projects by architects such as P. E. Blomstedt, Erkki Huttunen and Väinö Vähäkallio and later also Alvar Aalto. Exact information on individual projects and quantities of textiles produced in the weaving studio, which remained in function until 1974, remains unavailable due to a lack of documents. Nevertheless, the output of woven textiles during the interwar period must have been considerable, and the settings in which Skogster-Lehtinen's designs figured were not insignificant either. However, it is symptomatic that when one of her major projects, the headquarters of the paper mill of Enso-Gutzeit (fig. 3.4), was published in the magazine *Arkkitehti* (*The Finnish Architectural Review*, published by the Finnish Association of Architects) in 1935, her name is mentioned in the context of a unique decorative textile. The text points out a tapestry 'woven by the artist' but fails to notice the significant amount of furnishing fabrics, curtains and carpets she had designed, as if they formed a naturalized part of the architecture.[29]

It seems to have been common in architectural projects to label the textile designer as the executor of the practical work—as 'the weaver'. In real life, however, large-scale, high-quality production of textiles is not possible without the labour of skilled craftspersons. Furthermore, the training of textile artists at the Central School of Arts and Crafts, which engaged mainly students from educated families, did not aim at providing the professional skills of a weaver. In view of their background and networks the role of a craftsperson would not have been socially acceptable for the textile artists, either. On the contrary, many of them became designers and managers, outsourcing the manufacturing to professional weaving studios or home-based weavers or hiring craftspersons. It can be assumed that having even just one weaver 'of one's own'

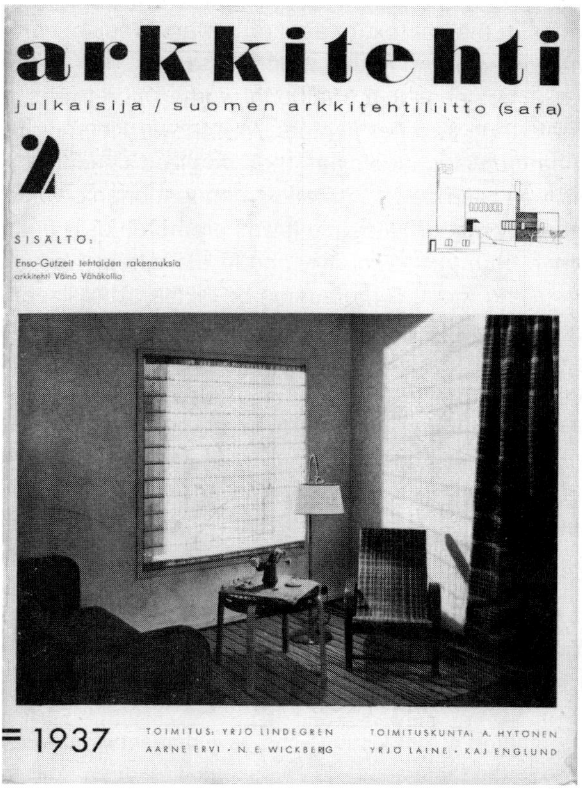

Fig. 3.4 An interior from the headquarters of the Enso-Gutzeit paper mill with textiles designed by Greta Skogster-Lehtinen, featured on the cover of the Finnish architectural magazine *Arkkitehti* in 1937. Image courtesy of *Arkkitehti—the Finnish Architectural Review*. (Association of Finnish Architects SAFA).

provided performance and continuity, and, for the textile artist, presiding over a weavery was a sign of status. It is noteworthy that many of them, like Skogster-Lehtinen, were in business under their own names.

I have used the term *entrepreneurship* to describe the activities of textile artists in the interwar period. This was not a contemporary notion but one that is widely used today to describe the work of independent actors organizing and marketing production. Kirsi Vainio-Korhonen has discussed the problematic role of women's traditional production of services and goods in economic histories conventionally concerned with large-scale production in industrial mills. Often based at home, and eschewing public records, the business of women selling food, cloths and nurture tends to remain invisible in accounts of economic development despite the indisputable significance and considerable scale of this type of manufacture and commerce.[30] The work of professional women designers who made a traditional Finnish craft into a business, organizing the production of their own designs and producing new meanings for crafted textiles in the context of applied art and design, can be compared to women's entrepreneurship in this wider context.

Pursuing design business in a traditional women's craft was certainly more readily acceptable than in other sectors. In interwar Finland, weaving fit well with prevailing nationalistic ideologies that idealized peasant and farmer culture. Handicraft was regarded as entailing unquestionable values amidst the anxiety brought on by modern life, and it was promoted as a useful spare time activity for women both in the country and in the cities. Weaving by hand as a core function in the modern profession of textile artists realized the ideal of self-sufficiency and rationality whilst also maintaining symbolically the traditional gender division in an age when more and more women were starting to work outside the home. A women's culture focused on the home and reproduction was created and mediated, for example through new magazines. For the textile artists it was of great importance to participate in this project, to be able to publicly address the female makers and users of textiles, who also were their clients.

FABRICS BY THE YARD AT THE FRIENDS OF FINNISH HANDICRAFT

> The emerging method of production—the development of standard types to be mass-produced in the thousands—is an essential feature of our age, just as the Grecian temples, medieval cathedrals, and Rococo chair types belonged to the civilizations of their own times . . . Contemporary woven products—which are also standard products, whether handmade or produced by industry—aim at the most monochrome hues possible and calm designed forms in order to suit, in an organic manner, the spirit of modern standardized, type-planned dwellings.[31]

This is how the architect Elna Kiljander in 1932 presented the 'mass-produced' furniture fabrics, window curtains and draperies made by the Friends of Finnish Handicraft (Suomen Käsityön Ystävät, est. 1879). She was addressing the readers of *Kotiliesi* magazine ('Home hearth', est. 1923), the first Finnish magazine for the housewife. Through this magazine the organization made a breakthrough in marketing their crafts products widely in Finland. Textiles for the home, mostly handwoven, and do-it-yourself (DIY) kits could even be ordered by mail via the magazine's supplement.[32]

The case of the Friends of Finnish Handicraft shows how the rise of handwoven fabrics for interiors and furnishing was not the result of the so-called breakthrough of functionalism-modernism exclusively. The Helsinki-based association was founded in 1879 with the Swedish organization Handarbetets Vänner as its model. From the beginning of the twentieth century the association promoted itself as an 'art organization' staging textile design competitions and regular exhibitions. The association was reorganized as a limited company in 1920. In the years following Finnish independence this organization enjoyed the status of a national actor, which undoubtedly contributed to the company's positive economic development. The functions of the Friends of Finnish Handicraft were then twofold: firstly, serving as a workshop that produced textiles commissioned by private customers or, very often, public institutions and architects for contemporary building projects; and, secondly, selling textile patterns and materials for hobbyists (DIY).

In the interwar years, woven fabrics by the metre became the company's core product group. Hitherto it had focused on presenting in exhibitions textiles that were more or less singular objects—woven carpets, bench covers and wall hangings, embroidered sofa cushions, curtains and tablecloths; compared to embroidered works and sales of crafts materials, woven products were economically marginal.[33] The design of fabrics by the yard received more attention from the end of the 1910s, when the designer name is sometimes mentioned in the studio's surviving documents. Before this, the fabrics were categorized mainly by structure and were listed according to the traditional bindings used in them. In the fortieth-anniversary exhibition in 1919, the company presented for the first time furniture fabrics designed by the new director of the weaving studio, the crafts teacher Valborg Madsén-Himanen. The following year, more than 800 metres of different kinds of fabrics for interiors designed by her were produced, most of them to be sold in the company's shop, but also as commissions for interior design projects, and some were offered for sale in the Helsinki department store Stockmann.[34] At the next annual exhibition the amount of woven fabrics was doubled, and there were new designers, such as Toini Kallio, Toini Nyström, Eva Anttila and Margareta Ahlstedt (later Ahlstedt-Willandt)—all trained at the Central School of Arts and Crafts.

In 1930 the company's weaving studio was for the first time headed by a trained textile artist, Laila Karttunen, who was recruited especially to renew the line of woven textiles. The company also hired trained designers to provide customer service and to assist architects in interior design projects. The Friends of Finnish Handicraft secured several important public commissions in this period. One of them was for the new Parliament House building in Helsinki, for which 750 metres of curtain fabric were woven in 1931, employing all of the company's weaving studio for the spring period.[35] Also, two design competitions were organized in 1933 and 1938, generating publicity for handwoven fabrics for interiors.

The production was now rationalized. While in the early 1920s all the fabrics woven were rather narrow (from 70 to 85 centimetres), a decade later most of the furnishing fabrics were much broader, although the width varied a lot (from 68 to 130 centimetres). At the end of the 1930s the standard width of all furnishing fabrics was 130 centimetres and for curtain fabrics 70 or 90 centimetres. Starting in 1935 the fabrics, probably all designed by Laila Karttunen, are listed with their individual product names—for example Niitty ('Meadow') or Vanamo ('Linnaea')—and the range of the assortment is astonishing. According to the 1938 inventory the company offered at least seventy-five types of furnishing fabrics and approximately seventy types of curtain fabrics, and some of the patterns were produced in different colours. However, the quantities made were mostly quite small, sometimes only 2 to 3 metres of each furnishing fabric, resulting in a total production volume of almost 700 metres. The curtain fabrics were—not surprisingly, given their use—produced in greater volumes, close to 3,000 metres in total.[36] These figures illustrate how seriously the Friends of Finnish Handicrafts worked to develop a new line of products for the consumer market, in this case the urban middle class of Helsinki.

The development can also be followed in the annual reports. In 1930 it was stated that the economic depression had lifted 'a domestic spirit',[37] and this boosted commissions and the sale of yarns. Now the studio also started making many of the fabrics used for the embroidery works themselves rather than using industrially woven ones. In a few years, increased competition in the weaving business and the decline of prices and buying power weakened the prospects—but only briefly. The situation changed again by the mid-1930s, and the new economic boom was made manifest especially in an increased demand for woven fabrics, 'this being a natural consequence of contemporary interior design favouring woven over embroidered'.[38] Furnishing and curtain fabrics, flat woven rugs and linen tablecloths were products that sold especially well.

The outbreak of war in Finland in 1939 changed the activities radically,[39] but the impact on textile production was not so drastic and sudden as is often suggested. There were public commissions for interior design projects, for example in the capital and in the reconquered areas of Karelia, and fabrics were ordered by the Finnish Army, by furniture companies and by radio manufacturers. These were woven using substitute and waste materials as well as paper and, in many cases, textile material provided by the customer. According to the annual report for 1943 the weaving studio had mainly produced fabrics by the metre, for example curtains and fabrics for dresses, coats and towels, altogether 6,752 metres. In the following year, artificial silk fabrics for clothing were the main products, also marketed in fashion shows.[40] This demonstrates the flexibility of craft-based production, even in wartime conditions. Also, as the supplier of all the flags for the Finnish Army since the nation's independence in 1917, the company was now harnessed to participate in the wartime action, as were other actors in art and architecture.

Just before the war broke out in 1939, the Friends of Finnish Handicrafts staged its sixtieth-anniversary exhibition at Kunsthalle Helsinki, presenting itself above all as a manufacturer of woven textiles. The exhibition featured forty different types of furnishing fabrics and twenty-one types of curtain fabrics designed by Laila Karttunen. In a photo from the exhibition the plain, 'functional' setting of draped fabrics with different structures and hues is contrasted with a unique tapestry woven after a painting dating from 1900 by Akseli Gallen-Kallela, the national artist hero who had died in 1931. The tapestry, picturing a motif from the national epic *Kalevala*, was a showpiece demonstrating the effort and skill of the weavers (fig. 3.5).[41] The exhibition featured no fewer than thirty-five *ryijy* textiles (decorative textiles with woollen pile based on a Scandinavian tradition), which had been the company's signature product since the early twentieth century, and also a wide series of ecclesiastical textiles, the company being the foremost producer also in this field.

The case of the Friends of Finnish Handicraft exemplifies how the focus of craft-based production changed with expanding consumer markets. The case also illustrates the broad scope of products offered through this particular design and manufacturing network in the 1930s, ranging from bespoke fabrics for individual and public commissions, to off-the-shelf products sold in the company's shop in Helsinki, to DIY craft kits delivered to the countryside through mail order. Thus, recalling the harsh criticism wielded against its Swedish sister organization by the modernist reformers in the *Acceptera* manifesto, the Friends of Finnish Handicraft's production was not all 'Rolls Royce'.[42] However, the 'Rolls Royces' were crucial in establishing and maintaining its position as a high-end national art organization. The *ryijy* textiles, modernized through design competitions, were used to symbolize the perpetual renewal of the company. Their artistic value and individual designs were underlined also when marketing them to Finnish consumers, notwithstanding the fact that the '*ryijy* taste' of most customers differed considerably from the ideas presented, for example, in exhibitions in Helsinki.[43] To the great irritation of design reformers who preferred textiles embedded in the architecture and interior design, the expressive and colourful modern *ryijys* became standard objects in international design exhibitions starting in the 1930s.[44] Compared

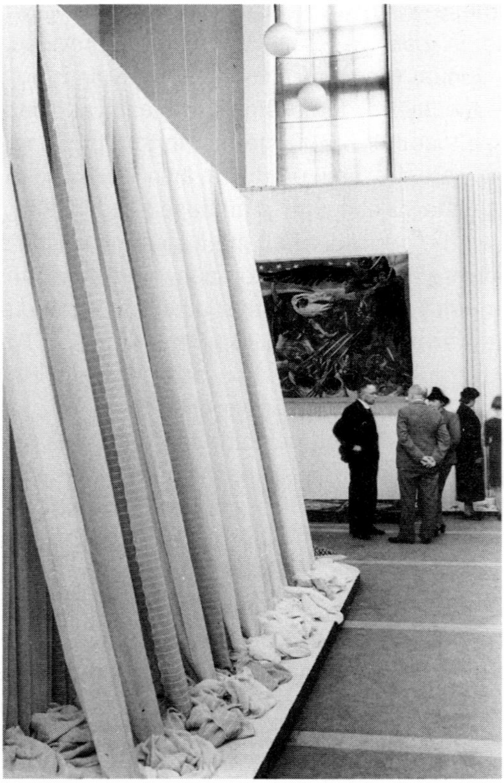

Fig. 3.5 Image from the sixtieth-anniversary exhibition of the Friends of Finnish Handicraft in 1939 foregrounding a range of handwoven interior fabrics designed by Laila Karttunen. Photograph courtesy of the Friends of Finnish Handicraft Ltd. (Suomen Käsityön Ystävät Oy.)

to these 'showpieces' representing the creativity of individual artists as well as the originality of the nation, handwoven fabrics by the yard stood timidly in the background when Finnish textile art was promoted abroad.

THE SCANDINAVIAN CONTEXT OF TEXTILE ART

> Of all the creations of Handicraft and Industrial Art in Finland in recent years, those of textile must undoubtedly be placed in the front rank. The most characteristic of them is the hand-knotted 'ryijy'. Its technique has a long ancestry in the art of the peasantry. The rich colourings and imaginative designs have, to a high degree, inspired the art of modern textiles.[45]

This quotation from the Finnish applied arts catalogue for the New York World's Fair in 1939 highlights the role assigned to contemporary textile art in the promotion of Finnish design. The 'renaissance of weaving art' in Finland,[46] the work of the newly established profession of textile artists, was conveyed as intimately linked with the national crafts tradition. This was to become the standard message in the international exhibitions of Scandinavian design in the 1950s, where the Finnish textiles shown were usually highly regarded but by no means representative of the full spectrum of Finnish textile design. This 'marketing ploy'[47] has idealized certain elements of design from the Scandinavian countries, and the narratives of a surviving tradition and individual artistic creativity have obscured the diversity and scope of the production, the modern practice and the breadth of the networks.[48]

Working hands-on with the material has become an idiom of Western textile art, and in that context weaving is connected to individual artistic expression.[49] Widening the object-centred idea of textile art to embrace serial production and entrepreneurship, this case study shows how Finnish textile artists of the interwar period not only made wall hangings and *ryijy*-rugs but also engaged in a wide array of different design practices and manufacturing systems. Also, in reference to prevailing modernist conceptions of craft-based production methods, it demonstrates that weaving by hand was not an outmoded reactionary phenomenon but rather a highly competitive mode of production that greatly contributed to modern design culture.

This essay has also discussed the role and impact of women in modern design. Textiles and textile art are often portrayed as a 'naturally' feminine sphere, which obviously is not the case: the female dominance in this craft tradition is a cultural construct that also appears in the strong presence of women designers in Scandinavian design history in general.[50] In Finland, hand weaving relying on existing craft networks involved possibilities of organizing production for new consumer groups in the modernizing society. The developing women's culture was key in creating the textile artists' networks of production and consumption: as entrepreneurs they benefited from existing peer networks and a manufacturing system with very modest technological or financial requirements; as designers they benefited from a large and increasing population of women devoting ever more resources to beautifying their homes.

The observed continuity and growth of handwoven fabric production during the interwar years confirms the view of economic historians according to whom handcrafted production prospered alongside industrial manufacture.[51] It is interesting that during the period of most severe economic regression in the early 1930s, applied art products, mostly ceramics and textiles, sold well in Helsinki galleries whereas paintings did not.[52] Did craft-based production, then, provide opportunities for other fields of design, too? Obviously, at that time there were a lot of craft activities in the factories; for example the processes in the furniture and porcelain industries were labour-intensive.[53] Also, there were smaller ceramics studios providing modern tableware and decorative pieces,[54] but compared to textiles, setting up a ceramics studio required larger investments and more mechanical equipment.

There is still very little research on craft-based industries in Finland, and, as shown here, such work has to face challenges like those of identification and attribution. Most work has so far concentrated on national institutions and big industry, and design histories tend to reflect the history of design promotion. However, changes in contemporary design practice, where there is an increased focus on individual designers working with small-scale production in complex networks, will perhaps spark an interest in design entrepreneurship in history writing, too.

–4–

Designing the 'Consumer in Infinity': The Swedish Cooperative Union's New Consumer Policy, c.1970

Helena Mattsson

> One almost cries when seeing the Coop bag . . . , all white, only printed with the blue symbol of infinity. No one had yet thought of grocery bags as something that needs to be designed.
>
> —Mårten Blomkvist[1]

The plastic bag for groceries referred to in the quote is one of many commodities that were part of a new corporate identity introduced by the Swedish Cooperative Union (Coop) in 1967 (fig. 4.1). As the quote shows, what was then the largest-ever marketing campaign in Sweden manages to this day to keep alive the myth of Coop products as being nonbranded and not designed. It only proves that the consciously designed strategy to debrand and to use a welfare state ideology to sell commodities was a successful marketing tool. This essay argues that Coop turned into an iconic brand through the use of their own history as one of the national popular movements crucial for the formation of the Swedish welfare state.[2] Interestingly, this happened at the very time when the welfare state otherwise was questioned and criticized as not fulfilling these values.

This case study investigates the new consumer policy introduced by the Swedish Cooperative Union in the late 1960s, one of the results of which was the debranded products. The campaign, as well as the consumer policy, is examined as part of a larger national process of identification with its roots in the formation of the Swedish welfare state. Coop was a large network in the 1960s and 1970s, controlling the process from production to consumption, owning factories, laboratories and shops as well as representing the consumers through customer ownership. This made Coop a powerful player in the political landscape, and, consequently, Coop had a great influence on the formation of a new national consumer policy established in the 1970s by the Social Democratic government.[3]

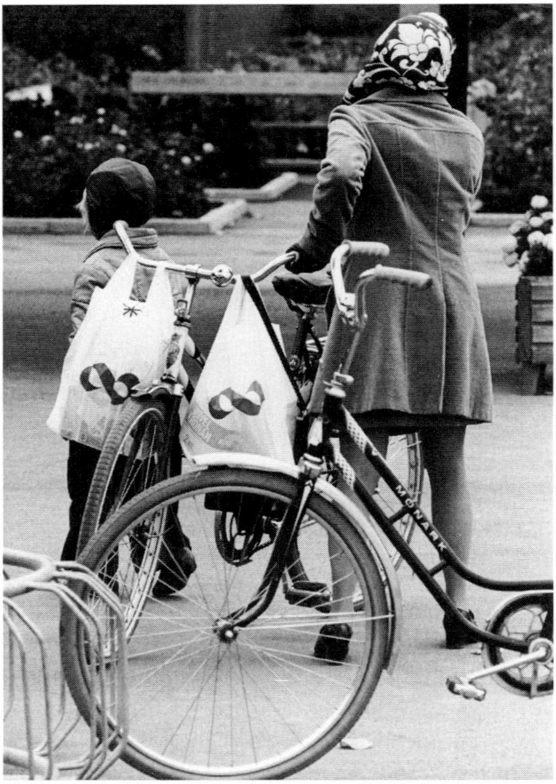

Fig. 4.1 Woman and child with bicycle and Coop plastic bags, 1970s. Photograph courtesy of KF Bibliotek och archiv (KF Library and Archive).

The Swedish case discussed here is one of many local expressions of modernism. Out of these microhistories, multiple modernities are continuously constructed. I choose not to use the concepts 'regional' or 'periphery' because these terms presuppose that a global centre exists from where theories and forms are diffused, thus consolidating the hierarchic view of modernism. The theoretical framework adopted here draws on Michel Foucault's model of analysis within which design appears less as a set of formal and aesthetic solutions and more as a tool for the production of subjectivity. Design is seen as an apparatus for the creation of order and discipline but also as a field for the creation of freedom and subjectivity. This does not mean that issues relating to form and aesthetics are left out. Rather, form and aesthetics are put in a larger context and analysed as a mediator between the individual and its surroundings. In this context the Swedish Cooperative Union's marketing campaign and consumer policy are emblematic examples of how design is used to create an identification program within a larger network consisting of producers, retailers, advertising agencies, marketing departments, politicians and the labour union.

CONSUMER PRODUCTION

A strong critique of the dominant modernistic design discourse was formulated from a consumer perspective in the early 1950s, and one of its first manifestations as a theoretical argument can be found in Reyner Banham's *Theory and Design in the First Machine Age*.[4] In his critique of modernistic design theory Banham argues for the replacement of ideal 'good design' with 'an aesthetic of expendability', and the new differentiated consumer market he applauds could be interpreted as a starting point for the postmodern paradigm.[5]

In 1960 the artist Richard Hamilton presented the idea that it was not only the product that should be designed but also the consumer.[6] This was stated in a period when modernism as the dominating design ideology was being challenged in most European countries, and American popular culture became a powerful influence. In the United States the concept of 'consumer engineering' had been introduced already in the early 1930s by the industrial designers Roy Sheldon and Egmont Arens as a process of shaping a product to fit the consumer's needs and tastes.[7] In the 1950s many voices stressed that the designer was losing his or her influence over the design process, which was increasingly related to the consumers' needs and desires. When Hamilton inverts the relation between the product and the consumer, saying that the consumers could be produced for the products, it should be understood as a reaction to the powerlessness expressed by designers and thus a reversion of Sheldon and Arens's concept. Hamilton's article started an intense debate in the English design press in which Hamilton was criticized, for example by Reyner Banham, who argued that the commercial market should be democratic and not a tool for 'producing' consumers.[8]

In Sweden the picture was very different. The consumer had been a central concern in the design discourse since the 1930s, as exemplified, for example, in the modernist manifesto *Acceptera*, published on the occasion of the Stockholm Exhibition in 1930.[9] Also, both governmental bodies and private corporations began coining more or less sophisticated consumer policies in the 1930s—a trend that continued into the 1970s. Consequently, I would suggest that the 1970s in Sweden could be seen as the pinnacle of the ambitions to construct a welfare state consumer. This was the period when the institutionalization of the Swedish consumer became particularly manifest through an unprecedented politicization of consumption. In 1971 the state-regulated consumer policy started to take form—but, interestingly, this is also the period when new strategies of marketing, advertisement and public relations (PR) were developing which could in fact be seen as the starting point for the more liberal consumer society that would fully emerge in the 1980s, and the rise of a postmodern material culture.

The idea of 'consumer production' refers to a conscious and well-worked-out strategy—formulated by state organizations as well as corporations—involving design, marketing and pedagogy as educational tools for how to become a well-functioning citizen through a process of identification. This was done through information, popular movements and regulations of the private economy through, for instance, state subsidies and loans. Both the consumer and the producer sides to this complex network surely merit attention; however, like several of the case studies in Part 3 of this book, my focus here is on the field between these two arenas: the intermediary actors—more specifically those operating in the marketing sector, busy designing Coop's infinite consumer.

FROM CONSUMPTION CRITICISM TO CONSUMER POLICY

The consumer policy constructed by Coop in the 1970s can be seen as expressing a dual understanding of the consumer. On one hand a consumer is imagined and constructed by Coop's advertising agency. On the other hand Coop's campaigns are intertwined with the formation of a new government consumer policy that had its roots in the critique towards the consumer society. Thus, with Coop as the intersection, two contradictory projects were taking form, one producing a consumer through marketing and the other protecting the consumer from the market. These two projects merged into one ideological message in the new corporate image.

The counterculture that formed in opposition to Western consumer society and became consolidated in the 1970s contained a strong design streak with the *Whole Earth Catalog* as its lifestyle bible and Richard Buckminster Fuller as its primary hero figure.[10] Consumer objects were discouraged in favour of a do-it-yourself philosophy—everyone could make their own things. Swedish manifestations of this counterculture in the aesthetic realm include the design collective and clothing brand Mah-Jong and the pedagogical experiments in the Moderna Museet (the Stockholm Museum of Modern Art) and its exhibitions without objects.[11] This was a design culture that derided consumer objects and proposed instead a culture *beyond* objects.

Sam Binkley has argued that the cultural processes forming around the turbulent year 1968, at least in an American context, highlighted the individual.[12] In this respect, Binkley claims to see a continuous development from the late 1960s hippie culture to the 1980s yuppie culture. Crucially, in the USA, this alternative culture quickly became commercialized—which also meant it became influential. One consequence of this process was the organization of consumer criticism into a differentiated culture of consumer movements.

In Sweden, as in the USA, the critique of consumerism became institutionalized rather quickly, but instead of a diversity of independent consumer movements, one national policy took form. At the same time as consumption was criticized, the consumer citizen was consolidated through official consumer policies and the establishment of new national authorities like the Consumer Ombudsman.[13] In the late 1960s advertising and consumerism were widely discussed in the media as well as in politics, and consumers, politicians and institutions, like Coop, all called for a more influential state consumer policy. At the same time official state investigations on issues like low income and the effect of advertising were in progress.[14] The year 1971 saw the establishment of both the Consumer Ombudsman and the Swedish Consumer Council, as well as the Swedish Market Court. In a way, however, these reforms were counterproductive. The effect of transforming consumer activism into a national policy, and thus a machine of bureaucracy, was that new marketing techniques evolved. This encouraged the media, market researchers and copywriters to come up with new forms and new strategies. In the end, then, consumer criticism could be seen as the best renewal of the logic of consumption.

THE SWEDISH COOPERATIVE UNION

The Swedish Cooperative Union started as a consumer organization in 1919 and became an important actor in the development of the welfare state. In 1924 Coop set up an architectural office that soon established itself as a driving force in marketing and producing Swedish functionalism.[15] Most leading figures in Swedish modern architecture passed through this office at one point or another, and its director was a pioneer of Swedish functionalism and a co-author of *Acceptera*: Eskil Sundahl.

The Coop movement was heavily politicized. There has been a close connection between the Social Democrats and Coop, even though the Coop director Albin Johansson often claimed that the coops were politically neutral. The movement was an essential part in the development of Swedish consumer behaviour, and early Coop grocery stores were the country's first case of standardized architecture. During his years as director (1924–56) Johansson—sometimes called the Henry Ford of Sweden—developed Coop into the largest company in Sweden, owning stores, factories and laboratories. The organization retained its prominent role in the postwar years as well, for example as the nation's largest producer of food and commodities. It was also an eager promoter of a global market.[16] Thus Coop formed a crucial part of Swedish politics and the economy.

Ever since the 1930s, Coop had developed strategies to shape and handle public opinion, primarily through a close collaboration with the advertisement agency Svea.[17] During the 1960s Svea's turnover increased dramatically, and towards the end of the decade it was the largest advertisement agency in Sweden, with more than 240 employees. The agency was acquired by Coop in 1968 (one year after the introduction of the new infinity logo). Svea developed marketing techniques combining advertising, art and architecture and informational campaigns. Coop's campaigns were characterized by the use of different media, a strategy the agency had developed since the 1930s. The exhibition Without Borders from 1957 is a clear example of this strategy. In this exhibition, directed by David Westman of Svea, the infinity symbol appeared for the first time but here in three dimensions.

Coop started as a popular movement and succeeded in establishing a company culture characterized by an efficient distribution of information, which to a large extent instilled in members a feeling of being part of a larger democratic movement providing a potential influence on a local (or even national) scale. This heritage was exploited to the full when the new campaign was introduced in 1967. Coop and Svea's goal was to shape public opinion, and in their construction of a new corporate image they honed in on a system of values—such as solidarity, the collective, community—associated with both popular movements and the welfare state. It seems clear that Coop aspired to be a 'manufacturer of consent', to use the term coined by Walter Lippman in his *Public Opinion* from 1922.[18] However, at the start of the 1970s Coop was also criticized for operating as a business like any other, distancing itself from its original idea of being of and for the consumers. Critics claimed that Coop was transformed into a corporation but still using the old slogans.[19]

THE CAMPAIGN

In January 1967, by means of the largest advertisement campaign to date in Sweden, Coop introduced its new corporate image centred around a new logo in the shape of the infinity symbol (fig. 4.2). The background for the campaign was a discussion at the beginning of the 1960s regarding a new corporate strategy to give Coop a unified identity. This meant that the heterogeneous company profiles and visual identities of 300 local societies were to be coordinated and redesigned into one collective aesthetic profile and identity. As part of this effort, Coop also planned to build thirty to forty flagship stores around Sweden, intended to become hallmarks of the values of the Coop movement, while at the same time drastically reducing the total number of shops. The process of centralization which characterized Swedish industries and national authorities in the 1960s also applied to Coop.

Preparatory work for the new corporate image had begun in 1964 when a 'structural investigation committee' was established with members drawn

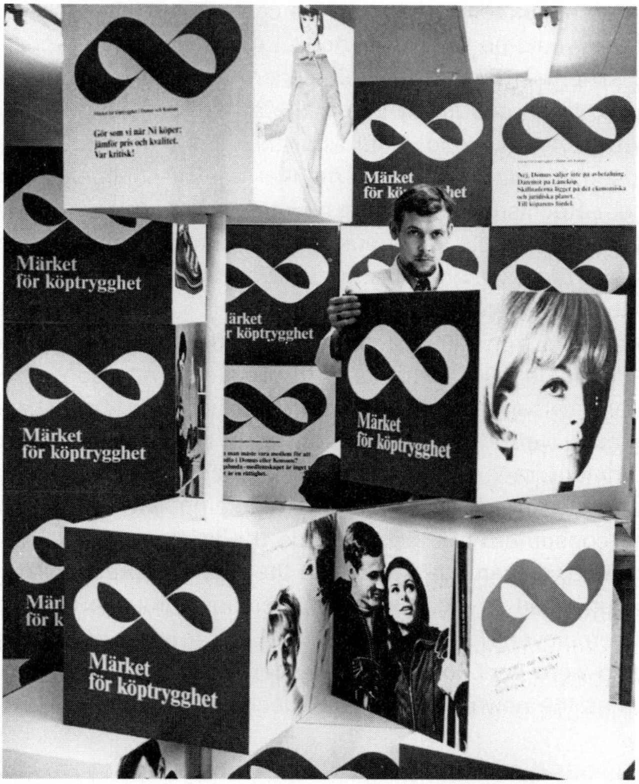

Fig. 4.2 Introduction of Coop's new design program with the infinity symbol on 1 January 1967. Photograph courtesy of KF Library and Archive.

from Coop's architectural office and Svea. The committee reinterpreted the infinity symbol from the exhibition Without Borders and presented the sign to the direction of Coop some months later as the new symbol that would make Coop 'infinitely recognizable'. Influenced by what they called the 'American expression, corporate image', they proposed an extensive campaign involving everything 'from the big goal and method to the personnel policy and the design of the brand'.[20] The final evaluation of the brand strategy had to consider a multitude of business aspects: purchases by consumers, production, distribution, local coop societies, retail outlets, information and social responsibility, education and dividends (bonuses). The committee ended the presentation with great pathos: 'Let us do something big and great with the program, something striking that gives an echo. To relate to the symbol of infinity: Let us state that "our ambition is without borders . . ."'[21]

The board made a unanimous decision to adopt the infinity symbol as the company's new logo, and Mats Erik Molander, Björn Petersson and David

Westman were appointed to manage the campaign. Main tasks in the development phase would be the actual design of the logo, new typography and a new colour scheme. Three graphic designers were commissioned to work in parallel before the board finally chose the artist Paul Persson's proposal for the logo design (fig. 4.3). To avoid what they call a 'symbol babeldom' they were supposed to produce a design manual—quickly dubbed 'the application bible' or the 'catechism'—regulating how to combine the symbol, typography, colour and materials. This ambitious project took form as a regulated combination of a set of designed parts, and the design manual became a crucial document holding this together.

The three years from the start in 1964 until the introduction of the new corporate identity in 1967 were used to produce a new consumer, much as Hamilton had envisaged. In the course of this relatively short period, Coop executed a massive redesign of virtually every element of its visual and material environment, ranging from receipts to trucks, from signage to factories, to conform to the new design program. This campaign was directed not only towards the consumers but also towards the local retailers, whose local visual idioms were discarded in favour of the new corporate identity. This had to be communicated to the 300 coop societies throughout Sweden, affecting 56,000 employees. In addition to the design manual, films introducing the campaign were sent to all local retailers explaining the rules of the design as well as the new rhetoric. It was declared in October 1966 that 'Svea

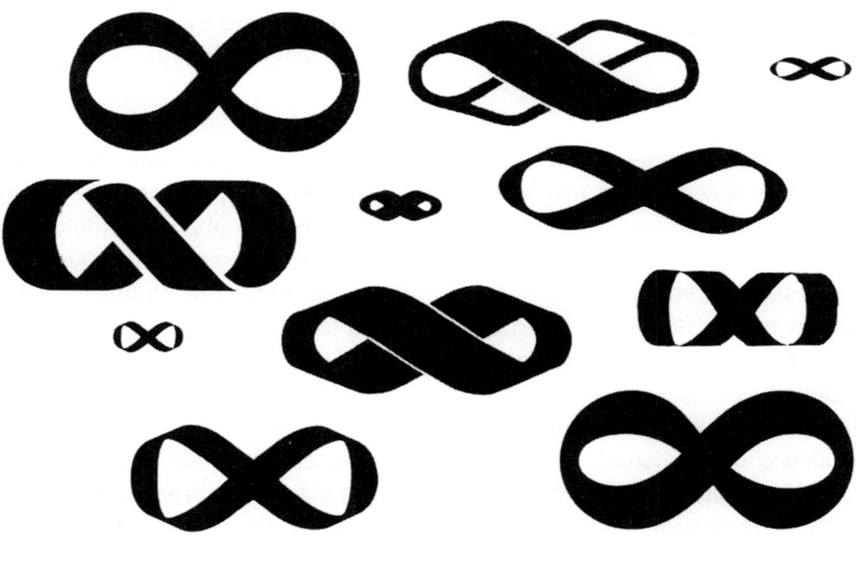

Fig. 4.3 Sketches for the infinity symbol. Photograph courtesy of KF Library and Archive.

must list all the correct expressions that we use'.[22] The weekly newsletter *Symbolinformation* was also a way of distributing information internally in the organization.

Instead of launching products Svea launched a consumer, 'Mrs Nilsson in apartment building number 37'.[23] She had an indefinite age, indefinite social status and indefinite consumer habits—but surprisingly her body had a concrete form: short and plump. The indefinite character of this consumer would later be described in more positive terms as something basic. This was a person who would never be materialized, nor feature in any pictures or verbal descriptions; she is just an imagined character standing in for the anonymous consumer in the abstract process of creating a market. Still, Ove Lundström of Svea formulated ten points explaining what Coop should do for this constructed consumer: I would listen to her; I would speak to her; I would defend her; I would make her feel good; I would thank her; I would try to gain her trust; I would introduce her to my friends; I would stop having secrets; I would try to get her to love me; I would speak up on her behalf.[24]

In a rather patronizing tone Svea formulated a strategy for catering to this consumer: 'Instead of offering candy to the kids, we will offer Mrs Nilsson a pair of glasses and the chance for a chat in our new "recreational corners" that will be set up in the shops.'[25] These small corners were supposed to feature information on consumer goods as well as small libraries containing literature on consumer issues. Consumption would be promoted as a democratic act, and the new logo in the shape of the infinity symbol was to function as a guarantee for rationality and consumer satisfaction. In short, this campaign can be seen as a reconceptualization of the established idea of the welfare state consumer, formed by functionalistic values, by means of a new imagery and mediated by new marketing techniques. As Björn Petersson put it a year before the introduction of the infinity symbol:

> Let us be grateful for the symbol, it gives us a wonderful opportunity to say the old things in a new and persuasive way. The intertwining of ideology and commodity advertising will be extremely interesting.[26]

According to Coop's market research, 42 per cent of Swedes recognized the logo as early as fourteen days after its introduction on 1 January 1967. By February the number had risen to 57 per cent, by April to 71 per cent and by December to 89 per cent. The introduction was considered a success by those involved in producing the campaign. But how was the response from the public and in the media?

The campaign got a lot of media attention and a diverse response. Severe criticism arose within the organization, especially from the local coop societies and members in the countryside, who saw the campaign as an expression of increased centralization: 'This will lead to a minority rule which means that Coop could not be described as a democratic movement any longer.'[27] In *Metallarbetaren* (a newspaper published by the Metal Workers' Union) it was stressed that the centralization would have a negative effect on life in the countryside. 'The year 1967 . . . the Swedish Co-op presents the new guidelines. They are so radical that the old Coop pioneers are turning in their graves. What did they know of concepts like efficiency, large-scale operation, rationalization? Not much . . . The old believed in idealism, solidarity and a yearly dividend.'[28] This criticism must be understood in light of how the campaign can also be said to have coincided with, or even catalysed, an ongoing restructuring of Swedish cities characterized by the centralization of consumption and the localization of shopping outside the cities. In 1967 there were 3,500 Coop stores, and the plan for the mid-1970s was to decrease the number to 920. However, the definite breakthrough for this transformation of the commercial life in cities, as well as of the consumer culture, had to wait another decade.[29]

Whereas the critics of the campaign made themselves heard, there was no shortage of positive responses. In one of the major national newspapers, *Aftonbladet*, the graphic designer Olle Eksell described the campaign as an excellent way of working with environmental questions through aesthetics, a simple, unified design that managed to connect different scales—from receipts to trucks and stores.[30]

HONEST ADVERTISEMENT AND EMPTY SIGNS

As already mentioned, at the end of the 1960s the debate on advertising and commercialism was intense, and in 1969 a Swedish commission on advertising proposed a marketing law. At the same time Coop invested more money than ever in advertisement, although the preferred terms were 'information' and what they called 'honest advertisement'.[31] In 1968 a Coop working group started to critically evaluate the accepted concept of 'advertisement', and the result turned 'a lot of things upside down and the group members felt like radicals'.[32] The group presented its ideas to the Coop board on 21 January 1969 with the following *ouverture*:

> In 1968 the 1960s disappeared, and we saw the 1970s. It happened more in one year than in the previous ten. A deep gap appeared between old and new thinking, and new manifests were sent over the world. No one escaped the demand to change opinion . . . Consumption and welfare are concepts that often are mentioned as contrasting elements to the material need in other parts of the world and have come to symbolize egoism. Shortly, new forces will emerge, forces that we never imagined only some years ago. However, there is a connection between the new forces and consumption.[33]

The working group acknowledged that in order to function in what it perceived as a new world order, advertising—and information in general—had to be reconceptualized. Some ideas on how this could be achieved were formulated as an 'Experiment in honest advertisement'.[34] One example was 'Planned purchase', where the text said, 'Warning! A trap! In the shop you get seduced to buy through tempting display of commodities.' Another said:

> In this space we thought of showing an ad for ham. But you already know that Coop has ham. Good ham also (SEK 9,20/kg). But when the world looks as it does we want to give you a tip instead: give some money to the charity you sympathize the most with. It could be social aid here or abroad, rescue actions, relief work in development countries.

So although the new, stricter law on advertising did not appear until 1971, some Swedish advertising agencies—including Svea—had already started what might be seen as a process of self-censorship in order to tap into the anti-commercialist attitudes emerging as a significant cultural force at the time.

However, it was not just the rhetoric that changed. New marketing strategies were formed that included different milieus, lifestyles, values and participatory politics. How the changing cultural climate and legal regulations for advertising and marketing affected marketing strategies is confirmed by Svea's CEO Lars Berg in an article from 1970: 'Seen from the advertising business the critique has been especially creative because it showed that it lacked resources and insights for understanding the value of soul-searching.'[35] Svea's own company history describes the effects of the political climate at the end of the 1960s much in the same vein: 'without doubt it [consumption criticism] gave something back to advertisement: many of us were raising the gaze from the drawing table and noticed the society outside the window'.[36]

In 1969 Coop ran an experimental advertising campaign consisting of huge posters showing graffiti-like slogans saying things like 'Power to the consumers', 'What power?' and 'Who are the consumers?' (fig. 4.4). The cultural journalist Leif Nylén reacted with resignation: 'everything can be exploited, even graffiti. Who expected anything else?' According to Nylén Coop left its original ideology a long time ago, and 'the moral has changed from being a program for action into an attitude, décor and rhetoric'. He also criticized the play with the 'real' and the 'image': 'When the posters end up on the big boards next to the real graffiti. A moment of vertigo, a crack in reality, big enough to get the whole Sergel's Square to collapse.' Nylén's view on this 'honest advertisement' is that it becomes even more false by claiming to be honest.[37]

Berg speaks of 'pseudo-phenomena': 'the contemporary word for the apparent, for that which seems to happen is that which actually happens'.[38] Berg's concept of pseudo-phenomena could also be seen in the light of Jean

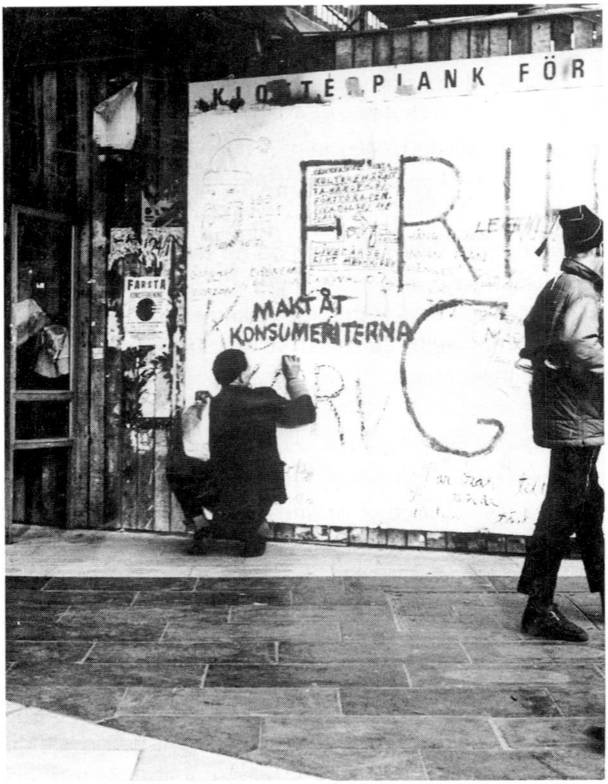

Fig. 4.4 Graffiti board. Photograph courtesy of KF Library and Archive.

Baudrillard's ideas on 'simulation', where the sign no longer refers to reality and the signifier takes the place of the signified.[39] Even the infinity symbol could be understood in the light of pseudo-phenomena (or a simulation). It was not supposed to symbolize a product, not even a company directly—instead, it was intended to evoke a set of values, represent customer guarantees or express cooperation without limits and borders, but at the same time do the job of advertising. 'It is clear that the new type of sign had to be a sign with the emphasis on advertising. It had to "sell" at night as well as day.'[40] Björn Petersson called the campaign 'a two-front operation. The symbol represented cooperation, but at the same time it had to be specific and sell goods.'[41]

The editor of *Fri Köpenskap* (the organ of private competitive merchants), Anders Byttner, criticized the campaign and the sign for its metaphysical peculiarities deprived of concrete meaning: 'Beautiful in design but devoid of content, impossible to associate directly or concretely with any idea or any activity which is specifically cooperative, should such exist any more.'[42]

Even if Byttner is impressed with the skilful advertising experts at Coop he claims that they have used questionable methods in the introduction of the symbol:

> The symbol conveys no message whatsoever which could stimulate people to make impulse purchases. It does not represent anything, a person, a firm of which we can approve or disapprove. Quite simply, and here I speak my mind, it is a piece of non-figurative art, and as such it goes completely over the heads of the great bulk of Swedes.[43]

This strategy of emptying a sign of any explicit meanings, and any connections to either products or producers, and instead loading it with abstract positive associations for the consumers—a consumer guarantee—makes the infinity symbol a typical sign in late capitalist consumer culture. As such, this free-floating sign without any signified reality can be framed in relation to both a pseudo-phenomenon, to use the Swedish term, and the postmodern logic of simulations.

CONSUMER IN INFINITY: AN EXHIBITION AT THE MODERNA MUSEET

Another critical response to the Coop campaign was the 1971 exhibition Consumer in Infinity by the artist Björn Lövin at the Moderna Museet in Stockholm. Lövin interpreted the logo as metaphysical, a simulation, lacking references to reality—much as Byttner had. In the exhibition Lövin constructed an imagined consumer who was building a 'hyper reality'—his own world produced by the symbol as abstract art.

The exhibition was staged as two different milieus: one was a ten-metre-long public street with shopping windows on both sides; the other was the private home of the fictitious Mr P, a low-income worker, and his wife and two kids. Mr P had no money to buy things, but he could enter 'his' shop, or his house, DOMUS (which was, befittingly, the name of Coop's department stores). Here he could collect cult objects to display and worship in his own house. The infinity sign became his identity, and the commodities in the shopping window turned into art along with the logo on the plastic bags, receipts, letters, envelopes and so on. Mr P had a salary of SEK 441 after tax per month at his disposal, and he made a painting of the sum—what he called a 'monument of freedom'. He realized that it was in the shopping windows that the 'Real Art' existed. He could not afford to consume, but he could develop a *lifestyle* out of the new culture. He displayed everything as art on the wall and said: 'I thought I found the truth! Consumer in infinity! . . . My life is a demonstration.'[44]

Crucially, it was the consumer who was portrayed in the exhibition, and not the commodities—which were very much present but remained props—and this consumer was presented as owned by Coop, almost like a brainwashed sect member. But on the other hand the public could see that this was only a facade, a pseudo-phenomenon, because Mr P made other paintings in the cellar that reflected him being a loving and desiring subject, although he never showed them.

The art critic Torsten Bergmark commented in the Stockholm morning paper *Dagens Nyheter* that 'the art is becoming more commercialized and the commerce itself is being lifted up to art which we now are experiencing in infinity. And a better symbol than the one KF [Coop] has adopted does not exist.'[45] This massive attention for a new corporate image, including a main exhibition at the Moderna Museet and extensive media coverage, must be considered as a marker of an extremely successful marketing campaign.

THE BASIC PRODUCTS AND THEIR BASIC CONSUMERS

In the early 1970s Coop entered a problematic economic period. Partly this depended on a campaign to keep prices down that Coop made together with the Swedish Confederation of Trade Unions in 1969—'The price stopper' (*Prisbromsaren*). The campaign was thought to be temporary, but the lowered prices could not be raised because the government issued a national price stop, which led to major losses for Coop. But they also started to lose market share, and consequently the factories were not used efficiently.

At the first Swedish Consumer Congress, organized by Coop in 1971, the problem of the lost market share was discussed.[46] Over four days 500 delegates met in Stockholm to discuss and develop recommendations and proposals that could be used as guidelines for the future policy of Coop. The first speaker was the Swedish Prime Minister, Olof Palme, who declared the establishment of a Consumer Ombudsman and presented plans for a Swedish Consumer Council (fig. 4.5). It was also the year Coop decreased its budget for advertising by SEK 20 million.[47]

The answer to the problem of decreasing market share was not for Coop, as for most of the retail trade, to differentiate the assortment, advertise more and have longer opening hours. Instead, a virtually opposite strategy was embraced. The idea was to create an alternative to the competition by defining Coop's products more as components in a new and ethically sound lifestyle rather than as commodities. This resulted in a new line of 'basic' products. One example is the Vinetta basic wardrobe for women with 'well-thought-out and timeless garments for all ages and all sizes'.[48] This was introduced in 1972 and consisted of nine garments in seven different colours. It was an immediate success: by 1976 one million garments had been sold.

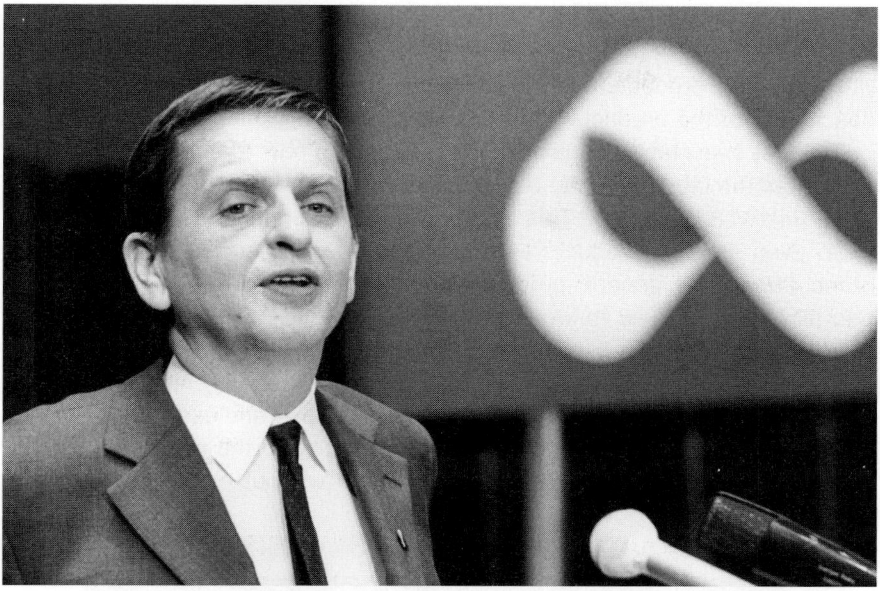

Fig. 4.5 Prime Minister Olof Palme speaking at the Consumer Congress in 1971. Photograph courtesy of KF Library and Archive.

The inherent paradox is, of course, that the Vinetta wardrobe was part of a larger strategy for creating a lifestyle of anticonsumerism by means of consumption. Although the emphasis was on values beyond the object, such as health, ecology and social relations, these values were to be evoked through buying objects. In the mid-1970s 'consumer corners' were set up in the larger shops, where people could gather to get information, discuss products and leave their opinions—advertising became relational, putting the *R* in PR, so to speak. As a continuation of this line of thought, the Coop Test Kitchen came up with a range of products labelled 'basic' food. A central didactic feature in the introduction of the new range was the so-called food pyramid—a figure that has since been widely exported and adopted in nutritional propaganda internationally.

The development of the basic products and their corresponding basic consumer can be understood as a continuation of the strategies developed in the campaign introducing the infinity symbol. The idea of infinity was replaced with the concept 'basic', and, like infinity, 'basic' had no specific reference to reality, not to any specific objects, clothes or other commodities, but rather to a field of associations around anticonsumerism. Like the new logo, it was a floating sign ready to work—to sell—but without any predetermined reference. This was also clearly shown when other brands also used the idea of basic clothes, like the clothing brand Twilfit. Basic was an anticonsumerist message aimed at selling more products. In contrast to the concept of infinity, which was based on a sign with a well-designed graphic form, the campaigns with the basic products never used one unifying sign; it was rather the very description of the products as basic that created the marketing effect.

The last important campaign made by Coop as part of their new consumer policy was the introduction of a new line of basic products known as 'blue and white' in 1978 (fig. 4.6).[49] This line had the same concept as the basic wardrobe. Even if these products were influenced by the success of the French brand Carrefour's generic products, which were introduced in 1976, Coop had already conceived this concept one year earlier with the blue-and-white toothpaste, which had a great impact on the market. Almost no advertising accompanied the introduction of the toothpaste, but it generated massive press coverage as the product that dared to be brandless. The blue-and-white products were supposed to be an alternative to the modern consumer culture by being debranded, or brandless, and without elaborate packaging

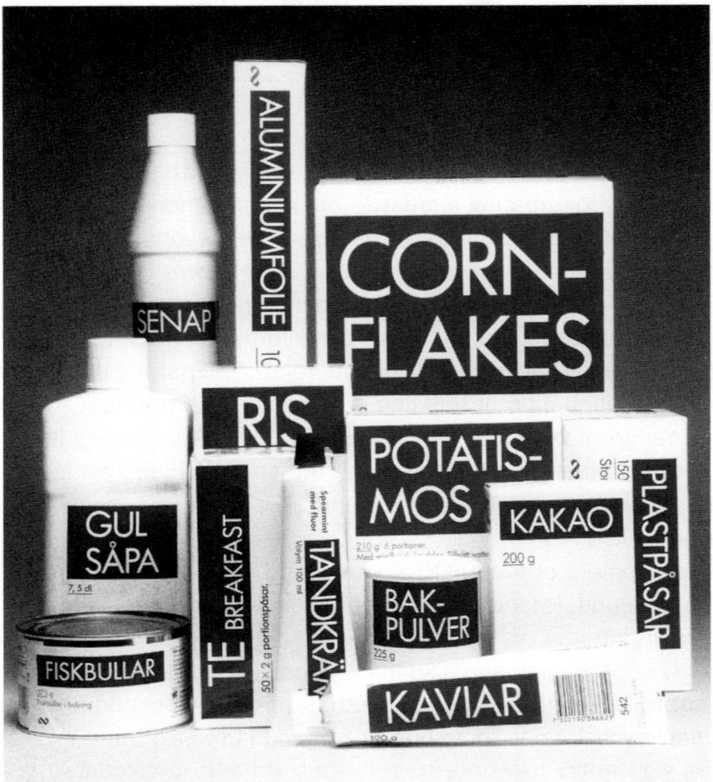

Fig. 4.6 Blue-and-white products. Photograph courtesy of KF Library and Archive.

or high expenditures for advertising and marketing. The contradiction is that this debranded brand, if you wish, became a very successful marketing tool.

The anti-aesthetics of the 1970s finally negated all the aesthetic hierarchies that had been preached to the welfare state consumer from the 1930s onwards. The ideology of the basic products did not emphasize form in the way early functionalism did—form itself was not something one needed to be taught to appreciate. Form did not have the same intrinsic value but was rather a means for negating contemporary consumer culture. Nevertheless, there is clearly a connection between the basic products and the functionalist ideology in the emphasis on rationality, with the significant difference that the idea of the basic did not comprise an ideal. If functionalist ideology implied a drive towards the most functional and rationally designed object, with beauty as a given result, the ideology behind the basic products aimed at a low price and a product that negated the commodity fetishism of late capitalist society. The focus had changed from functionality as *use* to functionality as *economy*. If the early welfare state design ideology had an ambition to cater to and educate the 'common people', the basic products could be seen as the end point for this project where the ambition more or less was fulfilled. In contrast to the functionalistic commodity, which often is considered elitist, the basic products actually became part of popular culture. The concept of basic was easy to grasp and had a coherent and rapidly perceived image and a low price. It was a pop version of the functionalistic ideal, without any hierarchic ideals of beauty or divine design.

CONCLUSION

This essay has argued that the Swedish Cooperative Union's campaigns introducing a new consumer policy around 1970 addressed acute contradictions in contemporary society and broke ground for a new strategy in marketing and design. The campaigns could, on the one hand, be interpreted as something new, but they could also be seen as the end point of a long project of producing a welfare consumer. It was the last big project in Sweden with the expressed ambition to produce a consumer with values related to the welfare state such as solidarity, rationality, democracy and collectivity. The consumer who was supposed to buy the basic products at the end of the 1970s could be understood as the final subject imagined by those who designed the welfare state.

The years around 1970 were characterized by contradictions. Western consumer society was growing to unprecedented dimensions while at the same time being subjected to severe criticism. In a Swedish context, both trajectories can be interpreted as symptoms of a welfare state increasingly under pressure. Also, both of these societal trends informed Coop's new corporate identity coined around 1970. It was a two-front operation, where two seemingly contradictory strategies merged into one ideological message to be expressed through the new corporate identity: Coop was a commercial business producing a consumer through its marketing efforts, while simultaneously honouring its roots as a people's movement by protecting the consumer from conspicuous consumption by means of 'basic' design.

In conclusion, the considerable efforts that went into designing the 'consumer of infinity' in 1970s Sweden illustrate the paradoxical break from the modernistic design tradition as seen from a consumption perspective. As protest culture was channeled into the establishment of a national consumer policy, consumption criticism became a productive force eventually paving the way for the liberalistic consumer society to come. The resistance of the late capitalistic society became the best renewal of the logic of consumption.

–5–

Designing a Hole in the Wall: The Reverse Vending Machine as Socio-technical System and Environmental Infrastructure

Finn Arne Jørgensen

Advertisements promoting beverage container recycling in Norway have one common feature: a consumer returns a bottle through a hole in the wall. This hole is a critical design component of the reverse vending machine (RVM), used for the returns of empty beverage containers in grocery stores, and has become a striking visual icon for consumer environmentalism and recycling in Norway. The design element of the hole in the wall has become embedded into the Norwegian culture of recycling. Yet analyses of the RVM as a designed artefact growing out of a Scandinavian context need to simultaneously look in through the hole in the wall, at the large technical system that makes the machine function, and out through the hole in the wall, at the position it has attained in the modern organization of beverage container recycling.

This chapter examines how the design of the RVM took place through a constellation of forces: technological development, the venturing into international markets, governmental policymaking and the onset of environmental concerns. By looking at three design parameters—inside, outside and systems—the article reveals how the RVM became both a visual symbol of and a key technical component in Norwegian recycling culture.

The Norwegian—and world-leading—RVM producer Tomra Systems is largely responsible for the creation of this technological iconography of beverage container recycling. We will look at three historical iterations of the company's RVM in this article: the Tomra I was created in 1971 to solve a specific logistical problem in grocery stores. The Tomra Can-Can, launched in 1982, marked Tomra's first attempts at involving professional industrial designers in the design process. Finally, in 1996 Tomra celebrated their twenty-fifth anniversary by releasing the Tomra 600 RVM, reaching what the company's founders had considered their design vision since the beginning.

In this chapter, I analyse the increasingly complex system character of the three machines, concluding with a discussion of the evolving design of the RVM as a fundamentally Scandinavian design process. In exploring what it means for a design to be Scandinavian, we need to ask whether the RVM could have been made elsewhere. What were the exact components of Scandinavian culture that were embedded in the RVM's design? And how was this done?

DESIGNING ARTEFACTS AND SYSTEMS

This is a case study of the design of technological products and the interactions between the engineers, designers and different users who were involved in giving the RVM its shape and functionality. Instead of examining designers or engineers as specific professions, or performing an ethnographic study of the relationship between engineers and designers, the article aims to keep a close eye on the object itself, Tomra's evolving RVM models. In order to analyse this product development as a design process, we need to understand the RVM as a functional technology, an artefact that is made to perform specific tasks for specific users, within clearly defined material constraints. A machine without users is a failed technology, as much recent literature in science and technology studies has argued.[1] It follows that we need to actively consider the role of these users in technology development. Recruiting users and guiding their experience of the technology is a question of design, of identifying what needs and values the user groups have and giving the machine a shape, an image and a set of functions that align with the users' interests. The RVM as a machine needs to process empty beverage containers in a reliable manner. The world of RVMs is far from glamorous; using it seldom gives its users aesthetic pleasure. It is a mundane technological artefact, yet the RVM has obviously been carefully designed with a function and the interactions with its many users in mind, making its design evolution of interest to design historians and historians of technology alike. As Barry Katz observed in his 1997 essay on the relationship between the history of technology and the history of design, these two fields have gone through a similar historiographic trajectory, from focusing on the great individuals, whether engineers, inventors or designers, to considering the broader context influencing technological development and design processes.[2]

The RVM is more than a free-standing, technological artefact. It is important to examine the relationship between its design, its designers and its users and, even more critically, to understand the RVM as an interface to a larger socio-technical system for handling packaging waste, an infrastructure that often aligns with national boundaries, cultures and mindsets. The history of the RVM reveals the complexity of the design process, how it reaches beyond the artefact itself and the formal designer, and how it extends over time, far beyond the point where the final product is launched and put up for sale. The RVM needed to serve many users, both over time and concurrently. Political finesse thus became one of its most critical design features. Throughout the different design iterations, the system served by the RVM grew increasingly larger and more complex. At the same time, the RVM engineers and designers sought to simplify this complexity in the meeting with the end users.

This hole in the wall is thus not only the place where the bottle-returning consumer meets the recycling system; it also serves as our analytical entry point into the machine and how its design has become so thoroughly embedded into the Norwegian culture of recycling. The social and economic context urged Tomra's engineers and design teams to pick the design they did, while at the same time the design itself created certain understandings of the way recycling works. A key question becomes how Tomra's personnel worked to integrate this design into Norwegian culture so much that the hole in the wall became equivalent with recycling.

The primary concern in this context is the interactions of engineers, designers and user groups in industrial design processes; this article is just as concerned with manufacturing processes, materials and technological limits as with aesthetics and product identity. However, the goal is not to study this as an ethnographic examination of specific work processes within Tomra but rather to examine how the company developed an idea of design as tied to action, making certain actions possible and others more difficult.[3] In this perspective, design both constrains and empowers the user. The RVM design process represents active, purposeful facilitation of the relationship between producer, machine and user groups.[4] The designer is a mediator, thinking about the needs of the user and the affordances of materials and technologies. As much recent literature within science and technology studies has pointed out, both users and producers can become designers, either by directly influencing the shape or functionality of the material product or by manipulating and changing the cultural references surrounding the product, thereby having an effect on the way it works.

INSIDE THE RVM: TOMRA I

The RVM has a longer history than one would think. As early as the 1920s, American inventors patented mechanical vending machines where customers could both purchase and return beverage bottles; the empty bottles went back into the slot where the full bottles had been. Several similar machines appeared in the 1950s, when bottled-beverage consumption increased dramatically in the USA.[5]

Why go to the trouble of getting customers to return the empty bottles? New bottles were quite expensive at the time. By getting the bottles in return, cleaning them and refilling them, bottlers could get as many as twenty-five to thirty uses out of each bottle. While there were costs associated with transportation, cleaning and storage of the bottles, it still made economic sense to keep reusing bottles. It is important to remember that while reuse and recycling activities have taken on a distinctly green tint today, neither producers nor consumers were inspired by environmental motivations in the early history of beverage container reuse; it was a matter of economics.[6]

When the grocer Per Fremstad installed Norway's first RVM in his store in Oslo in 1957, he primarily hoped the machine could help with bottle-handling but also attract customers and distinguish his store from competitors. He called this machine 'the bottle crusher', and not without reason. The machine was made by the Swedish company Wicanders, which mostly made bottle caps and machines for capping; it received bottles through a hole and used hydraulics to push the bottles onto a table in the back room, all the while making a hellish racket.[7]

The Wicanders machine had its issues, especially noise and insensitivity to the fragility of glass bottles, but it still presented Norwegian customers with a new way of returning their empty bottles and allowed the grocer to delegate some bottle-handling tasks to the machine. For each bottle returned, the consumer received a red or blue token according to the refund value. The store would count these tokens by hand and give the consumer a refund. The novelty effect of performing a common, everyday task in a new and different way most likely contributed to attracting new customers to the store. As such, the machine not only performed a physical task but also did work on a symbolic level. Automatic bottle return machines became a visible indicator of a modern, forward-looking grocery store. The practical effects, on the other hand, were limited by the inconvenience of counting tokens, the constant noise, the frequent broken bottles and the high maintenance costs.

As beverage consumption exploded in the postwar years, the problem of handling returned bottles intensified. In the late 1960s, customers lined up in Norwegian grocery stores to return their bottles. Norway had an industry-organized deposit-refund system, where a small deposit was paid upon purchase and refunded when the container was returned. Such an arrangement made sense for the breweries as long as purchasing new bottles was more expensive than handling and cleaning reusable bottles. For grocers, however, empty bottles were a nuisance. The staff were constantly interrupted by having to count and sort empty bottles, and the back room occasionally overflowed with empties. It could be hard to keep track of all the bottles and deposits, which encouraged fraud. The reusable bottles had to be made of thick glass, which made them very heavy. Fermenting drink leftovers complicated the grocers' bottle problem even further, leading many grocers to complain about unhygienic conditions.[8]

The modern, automatic RVM that we are going to consider here has its origin in the back rooms of grocery stores as a technology for handling empty-bottle logistics. A group of grocers got together and commissioned an improved

RVM from Petter Sv. Planke in 1971. He was a well-known salesman among the grocers, having introduced price-tag labeling machines to the Norwegian market. Petter, together with his brother Tore, who had recently graduated from the Norwegian Institute of Technology (NTH) in Trondheim with an engineering degree in cybernetics, founded a company to design and sell an improved RVM.[9]

The Planke brothers designed their RVM around clear user specifications. They asked Petter's grocer customers what they considered to be the most pressing bottle problems. What did they think the bottle problems would be in the future? Their questions were quite specific: how tall did the grocers think bottles would get, and how wide? What were the smallest bottles the RVM needed to be able to handle? At the time, Tomra did not have to consider different container materials since Norwegian grocers generally handled only glass bottles. Norwegian bottlers and brewers had long cooperated in using standardized bottles that could be returned to and reused by anyone. In the late 1960s, this cooperation came under strong pressure as some bottlers became interested in using disposable containers instead.

When consumers met the prototype of the RVM, they saw a metal plate on the wall, with a bottle-sized opening in it, large enough to handle one-litre bottles (fig. 5.1). They could place the bottle in a small box in front of the hole and then press a button to start a conveyor belt that transported the bottle into the machine. The production version of the machine used an automatic sensor to start the conveyor belt when a bottle was inserted—it turned out that the button confused many users. The RVM registered the deposit value and printed the total on a small paper slip. The bottle ended up on a storage table behind the machine, where the grocer could move the bottles into crates at a convenient time. This set-up was much simpler than for the older machines, where each bottle type had had a separate hole and the consumer received a token for each bottle. Still, a page of user instructions had to be posted on the wall to help consumers operate the machine. One of the things that the paper instructed consumers to observe was that the bottles had to be clean and empty, though in fact the first generation of the machine could not tell the difference. In short, the first-generation Tomra RVM was designed to address problems the grocers identified, primarily by getting the bottles out of the way while keeping track of exactly how many bottles had been received.[10]

The Tomra I RVM design clearly represented an engineer trying to make sense of an infrastructural problem. At this time, Tore Planke's engineering mindset focused on functionality and reliability rather than aesthetics and user experience. The most radical design choice Tomra made was to choose a high-tech approach to what most considered a low-tech problem. Tore's design process clearly followed a tinkering approach, where he tested out various technological alternatives for recognizing bottles. During his studies at

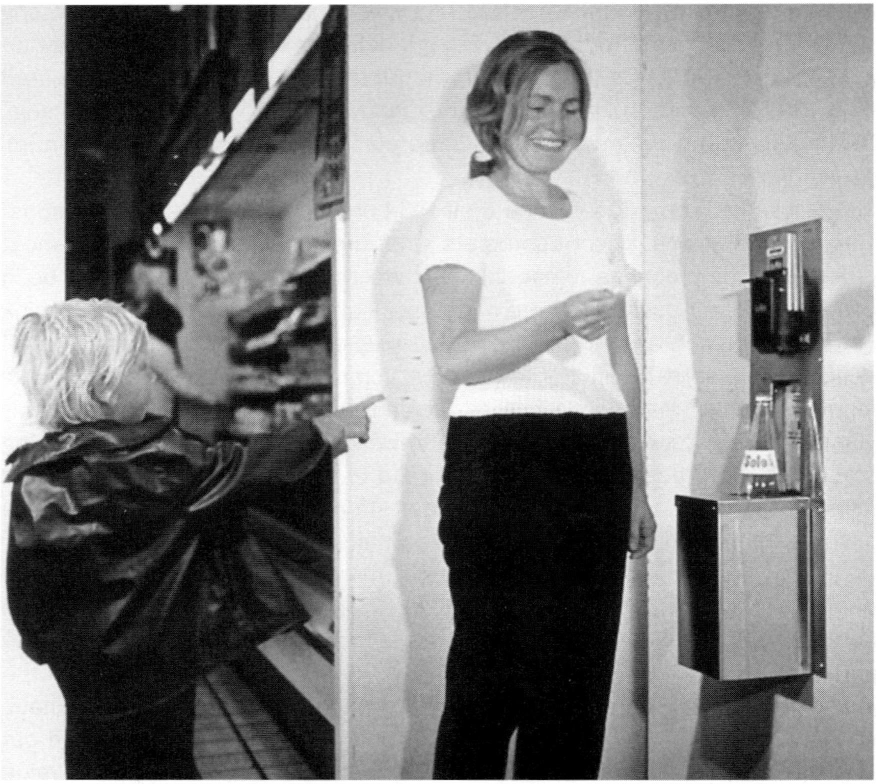

Fig. 5.1 Advertising image of the Tomra I, 1974. Photograph courtesy of Tomra Systems ASA.

the Norwegian Institute for Technology, he had been exposed to cutting-edge technologies that he now wanted to test. In the end, he chose a photocell recognition technology that let the machine recognize eight different bottle types, which was more than enough for the Norwegian market. We have to understand that at this time machines were sold on an individual basis, in a very personal relationship between the grocer, the machine and the Planke brothers. The Tomra I went through several iterations, selling a total of 2,200 machines, before being replaced by the dramatically more advanced Tomra SP in 1979.[11]

OUTSIDE THE RVM: THE TOMRA CAN-CAN

While the Tomra SP will not be discussed in detail here, this RVM model became a tremendous success for the company. By using new and advanced techno ogy like microprocessors, lasers and fibre optics to recognize and register bottles, Tore Planke and his small engineering team increased the number of bottles the machine could reliably recognize by orders of magnitude. While the development was time-consuming and costly, the SP gave Tomra an extremely strong position in European bottle return systems.[12]

As a result of their market dominance, a Swedish business consortium called Returpack invited Tomra to develop an RVM for handling aluminium can returns in Sweden in the early 1980s. These containers had grown very popular, but most ended up as litter since Sweden did not have a return system to handle them. The Swedish government responded to this problem by asking the bottling industry to increase the recycling rate of these containers to more than 80 per cent or face a ban on aluminium cans. After a few attempts at raising the recycling rate through informational campaigns, an industry consortium ended up organizing a deposit-refund return system called Returpack, modelled after the existing and very successful bottle return system.

The machine Tomra developed for the return of aluminium cans, the Tomra Can-Can, signalled a new company approach to product design. This was the first time Tomra employed professional industrial designers, in an attempt to improve their product development process.[13] At this time, industrial designers were aggressively targeting small Norwegian companies, arguing that they could not afford to stay with 'homemade design'. Nils Tvengsberg, the Chairman of ID, Norwegian Industrial Designers, at the time, argued that professional design was as important as research, development and marketing. Industrial designers had a strong sense of what type of design appealed to different users and so should come in early in the product development process in order to understand and discuss strategy, markets, product, development and economics.[14]

In making the Can-Can, Tomra cooperated closely throughout the entire product development process with Tvengsberg's design office. Both Tore Planke and Tvengsberg served on the first jury of the Council of Industrial Design's Mark of Design Excellence, a prize set up to recognize innovative and good product design. Planke had been recruited to the jury by Knut Yran, a graphic designer who had worked as the Director of Philips's design office in Eindhoven from 1966 until his retirement in 1980. After this he moved back to Norway, where he soon became president of the Council of Industrial Design in 1983.[15] The council's intention behind these awards was to increase the awareness of design as a competitive factor for Norwegian businesses.[16] They wanted to ensure that design became an integral part of product development and functionality, and not regarded as something that is added on top as fluff.

Tomra came to form a close cooperative relationship with the industrial designer Roy Håvard Tandberg, who worked for Tvengsberg at the time (fig. 5.2).[17] He had moved to Norway in 1974 after getting a degree in industrial design in 1970 at the Art Center College of Design in Los Angeles.

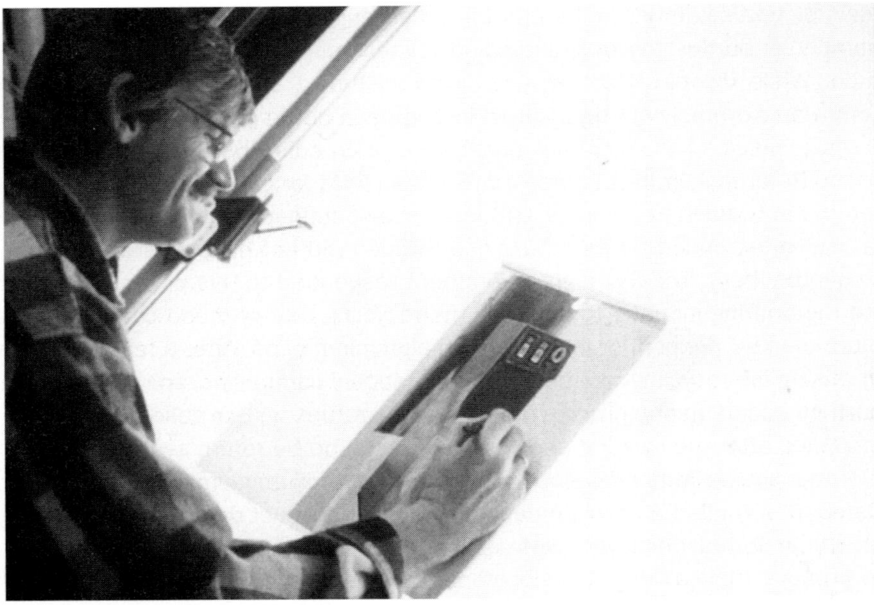

Fig. 5.2 Product designer Roy H. Tandberg working on the Tomra Can-Can. Photograph courtesy of Tore Planke.

Tandberg had worked with the Ford Motor Corporation during his education and with Volvo later on.[18]

Tandberg's design expertise made significant contributions to the Can-Can design that stretched far beyond the aesthetic. First, he had extensive knowledge of man–machine interaction. Tore Planke had worked on such topics during his studies at NTH, but Tandberg had received more thorough training and experience through his American education and work experience. Tandberg would consider such things as where to place displays in order for users to best notice them and the most ergonomic height for hand movements, and he implemented this in the design for the Can-Can and subsequent RVMs.[19] In other words, he rethought the relationship between the RVM as machine and the user's body.

Second, Tandberg demonstrated a profound knowledge of materials and their characteristics in the design process. The fronts of Tomra's machines had previously been made of steel or high-pressure laminate plates.[20] Tandberg used aluminium and plastic fronts on the Can-Can to give it a more rounded shape than Tomra's previous RVMs. He used an aluminium-casting process that he had learned from American car manufacturing. The darker top part of the front had more details and was made from molded polyurethane, a plastic polymer.

Finally, and perhaps most critical, Tandberg had gained his design experience in an industrial production setting. It had to be possible to manufacture the designs in an affordable way. This required a close knowledge of existing technologies, materials and production processes. Petter Planke later stated that this was the key reason why the cooperation with Tandberg went so well. While Tandberg was concerned with the visual appearance, he also paid close attention to the production process the artefact had to be a part of. Planke called this a concurrent engineering product development process that involved all relevant parties: the customer with the need, the salesman, the engineer, the producer and the designer, as well as the technological, material and financial limitations of the production process.[21] Tomra had been sensitive to this balance of user interests and material constraints since the beginning, even though they did not have a separate designer until they hired Tandberg.

The Can-Can's design also required some engineering planning. This machine was specifically designed for the Swedish aluminium can recycling system, and one of the political requirements of the Swedish Returpack system was that the RVMs that served as the front ends for the system had to be manufactured in Sweden. Tomra circumvented this requirement—which massively favored the RVM made by PLM, the main business organization behind the new deposit system—by producing the machine as individual modules in the company's established facilities in Norway and assembling them into RVMs in Sweden. The Norwegian design team termed this the *smokk-smokk* concept, reflecting the fact that the entire machine could be put together with one screw—the pre-assembled components only needed to be set into the cabinet and fastened tight to the frame.[22] This technique enabled fast and inexpensive final assembly and also made it easier for Tomra to use subcontractors in the production process.[23] Tomra's engineers thus circumvented Returpack's machine design demands by adopting the modular design concept. As a result of Tomra's design reorientation and the combination of expertise and requirements that shaped it, the design of the Can-Can was very different from the SP and miles away from Tomra's first-generation RVM. The Can-Can was a very compact machine—only 40 centimetres wide and 160 centimetres tall—designed to fit in crowded grocery stores (fig. 5.3). A small, round hole on the right accepted empty cans, and another hole under this one returned rejected cans. A LED display showed a welcome message and the total number of cans deposited. All in all, the outside of the machine looked sleek and polished. The inside of the machine matched the impression the outside gave through advanced and efficient technological solutions. The machine compressed the deposited cans and stored them in a container that could take 500–700 cans, weighing approximately 15 kilograms.

The Can-Can marked an increasing concern with how both grocers and the consumers returning bottles—the technology's primary end users—saw the

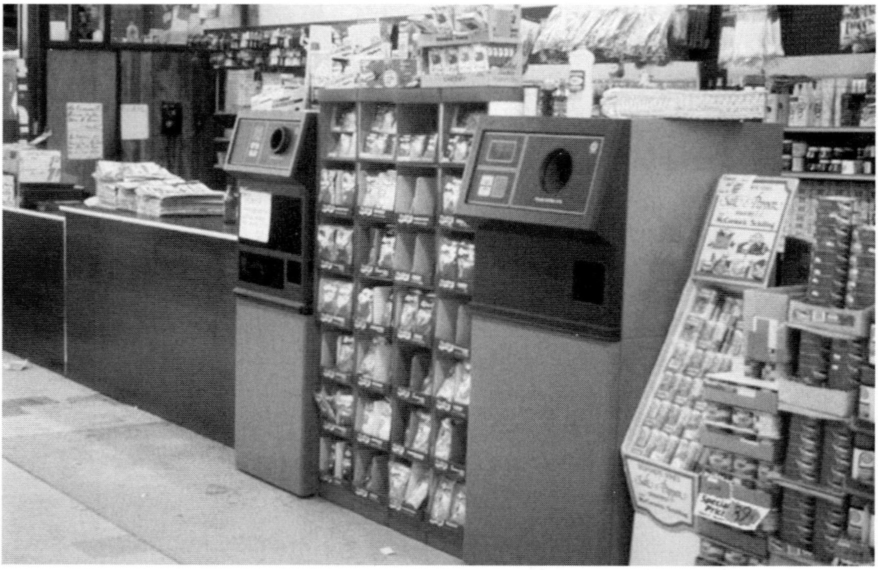

Fig. 5.3 The Tomra Can-Can in a store environment. Photograph courtesy of Tomra Systems ASA.

machine. Tomra wanted to give the Can-Can a softer expression that appealed to its users.[24] Grocers had begun asking for more aesthetically appealing RVMs, since they had become a prominent part of most Norwegian grocery stores.[25] Tomra also wanted to make an ergonomic machine that was easy to use at high speeds. Finally, the machines had to be easy to maintain and to assemble.

Tandberg's Can-Can design was one of the recipients of the Norwegian Council of Industrial Design's first (re-)edition of the Mark of Design Excellence in April 1984 on the basis of 'its concept, its functionality and reliability as well as the good overall impression' (fig. 5.4).[26] The Planke brothers were extremely impressed with Tandberg's contribution and offered to employ him under a retainer contract.[27] In practice, he became Tomra's in-house designer in a 50 per cent position and filled the rest of his position with external contracts. At times, Tomra required more of his time and at other times less, since the company's product development work was cyclical. Such contracts were quite unusual in Norway at the time, though Tandberg knew them well from his former work in the USA.

Tomra's move from having the company's engineers design the RVM to using a professional designer was a highly deliberate decision. The Planke brothers clearly recognized the limitations of their own design capabilities. At the same time, they were mostly thinking of design as the visual expression of the RVM and the user interface. Tomra's engineers excelled at designing

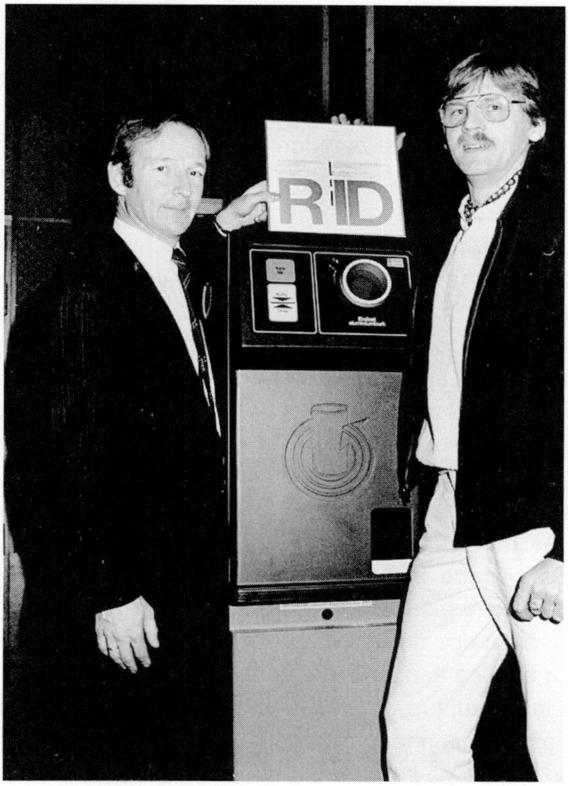

Fig. 5.4 Tore Planke and Roy H. Tandberg receiving the Mark of Design Excellence for the Tomra Can-Can in 1984. Photograph courtesy of the Norwegian Design Council.

technological solutions with close attention to function and the interaction between problem definitions and available technologies. Tandberg's design expertise was grounded in a strong knowledge of materials and production processes and allowed for a productive exchange of ideas and approaches that went far beyond aesthetics.

So far the Can-Can seemed like a perfectly designed machine; it performed well as a pure infrastructural technology, it looked sleek, and the modular design allowed Tomra to win a large part of the new Swedish market that opened up with the introduction of the aluminium can deposit. Around 1984, when Tomra was at its most confident, the company set its aims for the American market. The Can-Can seemed perfect for the American market but ended up demonstrating the limits of machine design.

The American beverage container recycling system required Tomra to modify the Can-Can design. In the US states with a bottle deposit-refund system, the bottlers were responsible for collecting the deposits and refunding them to the consumer. If a machine were to be used for this, it would have to be able to sort the cans by manufacturer. Tomra modified the Can-Can to fit these requirements by adding a laser scanner to enable barcode recognition. Tomra hired Andreas Nordbryhn, a young engineer who would become very valuable to the company, to design the barcode reader. The American version, called the Can-Can Wide, was bigger than the Swedish one. Tomra made this change because American grocery stores generally did not have the space limitations that Scandinavian stores had, enabling the machine to store more empty containers. When Tomra later introduced the bigger Can-Can to Sweden, the Swedes dubbed it the 'Tomra Jumbo'.[28]

Tomra's efforts to integrate the Can-Can into the American beverage container recycling system and the recycling habits of American consumers extended beyond technical modifications. In 1983 and 1984 the company spent NOK 8 million on marketing—an unprecedented amount in Tomra's history.[29] Their goal with the advertising campaign was to 'move from a position of relative anonymity to gain recognition as the leading supplier of reverse vending equipment'.[30] As part of the PR work in the American market, Tomra made a marketing video where Tore Planke demonstrated the features of the Can-Can. He directly addressed the American audience by highlighting features such as speed, accuracy, flexibility, compact size, safety, reliability, economic control, ease of service and software control.[31] The video presented the RVM as a high-tech infrastructural machine and clearly had American grocers and supermarkets as the main target group.

The advertising campaign seemed successful at first, since Tomra managed to get several large contracts for RVMs from Continental Can and Metropolitan Mining. Together, these contracts dwarfed the sales in Tomra's Scandinavian home market. However, two things happened to thwart Tomra's plans. First, the global market for recycled aluminium crashed as the Soviet Union dumped virgin aluminium on the market. Second, the alliance between grocers, bottlers and consumers that had formed the basis of Tomra's business model in Scandinavia simply did not exist in the USA. Bottlers in the USA got to keep unclaimed refunds, so it was not in their economic interest to support efficient recycling. Even in the states that had a bottle deposit and refund system, the RVM met with massive resistance.

Tomra's problems in the USA demonstrated the limits of the machine as infrastructure and showed that technology design needs to consider the social, cultural and political setting the product must function in. Because of the lack of system-wide support, the Can-Can machines did not receive anywhere near the return rates that had been achieved in Scandinavia. Although the Can-Can had been designed for the Swedish political environment, it was not adapted to the US environment when it was transported there. In other words, the needs of American users had not been embedded in the machine design, and this may even have been impossible to do at the time.

The combination of political and technological design that made the RVM so successful in Scandinavia was not sufficient to succeed in the USA. The machine design was the same in both markets, but the context was different. RVMs aimed to make recycling convenient, but US bottlers wanted recycling to be as inconvenient as possible. Targeting the grocers' logistical problem of handling bottles was not sufficient. By focusing more on the logistical aspects of bottle recycling and less on the political ones, Tomra failed to integrate their product into American beverage container recycling in the 1980s.

THE RVM IN A SYSTEM: THE TOMRA 600

The final iteration of RVM designs we will discuss shows how Tomra aimed to embed even larger contexts in its design. In many ways, as the technological platform of the RVM grew increasingly more sophisticated, managing the input and the output became the critical design question. The hole in the wall connected the interactions of users at the front of the machine with the larger recycling system design at the back of the machine.

The Tomra 600 Ultima (T600) RVM launched on 1 April 1997, on Tomra's twenty-fifth anniversary (fig. 5.5). It was the most technically advanced machine Tomra had ever made. The company had solved many of the technical problems the RVM had struggled with since the beginning. All types of beverage containers—glass and plastic bottles as well as aluminium cans—could be inserted lying down through a round hole in the wall, avoiding the stability problems that arose in the older machines where bottles had to stand up when inserted. A high-resolution CCD video camera paired with powerful computers scanned the inserted beverage containers at high speed and could identify all sorts of containers with a high degree of accuracy. In short, the T600 was an engineering marvel and looked well designed too. Like the Can-Can and several of the company's other RVMs, the T600 won the Mark of Design Excellence (1997).

However, the key design element was invisible to the end user. The T600 was just the front end to a new system. This was the ultimate RVM—completely integrated into a larger recycling system that electronically managed payments to grocers and bottlers for container returns. Tomra's goal was no longer simply providing rational handling of returnable beverage containers in grocery stores, but rather 'helping the world recycle'. This made the RVMs just as much green, environmentalist technologies as they were infrastructural machines.

Tandberg's involvement was critical to the T600 design. Tomra let him start the design process by first designing the front of the machine to create the best possible user experience. Since Tomra needed grocers to want the machine in their stores, the aesthetics of the T600 were important. It had to be

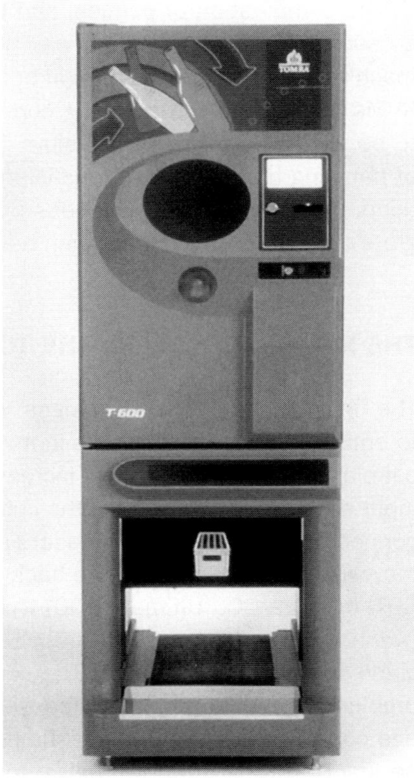

Fig. 5.5 The Tomra 600 Ultima, 1997. Photograph courtesy of the Norwegian Design Council.

durable and resilient. It had to handle spillage and sticky beverage residues without looking unhygienic. The display had to present information in a clear and legible way. And, most important, the beverage containers needed to be inserted lying down, so that they could not fall over. Tandberg addressed all these issues in his design for the T600 front.[32]

Furthermore, all this had to fit within a relatively compact frame, leading to negotiations between Tomra's engineers and Tandberg during the internal design process. For instance, Tandberg wanted the container insertion hole placed lower on the machine front, but Tomra's engineers could not make the internal mechanism work with the hole in this place. While ergonomics to a certain extent had to be sacrificed in order to make the machine function, this was the only major compromise between Tandberg and the engineers.[33]

At the same time, the back of the system was set through the design of the Resirk system. The T600 did not stand alone—it was the centrepiece of a new Norwegian deposit system set up by a business coalition to recycle aluminium cans after more than ten years of planning.[34] Tore Planke was the key architect behind the new system, dubbed Resirk, which plays on the Norwegian word for recycling, *resirkulering*.[35] He designed it around a new generation of RVMs with online capabilities—the T600—to provide more control and prevent fraud. The Norwegian Parliament finally allowed the Resirk system to start up in 1999 after a drawn-out legal controversy. In this system, all disposable containers carried a differential tax to be adjusted annually based on recycling rates. In other words, the higher the recycling rate, the more profitable disposable containers could be. Foreign beverage containers that were not part of the Resirk system would have to pay the full tax. Resirk then had a huge incentive to make the recycling system as effective as possible to benefit its members. Resirk was set up as a non-profit organization to handle the administration of the new deposit system. The deposit would follow the beverage container through the entire life cycle of the container, from producer to bottler to grocer to consumer and back again. In that way, the producer would lose money unless the container was returned and recycled. Resirk paid a small handling fee to grocers as well as to the recycling depot as compensation for handling the empty containers.

The consortium set up the new system as complementary to, not competing with, the old glass return system.[36] Resirk aimed to minimize the public distinction between different container types. Tomra specifically designed the T600 to handle all containers, be it plastic, aluminium or glass. The T600 launched for Tomra's official twenty-fifth anniversary in 1997, which was before Resirk got final approval, but the machine was clearly designed to be part of the Resirk plan. By using the same hole in the wall for all containers, Resirk emphasized the similarity of the containers as well as made recycling more convenient for consumers.[37] Resirk also subsidized grocery stores that wanted to upgrade their RVMs to ensure that as many stores as possible adopted the new technology. By choosing to use one machine to handle all beverage container types, even ones Resirk was not responsible for, the consortium made an explicit design choice to blur the distinction between the old and new containers. The glass bottle return habits were strong, so Resirk wanted to tap into the existing recycling habits.

Online functionality via a modem was key to the central position of the T600 in the Resirk system, as programming, monitoring, fault diagnosis, software upgrades and data collection could be done from a central computer. Tomra also upgraded its software, which could be retrofitted on old machines to add online functionality. The online capability was critical to the Resirk model because it allowed real-time monitoring and administration of can returns.

In designing the T600, Tomra came to reconsider the role of the indirect user group, the consumers returning empty bottles. It became critical for the company to understand what motivated these users to return empty beverage containers through the hole in the wall. The entire Resirk system was designed around this simple act, since the higher the recycling rate, the lower the tax. It was thus in the bottlers' and brewers' best interest to have a high recycling rate.

CONCLUSION: WHAT IS SO SCANDINAVIAN ABOUT THE RVM?

The historical evolution of Tomra's RVMs can tell us three important things about technology and design. First, Tomra's RVMs have become successful technologies because they have been designed for and by a multiplicity of users. Louis Bucciarelli discusses engineering design as a social process involving negotiations between a series of actor groups, which we see clearly in the Tomra case.[38] Tomra's evolving RVM design approach reveals an increasing concern with reaching and recruiting different user groups. While the first RVM mostly served grocers (where satisfied consumers were mostly a side effect), Tomra gradually included environmentalists, aluminium producers and policymakers among the users of the RVM. The design challenge is that it was fundamentally the same machine that did both these things. In the first version of the RVM, the design collective was quite limited, consisting mainly of Tore Planke, who had the technical expertise, and Petter Planke, who provided the sales expertise. Over time, different types of expertise became involved.

Second, we have seen how the RVM is a carefully designed object that was developed in an interplay between product technology, such as mechanical components, optical sensors and container types; political guidelines, such as deposits and taxes; industrial strategies, such as standardization, exports and competition; and cultural trends, such as environmentalism. Both engineers and industrial designers took part in this evolving development of the RVM designs, engaging in what John Law calls *heterogeneous engineering*, making no distinction between technical, social and aesthetic design elements and blending the front, inside and back of the RVM in order to make it work.[39] This blend of perspectives and approaches arises in situations where different competencies meet, as Birgit Jevnaker argues in her studies of the relationship between business and design. The design-related activities that take place in companies that have employed design expertise in their product development practices can be highly dynamic and create spaces for reflective learning and creativity.[40] It is in this meeting between different competencies, requirements and limitations that something new can be created.

Finally, the study has made a case for the value of following the design evolution of a technology in use, over time and through several iterations. A technology is not finished when it leaves the factory but changes over time, as the conditions of its creation and use change over time. Tomra was a somewhat atypical inventor-based engineering company since they were so closely focused on the needs of the customer when they designed the machine, and they came to realize that technologically advanced solutions were not sufficient. The path from having this insight through learning about the market and then implementing it in functioning machine designs, however, was challenging.[41] This was a gradual process where the RVM moved out of the back room and became integrated into society, politics, industry and everyday life. Tomra recognized that handling empty beverage containers required a complex socio-technical system.

One question remains, however: is there something particularly, essentially, Scandinavian about Tomra's RVM? Is the simplicity of using one hole to return all container types instead of many holes simply an engineer's idea of Scandinavian design? Another way to phrase the question is whether the RVM could have been invented elsewhere. Sure. In fact it was, as evidenced by the early American patents and the fact that there are RVM producers in other countries, particularly the USA and United Kingdom. However, Tomra's RVM differed from these, and not only because it used more advanced technology.

The Scandinavian setting, with a relatively cooperative relationship between bottlers and grocers who trusted Tomra, and the political support provided by the deposit-refund system, gave Tomra the stability to develop a fully mature technology. The problem with the older, manual RVMs was that they could not handle many different bottle types. The Tomra I could handle eight different bottles. This was sufficient for Norway and Sweden, with their standardized bottle types and sizes.[42] Markets like France and the USA, for instance, had huge potential but would most likely have posed an upstart RVM company too many challenges to succeed. With first Scandinavia and later Europe as a home base, Tomra today has between 80 and 90 per cent of the world market for RVMs.

Scandinavian design reaches beyond elegant furniture; the RVM was designed by engineers to grocer specifications and then grew increasingly more refined. The design in this context came to take its place in a large, complex socio-technical system. Yet it is a relatively anonymous design, which most of its users know only as a simple hole in the wall. The RVM has become part of the fabric of the everyday.

PART 2

APPROPRIATIONS

–6–

Just Decoration? Ideology and Design in Early-Twentieth-Century Sweden

Christina Zetterlund

'More than anything, Swedish interiors, architecture and design have been distinguished by a democratic intention.' This claim is found in a Swedish Government Official Report published in 2000, in a short passage with the heading 'A Democratic Tradition'.[1] Here, the use of the term 'tradition' points to an appropriation of the past to legitimate political strategies for the nation's contemporary and future development, both culturally and economically. Implicated in this is a notion of a past legitimizing a present, as well as a 'we' or, more specifically, a Swedish 'we'. The 'we' in the preceding statement is constructed in relation to a notion of the 'democratic'—an ideological trope that has played a crucial role in forming a tradition, a canonical Swedish design history. This notion of the 'democratic' in connection to forming a tradition is intriguing and worth interrogating further.

There are, of course, numerous ways to analyse this relation. In this essay, the Liljeblå ('Lily blue') pattern designed by Wilhelm Kåge in 1917 for the KG dinner service model—also designed by Kåge—manufactured by the Gustavsberg company, serves as an entry point (fig. 6.1). Art historian Gregor Paulsson used Liljeblå to illustrate his argument in the highly influential *Vackrare vardagsvara* ('Better things for everyday life') from 1919. This text is mentioned in the government report as a significant contribution to the formulation of 'the democratic tradition'. As 'the workers' service', Liljeblå has been given a canonical position within standard Swedish design history writing. Kåge also designed the patterns Apollo and Blå ros ('Blue rose') for the KG model, but they have not been granted an equally prominent position to Liljeblå. It is important that Liljeblå was already nicknamed 'the workers' service' in the sketching phase.[2] This fact makes one wonder what kind of idea of the 'democratic' 'the workers' service' implies. This essay does not analyse what has traditionally been the subject matter of Swedish design history. Instead, it asks the question: who is the subject implicated in this narrative as it is formulated in the Liljeblå case?

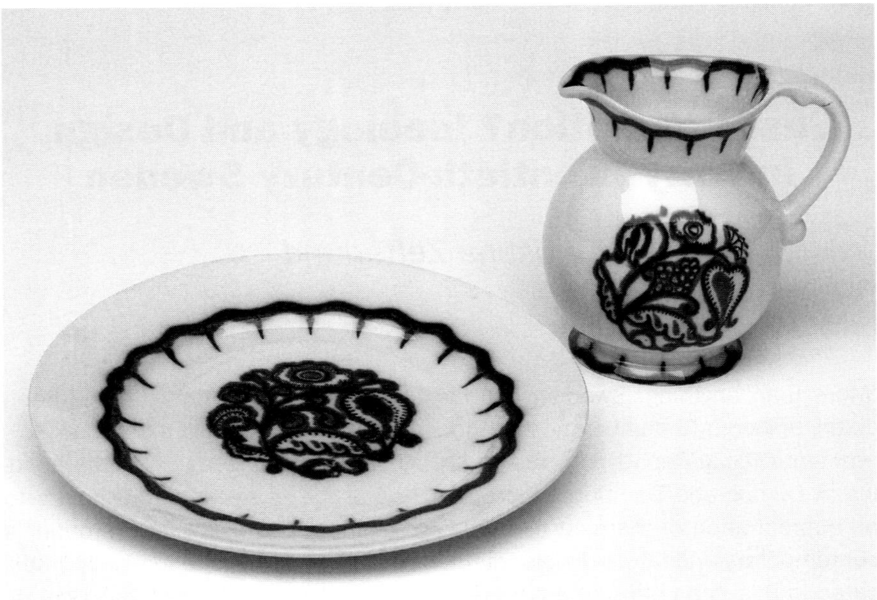

Fig. 6.1 Liljeblå, 'the workers' service' (1917), manufactured by Gustavsberg, designed by Wilhelm Kåge. Photograph courtesy of Röhsska Museum of Fashion, Design and Decorative Arts.

The 'workers' service' was designed for the 1917 Home Exhibition at the Liljevalchs Art Gallery in Stockholm. According to some design historians this event marked the birth of modern 'Swedish craft and design culture'.[3] This claim is founded on the fact that it was the first event displaying the efforts of the Swedish Society of Arts and Crafts' liaison office. The office was formed in 1914 with the aim of encouraging industry to hire artists and was modelled on a similar initiative by the Deutscher Werkbund. This was a big undertaking for the Swedish Society of Arts and Crafts that caused much debate and a reorganization.[4]

The year of the Home Exhibition, 1917, was a turbulent one. In the late spring, after years of war, and fuelled by the Russian February Revolution, the so-called Hunger Demonstrations were staged all over Sweden. Following the general election the same autumn, the Social Democratic Party entered the government for the first time, as part of a coalition headed by the Liberal Prime Minister Nils Edén. It was a coalition that reflected an aspect of the Social Democratic self-understanding. In 1917 the party had suffered a severe internal crisis resulting in the radical left-wing faction of the party being expelled. The party was to build the country by reforms, not to support and stage revolutions to topple the existing system. Within the Social Democratic Party there was an ambivalent relation to 'the masses', who many felt were 'difficult to discipline' and had a fundamental need to be educated. According to this would-be state-bearing party, then, the 'worker' should not be a radical subversive subject but a well-integrated citizen.[5]

PATTERN OF INCLUSION: LILJEBLÅ

Wilhelm Kåge was hired to the ceramics manufacturer Gustavsberg in late spring of 1917 following a meeting between him and the company's director, Axel Odelberg, set up by the Swedish Society of Arts and Crafts' liaison office. Kåge was given the assignment to design the Gustavsberg contribution to the Home Exhibition. This depiction of a quick and rather prosaic method of supplying the industry with artists, sketched by Nils Palmgren in his biography of Kåge, captures how this office—which is much discussed in the literature on Swedish design history—could work.[6]

A meeting held in 1916 by the National Association of Social Work (Centralförbundet för socialt arbete, CSA) to discuss 'the housing question' formed what could be seen as the immediate background of the Home Exhibition. The theme of the meeting was to improve the living conditions of 'people with small financial means'. CSA was a liberal political organization formed in 1903 to promote sociopolitical reform. In the published minutes from the meeting one reads that improving the living conditions was essential, not just for the underprivileged themselves, but also for a sustainable and prosperous development of Swedish society as a whole. The meeting stated that the housing question was one of the most important problems to solve, as the 'big tree of society' had its deepest and most sensitive roots in the home.[7] K. Starbäck, a lecturer, called for a revival of the beautiful Swedish home that had not been affected by what he considered the degenerating effects of industry. He also argued that handicraft used to play a vital role in forming the homes of the peasants before this decline induced by industrialization. This was confirmed by the architect John Åkerlund, who stated that people had left the traditional way of building for cheap frippery from abroad.[8] The ideas of Starbäck and Åkerlund were, as is discussed later, not unique but part of a discourse that was introduced towards the end of the nineteenth century. Improving the living conditions of workers had several purposes. It is important that aesthetics in the CSA discourse were placed side by side with the perceived need to improve the morals of 'people with small financial means', as part of a broader ambition to organize and control the 'other', the worker.[9] The CSA's engagement dealt not only with physical living conditions but just as much with improving the moral 'health' of the people. This is underlined in the introductory speech to the CSA meeting, which discussed the prevalent 'lodger system', not for its effects on physical conditions but as a moral hazard, a cancer, 'which erodes society's soundness'.[10] The CSA's engagement was rarely about rights but more about solutions, as Shamal Kaveh points out.[11] The Home Exhibition could be seen as one such solution.

The CSA meeting attracted people from various sectors of society. The list of participants is dominated by CEOs and engineers, but it also features union representatives, politicians, physicians, scientists, landowners and so on. Several architects attended the meeting, and some of these, like Carl Bergsten and Torsten Stubelius, had close links to the Swedish Society of Arts and Crafts. But, surprisingly, considering the substantial task the CSA was about to bestow on the Society of Arts and Crafts, no official representative from the organization is found in the list of participants. The society was asked by the CSA to organize an exhibition displaying homes for the 'people with small financial means', a proposal that grew into the Home Exhibition that opened in October 1917. Two years earlier, in 1915, the CSA had arranged a small exhibition of a two-bedroom apartment for low-income families in the housing complex called Framtiden ('The Future') in Gamla Enskede outside Stockholm. The CSA described this flat as 'practical and hygienic' as well as 'tastefully decorated'.[12] The organizing committee of the Home Exhibition consisted of Erik Wettergren, former assistant at the National Museum of Fine Arts, then Secretary of the Society of Arts and Crafts; Elsa Gullberg, textile artist and Director for the Society of Arts and Crafts' liaison office; Gregor Paulsson, Curator at the National Museum of Fine Arts; the architect Carl Bergsten; and Yngve Larsson, one of the invited speakers at the CSA conference.

Despite its origins, the Home Exhibition should not be understood merely as a philanthropic enterprise for the contributing companies; it was also a marketing event. Gustavsberg constitutes a good example of this fact. In a famous review of the 1914 Baltic Exhibition Erik Wettergren had criticized Gustavsberg's products severely for lacking artistic quality.[13] The Home Exhibition, then, provided a welcome opportunity for the company to display that an artistic renewal had taken place. The management at Gustavsberg was not indifferent to the conditions of the workers. But when the workers at the factory wanted to rally for a union, Wilhelm Odelberg, the owner of Gustavsberg, was furious.[14] For Gustavsberg, Liljeblå was part of the first step in a process of artistic renewal, and designing for the worker became a vehicle that communicated this process.

Liljeblå was inspired by eighteenth-century Swedish white-and-blue faience decorations but was to some extent a less refined version. The decoration was painted with a thick and somewhat floating blue line created by three different shades of blue. It was not a coincidence that the eighteenth century provided the inspiration for Liljeblå. August Brunius, art critic in the Swedish newspaper *Svenska Dagbladet*, proclaimed that the Gustavian period along with the widely mediated interiors by Karin and Carl Larsson in their own home, Lilla Hyttnäs, represented the quintessential Swedish style.[15]

This statement reflects the growing interest in defining and bringing forward a national character in design as well. The decorative gesture in Liljeblå included the workers in this Swedishness, but, as we will see, it was a highly conditioned inclusion. Liljeblå did not have the lightness of the more famous eighteenth-century designs produced at the large ceramics manufacturers Rörstrand and Marieberg. If anything, it resembles what could have been a rural version of these services. This aesthetic was also present in the ideal model flats shown at the Home Exhibition. A rural flavour is felt in most of the rooms, especially in the kitchens. Light white curtains, wooden furniture, rag rugs and open shelves are common features.[16] By the table in almost every kitchen was the kind of wooden sofa that would easily convert into a bed, very common in the Swedish countryside (fig. 6.2). Some of the flats also had a second room intended as a bedroom, furnished with two beds placed beside each other as would be found in any middle-class home.

The Home Exhibition drew considerable media attention. The Social Democratic women's magazine *Morgonbris* ('Morning breeze') stated that it provided an opportunity, not just for the 'people of small financial means', to learn how to build a home with 'harmony and style'. It displayed 'a democratization of beauty' with excellent design at affordable prices.[17] Carl Westman stated in *Svenska Slöjdföreningens Tidskrift* (the magazine of the Society of Arts and Crafts) that the displayed objects reminded him of household goods

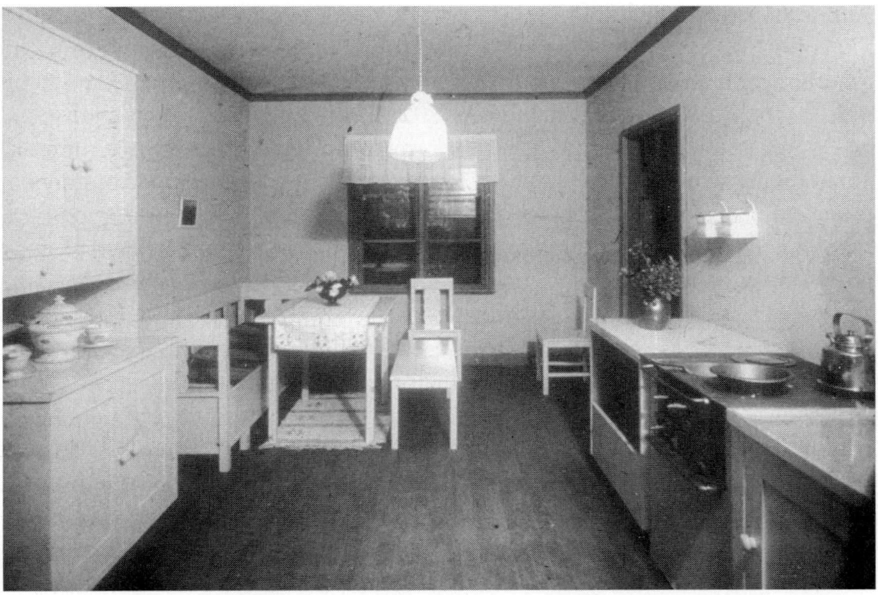

Fig. 6.2 Kitchen shown at the Home Exhibition (1917), designed by Uno Åhrén. Photograph courtesy of the Swedish Society of Arts and Crafts.

from an age of 'good culture'; they were representative of a Swedish culture, of objects in an age before industrialization ruined craft.[18] An aspect of the democratic gesture shown in Liljeblå as well as in the interiors of the Home Exhibition, as already stated, was turning the home into a battleground of the morals of the poor, an instrument of control. It was to be hygienic both in the sense of cleanliness and, just as important, regarding the interaction between the sexes as well as between parents and children in order to create a sound and sustainable living environment.[19]

The exhibited interiors show obvious references to the homes and texts of Karin and Carl Larsson as well as the writings of Ellen Key. Both Key and the Larssons were highly important in defining the modern Swedish interior. Both were widely published in such different publications as the Social Democratic women's magazine *Morgonbris* and the bourgeois interior decoration magazine *Svenska Hem i Ord och Bilder* ('Swedish homes in words and images'). By 1899 Key had already participated in organizing exhibitions of interiors for workers inspired by arts and crafts interiors.[20] However, several actors formed this discourse. One important institution is the open-air museum Skansen in Stockholm. Founded in 1891 by Arthur Hazelius, Skansen grew out of the Scandinavian ethnographic collection that had been established by Hazelius in 1873 with the aim of preserving a material culture that industrialism was rapidly changing. Peasant houses from all around Sweden were moved to the open-air museum.

The importance of Skansen is revealed, for instance, in one of the publications of the Housing Committee of the Swedish Parliament. In 1911 Gustaf Steffen, a Social Democratic Member of Parliament, was the first to raise 'the housing question' within the Parliament.[21] This resulted in the formation of the Housing Committee in January 1912. In his contribution to the Housing Committee's publications Steffen formulated historical examples largely based on houses found at Skansen. He was thereby trying to form references to an age preceding aspirations of upward social mobility, before the current state in which a social aspiration was—according to Steffen—evident in contemporary housing, which was no longer built with references to Swedish traditions.[22] However, copying historical examples was not an option. Modern housing should be developed in a modern spirit, requiring solutions that differed from those materialized in the historical examples witnessed at Skansen. Knowledge was to be found in the tradition and history 'of our people'.[23] Close to the endeavour of Skansen was the Association of Friends of Textile Art, established in 1874, and the National Association of Swedish Handicraft Societies, formed in 1899 with the aim of promoting Swedish handicraft traditions. These associations were important not just in forming the aesthetics of the Home Exhibition but also in the discourse of improving morals. In *Hemslöjdskommitténs betänkande* ('The report of the Handicraft Committee') from 1918, handicraft was proclaimed to be a suitable occupation that would prevent the workers from engaging in immoral behaviour.[24]

The Liljeblå decoration should therefore be seen as a pattern of inclusion. It can, clearly, be positioned in a discourse formulating a material culture in search of a visual tradition of Swedishness. The worker was to be included in this tradition by anchoring the constructed visual scheme in the past. This illustrative gesture was to give the worker a recognizable aesthetic expression. With this inclusion, the threats of the workers' poor moral and revolutionary tendencies were to be avoided. However, it is an inclusion that is highly conditioned. The worker inscribed in Liljeblå was not just any labourer. For people like drunkards and drifters, notably groups that did not contribute to production, or simply people of immoral behaviour, a severe instrument for exclusion was formulated in theories of eugenics. Such theories were invoked explicitly within the CSA as well as in Social Democratic discourse.[25] The worker, the 'other', is given a very conditioned presence but remains cut off from the subject position in this story. This is evident in the statement that people with small financial means should not aspire to move away from this given place and formulate something else through 'frippery from abroad'. The workers' material culture is never present in itself; instead, it is a culture known as that which is to be designed, educated, improved and controlled.

THE CONSUMER OF 'DEMOCRATIC DESIGN'

Not everyone agreed with the strategy chosen for the Home Exhibition. For instance, Erik Folcker, Curator at the National Museum of Fine Arts, claimed that looking back into history to find a way forward had never been a solution. He thought that workers, who acquired a natural sense for quality through their closeness to and knowledge of industrial production, would be unhappy with objects that reminded them of the underdeveloped production of their ancestors. They would not want household objects that marked their difference from the higher classes. Instead, according to Folcker, it was within the consumer cultures of 'highly cultivated' groups that 'a peculiar fascination for the primitive' could be found.[26]

The 'highly cultivated' people identified by Folcker were obviously not found among the workers but rather within the consumer groups of the fashionable department store Nordiska Kompaniet (NK). The NK catalogue of 1918–19 features the Apollo dinnerware pattern, where it is described as 'designed by the artist Wilhelm Kåge'. Several patterns shown at the Home Exhibition are also found in this catalogue. A blue-and-white washing set, also designed by Kåge, named Reklam ('Advertising') is offered alongside the Turbin ('Turbine') service designed by Edward Hald for Rörstrand—another object from the Home Exhibition, canonized in Swedish design history for pioneering abstract decoration inspired by industrial shapes.[27] The catalogue gives an indication of who appropriated the 'democratic design' of the Home Exhibition.[28]

Yet NK offers an interesting case. It clearly illustrates how a variety of styles are present at a given time—a fact not sufficiently acknowledged by historians.[29] Not only peasant-inspired design was sold at NK. In 1919, two years after the Home Exhibition, NK staged an ambitious show called Bourgeois Interiors. Whole rooms, like the ones at the Home Exhibition, interpreting the 1919 version of the bourgeois interior were staged within the department store. For instance, there was a parlour in the Gustavian style that included furniture with gilded detailing, a gilded clock, a sofa with finely patterned fabrics, a crystal chandelier and a large oriental carpet. It was a distinctly different version of the Gustavian style than the one referred to by Brunius. NK's Gustavian parlour represented an understanding of that style that differed from the prevalent interpretations founded at the beginning of the twentieth century. Among the architects contributing to Bourgeois Interiors we recognize Carl Bergsten and Carl Malmsten from the Home Exhibition. In a review found in the conservative home decoration magazine *Svenska Hem i Ord och Bilder* Carl Gernandt de Jossac praised the interiors for not presenting dull handicraft—*hemslöjd*—or far-fetched ideas of 'Swedishness'. Instead, he considered the NK interiors truly international.[30] Vice versa, one might say this magazine did not take an interest in the Home Exhibition. They did, however, publish actual interiors designed in the fashion seen at the exhibition. For instance, the homes of both the Larssons and Ellen Key were published here and presented as 'modern'. But the majority of the homes portrayed belonged to the Swedish elite and were closer to the ones presented in Bourgeois Interiors. This shows that the consumer of 'democratic design' cannot simply be located among the bourgeoisie but must be understood as part of a specific material culture within this group.

MATERIAL CULTURES OF THE WORKER

In practice, it was not the economically less fortunate who were given an opportunity to buy the 'well-thought objects' found at the Home Exhibition as a replacement for things 'already used', as Elsa Gullberg would put it in the 1940s.[31] One possible reason why the 'workers' service' did not become a common possession among workers is the simple fact that they might not have liked its design; many workers desired something else. But that answer is perhaps a bit simple because consumption is not just about taste. It is also about economic realities and material conditions. The lack of 'well thought objects' and the proliferation of used ones was, for many, not primarily a question of taste but of financial and practical means. An episode in the novel *Godnatt jord* ('Good night, earth') by Ivar Lo Johansson, a representative of the so-called golden age of worker's writers in the Swedish literary scene of the 1930s, illustrates the difficulties *statarna*—the landless farm labourers—had in accessing modernity.[32] Lo Johansson depicts how the main character's mother wins a modern lamp in a lottery. Initially it sits like a sculpture in the family's small home, until she is told that it needs a light bulb. With a tiring journey to the city she manages to procure a bulb. But the lamp still does not work. Her small and old-fashioned home has no electricity. In this depiction Lo Johansson illustrates the difficulty with which early-twentieth-century farm labourers would become modern consumers. This narrative forms a stark contrast to the idealism of Gullberg and the Society of Arts and Crafts. No matter how much education the family portrayed in *Godnatt jord* would get, certain circumstances made it impossible for them to take part in the design reforms. Perhaps it was not this particular group of people with small financial means that Gullberg implied. But, if so, this lack of clarity is in itself revealing about the reformers' rhetorical strategies concerning the worker. There is no homogeneous group that could be sorted under a single label such as the worker.[33] Despite all the designer attention targeting various people referred to as workers, they remained anonymous. The tendency of consumers in this social stratum to be unidentified or stereotyped has since turned into a historiographic problem persisting in Swedish design history to this day.

Looking closer at some groups that could be included in the elusive concept of worker, one is struck by the diversity of living conditions. There is no such thing as *a* material culture of the worker; there are several. For instance, servants living with their employers usually had very limited households of their own, as their lives were intertwined with the homes in which they worked. In the Stockholm City Archive, all that is filed as belonging to the estate of one household servant is a chest of drawers and some clothing.[34] Other Stockholmers listed as workers in the estate inventory have a longer record of belongings indicating a self-owned home, and these could probably afford to make a greater amount of consumer choices than the servant.[35] In the countryside we would find groups such as cottagers and farm labourers who had their own households. But even these groups were not homogeneous. A cottager was given a house and had to pay rent in kind by working for the farmer who was letting the house. The cottagers' lives depended greatly on the size of the cottage they were given and the size and quality of the land. The farm labourers, *statarna*, were married couples living with their families in rooms within houses at the farm. They got their payment mainly in groceries.

Cottagers and farm labourers acquired new objects for the home in various ways. In the countryside, local auctions seem to have been a frequent way of procuring new things. For non-used objects travelling salesmen were one supplier; occasional journeys to shops in the town provided another possible source. Furniture was usually bought from a local maker. Many goods were made at home, like towels, linens and rug rags for the floor. In questionnaires concerning the cottager and farm labourer found at the Nordiska Museum in Stockholm it is evident that what are called porcelain plates in these records are common in the surveyed households, whereas other utensils were made out of materials such as metal, wood and earthenware.[36] There are still other groups, many of them not as present in the archives as the farm labourers and cottagers. These groups would perhaps not fit a conventional description of worker, as they did not, for numerous reasons, have a job on a regular basis. For some of the people in this group it is possible that their income did not allow them to have a home or to own things on a long-term basis. Some of them would be found among the people without an estate inventory who, when they died, received a *Fattigbevis*—a certificate of poverty—as there were not enough belongings to make an inventory from when they died. It is, then, just the name of the deceased that is present in the Stockholm City Archive.

There is, of course, much more that should be said about the people who are called 'workers' or 'people of small financial means'. In the current context, it suffices to note that the observations regarding the material cultures of the 'workers' outlined here provide important information in relation to how design history has been written in Sweden. The historiography reveals how dominant the object-centred approach has been; very little effort has been made to contextualize the artefacts under scrutiny. 'The many' remain an anonymous mass in these narratives. In the case of the people who were the target of the 'workers' service', the actual living conditions and infrastructures are absent in the historical literature, as are analyses of consumer cultures (or the lack thereof). Swedish design history has mainly been written from a sender perspective. Admittedly, it is difficult to depict these material cultures. Some of the disciplines cognate to design history, such as ethnography, economic history and social history, have taken an interest in the material cultures of the workers at the time of the Home Exhibition. However, most studies concerning the living conditions of people 'with small financial means' are concerned with how housing was organized physically. Studies of this kind typically analyse issues such as housing location, costs, room size, the number of people who would share one space and the sanitation.[37]

In design history writing, moving beyond descriptions of material structures is important in order to—as far as possible—identify a sense of individuality in this group conventionally lumped together as 'the masses' or 'the people of small financial means'. Still, from the sources referred to previously it is difficult to gain knowledge about traditional design history concerns such as what kind of dinnerware patterns these people used. The majority of the archive records usually just state that such possessions existed, providing no information on their design or how they were procured. Detailed knowledge of the dissemination of dinnerware patterns is, of course, not always pertinent, but in some cases it certainly is—like in the present context, as a means to exploring why the decorative practices of certain groups are appropriated, canonized and sanctioned, thus constituting History, while the aesthetic preferences and consumer choices of others fall into oblivion. Ultimately, the selective appropriation at work here is a question of power.

EXCLUSION: NON-APPROPRIATED DECORATION

To the extent that new, non-used things actually were bought by low-income groups, a trace of their design properties might be found the mail order catalogue issued by the company Åhlén and Holm, which was one of the most wide spread of its kind in Sweden in the early twentieth century. This was at a time when the mail order system was crucial for the consumption practices of many Swedes.[38] Åhlén and Holm was a major player in this business and operated at the lower end of the market. The company sold everything from furniture and clothes to bicycle parts and gnome figurines. In the 1918–19 catalogue, a separate section was devoted to ceramics, including vases, coffee sets, washing sets and dinnerware. Because of Åhlén and Holm's position in the market, dinner services sold by the company give some indication of what kind of patterns many Swedes in modest- and lower-income groups preferred. Several different models of dinner services were on offer. It was not easy for the consumer to make an informed choice, or for the design historian to write about it, given the poor quality of the illustrations in the catalogue: small black-and-white images on an orange-and-white background. Accompanying the pictures were prosaic descriptions such as that for the N:r 14 U 30324 model: 'a fine porcelain with beautiful flowers in blue'; or, for the N:r 14 U 30298 model: 'made of genuine porcelain, matted roses with matted green leaves. Gustavsbergs Porcelain Factory well known brand. A nice, new model'.

Crucially, the Gustavsberg products featured in the Åhlén and Holm catalogue are miles apart from those from the same manufacturer exhibited at the Home Exhibition and somewhat different from what was offered at NK. A more elaborate description is given for another Gustavsberg model, presented as N:r 14 U 30296, 'Hawthorn pattern with gold. A very nice model. Gustavsbergs Porcelain Factory well known brand. Recommended as particularly beautiful and considered good quality and very low price'. Selling at SEK 125, it was one of the pricier dinner services offered by Åhlén and Holm. By then, Hagtorn, as the pattern was labelled by Gustavsberg, had been in the factory's range for almost twenty years. It was launched in 1899 following the introduction of new printing techniques that allowed a cheaper way of using four colours, a novelty evident in the delicate hawthorn twigs that were depicted on the porcelain with green leaves and small white and pink flowers. It was decorated with a golden line around the edges and applied on several

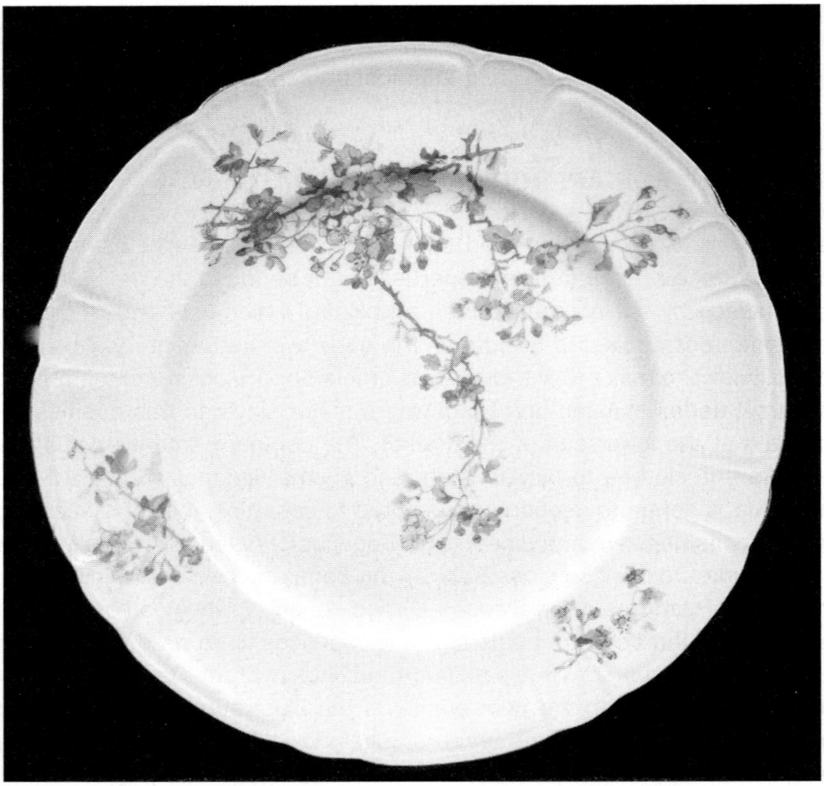

Fig. 6.3 Hagtorn (1899), manufactured by Gustavsberg. Photograph courtesy of porslinsbutiken.se.

models.[39] The one depicted in the Åhlén and Holm catalogue had a plate with a rococo-inspired shape (fig. 6.3).[40]

In terms of design, the dinner services sold by Åhlén and Holm were dominated by historical references. These references may not be as deliberate and direct as they are in the case of Liljeblå but rather express a simplistic historicism in which traditional forms are invoked more by allusion than by reproduction—resulting in a design idiom that may be described as *traditionalesque*.[41] In Hagtorn, for instance, a reminiscence of a floral rococo plate could be detected—and the same applies to the 14 U 30122 model 'of a nice flowery porcelain with golden lining. A really nice and splendid service'. These different applications of historical references in design provoke the question of why both in design reform propaganda and in design history writing certain appropriations of a past are considered aspirational and in poor taste while others are accepted as an expression of Swedishness and good taste. What makes the 'workers' service' 'democratic' and the Hagtorn pattern not?

THE SUBJECT OF SWEDISH DESIGN HISTORY

As suggested previously, the democratic gesture present in Liljeblå can be interpreted as concerning inclusion, at least from a couple of perspectives. First, the workers, 'the people with small financials means', are articulated and included in a certain kind of consumption. Yet it is an inclusion on a discursive or ideological level rather than a practical or actual one. It is evident that the 'well thought objects' did not, generally, migrate beyond the bourgeoisie. But rhetorically, at least, the workers are pronounced potential consumers of the 'modern'. It is also a gesture that can be interpreted as an intention that 'good design' should not be the preserve of the privileged but be within reach also for 'the many'—a notion that today is attractive within a political discourse, as demonstrated in the governmental report cited in the introduction, as well as within marketing. *Democratic Design* is the title of a booklet that IKEA published in 1995 to mark its fiftieth anniversary. The celebration took place in Milan and was marked by the launch of the first PS collection. This highly mediatized collection consisted of novel products commissioned from 'rising stars' amongst Swedish designers—a concept marking a distinct turn for this company, known precisely for *not* using designer names in its marketing. In the booklet, 'democratic design' is defined as an expression of values: everybody 'should be given the same opportunity in life. Everyone should be given a chance to enjoy it.' The democratic gesture in the IKEA context becomes 'designer objects' that do not have to be expensive and exclusive but rather are available to all. Not surprisingly, the Home Exhibition is included in the narrative of IKEA. The company presented itself as the 'present-day heirs of a long and typical Swedish tradition', the same tradition as defined in the governmental report.[42] Even if IKEA has been one of the more successful in this commercial appropriation, it has not been alone in promoting this version of Swedish design history.[43]

In this Swedishness, the 'we' of the 'democratic design tradition' is the second aspect of inclusion to be found. By formulating a recognizable pattern for the workers they are made observable. This is a visibility that seems to enable schemes for improving the physical living conditions, for the state to cater for the workers. At the same time, this becomes a mechanism of control demanding adjustment and adaptation. However, as argued previously, this is an inclusion mainly on a discursive level since the consumers of the 'democratic design' shown at the Home Exhibition were largely to be found among the clientele of the upscale department store NK.

This fact, concerning where the actual consumer of the 'workers' service' is to be found, gives some indication of the subject position implied within the Swedish design historical discourse dealing with the period of the Home Exhibition. Liljeblå is produced as well as consumed within a discourse formulated by an intellectual bourgeoisie. Therefore, it is the material culture of this specific group that is implied in the design historical discourse of this time. The intellectual bourgeoisie is to be the Swede, *the* subject, of the *Swedish* design history of this period—a fact enhanced by the reality of the 'democratic' intent. Despite the 'democratic' efforts invested in the 'workers' service', the group targeted, the worker, remains anonymous. It is never the actual material cultures of this diverse group that are made present in this discourse, not in the design of Liljeblå and the Home Exhibition, nor in the writings of Steffen or the CSA. The material cultures of the worker groups are never assigned any meaning; instead, the people that could be included in this group should be educated, their way of life altered and controlled.

The implication of this fact today depends on the role that we ascribe to history. Assuming that design history does affect how current practice is defined, this is not just an issue for the historian. One may ask, for instance, if the lack of multiple subjects in historical accounts is reflected in the difficulties Swedish design schools have in recruiting students outside the middle and upper classes. If so, it would seem that design history functions to confirm and establish norms that regulate student recruitment in design schools.

On the whole, norms are an issue that saturates this case study. In the 2010 autumn sale at Bukowskis, one of the leading Swedish auction houses catering to a high-end market, a complete set of the 'workers' service' was on offer at an asking price of SEK 15,000–20,000, effectively showing that design history also has significant monetary value. Hagtorn, on the other hand, was at the time of writing found in local second-hand shops and in a Salvation Army thrift store. This is a store generally not known for selling what traditionally is labelled as important design but rather objects discarded by some people and products that are not ascribed enough value to be sold at prestigious auctions.

The Liljeblå case also demonstrates how problematic the notion of creating or even claiming a 'democratic design' is. Today, when claims of a socially engaged design practice are ubiquitous—in part fuelled by the discourse on sustainability—it is wise to reflect on this difficulty. Planning a design process truly inclusive of more than just a few stakeholders is tricky, just as it is difficult to accept and work with the actual complexities that a socially engaged process really would entail. Likewise, writing a design history truly inclusive of more than just a few subject positions, select social groups and restricted material cultures remains a challenge to us all.

–7–

Goldfish Memories: Recounting Oslo's Streamlined Aluminium Trams

Kjetil Fallan

> Why do we love the tram? . . .
> Because it means solidarity. Because it reminds us of
> our conditions: a reasonable
> and vulnerable
> being, in an unreasonable
> time. A historic animal, in a history-weak
> time.
>
> —Jan Erik Vold[1]

On a late January day in 1937 something outlandish touched down on the streets of Oslo. Far removed from the research into aerodynamics carried out at American universities and the (pseudo-)science of eugenics that interested several American industrial designers at the time,[2] a streamlined tram that would soon be nicknamed *Gullfisken* ('the Goldfish') entered traffic in this city on the outskirts of Europe (fig. 7.1). In a setting where modern design was couched in the rhetoric and formal language of functionalism—at least in the realm of architecture and home furnishings, which is where professional design discourse took place in Norway at the time—the smooth yet dramatic shapes of the new tram must have been a remarkable sight. Yet its streamlined design was a sure sign of the times. The Goldfish remained in service for almost fifty years and thus became an iconic image of Oslo. A less conspicuous but equally significant feature of the Goldfish was its all-aluminium monocoque body. Lightweight, economical and technologically advanced, the innovative aluminium construction neatly dovetailed with the streamlined design into a potent symbol of modernity criss-crossing the streets of Oslo.

This case study explores a distinct episode in the history of Norwegian design: the development of the streamlined aluminium tram entering service in 1937.[3] The Goldfish represents an 'otherness' in several respects: Firstly, it has a formal language which does not conform to stereotypical images of Scandinavian design. Secondly, it was designed by a group of engineers, not

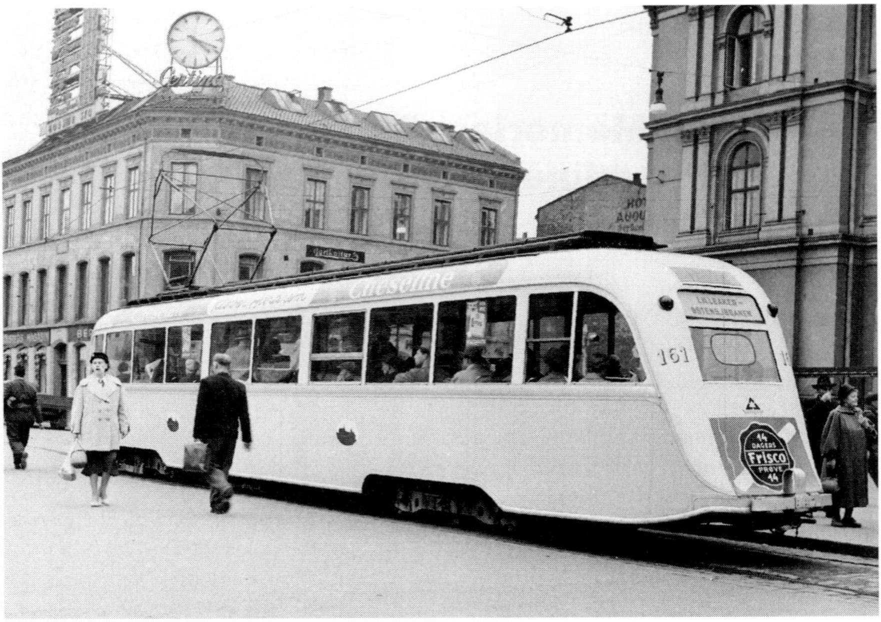

Fig. 7.1 Rear/side view of the Goldfish tram, manufactured by Strømmens Værksted for Oslo Sporveier from 1937 on. Unknown photographer. Oslo Transport Museum. Original in Oslo City Archives.

by an art school-trained designer. Thirdly, it is a type of artefact given little attention in histories of Scandinavian design. These aspects make the Goldfish an intriguing case through which to study both the less familiar hinterland of Scandinavian design and the design culture of streamlining as seen from its margins. The first section provides a brief account of how streamlining was mediated and appropriated in Norway in the 1930s. The second section discusses two earlier projects crucial to the development of the technology and design that would characterize the Goldfish. The third section analyses how the Goldfish was designed and examines its features. The fourth and last section situates the Goldfish in a discourse on the identity of its constituent material, aluminium, and how its cultural meanings are tied to notions of modernity and nationalism.

THE NORWEGIAN APPROPRIATION OF STREAMLINING

The mid-1930s, when the Goldfish was designed, might be considered the high point of streamlining as a formal language in industrial design. Although often portrayed as a particularly American phenomenon, the history of streamlining—especially in transport design—is riddled with European contributions. When the engineers at Strømmens Værksted were designing the Goldfish, the ideas of aerodynamics and streamlining and examples of streamlined vehicles were presented, mediated and interpreted in a Norwegian setting. Trade journals and special-interest magazines played a leading role in this intellectual and cultural appropriation of streamlining, and these mediations of both American and European novelties are essential in understanding the preconditions for developing a streamlined tram in Norway.

The primary arena for the mediation of streamlining in transport design was the motoring magazine *Norsk Motorblad*, an independent publication aimed at motoring enthusiasts and professionals in the sector. Streamlining was presented here as early as 1929 as the automobile design paradigm of the future. The report featured the predictions of the British race car driver Henry Seagrave, a heroic figure in the motoring world who had recently improved his world land speed record to 372 kilometres per hour in the aluminium-body Thrupp & Maberly Golden Arrow designed by J. S. Irving. Seagrave reportedly claimed that the car of the future would 'be built exclusively after aerodynamic principles, and only a small part of the wheels will be visible'.[4] While these remarks remained speculations, the magazine shortly thereafter presented an existing vehicle, albeit an experimental one: the streamlined car designed by British aeronautical engineer Charles Dennistoun Burney. The author of the article explained that 'wind tunnel tests have revealed that the exterior shape of the modern car . . . is very disadvantageous in terms of air drag' and lamented the failure of earlier streamlined experiments such as the German Edmund Rumpler's Tropfenauto (1921) and the Hungarian Paul Jaray's Lay T6 prototype (1922), placing great hope in the arrival of 'a new vehicle of the streamline type designed by Sir Denniston [sic] Burney'.[5] A piece from 1932 by a Dresden-based engineer by the name of Haase sought to explain the aerodynamic potential in streamlined design of car bodies. Crucially, Haase pointed out that the power loss caused by air drag 'increases with . . . the cube of the velocity' and that therefore 'streamlined bodies are justified primarily at high speeds'.[6] Erling Dale, a Norwegian engineer living in Germany, took it one step further: 'The so-called streamlined bodies appearing [in] the last years have nothing to do with the aerodynamically correct forms.'[7] It would be abundantly clear to the Norwegian audience even at this early stage, then, that streamlining had no or insignificant aerodynamic importance for slow-moving vehicles.

Despite this awareness of the limited benefits of moderate design changes towards a somewhat more aerodynamic appearance, the term 'streamlining' would from now on be used more and more frivolously. Even minor alterations like the removal of external sunscreens were explained as intended 'not only to make the vehicle more pleasing to the eye, but also to reduce air drag'.[8] Virtually every new car was described as streamlined, but *Norsk Motorblad* also singled out more radically streamlined novelties such as the Briggs 'Dream

Car' prototype (1933) designed by John Tjaarda;[9] the Volvo Venus Bilo prototype (1933) designed by Gustaf L. M. Ericsson;[10] the Chrysler Airflow (1934) designed by Carl Breer, Fred Zeder and Owen Skelton;[11] and the Tatra T77 (1934) designed by Hans Ledwinka, Erich Ledwinka and Erich Überlacker.[12] The latter two were met with special interest because they were commercial production cars. The Airflow was exhibited at the Norwegian Automobile Show in May 1934 and hailed as 'the modern vehicle' in a separate article shortly thereafter.[13] The T77 was described as 'the most beautiful and artistically harmonious vehicle ever produced by the automobile industry' despite the writer's claim that 'the Tatra body is not quite right in terms of aerodynamics, but the form is the best approximation possible without infringing [Paul] Jaray's patents which completely protect the correctly streamlined body'.[14]

In this sedimentation of a new design culture the imperfect adherence to aerodynamic principles is noted but met with acceptance, even acclaim, as long as the streamlining was aesthetically pleasing. Therefore, the magazine was only too happy to proclaim that 'the streamline principle is now implemented also on boats', presenting the stylish new 32-foot motor boat *Happy Days* which gave 'a grand impression with speed in its lines'.[15] The boat was built by J. Skeie at Maritim in Oslo and designed by engineer Richard G. Furuholmen. Equipped with a 30 bhp (horsepower) engine the boat would have a top speed of 13–14 knots, or about 25 kilometres per hour. While this is a respectable speed for a mahogany boat, requiring good hydrodynamic properties of the hull, it does not provide any rational justification for an aerodynamically motivated streamlined design of the boat's superstructure. But Furuholmen's most elegant design was nonetheless praised as a fine example of streamlining.

Although somewhat faster than contemporary leisure boats, buses of the 1930s reached only fairly moderate speeds, and their streamlining is equally difficult to rationalize by referring to aerodynamics. In keeping with this new design culture's transition from ideology to style it was a bus that seems to have been the very first example of a streamlined vehicle made in Norway.[16]

GEARING UP FOR THE GOLDFISH

In 1934 Oslo Sporveier (Oslo Tramway Company) entered a partnership with the coachbuilding company Strømmens Værksted with the aim of developing a new generation of lightweight buses and trams. The increase in private car ownership in the 1930s combined with harder competition from private bus companies led Oslo Sporveier to opt for a renewal of its rolling stock in order to provide improved and more competitive service. Larger, more efficient, modern units emerged as the most desirable strategy, forming the basis for the partnership with Strømmens Værksted. It was this collaboration that resulted in the launch of the Goldfish in 1937, but the groundwork for that product, in terms of both construction technology and design, was laid with the development of two generations of buses.

Strømmens Værksted was the country's largest coachbuilder, established in 1873—nineteen years after the first Norwegian railroad opened. In 1925 the company branched out into the construction of buses. Increased traffic required larger buses carrying up to sixty passengers, but such vehicles constructed by conventional methods would exceed the road load limitations in Oslo, which allowed only low weights. Strømmens Værksted's young director, the mechanical engineer and metallurgist Alf Ihlen, solved this problem by pioneering the aluminium monocoque body on a bus developed in 1929 that weighed only 6,450 kilograms—26 per cent less than the American steel bus upon which the design was modelled.[17] Reportedly, this bus was the first of its kind in the world. The innovative construction technology developed with this bus and its successors would form the basis for the subsequent development of the Goldfish tram.[18]

Alf Ihlen and his brother Joakim, one year his senior, were grandsons of Strømmens Værksted's founder and took over the company as soon as they had finished their studies. Both studied in the USA and graduated with a BS in mechanical engineering from the University of Wisconsin in 1921. Joakim received some business education in France and Germany before returning to Norway and taking over the family business in 1922, at the age of twenty-three. Alf Ihlen remained in the USA and received a MSc in metallurgy and business administration from Massachusetts Institute of Technology in 1923. He then returned to Norway and joined his brother as Director of the company, taking charge of research and development and product development. During his studies Alf Ihlen had a work placement at American Car & Foundry Co. (ACF), a leading manufacturer of trains and buses; he later secured the Norwegian agency for their products.

Whilst at the University of Wisconsin Alf Ihlen befriended a fellow Norwegian student, Einar Isdahl.[19] Upon his graduation (with a BS in mechanical engineering) in 1923, Isdahl went to work for Hall-Scott Motor Car Co. in California—a company that would be acquired by ACF in 1925 and later became the supplier of engines for Strømmens Værksted's buses. Returning to Norway in 1924, Isdahl got a job as a production engineer at Nordisk Aluminiumsindustri, a major manufacturer of aluminium products.[20] It was the rolling mill division at Nordisk Aluminiumsindustri that would supply the aluminium used to build the new buses and trams at Strømmens Værksted. When Oslo Sporveier started its bus operation in 1927, Isdahl, then twenty-nine years old, was hired to head this division. In the capacity of his new job, Isdahl would collaborate closely with his friend Alf Ihlen and the other engineers at Strømmens Værksted in the design and development of the new rolling stock.

Ihlen and Isdahl became close personal friends. They shared a keen interest in aviation and were both eager hobby pilots. So, when it became clear that the ACF bus that Ihlen intended to import or manufacture under license was too heavy for use in Oslo, the amateur aviators turned their attention to aluminium and visited British aircraft manufacturers to learn more about aluminium constructions.[21] Combining the monocoque principle from the American steel bus with the knowledge of aluminium alloys and profiles suitable for vehicle construction derived from British aircraft production, Ihlen and Isdahl went on to design the world's first bus with an aluminium monocoque body. Aluminium was considerably more expensive than steel, but the substantial weight reduction obtained through aluminium construction meant much lower running costs, and their choice would thus prove good economy for both their companies.[22]

The first delivery of the aluminium bus consisted of only ten vehicles, but it was nonetheless a construction that was remarkable enough to generate international attention: even the US trade journal *Automotive Industries* found Ihlen and Isdahl's design newsworthy and presented it under the heading 'Duralumin Shapes Used in Norwegian Bus'.[23]

ACF, who delivered the Hall-Scott engines for the bus, sent an installation engineer to Norway to oversee the installation of the engines. When he reported back to ACF mentioning the all-aluminium character of the design, the American company reacted by sending a letter to Strømmens Værksted advising against the use of aluminium in the floor frame. Based on its own experiments ACF had come to believe that due to aluminium's low modulus of elasticity—one-third that of steel—there was a great risk of fatigue failure. Ihlen and Isdahl disregarded the warning and trusted their design, and time proved them right: no such failure was ever reported.[24] ACF must have learned the same lesson too, because a few years later they contributed, in a joint venture with the Pullman Co., to the construction of the M-10,000 commuter train for Union Pacific (UP) Railroad based on the same construction technology pioneered at Strømmens Værksted: an aluminium monocoque body.[25] Completed in 1934, it is regarded as one of the first streamlined trains in the USA.

It is worth noting that although its construction technology was directly influenced by aircraft production, the body design of the 1929 bus did not bear any signs of streamlining—but then, this was years before streamlining emerged as a design principle for commercial products and five years before the UP M-10,000 train. Instead, Ihlen and Isdahl's first aluminium bus took its formal cue from the ACF steel bus, rather conventional and angular in shape—but, according to one commentator, 'the body is, as expected, executed solidly and in good taste'.[26] This was to change drastically with the second generation, completed in 1935—a redesign which also involved numerous technological advances (fig. 7.2). The weight was now trimmed down

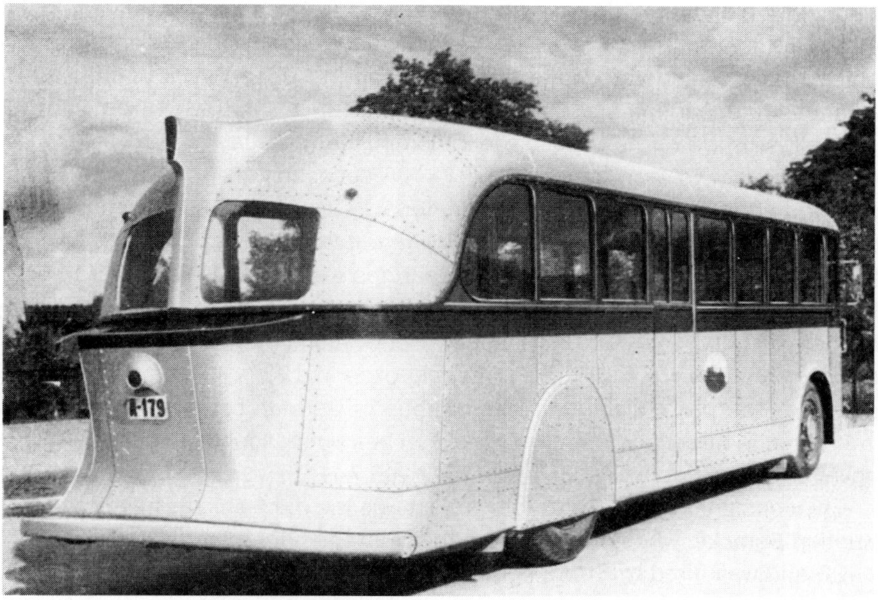

Fig. 7.2 The Hippo bus, manufactured by Strømmens Værksted for Oslo Sporveier in 1935. Unknown photographer. Oslo Transport Museum. Original in Oslo City Archives.

from the already-modest mass of its predecessor to a mere 5,080 kilograms, and the new bus could carry a passenger weight equal to 90 per cent of its deadweight. In a presentation of the new bus these advances were portrayed as a technology transfer from aviation, concluding that 'engineer Isdahl has had good opportunity to employ his knowledge of modern aircraft constructions'.[27]

Important and interesting as the constructional innovations are, it is the radically new body design that really commands attention in the present context. It was given rounded forms, sleek and streamlined. The rear end was particularly carefully designed, with an s-curved profile sloping down from the roof and ending in a 'duck tail' incorporating the bumper. Between the bumper and the rear window, neatly integrated in the overall body shape, was a compartment for skis and other luggage. The double-curved surfaces of the neatly modelled rear end were not an easy feat but the result of a complex working of the sheet aluminium and thus testify to the designers' determination to achieve a streamlined appearance.[28] A dramatic tail-fin housing the exhaust pipe, set as a protruding prolongation of the roofline, split the rear window in two, and the rear wheels were covered behind side panels.[29] In short, the new bus looked as though it was built for speed. But although it *was* faster than its boxy predecessor, the speeds at which it travelled were moderate even by contemporary standards. The swooshing streamlined design, then, was clearly not derived from rationalist notions or functionalist dogmas. Rather, its designers acknowledged the powerful emotional and symbolic meanings generated through design and inscribed their bus with overt allusions to speed, progress and modernity.[30]

In all, sixty-five of the second-generation buses were delivered to Oslo Sporveier over a two-year period. Like its predecessor, the streamlined bus received attention from abroad. The materials supplier Nordisk Aluminiumsindustri brought the bus to Copenhagen where it was described as 'gleam[ing] like it were made of pure silver' as its features were promoted to Danish politicians and representatives from the public transport sector and the coachbuilder industry.[31] Its parent company, Norsk Aluminium Company, included the bus in their exhibit at the Paris world expo in 1937.[32] Strømmens Værksted, on their part, negotiated with a group of German companies who were interested in manufacturing the Norwegian bus under licence, but these plans never came to fruition.[33]

Chief designer for the 1935 bus project was the mechanical engineer Johan Kristian Rømcke, who had graduated the Norwegian Institute of Technology in 1926 and was hired by Strømmens Værksted in 1930 from a job as a design engineer at the Norwegian State Railways' workshop in Trondheim.[34] As opposed to his fellow bus designers Ihlen and Isdahl, who had both studied and worked in the USA, Rømcke had no American experience to draw from. Yet it was with Rømcke as chief designer that Strømmens Værksted introduced streamlining—although according to Rømcke himself, his was a 'moderate streamlining'.[35] This fact may not be as paradoxical as it might appear. First of all, Ihlen and Isdahl had left the USA as early as 1923 and 1924 respectively, long before the gospel of streamlining had moved beyond the laboratories of experimental scientists and the workshops of eccentric inventors. Second, as we have seen, streamlining was not exclusively of American origin, leaving other possible sources of inspiration open to Rømcke as well as to Ihlen and Isdahl. By 1935 streamlining was also all the rage in European transport design. That being said, Ihlen and Isdahl kept cultivating their American contacts long after their repatriation and most likely shared any information running through their transatlantic communication channels with Rømcke and other involved parties. Whether their influences stemmed mostly from the USA or from Europe is ultimately of limited interest. Whichever is the case, the 1935 bus reveals that the engineers at Strømmens Værksted were utterly sensitive to international contemporary developments in industrial design in general and transport design in particular.

DESIGNING THE GOLDFISH

Based on the very positive experiences with the monocoque aluminium buses Oslo Sporveier decided to continue and expand the partnership with Strømmens Værksted and transfer the construction technology developed through the bus projects to the design of a new type of tram. The company's existing trams, about 150 motor coaches and 130 trailer coaches from the early 1920s, were getting old, and weight was a pressing concern. When the buses became such a success, then, it was hardly a surprising decision to develop a new type of tram based on the same construction technology and design principles.

This road-to-rail transfer of streamlined aluminium vehicle design has a little intermezzo in the form of a 'rail bus' ordered by Valdresbanen, a small private railway company, from Strømmens Værksted in 1935. This rail bus was, as the designation might imply, a small, combustion engine-powered, single-car train, only 13 metres long and seating forty passengers. Only one such vehicle was ever built, and it would come to lead a rather secluded life. The body design of this unique build very much resembled that of the second-generation bus developed the same year. According to the engineering journal *Teknisk Ukeblad*, 'The coach is beautiful, harmonic and comfortable, and built after the streamline principle.'[36] Although the rail bus was never multiplied, this curious case was in fact the first instance of road-to-rail transfer of streamlined aluminium vehicle design at Strømmens Værksted. Still, it was no matter of course that the body design of the new tram would be a continuance of the streamline vocabulary established with the 1935 bus and the unique rail bus. Early on in the project, in 1935, the engineers at Oslo Sporveier's own drawing office designed and built a full-scale model of what the new tram might look like. From the appearance of this study, it seems its creators had no knowledge of—or appreciation for—the streamlined designs coming out of Strømmens Værksted at the same time: with its completely vertical front and rear and ruler-straight horizontal lines with distinct band windows it had more in common with contemporary functionalist architecture than with streamlined transport design. However, mounted on what was probably the chassis of two old horse-drawn trams, this model was more likely intended as a mock-up for testing the general layout, floor plan, seating arrangements and so on than as a proposal for body design.

The design brief called for a vehicle approximately 15 metres long and 2.5 metres wide, with the capacity to carry 100 passengers, half of whom would be seated. Such a long rail car would clearly have to be built with bogies. The size was unusual in Oslo but not entirely unprecedented. Four cars of equivalent size built at Skabo Jernbanevognfabrikk had been servicing the Ekebergbanen line since 1933 (fig. 7.3). These trams, which were constructed of steel and wood, were designed with the assistance of the architectural partnership of Arne Korsmo and Sverre Aasland, leading figures in Norwegian functionalism, and were thus anything but streamlined.[37] The Skabo trams were considered light constructions, weighing 23 tons, and were powered by four engines yielding 77 kilowatt each. By comparison, the aluminium Goldfish weighed in at a mere 13 tons and achieved higher speeds with half the motor

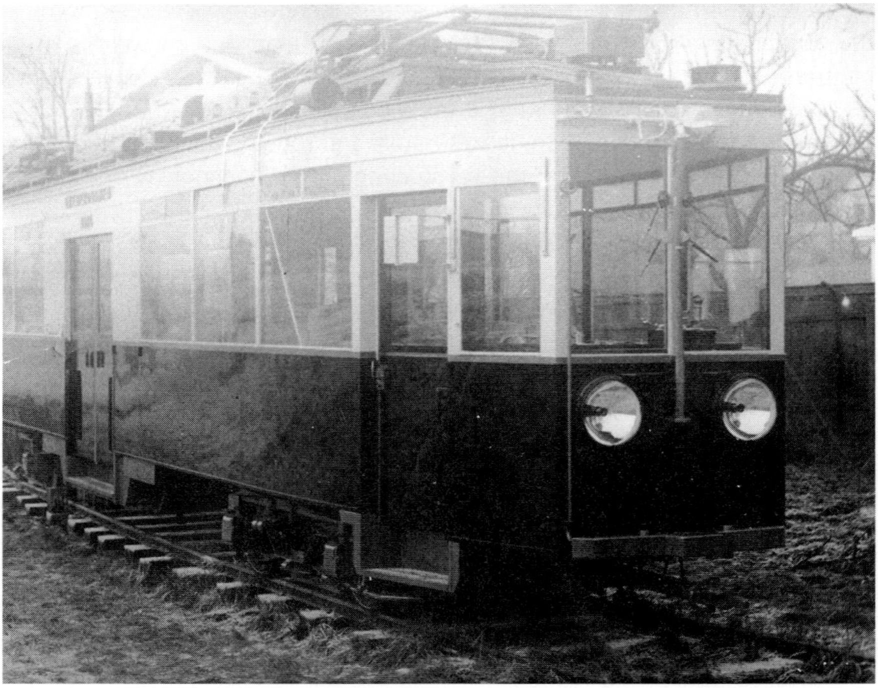

Fig. 7.3 Tram manufactured by Skabo Jernbanevognfabrikk for Ekebergbanen in 1933. Unknown photographer. Oslo Transport Museum. Original in Oslo City Archives.

power (4 × 37 kilowatt). The top speed was no less than 65 kilometres per hour—a notable figure for a tram in 1937.

The combination of a well-organized layout, large cars, low weight, high speed and low energy consumption held the promise of highly efficient service. Nevertheless, the Goldfish's early operation was troubled by problems with the technical equipment. The first six exemplars that were built were fitted with motors and electrical equipment from several different suppliers for the purpose of testing. This lack of conformity combined with the rather advanced character of the electrical equipment created many difficulties, resulting in both bothersome repairs and valuable experience to be fed back into later deliveries. Still, the client, Oslo Sporveier, was very pleased with the promise of modern, comfortable and efficient service they saw in the design of the Goldfish. The company thus ordered forty additional units, resulting in a total of forty-six Goldfish trams being built between 1937 and 1939.[38]

The design of the new tram was headed by a third Strømmens Værksted engineer: Ingvar Müller.[39] About twenty years older than Ihlen and Isdahl and twenty-five years older than Rømcke, Müller carried more experience than his fellow designers. Like the others he was trained as a mechanical engineer, graduating from Trondhjem Technical College, the precursor of the Norwegian Institute of Technology, in 1898. Before joining Strømmens Værksted in 1929 he had spent twenty-one years as a design engineer at the Norwegian State Railways.[40] His background, then, was similar to Rømcke's but with much more practice in rail transport technology and design.

Although Müller acted as chief designer for the project, many actors—including Isdahl, Ihlen and Rømcke—were involved in the complex process of designing the Goldfish (fig. 7.4). As such, the project is typical of most industrial design practice. Here, though, Isdahl's role is particularly interesting, as he was an employee not of Strømmens Værksted but of their customer, Oslo Sporveier. Of course, it was not unusual for public transport companies as customers to participate in the design of new rolling stock; after all, these were quite expensive products made in relatively small numbers and often subject to extensive tailoring. Still, such consumer participation is only recently being recognized in design history.[41] Although not an end user himself, Isdahl could be said to *represent* the end users (the tram's operators and passengers)—at least to a certain degree.[42] As such, his role resembled that of the grocers in Finn Arne Jørgensen's account in this volume of the development of the reverse vending machine—although Isdahl's participation in the design process was more hands-on. Also, Isdahl's involvement can be thought of as an instance of what is today termed 'participatory design'.

The design team came up with a body design for the Goldfish that is decidedly streamlined, but its forms are not as voluptuous as those of the 1935 bus and the rail bus from the same year. The characteristic duck-tail is still

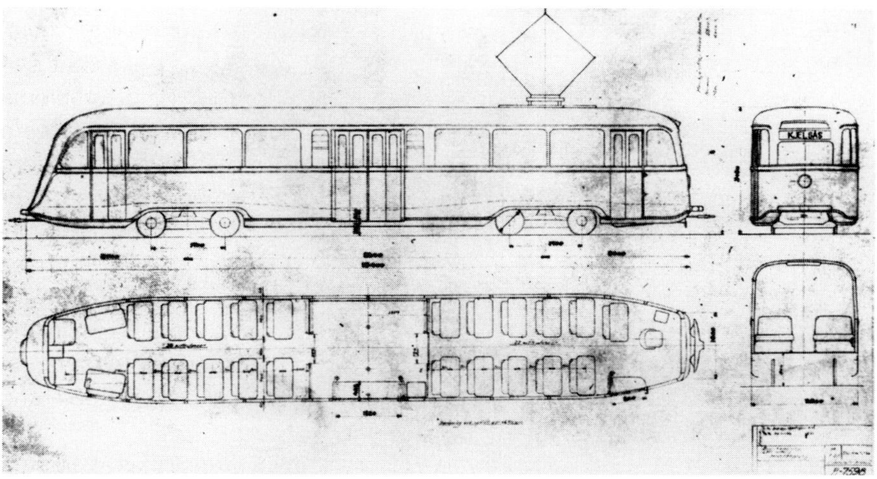

Fig. 7.4 Designs for the Goldfish tram. Unknown photographer. Oslo Transport Museum. Original in Oslo City Archives.

very much present, but on the tram it is less sinuous than on its predecessors and takes on a more sloping form, slightly tapered in width from top to bottom. The rather narrow front slanted slightly backwards and was equipped with a single, mid-mounted headlight. The sides are dominated by continuous band windows carried over from the 1935 full-scale model. A more distinctive feature is the bends by which the hemline of the side panels is raised at both ends to meet the front and rear profiles in the bumpers. Below the windows on the sides and front runs a waistband in the form of an aluminium profile that is integral to the monocoque structure (fig. 7.5). This waistband was painted silver and separated the white upper part from the light blue lower part of the tram, contributing to a harmonious, light appearance.

The Goldfish design clearly draws from the previous projects at Strømmens Værksted, but it appears more modest. Perhaps it is best described as a more temperate, refined form of streamlining. The formal language might be more refined than radical, but the ideology underpinning it was still very much present. This becomes especially evident if one is to accept one account's claim that the aerodynamic properties of the Goldfish were tested in a wind tunnel.[43] Such scientific methods of aerodynamic design were usually reserved for faster-moving objects like aircraft and, since the early 1930s, also trains and cars, and it is doubtful if it had any value in the design of a

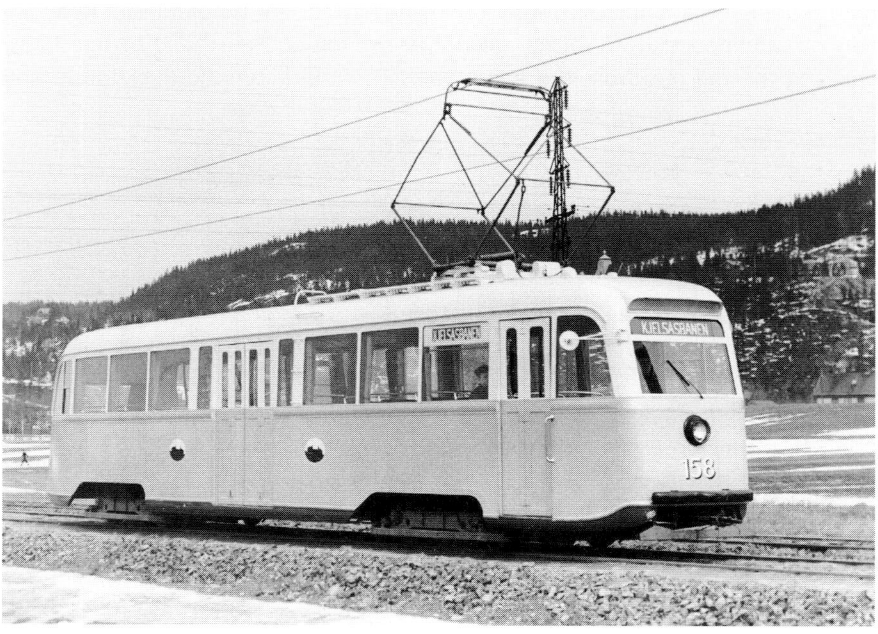

Fig. 7.5 Front/side view of the Goldfish tram. Photographer: A.B. Wilse. Oslo Transport Museum. Original in Oslo City Archives.

tram—even though the Goldfish was a fast tram with a top speed of 65 kilometres per hour. It is equally uncertain whether wind tunnel testing had any impact on the final design. Regardless of its scientific validity, the alleged wind tunnel testing strongly indicates that Müller and his fellow tram designers' devotion to streamlined design went beyond its aesthetic aspects.

Still, the design engineers at Strømmens Værksted acknowledged the sociocultural importance of modern, attractive design as well. As Alf Ihlen explained: 'Through its modern streamlined design and its modern colours, the modern high-speed train appeals to all those passengers whose judgement of modern means of transport is based on comparisons with the modern car and the modern airplane. This promotional aspect is easily underestimated by everyone—not least by us engineers.'[44] Apart from his repetitive mentioning of the adjective 'modern' (six occurrences in one sentence), this remark is interesting because Ihlen here exhibits a very non-instrumental, emotional understanding of design that may—at least partially—explain his design team's devotion to streamlining, even for slow-moving vehicles like a tram.

By the mid-1930s, when the first streamlined designs emerged from Strømmens Værksted, streamlining and its derivation from aerodynamics were well-known and not particularly controversial in engineering circles in Norway. Trade journals and magazines constituted an effective forum for mediating this design culture. The most specialized and business-related of these was Oslo Sporveier's company magazine *Trikk og Buss* ('Tram and bus'). As a chief engineer in the company, Isdahl was a regular contributor to this publication, and Alf Ihlen made occasional contributions. The magazine habitually featured reports from the USA but also from continental Europe, Britain and Scandinavia, resulting from study trips or recounted from international trade journals. These reports focused mostly on matters of bureaucracy, traffic and technology, but some touched on issues pertaining to the design of rolling stock as well.

The first reference to streamlining in transport design appeared in *Trikk og Buss* as early as 1930. The design principle was described in a presentation of the remarkable German propeller-driven high-speed train prototype dubbed the *Schienenzeppelin* (the rail zeppelin), designed by the engineer Franz Kruckenberg. In this text the streamlining is portrayed as a novel concept requiring explanation: 'One calls this form beginning with a round, wide head and at the rear ending up in a pointed tip streamlined. The shape is the result of lengthy tests, partly aerodynamic in nature, partly practical, in the construction of aircraft and airships.'[45] The following years brought reports heralding the application of streamlining to automotive design, a topic that was discussed less as a presage and more as a (unrefined) reality in a 1933 issue: 'The streamlining of the [production] car is far from sophisticated.'[46]

Also in 1933, Isdahl and his friends at Strømmens Værksted could read of plans to introduce into Denmark streamlined high-speed trains modelled on the Deutsche Reichsbahn-Gesellschaft's Fliegender Hamburger ('Flying Hamburger'), which had just entered service between Hamburg and Berlin.[47] One of the first American streamlined trains, the Burlington Zephyr, designed by Edward G. Budd, Albert G. Dean, John Harbeson and Paul Cret, was presented to Norwegian readers shortly thereafter, in January 1934—three months before it was even completed. A deeply impressed reporter said, 'It looks like a streamlined silver-shimmering torpedo.'[48] Interestingly, the stainless steel Zephyr was here erroneously said to have an aluminium body.[49] The rival to the Zephyr, the previously mentioned Union Pacific M-10,000, was portrayed a month after its completion, in March 1934, in a report that eagerly discussed its aluminium construction (correctly this time) and streamlined design.[50]

As compelling as these streamlined trains were, and as massive a cultural impact as they exercised, high-speed trains and trams are—despite both being railborne—worlds apart. It is therefore of greater significance that *Trikk og Buss* in 1934 brought news of a streamlined tram: a prototype of the American PCC streetcar designed by Otto Kuhler and manufactured by J. G. Brill & Co. (an ACF subsidiary) that was demonstrated to the press in Chicago. Brill later pulled out of the project, and the first production models were manufactured by the St. Louis Car Company and entered traffic in New York in 1936. The historical significance of the PCC streetcar lies primarily in the vast quantity built (5,000 between 1936 and 1952) and wide dissemination, but at the time of the prototype's demonstration in Chicago it was its design that held the greatest appeal: 'No movie star could have caused such commotion as did the streamlined car . . . Wherever the car materialized its appearance drew attention and people stopped at the sidewalk and looked at it.'[51] In the following years Kuhler made his mark on American railroads with his many and characteristic streamlined designs, but his PCC streetcar prototype was not amongst his most radical creations. But despite its somewhat ponderous appearance, Kuhler's prototype showed Norwegian transport engineers and tramway managers that streamlining was not necessarily the purview of trains and automobiles but might very well be the formal language of choice for a tram as well.

When developing the Goldfish, Oslo Sporveier and Strømmens Værksted singled out what they considered to be two of the most modern tram types at the time to be studied and evaluated in the concept phase of the process. One was the German Großer Hecht ('big pike'), designed by Alfred Bockemühl and manufactured by Christoph & Unmack for service in Dresden from 1930 on. The other was the PCC streetcar.[52] It is difficult to ascertain which—if any—features of the Goldfish might have been inspired by the German and American trams. What is certain is that it had virtually the same dimensions as the PCC and a related design language. When the steel-bodied PCC prototype was presented in Norway, it was described as light: 'only 18.5 tons'.[53] The all-aluminium Goldfish was much lighter—both physically and visually: it weighed only 13 tons, or 30 per cent less than the PCC, and boasted a more refined and slender body design than that of Kuhler's streetcar.

At the time when the first streamlined designs had left Strømmens Værksted and the Goldfish was under development, *Trikk og Buss* ran a longer piece entitled 'The Triumph of the Streamline', laying out the onset of streamlining as a rational development intrinsically intertwined with improvements in railroad technology and the introduction of high-speed trains. The alleged aerodynamic advantages are taken at face value, although the author is concerned with speeds above 100 kilometres per hour. A concluding remark states that 'the streamline is very popular. It has been employed even on typewriters and prams'.[54] Crucially, as opposed to later commentary on streamlining by a unison Norwegian design (applied art) community, this remark is not made in a derogatory manner—it reads more like an curious observation. It would seem, then, that although it was known that the aerodynamic benefits of streamlining were minor or negligible for vehicles operating at moderate speeds, there was no moral-aesthetic prejudice against designing a streamlined tram.

Still, streamlining did not seem to metastasize as aggressively in tram design as it did in train design. Most of the new trams to enter service throughout Europe in the mid-1930s were of a more conventional design. A couple of exceptions can be found in the United Kingdom, where Blackpool's Railcoach from 1933, designed by R. J. Heathman and built by English Electric, and Liverpool's double-deckers from 1936, built at Edge Lane Works, show certain streamlined traits. However, all new European tram designs mediated through the Norwegian trade press, such as those introduced in Milan, Copenhagen, Brussels and Bologna, were nowhere near a streamlining paradigm.[55] This indicates that there were few if any precedents for a streamlined tram, although streamlining was firmly established as a powerful design paradigm in transport design.[56] The Goldfish, then, would certainly have been an outlandish creature—but not an outrageous one.

The six initial Goldfish were ordered by Oslo Sporveier in the autumn of 1935 and were scheduled for delivery in late September 1936. However, delays in the supply of materials resulted in the delivery being postponed until January. To 'shorten the waiting time', as Oslo Sporveier's chief engineer Carl Witt put it, *Trikk og Buss* published a photo series of the Goldfish in production at Strømmens Værksted in the December issue. The body design was clearly subject to great expectation, because Witt stressed that from the photos 'one could get an impression of how they will look. As would be expected, they stand out from our existing trams like the children of the time they are, with their slightly streamlined design.'[57] Witt's characteristic does read like an understatement, especially given the evident excitement regarding the new tram's appearance, but at the same time it corresponds with the earlier description of the new tram's streamlining as more refined than radical, more mainstream than avant-garde. Although the qualifying adverb ('slightly') disappeared in the first presentation of the finished product, where it was characterized simply as 'streamlined' and as 'standing out *considerably* from our ordinary trams',[58] it was not the body design in itself that made the Goldfish remarkable—it was the combination of the radical monocoque aluminium construction, the excellent performance *and* its 'Most Advanced Yet Acceptable' design.[59]

'ALUMINIUM: THE MODERN ADVENTURE'—'OUR NATIONAL MATERIAL'

Aluminium as a material is both decidedly modern and, in a sense, particularly 'Norwegian'. When Paul T. L. Héroult and Charles Martin Hall in 1886 first succeeded in producing pure aluminium through electrolysis and the Pittsburgh Reduction Company shortly thereafter began production on a large scale, aluminium quickly became intimately linked with industrial manufacture.[60] Its properties, especially the impressive weight-to-strength ratio, were eagerly promoted by the industry, and designers and engineers soon saw great potential in the new material, making it integral to modern design and material culture.

Norway became an aluminium hot spot early on. The first production began in 1908, but it reached industrial scale only when Norsk Aluminium Co. (NACO, founded 1915) built the large works Høyanger Verk, operative from 1918.[61] Aluminium production is extremely energy-consuming, and the explanation for Norway's prominent role in the industry is to be found in her vast hydroelectric power resources.

The Norwegian aluminium industry is primarily an exporter of raw materials. But producers need consumers, and in addition to their efforts to make the existing manufacturing industry design products using aluminium, Norsk Aluminium Co. set up its own subsidiary, Nordisk Aluminiumsindustri, in 1917 as a means of creating an outlet for the raw material and profiting from the added value in semi-finished and manufactured goods.[62] As already mentioned, it was this company that delivered the aluminium of which the Goldfish and the other vehicles from Strømmens Værksted were built, and Nordisk Aluminiumsindustri took a keen interest in and saw great potential in the coachbuilder's aluminium designs.

The cultural identities of aluminium have been subject to stratifications and significant changes through space and time. So how were the modernity and Norwegian-ness of aluminium constructed and mediated in Norway in the 1930s? Taking a closer look at a few examples of how aluminium was portrayed in trade journals may provide at least a partial picture of this cultural identity construction. As the cultural identities of a material are of great significance for the identities of artefacts made from it, understanding the meanings of aluminium is paramount in understanding the meanings of the Goldfish.

During the 1920s the world production of aluminium increased rapidly, greatly strengthening both its physical and cultural presence in society. *Trikk og Buss* presented aluminium as 'the modern adventure in the kingdom of materials' and as 'a typical child of our time'. This intrinsic modernity of the material was explained by the power-consuming nature of aluminium production, a challenge overcome only recently by feeding the factories from large hydroelectric power plants. The explanation thus firmly connects aluminium both to Norway, by way of her natural resources acting as a midwife to the material's large-scale production, and to modernity. The latter connection is reinforced by references to aviation: 'Characteristically, it is one of the very youngest industries, the aeroplane industry, which has really opened up the eyes of the age for the significance of the light metals.'[63]

Sigurd Klouman, director of Strømmens Værksted's materials supplier, Nordisk Aluminiumsindustri, also referred to aircraft technology when, in a commentary on the first-generation aluminium buses, he wrote that they were made from 'Duralumin [which] is the same material used in the all-metal "Junkers" aeroplanes of the type employed in North Pole aviation'.[64] By way of this seemingly trivial reference Klouman effectively tied the bus design not only to the progressive imagery of aircraft technology and the adventurous ambience then associated with aviation but also to the theme of arctic explorations—a subject that in the 1930s was still saturated with heroic sentiment and national pride in Norway.[65]

Oslo Sporveier's publication continued informing its readers about aluminium: its history, production, properties and applications. A piece from 1935 entitled 'Aluminium—the Material of Our Time' announced that 'the world is about to leave the Iron Age and venture into the age of the light metals, where aluminium and its alloys will assume a leading position'. Here, then, aluminium was not only the modern material but even the material of the future. Interesting in this respect are two of the examples chosen to illustrate the advantages of aluminium: the previously mentioned Union Pacific M-10,000 train and Strømmens Værksted's buses—two decidedly streamlined designs. National pride is induced by reporting that 'Norway is third amongst the aluminium exporting countries' and by announcing that the most modern production method for aluminium oxide—employed for example at Høyanger Verk—was 'invented by Professor [of metallurgy] Harald Pedersen at the Norwegian Institute of Technology'.[66] The weaving of aluminium with modernity and Norwegian-ness continued, and in 1939 aluminium was proclaimed 'our national material' and portrayed as an important contribution to the national economy: 'As the light materials gain entry to more and more domains, al[uminium] production will become of greater and greater economic significance for our country.'[67]

The national economic significance of aluminium would to a large extent hinge on Norsk Aluminium Co. and Nordisk Aluminiumsindustri. It would be appropriate, then, to round off this discussion on the material's cultural identities by looking at an advertisement Nordisk Aluminiumsindustri ran in the motoring magazine *Norsk Motorblad* in 1938.[68] Under the heading 'Aluminium—for Speed and Progress', the company aimed to convince the manufacturing industries to use more aluminium. The accompanying illustration showed an airplane, an ocean liner, a race car and the Union Pacific M-10,000 darting out radially from a point somewhere in an urban centre only hinted at through a couple of skyscrapers. The Norwegian company thus sought to imbue aluminium with connotations of modernity, streamlining and transport design. The Goldfish may not have been depicted in the advertisement—although the streamlined train can be said to stand proxy—but such imagery nonetheless contributed greatly to the co-production of meaning encompassing the new tram.

CONCLUSION

This study has recounted the history of the streamlined aluminium trams that took to the streets of Oslo in 1937. Making use of advanced construction technology, a material couched as both absolutely modern and particularly Norwegian and a design language as typical of contemporary international transport design as it was atypical of Norwegian design practice, these Goldfish memories constitute a fascinating episode in Norwegian and Nordic design history. Moreover, this case study contributes to the debunking of the popular myth that streamlining is quintessentially American, supporting instead Nicholas Maffei's claim that streamlining is to be recognized, 'not as a purely American style . . . , but as a complex product . . . of a transatlantic collaboration that embodied the contradictions of modernity'.[69] The reading of motoring magazines, company newsletters and engineering journals has revealed that streamlining was appropriated and developed in Norway as an alternative face of modern design within the public transport business, the motoring trade and the mechanical engineering profession—completely on the side of the 'official' discourse on modern design being played out in the sphere of architecture and applied art. As some sort of 'freewheelers' the engineers designing the Goldfish thus have much in common with what Judy Attfield has termed 'trade designers',[70] who also figure in Minna Sarantola-Weiss's contribution to this volume in that they are not socialized into the community of art school-trained designers and do not feel compelled to adhere to the confines of 'sanctioned' design.

What makes the case of the Goldfish even more intriguing, though, is that in addition to representing an unsanctioned and outlandish form of modernism in terms of design, it also became a symbol of both Norwegian-ness and modernity by way of the cultural meanings shaped around its aluminium construction. The Goldfish may also be construed as an instance of using modern design to invigorate what was by many considered an outdated technology: In the 1930s improvements in bus construction and performance, perhaps aided by the allure of automobility, led many to consider the bus to be the future of urban public transport and spurred debates on the future of the tramway. Much as the prominence of streamlining in American trains of the period is often portrayed as an effort to revitalize this transport sector, greatly threatened as it was by the proliferation of cars and the onset of air travel, designing a gleamingly modern model like the Goldfish may be interpreted as an attempt to give the tram a new lease on life. The modernity of the Goldfish, then, was a complex and controversial but converging one.

In Fredrik Wildhagen's gloss, the Goldfish emerged on the streets of Oslo as an unequivocal symbol of modernity: 'The tram appeared as an image of the new, modern times—here were no reminiscences of horse-drawn trams and the olden days; here was the means of transport for the people of the time; busy, modern and efficient.'[71] In its exploration of the cultural meanings of streamlining and aluminium this article goes a long way in corroborating Wildhagen's rendering of the contemporary perception of the Goldfish. But: *sic transit gloria mundi*. Even the most glorious of worldly things are fleeting. In service for almost half a century, Oslo's streamlined trams witnessed design trends come and go and survived many plans for closure of the tram network. Audaciously modern in 1937, the Goldfish eventually became an aesthetic anachronism, embodying more than anything a faded past vision of the future. In 1971 the poet Johan Fredrik Grøgaard expressed his love for the ageing Goldfish, caring particularly for its characteristic 'duck-tail', a mainstay of its by then unfashionable streamlined design:

> we are older now
> reason has at times trumped fortune
> but we bear our age well, right
> when you're passing by on Drammensveien and I
> gently caress your sloping back
> with a giant child's hand.[72]

–8–

Creature Comforts: Soft Sofas and the Demise of Modernist Morality in 1970s' Finland

Minna Sarantola-Weiss

In 1972 the Finnish furniture manufacturer Sopenkorpi advertised its new Tower sofa group as follows:

> In recent years we have lived in a freely developing society with its hurried life and worries. These rapid developments have definitely given us a higher standard of living and thereby the opportunity to spend more on decorating our homes. Perhaps this spirit of our times has matched the harshness of everyday life with the need for a more romantic and liberating setting and way of thinking in our leisure moments at home. With these ideas in mind, we set out to develop a furniture suite responding to this romantic need. The first details of our present Tower products were outlined through long-term research and design.[1]

The Sopenkorpi company was a large furniture manufacturer by Finnish standards, with 300 employees in the early 1970s. With decreasing sales in the late 1960s, it began to look for a new product for the mass market.[2] Product development led to Tower, which became one of the most widely sold Finnish sofa groups of the 1970s (fig. 8.1). Taking this design-politically incorrect product as a case, this study explores how the remarkable popularity of such mass-produced sofas contributed to the demise of modernist morality in 1970s Finland.

The process of designing Tower began with a market analysis. The factory's representatives first considered the products currently being offered on the domestic market, followed by a review of international trade fairs in the furniture sector. A source of inspiration was found in a Czech sofa suite of a kind that was not offered on the Finnish market. Back home, the company's production and marketing experts pooled their skills to create the Tower sofa group, which was introduced for Christmas 1971. The chipboard frames of the pieces were lined with dark-stained oak veneer, and the upholstery was in green Dutch furniture plush. The items employed a sumptuous and bourgeois idiom of form, resembling, for example, furniture seen on the British television series *Upstairs, Downstairs* (1971–5), which was highly popular in Finland.

The process of designing Tower was typical of the Finnish furniture industry at the time. Sopenkorpi partly relied on professional designers, designing and producing, for example, seating for Finlandia Hall in Helsinki (architect Alvar Aalto, 1971). These products were featured in interior design magazines, but the revenue generated by such special commission products was fairly limited. Therefore, products of a more commercial nature destined for private consumption, like the Tower suite, were often designed as described earlier, in a process continuing a tradition established before professional design education. The company management's notion of product quality in this case did not hinge on uniqueness in design but rather on production technology and the finish of the work. Ultimately, however, quality was gauged with sales figures. The mismatch between designers and industry has been a recurring issue in Finnish design, particularly in the 1970s, as Pekka Korvenmaa observes in his contribution to this volume.

In the history of design, mass-produced sofa suites such as Tower form a parallel to the notion of 'history from below', as phrased by Edward P. Thompson.[3] Anonymous mass products challenge the grand narrative of modern design, good taste and rational consumers in the welfare state. The demand for sofa groups peaked in the Finnish market around the turn of the 1960s and 1970s, and the growth of sales was terminated only by the economic downturn that followed the oil crisis of 1973. From the perspective of design history, we may speak here of the relationship of high and low. The former consists of products enshrined in the canon of sublime objects and celebrated designers appreciated by a cultural elite, while the lower realm is the domain of mundane, anonymously designed, mass-produced objects catering to the pluralistic tastes of a broader public.

This case study sets out to explore the factors behind the remarkable success of products that do not conform to contemporary notions of 'good design'. Such 'non-appropriation' of design propaganda and the complementary appropriation of the comfortable sofa group may offer an object lesson on the preferences and power of consumers. Furthermore, the Tower case opens an alternative perspective on a decade that—at least in terms of home furnishings—is often described as a rather uninteresting, even ridiculous, interlude between the more dynamic 1960s and 1980s. In design history, the 1970s are not remembered for interior decoration but rather for an increasingly politicized design discourse. This, however, does not detract from the significance of sofas. Underlying the success of sofa suites was the acceptance of a more hedonistic and comfort-oriented lifestyle. Tower, in particular, also involved the rise of nostalgia as one of the main commercial trends of the 1970s.

FROM LUXURY PRODUCT TO EVERYDAY NECESSITY

The sofa group is a good example of a bourgeois luxury product that has become an everyday necessity. The sofa group became an established feature of bourgeois salons during the nineteenth century. In Finland, it was for a long while a product made to order, and it included not only the actual sofa but also several matching pieces of furniture, such as chairs, armchairs and a table. The production process is best described as machine-assisted craftsmanship.[4] From the 1940s onwards, the set of furniture was standardized to a three-piece suite consisting of a sofa and two armchairs. By the 1960s, the production process, technology and materials had become so different that the modern mass-produced sofa groups had very little in common with their bourgeois antecedents. Prices had also declined significantly during the process.

The use of the sofa group also changed during the twentieth century. The bourgeois sofa group was a highly social set of furniture emphasizing a feeling of community. It was a symbol of sociability and lifestyle, marking the owner's status and taste. Åke Daun points out that the phrase 'please, have a seat' is the first step in a social process in which the person seated is included in the social dynamic of the interior and its social order. To sit on a sofa is different from sitting on a chair.[5] The bourgeois sofa and its successors are involved in a complex social act intertwining identities, social hierarchies and gender roles.

The sofa group of the 1960s gained new functions and meanings, with the emphasis shifting from community to private pleasure. Leisure was increasing amongst the lower and middle classes, and people spent more time at home. A great part of this time was spent watching television or listening to music. While the introduction of radio in the 1920s had already provided a new function for the sofa, television changed its role entirely because it required the transformation of the seating group to an auditorium. Many families bought their first sofa together with their first television set.

The spread of television evoked plenty of moralizing comments from the university-educated elite, in Finland as much as elsewhere, because television symbolized a commercial and passive lifestyle. On the other hand, the Finnish market saw in 1968 the first sofa suite that was specifically designed for the ritual of watching television. The Bonanza seating group had wide armrests with space for the coffee cup and sandwich plate.[6]

The sofa combined comfort with the private escapism offered by television. This combination was by no means a modern phenomenon. Theodor Adorno pointed to this escapist dimension of the sofa in his reading of Søren Kierkegaard (1813–55). In Adorno's analysis, the sofa serves as the comfortable base from which the creative mind of the genius wandered to consider the wonders of the world. Many more ordinary readers also spent their time on bourgeois sofas. But it was not until the mass production of consumer goods that the combination of comfort and escapism became a mass phenomenon.

LIMITS AND LIBERTIES OF HOME DECORATION

A three-piece sofa suite is among the more expensive purchases when furnishing a home, and it also requires a great deal of space. Although economic and spatial restrictions set limits for the home decorator, these resources increased considerably in Finnish society from the 1960s onwards. In the international perspective, the transition of Finland into an urban consumer society took place late but very rapidly. In the early 1950s, a typical family home consisted of two rooms and a kitchen and was located somewhere in the countryside. One generation later, a typical dwelling was a flat with three to four rooms in a suburb or urban housing area.[7]

With increasing space, the activities of habitation could be separated within the dwelling. Parents and children finally had separate bedrooms, and some lucky teens even had a room of their own. A new and important space for the home decorator was the living room, which had been introduced in the functionalist apartments of the 1930s but became a standard feature only with the large-scale housing schemes from the postwar reconstruction years onwards. The design reformers intended the living room to be the shared space of the family, but to a large extent it remained a representational space. In many homes, the doors of the living room were opened to everyday activities only when television became more widespread.

Space was thus no longer a limitation if one had money, and growing numbers of people now had it. Like other Western economies, the Finnish economy expanded almost without interruption from the end of the Second World War until the oil crisis of the early 1970s, resulting in an enormous growth in real household income. Private consumption trebled between the 1950s and the 1970s. A major portion of the new wealth was used to improve the standard of housing, with the dwelling as one of the most important arenas of Finnish consumer culture.

THE SOFA DISCOURSE

This chapter began with a quotation from an advertisement for the Tower sofa group where the manufacturer described the product and the needs to which it was to respond. The text tells us that everyday life is hard and hectic and that romantic products could soften up this unpleasant side of modernity. The quotation also alludes to the commonplace middle-class idea of the private sphere as a refuge from the harsh world outside. The home is discussed as a space of consumption, with the presumption that consumers want to use their income to decorate the home.

If we take our cue from the systemic approach laid out in Part 1 of this book, Tower and other three-piece suites can be understood as actors in a network that consisted of various players in the furniture market, designers and other arbiters of taste, and the actual users of the sofa groups. Together, these actors created the discourse of domestic interior decoration. In its Foucauldian sense, discourse is not only textual but also material and can therefore encompass objects such as sofas. The mute object can act as a subject that can use and create power in the same way as texts or speech do. Foucault was not alone in presenting this idea. Several writers, among them Michel de Certeau and Jean Baudrillard, have suggested that objects and their order reflect and generate the prevalent practices and value judgements of our everyday lives. In consumer society, commodities, debates, market mechanisms and changing everyday practices have been woven into dynamic interaction.

For many years, the Finnish discourse on architecture and design was marked by discussion of ideal homes, good taste and rational consumers, all of this being merged with discourse on the nature of Finnish culture and modernity. As late as the 1950s, the debate was dominated by nationalism and an ethos of popular education following the ideal of creating a modern and rational society. The modernist ideal was not just a rhetorical device; considerable efforts went into its realization both in architecture and in consumer goods. Like other concepts in design history, the modern is at the same time an analytical category, an ideology and simply a fashionable style. The Finnish elite was quite small, and Finnish society was relatively homogeneous, which meant that a single style could permeate the whole of society in an effective manner.

As in other countries, the Finnish design discourse was dominated by a small yet influential group of design professionals and other university-educated members of the middle class. They formed an elite in matters of taste, and their opinions dominated the arenas of discussion on interior design such as published guides for home decoration and the trade press. The consumer/home decorator was addressed from a position of expert authority, and the discourse often had the character of advice. However, as the post-war reconstruction effort was gradually completed, competing ideals began to emerge alongside rationalism and modernism.

In the 1960s, the balance of power within the home decoration discourse began to change. The prevailing ideals of rational modernism were now challenged by new, more hedonistic approaches to interior decoration accepting a variety of different lifestyles. The furniture industry became a more dominant force in design discourse through the sheer volume of advertising and other expanding media. The debate and the players can be found in the pages of the interior decoration magazines, women's magazines and mail-order catalogues of the time, which are the sources of this study. These publications functioned as an interface where consumers, products, producers and design professionals could meet.[8]

This change was manifested in the discussion on sofa suites, with the gatekeepers of good taste, commercial players and consumers pitted against each other. The modernist ideal was a flexible and rational home, yet the sofa group was neither. A guidebook from 1953 recommended a form of habitation proceeding from the needs of everyday life:

> A sofa is by nature best suited to a sitting room or other spaces for representation. A sofa that would be in daily family use is a rather rare phenomenon in our homes. An old-fashioned three-piece suite is voluminous and needs a lot of space. A small two-seated sofa is the modern favourite.[9]

In the 1970s, sumptuous sofa suites continued to annoy the elite. In October 1971 the interior decoration reporter of a Finnish newspaper noted the enthusiasm of Finnish furniture retailers to sell 'status furniture', that is sofa suites, to consumers: 'If one were to look only at the display windows of furniture retailers, one would think that over-upholstered, cushioned status furniture was the main thing.'[10] A year later, another journalist noted in the same newspaper: 'In principle we are all fed up with this combination of a sofa and two armchairs.'[11] But consumers disagreed. Growing numbers of Finns bought precisely the 'sofa and two armchairs combination'. Fashion clearly was of importance here, but the comfort offered by the sofa played a significant role.

COMFORTABLE MODERNISM

The celebrated Finnish, and more broadly Scandinavian, modernism is quite sparse, even ascetic, in its formal language. The prevailing ideal has been that of light weight, light colours, functionality and hygiene. Modernism, however, has another, more hedonistic dimension, associating it with industrially made sofa suites, namely mass-produced comfort. Tomás Maldonado suggests that industrial comfort of this kind is specifically a modern idea.[12]

Comfort has always been an essential feature of the sofa, and this trend peaked in the 1960s. Production technologies, materials and forms have naturally varied. The softness of nineteenth-century sofas was created with cushions and textiles. In the 1960s, this was achieved with foam rubber, which had become the main raw material of sofa groups alongside chipboard. It permitted the making of sofas that were softer than ever before. This mix of hard technology and soft sensorial qualities was typical of both high design

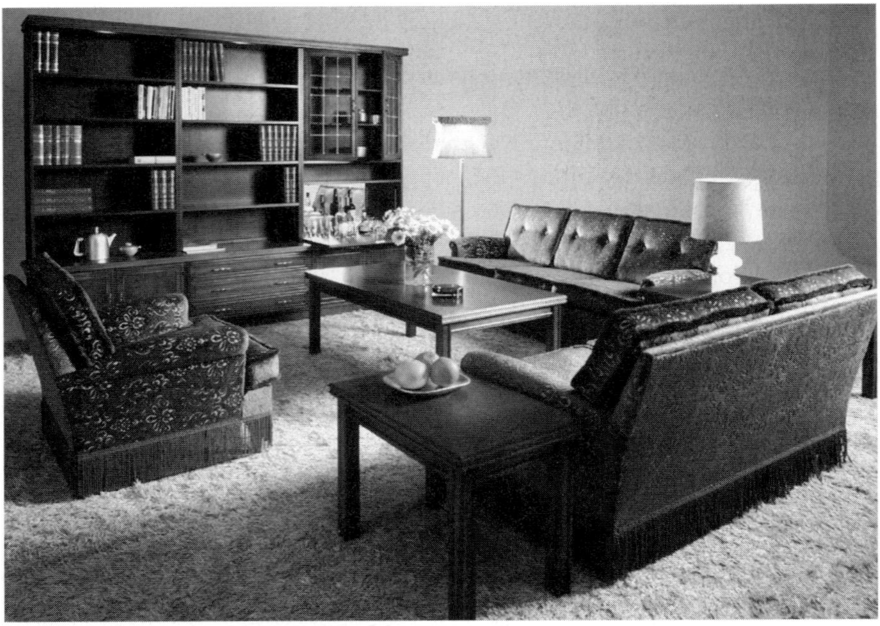

Fig. 8.1 The three-piece sofa suite Tower, launched by the Sopenkorpi Company in 1971. The collections of Lahti City Museum. Out of copyright.

and conventional mass-produced items. Examples from high design include living spaces and furniture made of plastic and fibreglass yet thoroughly upholstered, such as Verner Panton's polyurethane seating system (1970) or the Sacco beanbag by Cesare Paolini and Franco Teodoro (1968). The Ball chair by Eero Aarnio (1963) is the best-known Finnish example.

Soft appearance was not just a technological and aesthetic matter. The use and design of the furniture were also influenced by a change in body language. In the 1960s, people sat differently than they did in the 1850s. An informal laid-back slouch was no longer a private act but could be practised in front of guests and friends, at least at home. Low furnishings were also part of a 'young' lifestyle formulated in opposition to the previous generation. Radicalism and the rejection of bourgeois habits were intertwined with softness.

Maldonado points out that the concept of comfort may be understood as a device for social control. It has a compensatory function that resembles other modes of *Entfremdung* (alienation) associated with the modern lifestyle. On the other hand—and Maldonado discusses this extensively—comfort is a very complex phenomenon. Of particular interest in the present context is that the notion of comfort may shed some light on the consumer's point of view. Consumer preferences were easily left behind when the taste elite discussed comfort, sofas and the beauty of the home.

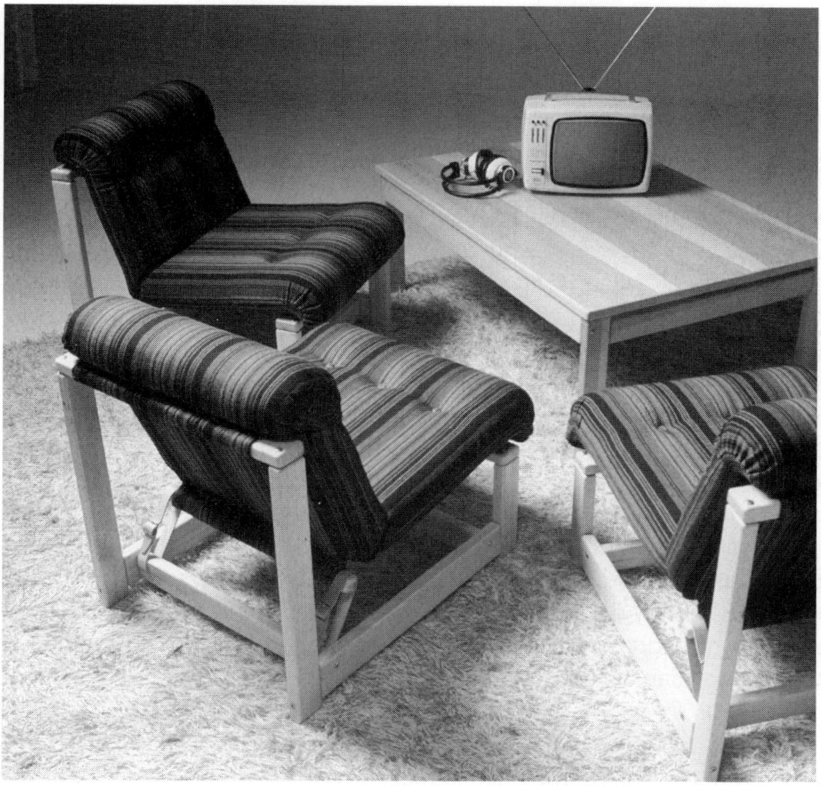

Fig. 8.2 The three-piece sofa suite Esikko was inspired by the vernacular tradition. It was launched by the Sopenkorpi Company in 1974. Designed by Ahti Taskinen. The collections of Lahti City Museum. Out of copyright.

THE TOUCH OF THE SOFA

Comfort is a physiological experience passed on through the sense of touch. The philosopher Gaston Bachelard presents a phenomenological reading of the home and its objects in *La poetique de l'espace* (1958), underlining the importance of the sense of touch for understanding the value of daily life. In his essay, humans and objects repeatedly meet through touch, for example in everyday cleaning, forming a connection that at the same time is both intimate and above the level of the everyday. Touch brings objects to life, and a similar deep, unverbalized connection can form between the sofa and the person sitting on it.[13]

The senses affect our understanding of the world and even times past. The argument put forward is that our experiences are culturally constructed and bound to certain historical moments. Different senses are presumed to have played different roles at different times. According to Mark M. Smith, interest in the senses closer to our body—smell, taste and touch—gained new importance in the postmodern era with its greater attention to the body, whereas modernism prioritized the more abstract sight and hearing.[14] If we really want to understand the enormous popularity of modern mass-produced sofas, we need to consider the senses, especially touch and the meaning of comfort and softness in the everyday life of people living in Finland circa 1970.

The sense of touch is hard to trace in the textual sources usually used by historians. We can, however, find a hint in the visual representations of sofas. The development of photography has played a crucial role in this respect (the significance of product photography in mediating design is amply demonstrated in Malene Breunig's contribution to this volume). The drawings typical of the advertisements of the 1950s do not convey much of the actual sitting experience, while the close-ups of the 1970s do not leave much room for imagination. The smooth velvet and the softness of the cushions are almost palpable. Softness is often emphasized by a woman reclining against the cushions. Irene Nierhaus points out that the subject is typical of nineteenth-century art in which comfort, privacy, idleness and eroticism associated with fabrics and softness converge in the figure of a woman.[15] This interpretation can also be applied to visual representations of the sofa groups of the 1970s.[16]

But what about the people who actually used the sofas in the late 1960s? What do we know about their experiences and preferences? In Finland, ethnological surveys have produced valuable sources that can be used for tracing people's experiences of habitation and of their sofas. Photographic material collected in Hämeenlinna and Helsinki between 1965 and 1975 shows that most of the documented families had bought a sofa within a period of ten years.[17] The trend here was from simple bed-sofas towards larger and softer furniture.

The same changes are verified verbally in recollections collected by the Finnish Literature Society in 2004.[18] The informants recall a society in rapid transformation, although the standard of housing was still often very poor. The narratives tell a great deal about the problems of finding a decent dwelling. The most common comment concerned cold and draughty old dwellings. The narrators, however, also reflected on pleasant and unpleasant experiences in terms of touch. A young couple discarded their sofa of imitation leather because the material did not breathe and felt cold. Another couple found the upholstery of their first sofa to be ugly and coarse. All materials that were soft and warm felt comfortable and cosy, and even luxurious. A sheepskin on a bed, a grey wool carpet or a black-and-red fitted carpet transmits this kind of experience. The owner of the fitted carpet was an enthusiastic home decorator for whom the climax of her own history of habitation was the opportunity to hang lace curtains in her window. For her, the sensory abundance of the fabric masses represented comfort and luxury.[19]

These stories of increased comfort and the desire for it are common to the histories of habitation of the baby-boom generation and their parents everywhere. In the late 1990s, Birgitta Rydberg Mitchell interviewed several Swedish home decorators and found similar stories. Childhood memories were full of hard and uncomfortable sofas on which children were allowed only occasionally and where they were to sit quietly and with their backs straight. In the narratives, the new, soft and comfortable piece of furniture that arrived together with the television set represented freedom and a better life.[20]

THE POWER OF TOWER

Comfortable, plush-upholstered softness was, of course, also the Tower suite's secret of success, but the buyer gained something else in the bargain. When it was launched, Tower stood out compared with many other sofas on the Finnish market. There was a wide range of sofas on the market, but no medallion-plush upholstered British-style suite of this specific kind. Such products, however, soon began to appear, which also reflects changes in the design climate and the design processes of furniture manufacturers. The Asko company, Finland's largest furniture manufacturer at that time, introduced its Kensington plush suite in the same autumn as Sopenkorpi launched Tower and was thus in the same market from the very beginning. Like Tower, Kensington became a commercial success. Owing to competition, Tower began to be advertised a few years later as 'authentic'.[21]

Tower, Kensington and similar furniture conveyed feelings of bourgeois affluence and a great deal of nostalgia. Design reformers considered such allusions both aesthetically corrupt and politically incorrect—which only makes them more interesting. Nostalgia was one of the main trends of home decoration in the 1970s. One might argue that whereas the fashionable interiors of the 1960s looked towards the future, the 1970s turned to the past, as the future was suddenly filled with threatening scenarios such as the energy crisis, overpopulation and terrorism. After the pristine white space-age interior utopias of the previous decade, women's magazines were now full of various decorative and romantic ideas, often complemented with do-it-yourself instructions. Romantic curls, long dresses and folklore of all kinds flourished on the pages of magazines, and bright primary colours were replaced by hues of green and brown. The popularity of furniture in historical styles grew, along with retro objects borrowing stylistic features from the past. Like Tower, most of these nostalgic items were specifically stylized and did not purport to be copies of traditional pieces such as the reproduction period furniture discussed by Judy Attfield.[22]

The nostalgia of the 1970s was largely a fashionable phenomenon. Georg Simmel wrote already in 1906 that fashion was fuelled by the desire for variation, maintaining that it was a form of escapism, a flight from everyday life. One might suggest, then, that in the 1970s, nostalgia helped people escape two opposing trends of this conflicting decade: a mania for planning and insecurity.

In Finland the 1970s saw the ideals regarding social justice formulated during the preceding decade become implemented as key components in the welfare state. The construction of large-scale systems in all spheres of society resulted in an expanding technocracy that brought its rationalist outlook and faith in planning into the discourse.[23] The welfare state affected the everyday lives of people primarily in the form of social benefits but also as control and through the growing role of public authorities, focusing, for example, on citizens as consumers. Elsewhere in this book, Helena Mattsson describes the efforts of the Swedish Cooperative Union to educate Swedes to become 'infinite consumers' whose rational choices would lead to free self-expression in consumer behaviour. The material manifestations of this way of thinking were also rationalized and sparse. Nostalgia, then, can be seen as an antidote to this modernist morality.

The daily lives of Finns underwent drastic changes in this period. Many had changed their livelihoods, domiciles and social frames of reference within a brief period, as Finland's evolution into an industrialized and urban society was faster than that in any other Western nation. Such drastic change often spurs insecurity. The Finns of the 1970s wanted their lives to have, at the same time, freedom and individuality on the one hand and security on the other, and many found these properties in the past. This affinity with the bygone found an outlet, for example, in an increased interest in the rural communities of one's childhood and an idealization of the era of one's grandmother. While national romantic art nouveau experienced a comeback both in Finland and internationally,[24] commercial forces drew inspiration from a wider set of sources, resulting in designs paying tribute to both Finland's own rural roots as well as international trends of romanticism.

Nostalgia was first diagnosed in the late seventeenth century and was long regarded a physical illness. The nostalgia of the late twentieth century, however, was part of consumer culture, since—as noted by David Lowenthal—people's longing for things past makes for excellent business.[25] The design of consumer goods, then, becomes a shorthand for a more profound historical sensibility. Acquiring and owning certain items or goods appear to be more important—and are certainly easier—than adopting, or even knowing, the culture of a given period. In the English-speaking world in particular, nostalgia became one of the most popular trends in home furnishing, and the antiques and second-hand trade grew considerably. Retro culture, understood as interest in the material expressions of lifestyles of the recent past, obtained its current connotations in the early 1970s. However, as Jonathan Woodham points out, as a cultural practice this was not a new trend in the design world, as nostalgia had played a significant role in design and consumption throughout the twentieth century.[26]

English nostalgia drew upon the past greatness of the British Empire, which was lost after the Second World War, and on an idealization of rural life. Owing to the entertainment industry, and television in particular, this nostalgia of a British type and its manifestations as material culture also became the dominant model internationally. In Finland, the USA and American consumer culture were much admired in the 1950s and the 1960s but were out of reach for the majority. In many ways, British television series set in the Victorian world felt more familiar and thus became a good counterforce to modernism. One of the first was *The Forsyte Saga* (1967).

Finnish nostalgia mostly referred to the rural lifestyle of the past that the majority of the population knew through their own family backgrounds and to its accompanying aesthetic. Apartments in housing areas were filled with pine furniture, rag rugs and folk handicrafts, mostly homemade. Imported goods were mainly of British style. Department stores and mail-order companies offered Victoria polyester lace curtains and Chelsea tableware services with rose patterns.[27] More expensive alternatives were provided by Laura Ashley and Sanderson. Russian-style folklore with floral-print scarves and samovars was also typical of Finnish material culture of the 1970s.

As such, there was a long tradition of idealized rural life in design, since romanticization of the peasant heritage had been typical of both Finnish design and the related discourse ever since the nationalist project of the late nineteenth century. The specific character of the Finns had been regarded as manifested in the rural way of life and the relationship with nature.[28] The renowned 'golden age' of Finnish design in the 1950s gave the vernacular tradition largely a very abstract interpretation, while the 1970s' iterations of the same theme were more concrete. The vernacularly inspired furniture of that decade was made of solid pine and upholstered with simple cotton or woollen fabrics. The wooden construction of the pieces was left visible. The names of the products often referred to Lapland or the wilderness. The enthusiasm over the Nordic wilderness was also one dimension of the ecologically inspired design discussions in Europe, and Finnish pine furniture was exported to Sweden and Germany. On the whole, then, the idealized rural community of the past was a very strong mental construct and a lucrative source for commercial exploitation despite the fact that the often-poor and even backward reality of the countryside was still very close to most people—not further away than their own childhood and youth.

The Tower sofa suite did not belong to this rural continuum with its close ties to nature and national heritage. Instead, it belonged to the other major nostalgic trend discussed earlier, referring to a more cosmopolitan way of life and to bourgeois culture. Its style was definitively not Finnish or Scandinavan, nor was it international—but it was decidedly foreign. If anything, one might describe its essence as Central European, down to the country of origin of its upholstery plush. But perhaps this generic nature of its references is the very key to the remarkable success of products like Tower, offering allusions to an elusive exoticism and a lush life without the restrictions on flexible interpretation that more specific connotations would entail. Perhaps this is the power of Tower.

NOSTALGIA, CLASS AND MODERNIST MORALITY

The Tower suite's formal language was, as already mentioned, not only nostalgic but also bourgeois and middle class. The elite arbiters of taste of the 1950s represented an educated, conservative middle class. By the 1970s, the design reformers still belonged to the educated middle class, but their thinking was now marked by a radicalism that included opposition to an integrated bourgeois culture and its values, even when this radicalism was not always of a left-wing nature in political terms. To these new radicals, the middle-class nuclear family and its practices of interior decoration represented an outmoded relic. However novel per se, this attitude belonged to the heritage of modernism, since criticism of the bourgeois lifestyle is a key feature of modernism in all its iterations.[29] Writing in a home decoration guide in 1972, an architect criticized the tradition of representation in interiors: 'Artificial representativeness mainly appealing to outsiders does not create comfort. A peaceful bedroom is more important than a living room for entertaining guests.'[30] In her opinion, sofa suites were superfluous, as they hampered flexibility—an argument repeated by design reformers since the 1950s:

> A sofa and two armchairs is a common set of furniture in living rooms. But it might be more practical to buy different kinds of seats for different uses. In a small room, a suite consisting of a sofa and similar chairs may dominate too much and give a monotonous impression.[31]

As good modernists, these tastemakers were suspicious of anything that they regarded as unauthentic. Ever since the heyday of nineteenth-century design reform, the primacy of authenticity has discredited liberal uses of historical styles, retro and nostalgia as kitsch. Modernists could accept genuine antiques and old vernacular objects if they were combined elegantly with modern interiors. Interiors of this kind, which Reyner Banham called the gentrification style,[32] were frequently showcased in interior decoration magazines. Non-sanctioned use of historical styles, however, especially when eclectically applied in the design of new products, was considered the hallmark of social climbers. In 1974 a design critic observed: 'The new urban dwellers have lost their contact to the inherited norm systems, and mainly adopt their guidelines from contemporaries and the media, they thus absorb examples that are characterized by the tradition-free use of revived styles.'[33] This way of thinking harks back to the eighteenth-century discourse on good taste as a trait of the elite.[34]

Even nostalgia involves a class perspective. Karin Johannisson describes how nostalgia was originally defined as a trait of innocent, uneducated rural dwellers. As the ideology of modernity began to make progress in the nineteenth century, nostalgia began to be understood as a sign of resistance to change and in particular of the inability of the lower classes to adapt to modern requirements. Nostalgia was not suited to the enlightened modern age, and therefore it could not be a characteristic of the elite or the world of material culture approved by it.[35] This understanding of nostalgia has been a prominent feature of modernist morality ever since and had by no means been abandoned by Finnish arbiters of the 1970s, who harshly criticized nostalgic design and retro furniture as superficial and the commercial utilization of old ideas.[36]

However paternalistic in tone, the design reformers' critique of the quality of furniture and its uses may not have been entirely unfounded. Interior architect Ahti Taskinen designed a number of sofa suites for the Sopenkorpi company that responded more closely to the modern ideal (e.g. the three-piece suite Esikko, fig. 8.2.) without achieving the same sales figures as Tower. His opinion of the latter was not flattering:

> *Tower* was a typical product exploiting people's yearning for antiques. It was cheaply produced industrially out of chipboard and given a spirit that pretended to be antique. I think it cheats people, leading them on to think that it's an antique. And that it's valuable because it has the touch of something Old English or of historical style. I think it's immoral.[37]

Taskinen was one of the few interior architects who engaged in active, long-term collaboration with the private-market furniture industry throughout the 1970s. At the same time, Taskinen's education and role made him a member of the expert elite, and the modernist morality he reveals reflects his commitment to the professional self-understanding of his occupation. Seen from this perspective, the expert's task was to protect consumers against inferior products such as faux antiques. On the other hand, genuine antique furniture was a rare commodity in Finland at this time. Only a few families had heirlooms, partly because a great deal had been destroyed in the war. Also, in a country of extensive internal migration, old furniture had not been taken along when people moved into the cities. Buying furniture in a historical style and imitations of various kinds was one way of acquiring roots and memories, providing the living room with respectable middle-class interior decoration, whether the elite liked it or not.

THE NEW PLURALISM

The 1970s was the decade when Finns finally entered the consumer society—although there have been attempts to date this change to various moments from the 1930s onwards.[38] By the 1970s, at the latest, the vast majority of Finns had the opportunity to buy consumer products more or less freely and to participate in consumer culture in the creative sense as defined by, for example, Daniel Miller and Colin Campbell.[39] In addition, the nature of the middle class changed. The old educated middle class was now usurped by a new middle class made up of people engaged in the numerous administrative and service tasks of the welfare state, whose class consciousness was expressed above all as consumer behaviour. With this massive expansion in the consumption of mass-produced goods and experiences, the relative homogeneity of the market broke down, and the role of experts declined.

The new, enlarged middle class developed an immensely varied material culture and rejected old notions of class-bound consumption and good taste. The ideal of ascetic consumption that had long prevailed became old-fashioned and was replaced by a new, hedonistic consumer. The reason why the importance of experts in the discourse on home decoration decreased is not found only in the ever more diversified material culture and increased confidence on the part of consumers—the experts themselves found greener pastures. The design elite—at least its more radical faction—had by now focused their attention elsewhere, for example towards issues of ecology and ergonomics, and the home decoration discourse was to a greater extent left to commercial actors, whose interest in consumers' tastes and preferences were considerably less condescending than that of most design reformers.

The phenomenon of nostalgia must be understood as part of this empowered consumer and expanded consumer culture. It did not necessarily refer to one's own experienced past or roots but rather reflected an imaginary, idealized and generic past. Part of the appeal of Tower stemmed from pre-war Finland, where the salons of the bourgeoisie were accessible to only a few. The yearning for a more comfortable, lush life was an old and prominent desire that people could now satisfy in a new consumer environment.

Nostalgia tends to project a maudlin and backward-looking image. However, it is not necessarily an engulfing sensation immersing its harbourers with alienation or a quest for security. Someone who collects kitsch may well be a pragmatist and future-oriented in everyday life. Anneli Juntto and Anni Vilkko have observed how the nostalgia of Finland's baby-boom generation largely involved addressing one's own identity.[40] Finland changed faster than ever before or since, and nostalgia was one of the means to internalize this change.

The new plurality in home decoration can also be seen as part of what, for example, Orvar Löfgren and Mike Featherstone have called the aestheticization of everyday life, understood as people's increased opportunities to shape their identity with the aid of consumer goods.[41] Especially in the 1970s, the rising standard of living offered consumption as a creative activity to a large number of people who had previously only dreamed of having their own living rooms, not to mention decorating these. Commercial players soon recognized this new segment of the market.

The success of the Tower sofa group resulted from a combination of all of the previously mentioned factors. Tower was not an example of the tradition-conscious reproduction furniture, nor was it a retro product explicitly copying the recent past. It was a hybrid with an indefinite language of form. From the perspective of the elite, Tower's urban middle-class, un-Finnish and nostalgic character made it alien, an 'other' in the discourse of interior decoration, but consumers loved it. Therefore, it was not displayed among other new products on the pages of interior decoration magazines or even advertised in the trade press like other furniture made by the Sopenkorpi company, although it was widely advertised elsewhere.[42] To most consumers, Tower represented status and traditional values, among which a sumptuous sofa suite for the living room was an important social marker. Tower was perhaps not primarily bought by members of the baby-boom generation but instead by their parents, whose standard of living also improved significantly during these years. The sofa suite sold well, and according to the manufacturer it did not even have to be especially advertised when it was launched. 'All the mink farmers rushed to buy it,' claimed Sopenkorpi's managing director of the time. The suite gradually expanded into a whole family of products, including a dining-room suite and bedroom furniture. Tower was also exported to the Soviet Union, which was an important market for the Finnish furniture industry in general. The most definite sign of success, however, was the large number of copies of the suite that appeared on the market within a few years.

–9–

Jacob Jensen and the Lifa Kitchen: Branding the 'Lifestyle Kitchen' with Designer Personality and Mythology

Hans-Christian Jensen

In 2005 a new chain store for kitchen, bathroom and wardrobe furniture was launched in Denmark by the newly merged companies Tvis A/S and Modulia A/S. The central prop in the heavily mediatized event was the Lifa kitchen designed by the renowned design consultancy Jacob Jensen Design founded by Jacob Jensen (1926–), who holds a certain international acclaim, especially due to his designs for the audio/video manufacturer Bang & Olufsen (B&O) in the 1960s and 1970s. This cooperation rendered possible a leap into a sphere quite uncommon for kitchens, the sphere of 'star' designers and iconic designs. The branding of the Lifa Design chain of shops was thus in the main sought through a 'positive contamination' between an array of new designs and commercial settings in the kitchen trade and the well-known identity of one of the heroic figures of Danish design.[1] This chapter examines how the design consultancy appropriated and conventionalized a visual language identified with its founder and how the Lifa kitchen can be seen as an example of this and—by extension—as an appropriation of the 'aura' of the heroic designer personality, while also proposing that this strategy constitutes a pre-appropriation of the kitchen as a commodity on behalf of the consumer.

THE LIFA KITCHEN

The Lifa kitchen showed a remarkable and much-commented-on seven-degree tilt inwards towards the floor on the base unit and inwards towards the ceiling on the top cupboard, resulting in an unusual visual profile (fig. 9.1). It was equipped with innovative technological features like LED lighting in drawers and panels, possibility for integration of flat-screen TV and a central control panel for these. The kitchen was allegedly the first 'designer kitchen' to appear in Denmark. The Lifa kitchen served a flagship function for the fifteen initially planned Lifa Design outlets in Denmark and the ten to come in the following years. Some of these were to appear in Norway and Sweden and even in other European countries like Poland and Spain. Simultaneously, Tvis/Modulia introduced the Modux series of kitchens, also to be retailed through Lifa Design. These were more conventional in terms of form, function and aesthetics, bidding for the middle-range market, and generated considerably less media attention.

With the technologically and aesthetically sophisticated Lifa kitchen, Tvis/Modulia aimed at a share of the high-end kitchen market—an optimistic and expanding market with a turnover of DKK 3 billion a year. On the production side the initiative was prompted by a concentration of companies and capital, with several mergers and acquisitions by venture capital firms. In 2003 the Swedish kitchen manufacturer Ballingslöv had bought Svane Køkkenet A/S, a chain of kitchen retailers previously supplied by Tvis/Modulia, to expand its distribution in the Danish market. The Svane Køkkenet contract had been Tvis/Modulia's main source of revenue, and its cancellation more than halved the company's DKK 300 million annual turnover. With the initiation of Lifa

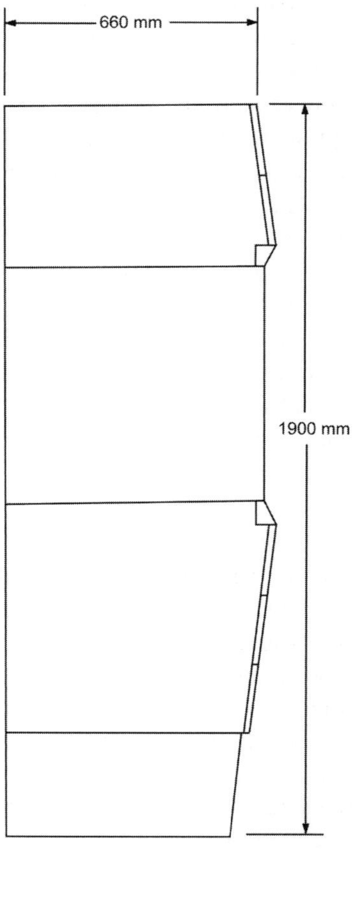

Fig. 9.1 Line drawing showing the sloping fronts. From the first Lifa catalogue. Image courtesy of TMK (Tvis/Modulia Koncernen A/S).

Design, Tvis/Modulia sought to secure a channel of distribution under its own control and regain an outlet for its line of production.

The market for kitchens was expanding, but evidently the competition was also intensifying. This was not least due to the introduction of nationwide TV commercials from 1996 onwards by the leading domestic manufacturers HTH, Invita and Kvik. But in contrast to this conventional marketing the Lifa project and its collaboration with a renowned design consultancy was referred to as a focus on a design strategy rather than marketing or rationalization. Although it is fair to say that the emphasis was on design before marketing, this was done with awareness of the media potential and thus marketing effect of innovatory design. Before the launch on 1 April 2005, the collaboration was effectively 'leaked' to the press, resulting in considerable advance publicity about the 'remarkable' cooperation between Tvis/Modulia and Jacob Jensen Design and the 'revolutionary' kitchen. That a 'breakaway from tradition', an 'alternative' and 'never seen before' approach to kitchen design was under way due to this cooperation was known to the public a year in advance of the actual launch, whilst the form and features of it were kept secret. Allegedly, a full-size model existed, but it could not be seen or photographed.

The Lifa kitchen caught on well in the market, and in the course of 2005 and 2006 it gained recognition as one of the 'luxury' or 'exclusive' kitchen brands in the Danish market along with the range of high-end kitchens which are colloquially referred to as the 'form market' due to the brand names Uno form, Multiform and Boform. The design project manager had previously referred to Lifa as intended for the upper section of mid-range kitchens just below the high-end kitchens. However, in the marketing and the wider publicity it was presented as a luxury kitchen (fig. 9.2). The design brief might not have been quite clear on this point, or the expenditures of the production and the portfolio strategy of the venture capital fund behind Tvis/Modulia prompted such a placement. The funds entering and concentrating the ownership of the kitchen business in the twenty-first century all pursued a portfolio strategy where the companies or brands under their control were distributed all over the market space, whereby low-end, middle-range and high-end kitchens were offered to consumers by the same company.

In 2007 the Lifa Design chain of stores introduced the Jacob Jensen Kitchen 2. This kitchen also bore the distinctive mode of expression of Jacob Jensen Design with the units divided into distinct compartments with wooden, metallic and treated surfaces but this time on the basis of a traditional upright front. In this way they were aiming at a broader target audience than with the Jacob Jensen Kitchen 1, as the Lifa kitchen was called from this point on. Actually, in some respects the story of the Lifa kitchen ends here. The kitchen changed status and function within its immediate commercial environment along with the change of name. It no longer served the flagship function for the Lifa Design chain of stores, and it became a brand among others

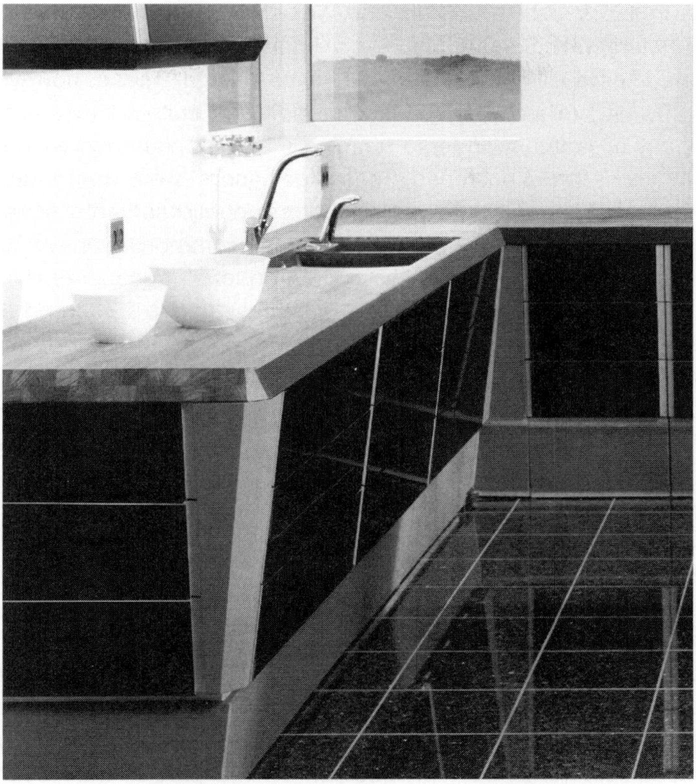

Fig. 9.2 Lifa in a 'real-life setting'. From the first Lifa catalogue. Photograph courtesy of TMK (Tvis/Modulia Koncernen A/S).

in the brand portfolio of TMK. The ownership had just recently changed from one venture capital fund to another, and so the name had been changed too, to Tvis Modulia Koncernen (TMK). The Modux brand which accompanied the Lifa kitchen was discontinued as well, and the company resurrected previous brand names, which from this point on were marketed along with the Jacob Jensen Kitchens. Both the Jacob Jensen 1 and Jacob Jensen 2 are still in production and for sale (in 2011).

DESIGN, DESIGNERS AND 'DESIGNER KITCHENS'

The claim that the Lifa kitchen is the first Danish designer kitchen is fair in a certain sense which might be worth reflecting on to pinpoint the case more exactly. Obviously it is not the first designer kitchen internationally. Georg Muche and Adolf Meyer's kitchen in the Haus am Horn at the first Bauhaus exhibition in 1923; J.J.P Oud's for the Weissenhof Settlement, Stuttgart, in 1927; and Margarete Schütte-Lihotsky's 'Frankfurt kitchen' of 1926 are regularly referred to as early examples of kitchen design. These, however, differ from the Lifa kitchen in being models intended for built-in kitchens to be realized, ideally or factually, in large housing programs, not sold as a branded commodity in the retail business. These 'designers' were in fact also all architects by training and served as educators, public servants or reformers rather than performing design as a vocation and commercial enterprise. Thus the Lifa kitchen is closer to more recent international precedents like Joe Colombo's Minikitchen unit for Boffi, which was designed in 1963 and earned a Gold Medal at the Triennale di Milano in 1964, or Otl Aicher's renowned design collaboration with Bulthaup and the launch of system b in 1982. The Minikitchen, however, was primarily an exhibition piece, and Aicher was a consultant for Bulthaupt doing design research and supervising development of systems rather than creating specific designs for actual kitchens. The release of system b followed his 1980 publication *Die Küche zum Kochen: Werkstatt einer Neuen Lebenskultur*, which was an impressive outburst of modernist design intervention into the poor state of things that he considered to be hampering values such as no-nonsense, rationality, simplicity, truth to materials and ergonomics in kitchen design.

In a certain respect all kitchens could rightfully be called designer kitchens. For all of the individual products, elements, features and forms which together make up a kitchen it would be possible, although not easy, and only with an considerable amount of research on the part of the design historian, to point out a single originator or team of originators who at some point conceived the design. These, however, would turn out to be of professional backgrounds other than designers in the conventional sense; they might be engineers, foremen, operators or craftsmen. These 'anonymous designers' are the true designers of the absolute majority of the stuff that makes up the fabric of everyday material culture in Denmark—kitchens in particular. Following this perspective we would have manifold candidates for the title of Denmark's first designer kitchen or kitchen designer. Arne Munch, who designed the Uno form kitchen in 1968 and founded the company by the same name, considered one of the top-range brands today, would be one of them, although he was a banker by training and had a career as a salesman before venturing into design.

Pushing this argument further, the consumers could just as well be considered the true designers of kitchens. Built-in kitchens have been a mainstay of the welfare provision in council housing since the 1930s, but the majority of Danes live in privately owned single-family housing with fitted kitchens. Consequently, a large number of consumers have had a great say in the final appearance of their specific kitchen for several decades. This tendency has become ever more pronounced, and a veritable kitchen boom can be detected from the beginning of the 1990s. Today, regular kitchen renewal is common, and when one buys a house, replacing the existing kitchen with a new one has become the norm. Making choices from an abundant array of products and combining these into an 'individual' kitchen of one's own creation is key to this process.

What makes the claim to status as a designer kitchen especially apt in the case of the Lifa kitchen, however, is the combination of the two facts that Jacob Jensen is a 'proper' designer in the sense that he has the formal education and training to make him a legitimate member of the design profession and that he is one of the few Danish designers who truly can be said to have become a household name. Had either or both of these features been missing, the claim could not have been pushed as convincingly or successfully.

A crucial point here is that the rightfulness of the claim to be a designer kitchen has less to do with the way the process of designing was performed or the final form resulting from this but predominantly rests upon the conquest of a position within a system of meaning, based on celebrity and differentiations in professional status. Several professions and occupations conceive forms within an industrial context, but in the course of the twentieth century the industrial design profession has successfully promoted the belief that its contribution basically and ultimately is the most adequate in terms of function, symbolism and aesthetics. No matter how biased the hegemonic depiction of nineteenth- and twentieth-century design history is towards designers at the expense of engineers and other designing actors, and how often some design historians point to this privilege, this general picture is unlikely to change. This bias has been critiqued within academia for several decades, and numerous highly commendable studies have been published and brought about a fuller and more comprehensive picture of the multiplicity of design and designing actors. In fact, this volume is a contribution to this academic tradition and endeavour. Still, during the same period, the bias seems to have only increased in dominance in popular conceptions and depictions. That the occasional engineer or self-taught designer has risen, and will rise, to stardom does not alter this situation. Surely popular design history will continue to expand its canon, and the proliferation of designer names within commercial design culture is bound to carry on as well, but there are limits to the array of designer names that can be brought to and kept in public recognition. The absolute majority of 'designers'—formally trained or not—will remain anonymous. However, consumers will differ in how many names or personalities they are able and willing to familiarize themselves with and appropriate into their daily lives.

FROM INDUSTRIAL DESIGNER TO BRAND

The quality and status of the Lifa kitchen, described by the manufacturer as outstanding, were portrayed—at least implicitly—as a direct result of the innovative and uncompromising spirit emanating from Jacob Jensen, the founder of the design consultancy Jacob Jensen Design, which was by this time run by his son, Timothy Jensen. The blurring of the demarcations between person and company is of course highly deliberate. The entire mediation of the Lifa kitchen was saturated with the perception that the personality of Jacob Jensen, with equal amounts of originality and a steadfast, almost provocatively uncompromising dedication to aesthetic purity and functional order in life as well as design, was somehow present in the kitchen. Still, the design was ascribed to the Jacob Jensen Design consultancy as a whole, and from the outset it was made clear that Lifa was not actually designed by Jacob Jensen personally. He didn't even oversee the process although he reportedly did cast a glimpse at it.

For this kind of transference of a designer's disembodied and distributed personality to a product to be done successfully the prerequisite is a well-established standing in the symbolic system of objects known to the general public. In the case of Jacob Jensen such an acclaim was built over fifty years of commercial and cultural activity. The biography of Jacob Jensen, not as an individual person but as a cultural figure, could be outlined as a development from an anonymous industrial designer in the 1950s, to the leading consultant designer at B&O and the originator of the B&O corporate identity in the 1960s and 1970s, to an independent designer sufficiently famous to punch signature designs for national and international firms in the 1980s and 1990s, to, finally, a brand identity encompassing a set of values and distinct visual nodes at the turn of the millennium. In 1998 Jacob Jensen Design was transformed from an outright design consultancy to a company spanning other activities. Most notably, the Jacob Jensen brand was formed in 1999 with its own registered trademark, Jacob Jensen™, and its own line of products within the mainstay of the Jacob Jensen portfolio in product design. Examples include a telephone, a smoke detector and various other kitchen and home appliances and new areas within personal apparel like watches, glasses and jewellery.

The historicization and historicity of Jacob Jensen's career form a decisive precondition for the development of the Jacob Jensen brand. From the mid-1970s he has featured in numerous exhibitions and publications, at first as chief designer at B&O, but eventually in his own right as one of the 'star' designers of the twentieth century and the originator of a staggering array of 'masterpieces'. In the course of this process, design historians have contributed to the pronunciation of a distinctive visual language (in Danish, *formsprog*) of Jacob Jensen.[2] However, auto-historicization has also played a major part in this process. In 1997 Jacob Jensen published his autobiography, handing down equal amounts of accounts from his life and work.[3] It has served as the main source of the following biographical works. Most recently, the success of the auto-historicization has even led to auto-musealization with the opening of the House of Jacob Jensen in 2008 as a permanent exhibition of the Jacob Jensen collection.

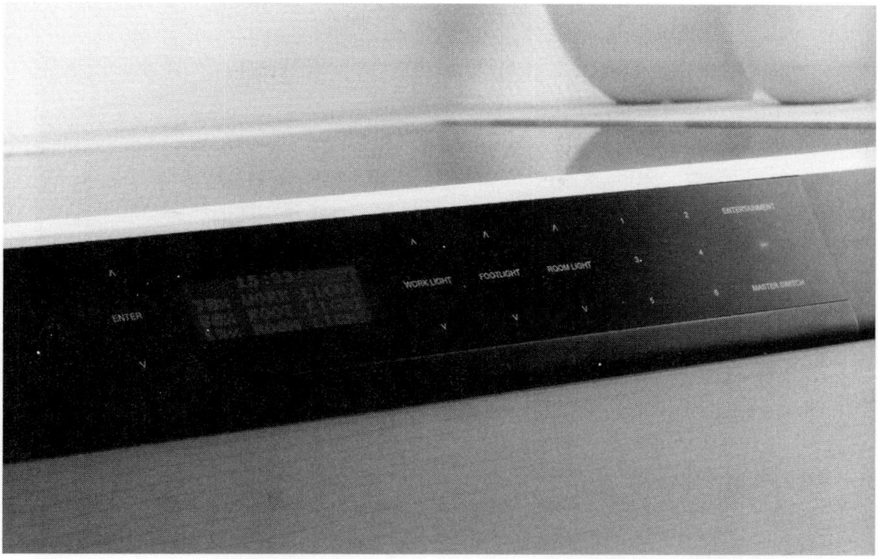

Fig. 9.3 Close-up showing the central control panel, clearly reminiscent of B&O interfaces. Image from the first Lifa catalogue. Photograph courtesy of TMK (Tvis/Modulia Koncernen A/S).

In the sales promotions, it was stated over and over that Lifa was different. Already during the design phase it was an explicit strategy to aim for a different but not odd kitchen. This discursive figure emanates from the leitmotif of Jacob Jensen for design and life alike. His autobiography bore the title *Anderledes, men ikke mærkelig: En designers erindringer* ('Different but not strange: Memoirs of a designer'). The phrase owes a great deal to Jensen's early experiences in American industrial design; he worked in Raymond Loewy's office in the late 1950s. Loewy's famous MAYA principle—most advanced, yet acceptable—clearly rings through here.[4] In the sales promotion a connection was drawn to other well-known products by Jacob Jensen Design as well. Telephones, watches, cable drums and not least B&O products were consistently and explicitly mentioned (fig. 9.3).

Initially, it was Jonas Gaarde, chief designer at Jacob Jensen Design, who was listed as the project manager and responsible for the kitchen. But soon Lifa was increasingly ascribed mainly to Timothy Jensen, and his previous engagement as chief of design at Gaggenau Hausgeräte GmbH, a German manufacturer of high-end kitchens, was enrolled as a precursor. A year later, in 2006, Timothy Jensen was presented as the originator of the kitchen (fig 9.4). Still, it was never doubted that his father's persona was actually somehow embodied in the kitchen. In fact, Tvis/Modulia made it clear before the launch that its prime motive for the cooperation was that this embodiment would and should be apparent. It was never specified which qualities the company

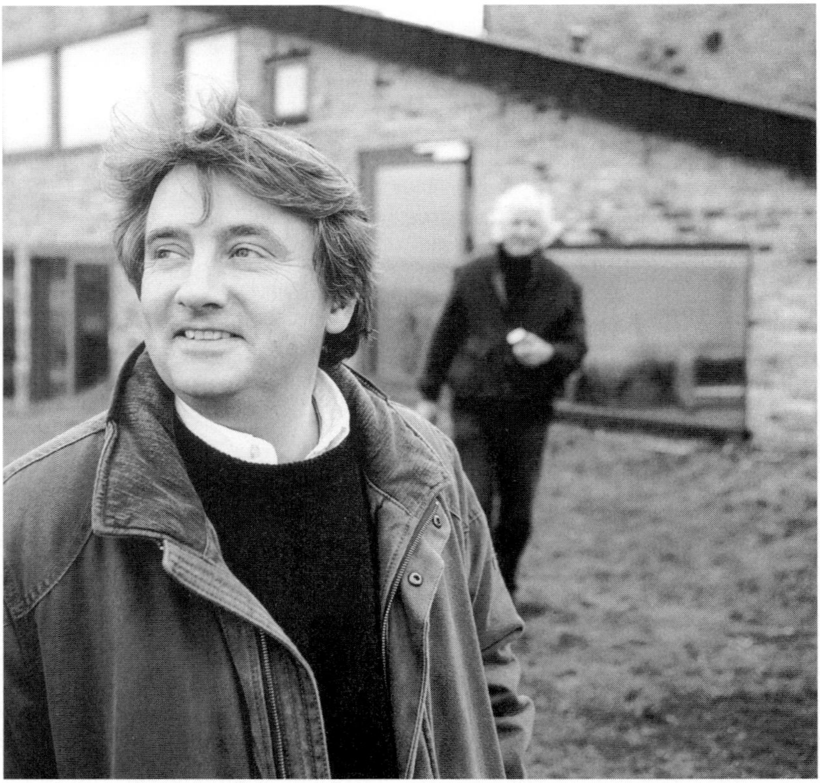

Fig. 9.4 Timothy Jensen and Jacob Jensen. Double portrait in front of the combined drawing office and home. From a recent Lifa catalogue. Photograph courtesy of TMK (Tvis/Modulia Koncernen A/S).

sought to convey in their new kitchen. Was it a 'look' or personal style, a distinct way of solving a functional, constructional and aesthetic problem, or a symbolic status? Probably all three at the same time. Tvis/Modulia was well aware of the signature value of the designer name Jacob Jensen—a value the company reported 'sold' in Scandinavia, Great Britain and the USA. So it is fair to say that the prime goal was to secure some degree of recognition in the market, and since neither appearance, construction nor name would be sufficient to make the Jacob Jensen persona apparent and convincing on its own, the triumvirate was necessary.

PERSONALITY AND SIGNATURE

Russell W. Belk is widely acknowledged for his idea of extended selves.[5] Belk mainly theorizes the way in which consumers tend to extend into their objects so that the idea of a discrete demarcation between object and subject is hardly obtainable in practice. In this particular case an equivalent tendency could be argued to be at work within design and production, with the Jacob Jensen persona extending across time, places, persons and things. The idea that brands can take on personality is commonplace within branding research and literature. In *Building Strong Brands* David A. Aaker defines brand personality as the set of human characteristics associated with a given brand.[6] Aaker argues that objects have the capacity to show general, universal personality traits that can be found in different combinations in an infinite number of concrete instances. Still, products also seem capable of taking on personalities particular to specific persons. Chanel No. 5 and Nike's Air Jordan basketball shoes are excellent examples. The latter is a case of what is commonly known as celebrity endorsement and can be studied in detail as a movement of meaning from celebrity to consumer.[7]

Many different types and degrees of personalization of brands could be said to occur between these two poles. To illustrate this, one of the leading Danish kitchen brands, Invita, seems an appropriate example to mention in this particular context, since it has pursued at least two different strategies to attain personality. For several years from 2005 onwards the brand ran an advertising campaign on TV depicting 'real' kitchens fitted by 'ordinary' Danish couples. In the series of mock-documentary ads the main ingredient was the testimonials by the couples about how they had achieved a kitchen truly unique to them by picking and choosing from the range of Invita products and by using Invita's ability to deliver tailored solutions to fit their individual and specific need. In fact, this was possible and had been done to a degree that these were no longer Invita kitchens but kitchens which could rightfully be named after the couples instead. The couples were presented by their first names, which were Lone and Christian, Rikke and Lars, Bente and Peter and so on. At the end of the TV spot the couples proudly stated, for example: 'It's not an Invita kitchen. It's a Lone and Christian kitchen!' These kitchens, then, were utterly personal to their owners, and it follows that such a truly personalized kitchen was only a fair expectation on the part of every other consumer. These couples, however, were also representative of a range of typical lifestyles. Their combinations of first names were easily readable as indicators of social, generational and cultural groupings. So the kitchens might have been personal but also specific to larger groupings or segments that the viewer could identify with.

In 2010 Invita launched a new TV campaign pursuing a rather different type of personalization. This time a kitchen by Invita is praised by the well-known public figure Mads 'Blærerøv' Christensen, who is known for his verbal eloquence, wit and humour and distinct mode of dressing, combining classical male apparel with fashionable and luxury items in a flamboyant and highly personal manner very unusual for Danes. This is no simple case of celebrity endorsement, however. Christensen owes his nickname 'Blærerøv', which means 'braggart', to his 1998 book *Den Store Blærerøv: En guide til manden* ('The big braggart: A guide for men'), where he gave advice on classical and fashionable male clothing. Christensen's celebrity thus rests on his status as a style leader and connoisseur of taste with the ability to make authoritative judgments on things and forms.

In relation to these four instances of personalization, we see that what is distinct about the way the Lifa/Jacob Jensen Kitchen 1 attained personality is that it drew on a specific designer's personality by appropriating his aura and using his name as a brand. There are several prerequisites that had to be in place before such branding could be expected to result in the desired personalization. The first of these is the establishment of a national and international design heritage. A central tendency of Danish design culture from the early 1990s onwards has been the canonization of a handful of designers and the rise of their names, key works and distinct design idioms to the status of, if not common knowledge, then at least intense public interest. This tendency is accompanied by the sedimentation of a series of design classics and a retro revival of the golden days of Danish design in the 1950s and 1960s. The obvious commercial opportunities following such privileged cultural status have led to the promotion even of less well-known designers and claims that their products are 'classics' of modern design as well. The apparently successful strategy has in turn made it common practice to use the names of designers as part of the promotion for new products as well, even in sectors of the industry with no tradition of such a designer personality cult. One might argue that the obsession with 'signature design' seems to have been the most prominent general trend in Danish design culture around the turn of the millennium. Assigning a signature to well-established products to boost their market performance, relaunching old products by signature designers and launching new products with designer signatures—pedigreed or not—have become everyday occurrences.

Another prerequisite has been the increased attention to the mediation of design in the public sphere. The production of fame and celebrity within the design field of course depends on media exposure just as it does in the entertainment industry. The amount of glossy books available on Danish design and designers has seen a tremendous rise over the last ten years, and newspaper and TV features on design have become commonplace, accompanied by a staggering array of magazines and Internet resources dedicated to design. A frequent and recurring motif in this type of mediation of design is the eulogization of key figures and products in the domestic design heritage. Their names and products have become common knowledge not only for the new cultural intermediaries or the creative class but even for ordinarily well-informed mainstream consumers.

A third prerequisite is the emergence of design as a para-art field, where the key features of the culture of art—signatures and masterpieces identifiable within a line of progress—are transferred to design. The tendency is as of yet less pronounced in Denmark than internationally, since design as para-art is heavily dependent on the presence of an institutional framework composed of museums, exhibition spaces and galleries, and Denmark has thus far been too small to really keep such a framework specific to design going. But the tendency is clear.

The transformation of Jacob Jensen's design consultancy into Jacob Jensen Design and the formation of the Jacob Jensen brand demonstrate a particularly clever and intensive harnessing of the opportunities of this particular design culture. Jacob Jensen Design has expediently exploited and benefited from the general and external historicization of design which has offered Jacob Jensen a place in the hall of fame of the Danish design heritage. This has been done through investment in autobiography, auto-historicization and auto-musealization, as already mentioned, whereby the necessary information and props for the production of celebrity were provided.

With this in place the extension of Jacob Jensen across a range of objects and persons was possible. In the course of this process the conception of a visual language unique to Jacob Jensen plays a significant role as the vehicle by which it is possible to step into and distribute his persona. If Jacob Jensen Design succeeds in both reproducing Jacob Jensen's fame and materializing his visual language, henceforward the Jacob Jensen brand will be able to transcend the ordinary limits of the lifespan of a designer and live on for years. What is captured with the concept 'visual language' is by no means a new phenomenon. It is basically the same as that which would previously have been denominated 'style', and in our context corresponds quite closely to Heinrich Wölfflin's notion of 'personal style'. This long-established but by now unfashionable term has lost its academic and professional attraction due to its association with surface and lack of depth. However, it has also in some instances been known to characterize the deepest and most authentic mode of expression of a person and even a whole culture with the ability to transcend the limits of lifetimes and embrace large collectives of makers and producers of form. What is new, then, and might justify the neologism is that such a diffusion of personal style into regional or period style can now be hindered and controlled by making the visual language the property of Jacob Jensen Design, protected by the Jacob Jensen trademark. In this sense, the appropriation of a designer persona becomes the trademarking of style.

DESIGN IN A MEDIATIZED WORLD

The symbolic and material merging of the Jacob Jensen Design and Lifa Design brands in the Lifa kitchen can be studied through several types of media including press releases, catalogues, newspaper features, advertisements and TV appearances. All of these could be said to be instances of an endeavour to manage meaning.[8] The management of meaning was attempted in two ways: firstly, by immediate identification with Jacob Jensen and the array of previous classics of his and thereby also with the special category of design with a capital *D* constituted by the universe of canonical designs and designers; and, secondly, by *differentiating* Lifa from other kitchens in general and especially from mainstream and mid-range 'lifestyle' kitchens. In this way Lifa was drawn into 'Design' and set apart from 'lifestyle' in several respects.

At the time of the launch of the Lifa kitchen, TV advertisements had become the norm for suppliers of mid-range kitchens. The main assertion in these commercials, and in other types of kitchen advertisements, is that the truly unique and thus individual kitchen is possible and obtainable due to infinite variation and possibilities in the combination of forms, features, surfaces and appliances. Although in the strict sense a contradiction in terms, since what is genuinely singular could not share a style with anything else, the quest for individuality is commonly referred to as an expression of 'lifestyle'. Even though the launch of the Lifa kitchen was not backed by a full-blown TV campaign, this media context played a substantial role herein. In the various other kinds of promotional releases the Lifa kitchen was positioned against this backdrop of lifestyle kitchens. These, allegedly, showed an overall conformity despite, or perhaps because of, their origin in infinite variation and individual solutions, whereas the Lifa kitchen was truly unique. The design feature offered as evidence for this claim was the seven-degree tilt of the fronts of the furniture. However small this reorganization of material form might seem, more of a style modification than a design innovation, it rendered possible the leap into the sphere of star designers and iconic designs.

With the material form thus in place the quest for a cultural form aspiring to the status and value of 'high design' was mainly fought for at a discursive level in several ways. First of all, it was inscribed into the modernist mythology of design as a practice of intervention into and civilizing of commercial chaos. Secondly, two streams of discursive claims of designer ideology and promotional jargon with a modernist ring were effectively played out. The design of the Lifa kitchen would allegedly break away from both tradition and mainstream design associated with low functional, formal and aesthetic quality, thereby enrolling the idea of societal reform and progress. Furthermore, the design would place the kitchen well before its time and be both future-proof and avant-garde. Its originator, Timothy Jensen, even foretold that it would become another 'icon' of Jacob Jensen if only Tvis/Modulia was able to exercise the necessary courage and persistence in keeping it on the market long enough.

This strategy was especially apparent around the launch in 2005. At this point Lifa was mainly presented as a case of form following function. In a traditional modernist manner the sloping fronts were pointed to as delivering functional advantages (clearance for the feet, more working area due to the larger counter top, more storage area in the top drawer nearest at hand) as well as extraordinary beauty. The obvious possibility of differentiation of taste and identity and effective demarcation of distance to the mainstream was never even implied in the mediation at this point, but it is only fair to assume that such issues were considered a key attraction by consumers in the actual encounter.

So whereas the seven-degree sloping fronts were also functionally motivated, products do function in several other respects as well, most evidently economically and symbolically. As Tony Fry has argued, 'products are clearly central to the building of identity, image and reputation of a manufacturer'.[9] Exactly this kind of broader function also seems to have been a prime motive for Tvis/Modulia. What the company obtained from the collaboration with Jacob Jensen Design was also a kitchen with an unusual visual profile that invited both visual consumption and discursive notice and thus catered to media exposure. In this way it could function as the central prop in the establishment and staging of the Lifa Design chain of shops and serve a flagship function in the longer run.

After 2007 and the metamorphosis of Lifa into Jacob Jensen Kitchen 1 a rather different type of mediation than the quasi-modernist adherence to form following function can be discerned. It featured, somewhat paradoxically but cleverly in terms of product placement, as a central prop in the set design of the Danish soap opera *2900 Happiness* depicting the lifestyle of the absurdly and demonstratively rich in the suburbs north of Copenhagen. Thus the luxuriousness and exclusivity of owning a Jacob Jensen Kitchen 1 were firmly stated and heavily instilled into the public. The disengagement of the kitchen from the flagship function made way for a more singular status as another masterpiece of Jacob Jensen Design and the cultural profile usually conferred on such an object.

As discussed in the introduction to this volume and exemplified by the case studies making up Part 3 of this book, there is an emerging trend within design history to consider questions of mediation along with those of production and consumption in the study of design. According to Grace Lees-Maffei there are three categories of mediation studies in design history: the role of different media in the mediation between production and consumption, the design of mediating channels and, finally, mediation in or by designed objects.[10] In continuation thereof it could be argued that this particular case study points to the ever more pervasive presence of media as a calculated and integrated factor in design. A growing mediatization of design could thus be said to be taking place.

PREPARING APPROPRIATION BY DESIGNER PERSONALIZATION

The engagement of Jacob Jensen Design by Tvis/Modulia seems to have been prompted by a need to shortcut the mediation between production and consumption in a situation where the connection had been lost overnight by

Ballingslöv's acquisition of Svane Køkkenet A/S and had to be re-established fast for Tvis/Modulia to stay in business. The shortcut could be said to have been obtained by a brand marriage between a plain and reliable company in the kitchen trade in unfortunate circumstances and a high-profile design consultancy with an international reputation, with Lifa Design and the Lifa kitchen as the offspring with some degree of claim to 'designer' status and meaning. Furthermore, a key component in making the shortcut possible could be described as a pre-appropriation by the producer on behalf of the consumer. The concept of appropriation is rather broad in colloquial use and has a great many specific meanings within academia. The meaning drawn upon here is the one developed within some realms of anthropology and material culture studies in particular. The concept refers in this tradition to the active and culturally productive process of rendering anonymous commodities meaningful in the course of consumption in the face of the modernity's general tendency to alienate objects of production.[11]

Drawing on this conception, Guy Julier has made the case that what designers deliver within the framework of a design culture is the smoothing of this appropriation by 'de-alienating' products in advance for the consumer by anchoring them in networks of meaning by 'sophisticated construction of meanings to be supplied with the object and to be identified with it'.[12] The designer thus frees the consumer from part of the burden of interpreting and rendering alien consumer goods meaningful. This is, however, as Julier points out, also a strategy whereby not only the physical content of goods but also their interpretation is considered and sought to be controlled within the design and production process.

The phenomenon appears to be central to modern and, maybe even more so, late-modern design culture. Parallel to Julier's conception of design as a facilitation of appropriation, inspired by material culture studies, media studies and cultural studies in general, similar but different analytical conceptions have been developed within and influenced by science and technology studies (STS). Most notably, Kjetil Fallan, drawing on Madeline Akrich's ideas, has shown the pertinence of the concepts 'scripts', 'scripting' and 'subscription' in the study of design as mediation of meaning in design history.[13] Also, Steve Woolgar's idea of the 'configured user' could be cultivated in a similar fashion.[14]

Returning to Julier, the idea of design as 'de-alienation' supports his general point about the leading trend within current design culture being a closer and closer integration of design, marketing and advertising. By extension, the design consultancy could be said to be moving away from its former model, the architectural firm, and identifying and sharing more traits with the advertising agency. In this environment Julier describes the meaning management taking place as follows: 'The designer, in combination with other professionals, must take decisions regarding the degrees and mechanisms of de-alienation. The designer can entirely hand over the object to be received "as it is", to allow the consumer to build their own meanings or none at all.'[15]

Following this, the case of the Lifa/Jacob Jensen Kitchen 1 appears to be a result of the highest possible degree of de-alienation, strived for by infusing Jacob Jensen's persona into the product and thereby at the same time drawing the kitchen into the extraordinary and distinct category of 'designer goods', leaving only a tight margin for interpretive creativity on the part of the consumer. This pre-appropriation was facilitated by the consultancy's strategic move in which the tendency of convergence identified by Julier was taken a step further: becoming a brand itself.

PART 3

MEDIATIONS

–10–

Something Old, Something New, Something Stolen, Something Blue: Designing a Chocolate Bar

Stig Kvaal and Per Østby

Design history often focuses on objects such as furniture, cutlery and lamps. So why choose a chocolate bar as the object for studying design? Chocolate is a cheap and relatively modest mass product. It represents short, stolen pleasures, in contrast to the manifest visibility and durability of consumer durables. Furthermore, chocolate design has not been regarded as a particularly prestigious or challenging task for design professionals. With the exception of Nidar's chocolate box Sfinx, whose pieces of confectionary were redesigned by Johan Verde in 1999, and Freia's chocolate bar Lohengrin, designed by Henrik Bull back in 1911, few prominent designers are associated with Norwegian chocolate manufacturers. This, however, does not by any means imply that chocolate design is an 'inferior' form of design practice, nor that it is any less worthy of scholarly attention than more formalized sectors.

In the context of sweets production, design seems to have been an in-house and ad hoc process conducted by a variety of people belonging to different trades.[1] And what has been regarded as design within the stimulant sector of the food industry? The taste, smell, colour and shape of the chocolate? The design of the packaging? The designing of brand identity and advertising material? The concept of design might therefore be opened to a wide variety of various activities and processes that could be examined.

In this case study of the continued development of one particular chocolate bar, designed in 1936, throughout its lifespan, we want to describe and analyse a range of processes that appear to have played an important role in designing the chocolate. To fully appreciate the complexity and cultural significance of chocolate design, we must take a systemic approach—as exemplified by the chapters in Part 1 of this book—to our humble object of study. The theoretical backdrop underlying our analysis is collected from a wide spectrum of sources, but mostly from the field of science and technology studies (STS) and the history of technology.[2]

Most immediately, it must be analysed in the context of the food industry, but an even wider perspective is required: How does this chocolate interact with broader historical developments, such as changes in economic situations, political ideologies, patterns of consumption, lifestyles and health policies? How do these aspects relate to chocolate design? What is Scandinavian chocolate design?

With these questions as starting points we propose an analysis of chocolate as design culture. The investigation focuses on how the Stratos chocolate bar was created, developed and redesigned, thereby exploring the many mediating capabilities of design. Much of the design work we will encounter is focused on mediating the commodity with the aim of generating profit, but the designed chocolate itself also becomes a mediator as it co-constructs everyday cultural practices.[3] We shall be examining this chocolate as part of various 'collages' dependent on time, place and design with the aim of understanding how and why these collages changed over time and assessing the implications of these changes.

STRATOS: A HEAVENLY NEW CHOCOLATE

The candy company Nidar was established in Trondheim in 1912 and expanded rapidly during the postwar business boom. This expansion came to an abrupt end with the global financial crisis in 1921.[4] As if the situation was not bad enough, a tax on the sale of chocolate was introduced to raise fresh funds for the ailing Treasury. In 1922 the Norwegian Parliament agreed to a 33.3 per cent tax on eating chocolate and a 10 per cent tax on cooking chocolate.[5] More expensive chocolate at a time when most people had less money to spend was an unfortunate combination of circumstances for the chocolate manufacturers. The crisis, however, gave rise to great creativity, and this influenced chocolate design. Price was important, but offering new and striking products was also an important strategy in the endeavour to strengthen the market position. Nidar's price lists from the 1920s and 1930s reveal an explosive expansion of the range of products. In 1922 the factory marketed 88 different products; by 1935, however, the number had risen to 269.[6] Like many of Nidar's products, the Stratos chocolate bar was created in the 1930s. Nidar had survived a very difficult period, and the financial prospects were beginning to improve. It was under these conditions that the Stratos chocolate was created.

It all started at a trade show in Germany in 1935. One of the visitors at this particular show was the operations manager at Nidar, chemical engineer Jørgen Holmsen. He noticed a chocolate from the British Rowntree factory which was different from the rest.[7] The chocolate was porous and was produced using a new process, part of which was a great reduction of the air pressure to create a vacuum. Since the production method was patented, it could not be adopted by Nidar just like that, but Holmsen was determined to find a solution. Back in Trondheim, he started experimenting to find his own way of producing a porous chocolate. After six months of trial and error he succeeded, and in 1936 the Stratos was ready for the Norwegian market.

In Nidar's company newsletter, *Chokolade Bladet*, the wrapping was described as 'simple and straightforward'.[8] The bar was wrapped in silver foil and a corn blue paper band. There were no drawings or ornamentation, only a plain white text, which in pure style and simple letters provided the information that this was NIDAR, STRATOS, MILK CHOCOLATE. There was no mention of this being a porous chocolate, which after all was what the invention was all about. At a time of heavy price competition between chocolate factories, Stratos was instead presented as a good bargain with its great volume in relation to the price. The encapsulated bubbles of air increased the volume of the bar and gave consumers the impression that Stratos was better value for the money than other chocolates. This was a strategy tailored specifically for the targeted customer segment.

The launch of this chocolate was regarded as sufficiently important by general manager Karl O. Karlsen for it to be given a prominent place in the editorial of the previously mentioned issue of *Chokolade Bladet*.[9] Under the headline 'We are up to date!' Stratos was presented as an example of Nidar keeping up with 'the strong developments currently taking place'. Karlsen was not primarily referring to developments in the chocolate industry, although the 1930s were a decade during which many great chocolate brands were created. He was using the activities taking place in chemistry laboratories 'all over the world' as his frame of reference. In Karlsen's picture, this was where all innovation was taking place, and, he added, 'these improvements have become such a common occurrence that we would probably be astonished if they should fail to appear all of a sudden'. This understanding of change as continuous and necessary can be related to the contemporary perception of living in the age of modernity, where change, development, science and new technology appeared as an indivisible unity.[10] The fascination with scientific and technological advances provided the backdrop for Nidar's tactical approach in their advertisements for Stratos. Not only was Stratos a new chocolate, it also provided proof that Nidar was taking part in the general progress and the technological development.

The choice of the name for the new chocolate bar connected it directly to the spirit of the times. Stratos is an abbreviation of 'stratosphere'. Shortly before, the Swiss physicist Auguste Piccard had developed the stratospheric balloon. This was a very large balloon with a round, airtight aluminium capsule, or gondola. In 1932 he had succeeded in reaching an altitude of 16,770 metres. In 1935 this record was beaten by the Americans Anderson and Stevens, who ascended to 22,066 metres.[11] What better name for a chocolate developed according to scientific methods, and described as proof that Nidar was keeping up to date, than a name inspired by the most spectacular pioneering scientific achievements of the day and age? Like those pioneers, Nidar aimed for ever new heights.

THE MODERNIST CHOCOLATE

In the first issue of *Chokolade Bladet* in 1937, Nidar was able to announce 'News on Stratos'.[12] By then it had been on the market for a while and had clearly become a success. However, the engineers did not rest on their laurels. Through new experiments they had improved its appearance, so that Stratos now had a 'completely smooth underside'. The paragraph gives us an impression of their triumphant laboratory activities when we read that Nidar had originally thought it impossible to produce tiny bars of Stratos but that the engineers had tackled 'even this task'. With this change the ambitions in relation to sales also seem to have become higher. In any case it is announced that since Stratos stood out as something 'completely new', it had 'without a doubt the greatest prospect of becoming one of the best-selling eating chocolates of the entire country'.

In 1938 Nidar launched a new campaign to promote the Stratos chocolate. While initially focusing on the novelty, size and porous texture of the chocolate, the new campaign used its name as the focus point. The poster was designed by illustrator Per Frenger and shows a large Stratos bar descending from a starry but nonetheless blue sky (fig. 10.1).[13] At the bottom of the poster, a golden glow indicates that the sun is about to ascend over a row of snow-capped peaks, and lights from holiday cottages or homes can also be glimpsed. Red lettering below the illustration announces: 'All good things come from above'. The porous texture that had been the most prominent feature was no longer in focus.

In another advertisement from this period, the connection to the stratospheric balloons becomes very evident.[14] Here they are even described as the 'Stratos balloons', which have 'reached higher altitudes than anything else'. The illustration, again designed by Frenger, shows a stratospheric balloon with a Stratos bar hanging below it (fig. 10.2). We get the distinct impression that the balloon is very high up—in the stratosphere. This supports the message trumpeted in the text, which relates that 'the Stratos balloons have reached higher altitudes than anything else. The new Stratos is the highest product produced by the chocolate industry to date.'

This 'Stratos balloon' was in frequent use in different promotional campaigns. One example is the fishing industry trade show in Trondheim in the autumn of 1938, during which the balloon featured as a ceiling decoration and eye-catching device above Nidar's booth. One of the 'very most recent packing

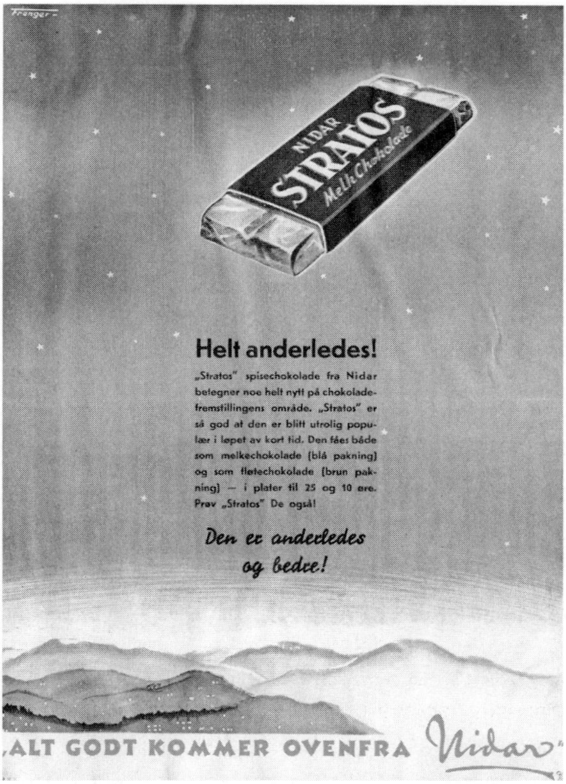

Fig. 10.1 Advertisement for Stratos, designed by Per Frenger, 1938. The copy reads: 'Completely different!—All good things come from above'. Photograph courtesy of Nidar AS.

machines', which was used to pack Stratos bars, was displayed at the booth. According to *Chokolade Bladet* the 'grand and high-speed' machine had generated great interest among the visiting public, with crowds gathering to 'admire the ingenious machinery' packing Stratos without the chocolate being touched by human hands.[15] At the time, chocolate production was based largely on manual work, with the packing process being particularly labour-intensive. This was about to change with the introduction of the new packing machinery, and Stratos, the modern chocolate developed by chemical engineers using scientific equipment, led the way.

Stratos was not only a chocolate among many others in Nidar's assortment; it was a spearhead and proof that Nidar was keeping up with the new developments and indeed leading the way in terms of introducing new methods in the development and production of chocolate. The development of chocolate was, and still is, largely a matter of combining familiar elements in new ways—as is so much design.[16]

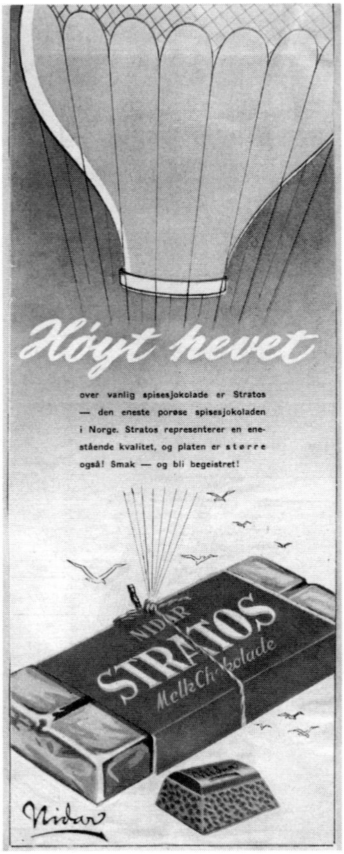

Fig. 10.2 Advertisement for Stratos featuring the Stratos balloon, designed by Per Frenger, *c*.1938. Photograph courtesy of Nidar AS.

THE BALLOON DEFLATES, BUT THE AIR IN THE CHOCOLATE BECOMES MORE VISIBLE

Stratos sold well from the very beginning, and the sales figures remained high during the early years. However, the progress was to be brutally interrupted. On 9 April 1940, German soldiers invaded Norway. This immediately put an end to the import of cocoa beans, sugar and other vital raw materials for chocolate production. When the stocks of cocoa beans were gone, the production of chocolate came to a halt. Cut off from its primary business, Nidar survived the war by producing various substitute products. When the war ended, raw materials for chocolate production did not feature at the top of the government's list of priorities, and when cocoa beans were again imported, the quantities were not nearly large enough to cover the needs of the chocolate factories. Due to a combination of this shortage of raw materials, rationing and an increase in the chocolate tax, Nidar was unable to put Stratos back on the market in the first postwar years.

In 1952 the Stratos was relaunched hanging below a 'Stratos balloon' as 'Nidar's big hit before the war'.[17] But while this illustration was not unlike the pre-war artwork, times had changed, and the imagery might now give new associations. Through the illegal Allied airdrops over Norway during the war, many good things had come from above. Whereas the porous quality had not been greatly communicated as added value in the pre-war advertising, it was now becoming the most prominent element. In this new advertisement, Stratos was presented as 'the porous milk chocolate'.

The greatest change at this point, however, was invisible—but it was nonetheless a noticeable one for any lover of chocolate: the price had increased from NOK 0.10 and 0.25 to NOK 0.65 and 1.20 for 22- and 42-gram bars respectively.[18] There were several reasons for this, but the major factor was the skyrocketing of the chocolate tax. In 1950 this tax was increased to 150 per cent of the price of the chocolate.[19] The background for this 'world record chocolate tax' was the government's need for funds to finance extraordinary contingency measures in connection with the Korean War, which many feared would escalate into a new global conflict. The tax increase not only made chocolate drastically more expensive for the consumers but also made many chocolate manufacturers look for alternative products to earn their money from.

Nidar found such alternative business in household products, such as instant soups, sauces, desserts and essences. At the same time, the main product range was considerably reduced. In 1939, Nidar had 230 varieties of chocolate in production. In 1950 the number was only 41.[20] This rationalization also had its advantages. A smaller range of products gave a more rational utilization of the production equipment and represented savings in relation to advertising and publicity. Until then, the Nidar logo had been an important feature of the advertisements, but a new approach was developing whereby the product brand—the name and logo of the actual chocolate advertised—gained prominence at the expense of the company brand. The Nidar company, which had guaranteed the quality of the goods, was replaced with the brand name Stratos, and we see a clear indication of what was to become a long-term development: that the product brand would 'lift' the chocolate and make it visible.

GIRLS, GIRLS, GIRLS

Two factors had an important impact on the promotional work of Norwegian manufacturers of sweets and chocolate in the postwar era. The first of these was the influence of American popular culture. The second, which is related to the first, was the use of pin-ups to advertise merchandise. In an advertisement for Stratos printed in the weekly women's magazine *Norsk Ukeblad* in early 1953, a drawing of a pretty woman eating a chocolate was the focal point.[21] The distinctiveness of the chocolate had been toned down. Brave men high up in the air no longer did the job; this was the time for beautiful women. Judging by the postwar advertisements, the age of the pin-ups had arrived.

In 1961, when Nidar relaunched Stratos in new packaging, a woman was again the focal point.[22] The exposed silver foil had now disappeared, and Stratos was wrapped in a deep blue colour. The slogan was changed to 'fancy something different?' The advertisement explained that the 'delightful aroma is brought out because STRATOS is porous'. Up to this point, there had been more emphasis on the larger size resulting from the air bubbles. Now, Nidar seems to have decided that there was no point in sharing this information with the consumers. After all the problems with heavy taxation, strangely enough, price seems to have become less important. This must be understood in light of the increasing prosperity of the postwar era. In the prosperous 1960s—the golden age of social democracy and the welfare society—everyone could afford to buy a chocolate now and again.

These changes can be regarded as minor adjustments. The posters and advertisements used to promote the chocolate changed more dramatically, however. Soon the women were gone. Instead, the chocolate bar was 'put centre stage'. In a newspaper advertisement from 1966, parts of an opened chocolate bar take up about one-third of the space.[23] A piece has been broken off, clearly showing the porous texture of the chocolate. The text proclaims that Stratos is 'the only porous milk chocolate'. The Stratos bar had descended from the sky and emerged as 'pure', free of stratospheric or womanly trimmings. The brown porous chocolate bar with the Nidar logo embossed on each piece was now meant to catch the attention on its own. Thus we may say that it emerged as more 'honest' than before. Was this a signal that the Stratos had 'landed'; that it was no longer hovering in the stratosphere but had become a 'natural chocolate'? It is possible to conceptualize this as a commercial parallel to the nascent youth rebellion, with its waning belief in progress and the dream of 'returning to nature'.

Nidar's declaration that Stratos was the only porous milk chocolate was nothing new. This had been part of the message of the advertising since the war, albeit then with the reservation that this applied to Norway. Now this message was emphasized. It is natural to see the strong accentuation of the message as a positioning in relation to Freia's Melkesjokolade ('milk chocolate'), which was the market leader among milk chocolates.[24] Freia chose to link its milk chocolate to the folk tales and national romanticism. In contrast, Nidar linked Stratos to the great narratives of scientific and technological progress. The early 1970s were the era of space travel and lunar excursions and of

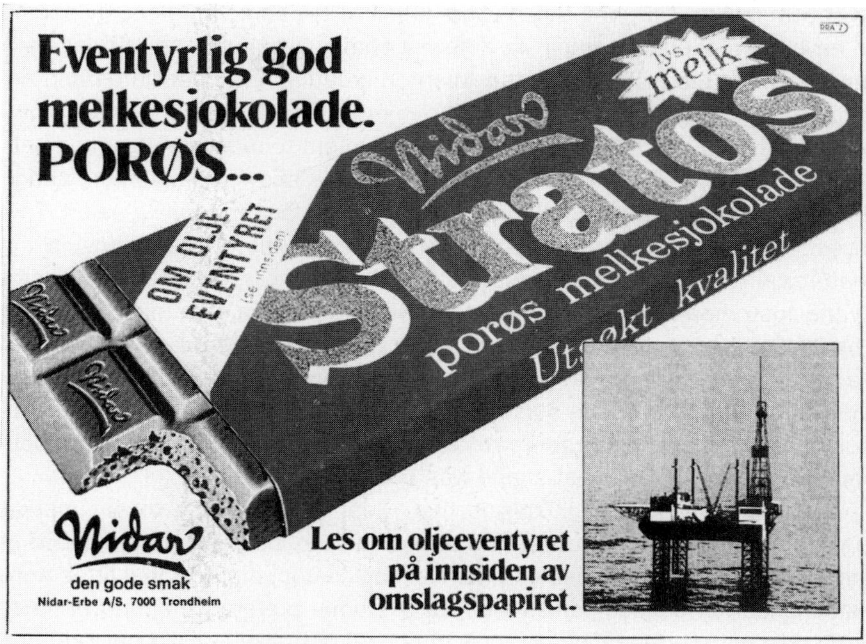

Fig. 10.3 Advertisement for Stratos, early 1970s, playing on the fairy tale-like qualities of the then-emerging Norwegian oil adventure. Photograph courtesy of Nidar AS.

increasing Norwegian affluence following the discovery of oil on the continental shelf. Nidar knew how to play on this (fig. 10.3).

Stratos was to stay more or less the same for a long period. And perhaps no good reasons could be found to change a winning formula: in 1970 Stratos achieved a sales increase on the previous year of no less than 40 per cent, and, for the first time, it was described as an 'everyday commodity' in *Sjokolade Bladet*. Stratos was now Nidar's bestselling product and among the bestselling chocolates in Norway. No wonder it was described as a 'winner'.[25]

BRIGHTER TIMES

Whereas the 1960s had been coloured by the prospect of strong foreign competition resulting from new international free-trade agreements, the 1970s were for Nidar a decade dominated by domestic takeovers and mergers. In 1970 Nidar merged with the Trondheim firm Lorentz Erbe & Søn, and the name was changed to Nidar-Erbe. Five years later, in 1975, Nidar-Erbe acquired Kielland fabrikker. Finally, in 1980, a merger united the company with the long-established Oslo firm Bergene A/S. The merged company, Nidar Bergene, employed 1,000 people and had annual gross sales on the order of

NOK 500 million.[26] During these years much of the company's energy seems to have been used on combining different company cultures and tidying up a mushrooming product range rather than on creating new chocolates and developing existing ones.

The mergers and takeovers were an adjustment to meet stronger competition. In the mid-1970s, however, the sales figures showed stagnation, and in 1980 Nidar initiated an investigation into what caused the failing sales. This investigation showed that the porous consistency, one of the distinguishing features of the Stratos bar, was no longer perceived as an important factor by the customers. Neither did they perceive Stratos as a pure milk chocolate. The explanation suggested by those who conducted the survey was that this had to do with the fact that the packaging had gradually become darker over the years. According to the survey, it was above all the young who had 'abandoned' the Stratos.[27] In order to recapture its position, some smart manoeuvring was required, but what shape was this to take?

An important element in this is that Nidar applied more recent market survey methods in this process. As a result of the increasing prominence of the social sciences and their commercial application, professional firms were established to help companies test out customer preferences in novel ways. From now on, the feedback on what the customers liked or did not like, and why, no longer came exclusively from internal taste panels; it was collected from a larger sample of consumers 'out there'. This provided a new and better basis for product design, while at the same time challenging the boundaries of what could actually be observed. To what extent consumers actually had opinions about the connection between colour and taste, or whether this was among the questions designed by the market survey experts, is an entirely different matter.

In the wake of these investigations, in 1982 Nidar decided to relaunch the Stratos. Rather than change the product or shore it up with advertising campaigns, the management chose to relaunch the brand with a new profile. So what was done? The most apparent change was the design of the paper wrapper, which was given a lighter hue of blue. Navy blue was replaced by cornflower blue. It is worth noting that the packaging was not 'reset' to the original shade of blue; instead, a much lighter variant was adopted. Another conspicuous modification of the wrapper was that the white, star-shaped section with the text 'light milk' was substituted by a drawing of a wooden milk pail. Why was this done? Here it is obvious that an image gives a stronger and more immediate impression than words. Nidar went further than changing the visual expression, however. The text on the wrapping paper was also altered. The words 'porous milk chocolate' were replaced by 'the porous, blue milk chocolate'.[28]

The latest changes meant, first of all, that the chocolate was described in the definite singular. There was to be no doubt that this was a unique product.

Furthermore, whereas the previous packaging designs had described the actual chocolate bar, an additional quality unrelated to the physical and tangible chocolate had now entered the description, namely the colour blue. The colour of its wrapping paper was included in the understanding of the Stratos. The Stratos bar had always had blue packaging, but now this property was emphasized as part of its image. Not least, this 'blueness' gave associations to air and thus represented the air bubbles giving the chocolate its porous quality, as well as the stratosphere that had provided the inspiration for its name. At the same time it also says something about the significance of packaging design in the marketing and consumption of chocolate.

However, the most significant change in this radical rebranding campaign was not the alterations to the shade of blue, nor the designation of this chocolate as 'blue'. The boldest innovation had four legs, two horns and an udder—and it was blue: the Stratos cow. The advertising campaign which was part of the relaunch featured a 'feminine' cow wearing light blue court shoes and bright red lipstick (fig. 10.4). The appearance of this figure was

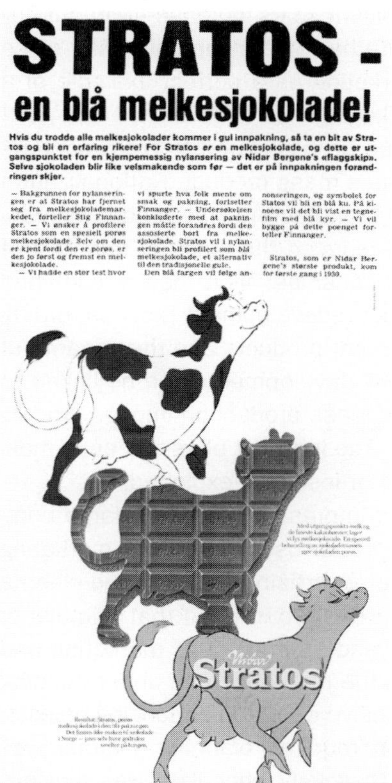

Fig. 10.4 Advertisement for Stratos, 1982, introducing the blue cow. The copy reads: 'Stratos—a blue milk chocolate!' Photograph courtesy of Nidar AS.

not particularly 'bovine'. She was an anthropomorphic, almost sensual character with her long lashes, closed eyelids and casual pose.[29] Nidar described the Stratos cow as 'innocently blue and friendly'.[30] This striking combination was definitely an eye-catcher. With this device, Nidar created an association between the 'blue' chocolate and the cow, underlining that this was a *milk* chocolate. This would turn out to be a very successful move, and soon the blue cow was one of Norway's best-known brand symbols. Furthermore, the use of a blue cow demonstrated that it was possible to challenge the naturalistic approach that dominated much of the advertising at the time by introducing paradoxical and artificial elements. On the one hand, this was a milk chocolate; on the other, the milk chocolate was disconnected from traditional conceptions of milk, cows and nature.

The primary aims of the rebranding were to highlight Stratos as a milk chocolate and to give the brand a profile of its own: 'Stratos. The blue milk chocolate'. There was no emphasis on the porous texture in this campaign. This was considered an already-familiar feature. The objective was to reach new target groups. All in all, this must be said to have been a very successful campaign. The campaign resulted in a significant sales increase—without any changes having been made to the chocolate bar.[31] This campaign has since been cited by an introductory guide to marketing as a perfect example of a successful reformulation of profile and packaging.[32]

The changes Stratos was put through can be connected to many contemporary conditions. For one thing, Stratos was a mass product. Rationalization of the production had made it cheaper to manufacture the goods. Increasingly automated production machinery had reduced the costs of this part of the business operation. Like many other companies, Nidar had streamlined its product range through a so-called product redevelopment process, drastically reducing both the total number of different products and the variants of each type of product. One aspect of the new developments can be linked to changes in the production process. Modern mass production implies production of a large number of identical products. The inherent possibilities of making savings in this area had now been more or less fully exploited.

Stratos had problems creating a distinct impression among a large number of apparently similar chocolates. Here, Nidar used traditional marketing channels such as newspaper and magazine advertising, posters and cinema commercials. In this context it is important to keep in mind that stimulants like chocolate were cheap mass products, and as such their marketing and the way they were understood differed from the marketing and understanding of, say, a car. Unlike the purchasing of expensive or status-enhancing objects, buying mass products was not an act that required planning. Neither was chocolate a necessity like milk or bread. Obviously, chocolate was typically bought on impulse. With increasing affluence among Norway's population, impulse buying became more and more common. Consequently, the packaging design and its context became increasingly important.

BUT INSIDE, THEY ARE ALL THE SAME?

When Stratos was first introduced, the innovative effort was primarily directed at creating new types of chocolate. The packaging received less attention. If a label did not sell well, it was removed from the product range and replaced by a new one. Rebranding through extensive campaigns and redesigned packaging and advertisement material in the style of the 1982 Stratos makeover was not an obvious strategy. It was only in the postwar era that the packaging gained a significantly important role as a competitive tool in the consumer product market. During this period, the design of the packaging gradually became an integrated part of the product development.[33]

The packaging has several functions. Originally, its primary function was to protect the product. It also has the function of facilitating the handling and use of the product. Furthermore, it helps the consumer identify the product and provides information about it. In addition, it can be used as a means of competition—as a medium for signalling what we may call additional properties or added values. The increasing significance of the packaging was above all a result of four factors. First, the new self-service shops had made the consumers' buying patterns much more dependent on the direct encounter with the product. Thus, the shape and visual character of the packaging became more important than it had been during the time when most products were sold over the counter. Second, the higher standard of living had made consumers less price-minded and more willing to pay for other qualities than the ones primarily satisfied by the product. Third, the increasing brand name competition made it necessary for the companies to differentiate their products, in order to set them apart from those of their competitors. Fourth, the product lifecycle had become shorter, among other things as a result of the technical development and stiffer competition. In order to prolong the lifecycle of a product and thus improve the financial result, relaunching the product often makes sense. This requires modifications that show that new value has been added to the product. This may be a matter of new packaging adding positive value, as we have seen in the case of the Stratos bar, or design features helping convince the consumer that this is a new product.

During the early years of the Nidar company, the confectioner was the pivotal figure in the work of innovation. The confectioner's ability to create new products based on craft traditions and experience was decisive for the company's ability to present chocolates which won approval amongst consumers. With time, the laboratory, often as a rhetorical source, was to play an increasingly important role. The making of the Stratos is a good example of how the laboratory engineer, with his or her scientific tools and knowledge, became a driving force in product development. The rebranding of the Stratos in the 1980s shows that new groups had acquired a central position in the activities of innovation: among them were marketing experts, designers, economists and advertising professionals.

REDESIGN AS RESUSCITATION

In 1987 an incident occurred that might have meant the end of Nidar. In March, doctors and hospitals were contacted by people who had fallen ill. They reported severe digestive problems, and tests showed that they had been infected by salmonella bacteria.[34] Since these bacteria are rare in Norway and since they can sometimes be life-threatening, the Food Control Authority quickly sounded the alarm. Very soon the source of the infections was found. A press release announced that the salmonella bacteria had been detected in chocolate produced at Nidar's factory. The bacteria were first found in Stratos, but soon they were also detected in two other products.[35] The case became hot front-page news in the national newspapers, and it was given extensive coverage in the radio and television newscasts. The newspapers reported sick children in hospitals and various problems tied to food safety. The fear stirred by the incident was tangible, and the coverage was extensive.

This controversy, which must be the worst nightmare of any food manufacturer, contained a twofold problem. First, the source of the salmonella infestation needed to be identified and eliminated. This, however, was probably not the greatest problem. It was a challenge in the short term, and it would require great effort and cost a good deal of money, but according to all experience, it would be solved relatively quickly. A more serious challenge was connected to the fact that a food manufacturer always needs the customers' support. Consumer confidence was at stake, and in the worst case this could be a problem with long-term implications. Therefore, Nidar stopped production, and all chocolate produced at the factory after the outbreak of the epidemic situation was supposed to be brought back to the factory and destroyed. The slogan 'Dangerously good', which was used to promote one of Nidar's chocolates, had suddenly acquired an aftertaste.

In the beginning of April a small army of company employees and hired hands were mobilized to relieve all shops and sales outlets of the recalled chocolate. The production of chocolate was suspended, and the premises were disinfected.[36] Parallel to the emptying of all Nidar products from the shop shelves, the Food Control Authority together with Nidar examined all production lines.[37] Other measures followed: Nidar started its own bacteriological laboratory for product testing and analysis. Furthermore, all chocolate was to be manufactured from externally purchased chocolate paste with a certificate guaranteeing its conformance with health and safety standards. The cocoa beans from Ghana were replaced by cocoa paste carried by tank lorry from Belgium.[38] Upon arrival, it was sent via a closed system to different mixing and production stations. One last consequence of the incident, for both Nidar and other chocolate manufacturers, was more frequent visits from Food Control Authority officials.[39]

Late in April, the Food Control Authority gave the Nidar premises in Trondheim the all-clear. Nidar was able to resume its chocolate production.[40] By summer, Nidar's sales manager Stig Finnanger could finally breathe freely, having established that sales were back to normal, and one of the 'salmonella chocolates', Stratos, was again the top-selling brand. He concluded that 'the market has a short memory, and the chocolate eaters are not easily excited'. However, the explanation for the restored market trust and acceptance was not quite that simple.

The practical safety measures implemented to safeguard the products against actual contamination were only one part of the effort to restore the chocolate to full health. After the incident, Nidar contacted the advertising agency Nordskar & Thorkildsen LB. What to do now? One possibility was to discontinue the labels involved in the controversy, replacing them with new alternatives. Another was to go on the offensive with new and powerful marketing of the existing chocolates. The latter option was chosen, and the outcome of this strategy was to prove very successful. The design of this campaign thus merits a closer look.

The planned campaign was intended to last for five weeks and cost NOK 6 million. The last stage of this campaign was a screen advertisement set in Harlem, New York. Here, an African American man made jokes about Stratos and salmonella. After reporting that Stratos was back, he looked straight into the camera while giving his concluding comment: 'No shit, man!' Nidar made no attempt to cover up the facts; instead, humour was used to disarm the critics. 'No shit' referred, of course, to the stomach problems many people had experienced as a result of eating chocolate contaminated by salmonella. In short, the strategy adopted by the Nidar management, namely to accept full responsibility and maintain an open attitude to the problems, was rewarded with success. The newspaper press, whose reports had initially been rather sensationalist, undercutting the company's credibility, started to express a much less critical approach. Nidar's management took pre-emptive initiatives in relation to the media and invested much effort to create an active and positive dialogue with the press.

Nidar's campaign went beyond recapturing customer trust in Nidar and Stratos. Following the first 'fire-fighting campaign', Stratos was modified. As had been the case at the previous crossroads, the recipe was kept unchanged. The cocoa paste was no longer produced by the Nidar factory, but, otherwise, the chocolate bar remained the same. The greatest change was to the brand image of the Stratos and its market profiling. The Stratos cow had become a well-established trademark, with a high degree of market recognition. Consolidating and evolving this trademark was Nidar's chosen strategy for the way forward. Part of the suggested strategy was to create a new expression. As a counterweight to the concerns tied to the contamination of Stratos, a wild and daring, almost masculine cow was created (fig. 10.5). It is difficult to determine to what extent this amounted to a sex change or simply to a wish on Nidar's part to add other expressions to what had up to then been a somewhat sedate bovine character. In late May, the sales figures had already recovered to

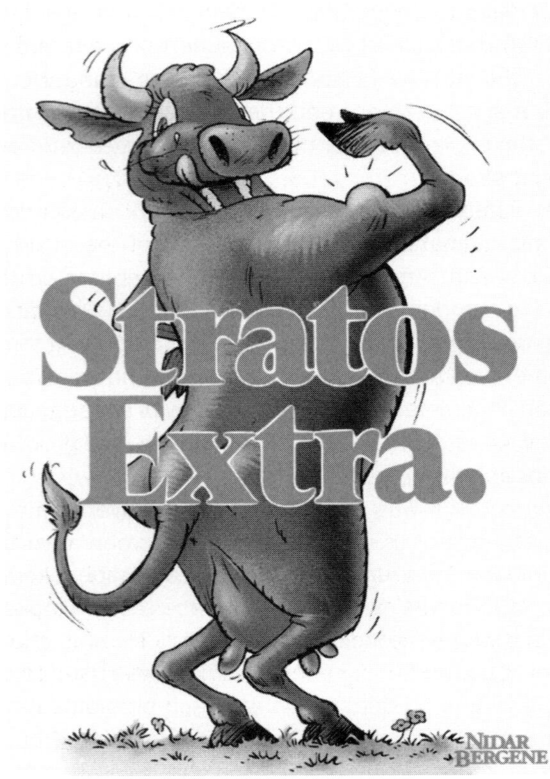

Fig. 10.5 Advertisement for Stratos, 1987, featuring the transformed bull-like cow. Photograph courtesy of Nidar AS.

90–95 per cent of normal levels, indicating that the company had managed to recapture market confidence by its redesign.[41] In the following years, Stratos was again Nidar's most important product.

DIFFERENT BUT STILL THE SAME?

In this essay we have explored how the Stratos chocolate bar was created and developed during times of both expansion and crisis. The biography of the chocolate tells us the story of a successful product that has undergone small modifications as well as more dramatic transformations. The taste and appearance of the actual chocolate have been subject to assessments and adjustments, but in the end, the original recipe has been retained. The physical shape of the chocolate itself, on the other hand, has been redesigned ad infinitum; the conventional bar has appeared in numerous different sizes over the years, and more recently it has taken the shape of 'gold bars', small pieces wrapped in cylindrical rolls, cow-shaped figurines, and so on. Still, the packaging and marketing have probably been the most important elements in designing the Stratos. The packaging has been used to focus on small details, making them visible, whereas the marketing has interacted with the greater societal discourses and trends. A very important aspect is the interaction between producer and consumer. From the 1980s onwards, Nidar has put great emphasis on surveying and listening to consumer reactions.

This study also indicates how various social changes materialized in production and consumption. Our starting point was that design has been, and remains, a complex process, where it can be difficult to delineate what is design and what can be conceptualized by other terms. We have also seen how design started out as an informal process carried out by confectioners and has developed into a specialized task performed by professional industrial designers and advertising agencies—and, one might say, with additional input from consumers. As suggested in the introduction, it has been difficult to pinpoint any impact from the overall development in the broader field of design during the period in question. Nevertheless, the biography of the Stratos chocolate suggests that its fate has been connected to important social currents. Thus, it is possible not only to regard the life of the chocolate as a mirror image of the minor and major events of Norwegian society but also to use it as a lens through which central features of social change can be explored.

–11–

Exhibitable Furniture: Interpreting Images of Design

Malene Breunig

Artefacts of international modernism are often portrayed in white, airy spaces with few distracting elements. Yet this visual framing of aesthetic purity contains a historical and ideological meaning that is anything but neutral. It is bound to an ideal conception of the near empty, uncluttered, dematerialized and abstract spatial setting as defining features of modernity. This was partly driven by a shared distaste among modernist architects, artists and designers for bourgeois domesticity and partly by a desire to create classless houses and material objects that, they believed, would replace the values of middle-class Victorian interiors with more democratic ones of efficiency and utility.

What this type of display shows is that artefacts do not get their meanings by their materiality alone but also by the way they are mediated. This mediation occurs through language as in the case of criticism, promotion and review, but in the following I examine how the framing of design as artefacts of high modernism occurs through the physical framing of modernity's medium of choice, the photographic image. Thereby I will reconsider some of the meanings usually ascribed to modernist artefacts, not according to their form, but according to their visual and spatial display in images.

The mediation or mise en scène of design through photographic images is explored through an analytical case study of the Danish photographer Keld Helmer-Petersen's collaborative work with the Danish furniture designer Poul Kjærholm during the years 1954–80. By working closely with Helmer-Petersen, Kjærholm not only developed his design practice and promotional strategies within the twin forces of rationality and efficiency rooted in modern technology and industry but also found valuable inspiration and aspirations in the highly irrational sphere of contemporary art. By embracing a minimalistic and self-referential mode of expression, Kjærholm thus aligned his furniture with 'the spirit of modernity', which many modern artists conceived as both fascinating and forbidding, emancipating yet alienating. He was concerned with abstraction and materializing internalized conceptual ideas rather than narrative, representation or ornamentation. As such he found a kindred soul in Helmer-Petersen, who contributed to making photography more than a journalistic enterprise; instead, he saw it as a modern art form.

This essay first introduces the scenography of Helmer-Petersen's photography, which provides the basis for interpreting his mediation of Kjærholm's design, before analysing in more detail the result of this collaboration—that is the photographic display of Kjærholm's furniture—in its various aspects. This is done in relation to Brian O'Doherty's observations of the visual and spatial dogmas of modernist art as expressed in his collection of essays *Inside the White Cube*. The concluding discussion centres on the implications of the photographic display of Kjærholm's design, seen as an aesthetic expression of the immaterial modern values of defamiliarization, or 'the uncanny', as it emerges in the mediation of Kjærholm's design for the modern home as photogenic and exhibitable furniture.

PHOTO GRAPHICS

Helmer-Petersen developed a distinctive photographic style in the 1940s, working with physical elements from contemporary urban industrial culture. Yet it was not the human consequences of new production forms nor, later on, the impact of prosperity, as in the overflow of material goods and destruction of the environment, that were portrayed through a critical lens. Instead, the motifs were based on the aesthetic diversity of modern anonymous daily objects as in the form, structure, patterns, materiality and texture found in, for example, road signs, oil barrels, electricity poles, cranes, railroad tracks and factory buildings. This was done without any picturesque or anecdotal effects but solely through a perceptual sensibility towards the qualities of the visual phenomenon. Helmer-Petersen was able to render daily life familiar but obscure it in a way that partly removed the motifs from their context and partly removed photography from the medium's traditional documentary function.

The objective was instead artistic and motivated by a search for a modern, yet classic sense of beauty. With light as the direct source, Helmer-Petersen cropped and abstracted his visual impressions as graphical compositions of well-defined form, line, space and texture. Verbally, he expressed it as an aphorism: 'Contemporary Art is the Experience of Contemporary Forms and Contemporary Materials expressed in Contemporary Materials and Contemporary Forms'.[1] The images thereby came to touch on the conception of a confrontation with modernity, referring not to an opposition but to a situational encounter: standing face-to-face with a new world absorbed in detail and single pictures and, in a particular moment, seeing and recognizing its aesthetic potential.

The simplification and abstraction of the images, which were not completely non-figurative yet in all cases distant from the motif's contextual grounding,

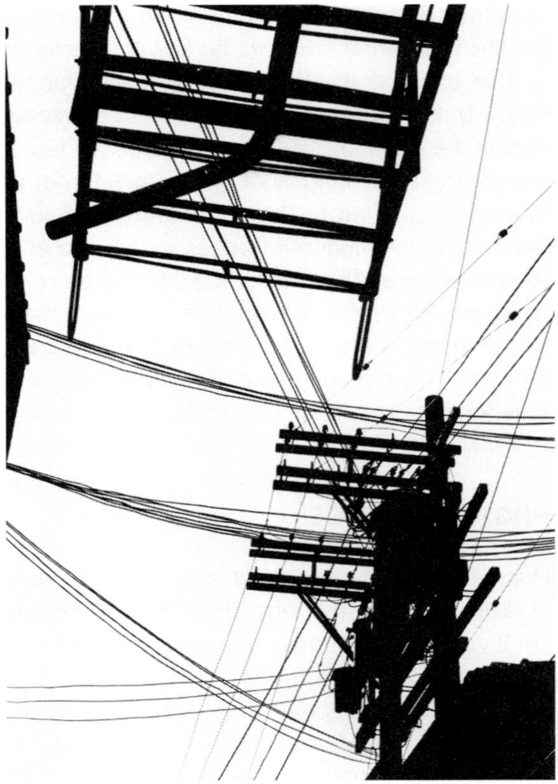

Fig. 11.1 Keld Helmer-Petersen, 'Wires', *Fragments of a City*, 1960. Courtesy of Keld Helmer-Petersen.

are characteristic of Helmer-Petersen's *122 Color Photographs* (1949). The book created a great deal of attention and brought a prestigious spread in the American photo-magazine *Life*.[2] Like many other European artists, Helmer-Petersen traveled a year later to the United States to study at the Chicago Institute of Design. Here he acquainted himself with and was inspired by photographers such as Harry Callahan and Aaron Siskind, and a year later he received a temporary teaching position there. During his stay in Chicago, Helmer-Petersen developed his high black-and-white contrast photography creating a graphic expression with sharp silhouettes. In 1953 some of these pictures were admitted to the exhibition Post-war European Photography at the Museum of Modern Art (MoMA) in New York. A selection of these images was published in his 1960 book, *Fragments of a City* (fig. 11.1).

Despite an obvious affinity to the prevalent constructionist art of that time, Helmer-Petersen had not yet experienced his artistic breakthrough in Denmark. Due to a conservative art institution, photography was seen for a long time as a journalistic medium and as such could not express topics of an individual or universal character but merely a situational, specific content of daily concerns. However, after building up a niche for himself as a photographer of modern architecture and design, Helmer-Petersen was hired in 1964 as a teacher of architectural photography at the Royal Danish Academy of Fine Arts, where Poul Kjærholm held a position as a lecturer on furniture and spatial art.

Helmer-Petersen's own generation of Danish architects, such as Jørn Utzon, Finn Juhl and Jørgen Bo, had found in him a congenial interpreter of their different modern visions. And they understood the importance of the meaning-constructing function of photography's visual mediation. According to these young architects, Helmer-Petersen's focus on the objects themselves, in particular their construction principles, proportions, materiality, palette and variable patterns, contributed to developing a sensibility towards a modern, transparent and disciplined language. They believed this to be without illusions and myth. Similarly it was the reverence for and the careful configuration of a presumably objective aesthetics as a modern, unromantic beauty ideal which provided the foundation for a mutually inspired collaboration between Helmer-Petersen and Kjærholm. However, this partnership, established in the first half of the 1950s and lasting until Kjærholm's death in 1980, did in fact obey the modernist myth of the White Cube's superior aesthetics.

AN ARTISTIC ACCORD

The emphasis on the material qualities of things and their aesthetic appeal meant that Helmer-Petersen and Kjærholm, as collaborators, were not exactly loyal custodians of the social welfare project of early functionalism. The reforms of the interwar period in Denmark as well as in the other Scandinavian countries, which aimed at bringing a large degree of social equality and cultural homogeneity to society, was for them a decrepit utopia. Yet they did find the holistic-oriented drive for an egalitarian material culture sympathetic. And Kjærholm's spare statements about his work show that, in much the same way as the older generation of Danish designers such as Poul Henningsen and Børge Mogensen imagined it, he thought it possible to provide the majority with better and more suitable furniture than the free market and what he considered to be the unrefined taste of the hedonistic consumer—as described in Minna Sarantola-Weiss's contribution to this volume—could generate.[3]

What set Kjærholm's conception of design and its role apart from earlier functionalist notions of social reform was that he was witnessing the welfare society becoming a reality. For Kjærholm this meant the abundance of imported and mass-produced goods could be constrained neither through idealistic appeals to the public about the blessings of 'good design' nor through polemic statements about society. According to Kjærholm, it was through a qualitative aesthetic superiority and formal discipline that an alternative could be proposed to the conspicuous consumption and 'bad taste' of the petty bourgeoisie, as well as to functionalism's promising ideology and rather uncritical adaptation to industrialization. His contribution therefore remained predominantly nonverbal and never really became a factor in a new public opinion. Completely devoid of the ambition for mass popularity and easy commercial rewards, he acknowledged laconically, 'I only leave a choice to the user if it does not damage the piece's intrinsic value.'[4] The physical-material features of a design were qualities in their own right, and the furniture should be photographed and exhibited accordingly.

The spatial and visual mediation of Kjærholm's furniture thus marked a revolt against the conception of design as a means to social reform so prevalent in Scandinavia throughout much of the twentieth century—the demise of which is pithily analysed in Helena Mattsson's contribution to this volume. This revolt was strengthened by the fact that Helmer-Petersen's artistic acquisition of the photographic medium was not in accordance with these promising visions and hopes for an aesthetic democratization potential in modernity's mechanical production processes, as declared for instance by Walter Benjamin.[5] According to this critical notion photography was seen as one of the new visual media that would irrevocably eliminate the aura of art with its distinguishing values of the original and the ideal, which according to tradition surrounded the work of art and preserved it for a narrow privileged elite. Benjamin did not, however, describe in any detail how this democratization would actually work within photography. And, more important, he avoided the question of how photography, as an aesthetic mode of expression and not only a medium for commercial purposes, might itself possess or mediate properties of aura.

Assigning aura or value to mass-produced things as self-legitimate, unique entities was in fact exactly what Helmer-Petersen and Kjærholm attempted to establish. Together they endowed the spatial presentation and photographic styling with an aesthetic and somewhat existential objective as well, which elevated the furniture to cult status, as in modernism's realm of fine art. This strategy took place in continuation of the practice among modern architecture and design photographers of the 1920s and 1930s, who had strongly accentuated the diagonal lines and smooth surfaces in black-and-white photos. The motifs were presented as pure graphical patterns or abstract compositions with a slight tendency towards a fetishism of industrial culture's formal language, thus manipulating the fact that the modern architects in many cases used a wide palette of colors. This prevailing impression given by the extremely aesthetized visual mediation of modernism's spaces as purely white marks what has been termed 'a photographic fallacy'.[6]

The formally reduced visual features of modernism thus became a myth sustained by the strategic deployment of mass culture's advertising techniques and artistic promotion. In these pictures, the furniture is placed exclusively in closed white spaces without people and ordinary daily objects. Neither are there references to the outside world, nor any visible concern for the average consumer's practical needs, and the immaterial message is not mediated to the consumer by any additional texts. Instead, the photographs dwell on the reduced expression of the things and their distinct details, while accentuating the visual leanness and lightness of the furniture through a diffuse, almost shade-free lighting contrasting with the heavy weight of the materials. According to Helmer-Petersen and Kjærholm's ideal conception, the furniture would thereby appear easily comprehensible although pictured in asymmetrical, almost abstract planes and singular pieces, revealing only its skeletal, anatomical parts. The only thing added was a sacral aura of sublime 'furniture as art' aspiring to transcend time and space. However, this photographic presentation and rendering is by no means timeless. Indeed, it is historically conditioned and grounded to a specific cultural set of values, which were only understandable to a select group familiar with the required cultural code.

PHOTOGENIC DESIGN

Shortly before Helmer-Petersen began his collaboration with Kjærholm, he articulated a number of principles regarding artistic photography. In his view, photography was characterized by a process of abstraction suspending the medium's quotidian function as a way of representing something else, while at the same time establishing photography as an aesthetic mode of expression in its own right. What the genuine artistic photography rendered was thus not identical with the object, which could be a prosaic clip from reality. It was an autonomous, interpretive mediation of the depicted object, developed in a complex graphic process:

> The time of the photographer is at dusk or in foggy weather, when the silhouettes of objects stand clearly and distinctly against the white background. The stem of the plant and the crane unveils with remarkable clarity its incredible structure, its contours and hollow spaces, its play with lines and the distribution of surfaces. The commonplace is literally displayed in a new light; revealing many new and bizarre sides of its being, unknown features and proportions; and moved by such new and peculiar grace the photographer lays down his pictorial rectangle around the black patterns, lines and fields of forces, frames his experience on the celluloid membrane of the film, projecting, finally, in the red dusk of the darkroom his enlarging cone of light through the magic ghostlike negative, and reproduces in enlarged scale and strengthened contrast his graphic symbol on the white, glossy paper.[7]

Helmer-Petersen's description of his photographic approach establishes a split optic in relation to physical-material phenomena. A sharpened perceptual presence and a hermeneutic reflection are required at the same time. A fascination with the reality of the concrete features of the original is essential but cannot stand alone. As pictures, these features become interesting only when a process of abstraction has taken place in the decontextualization of the source motif from its context, that is in the choice of framing, focus, perspective, editing, cropping and format.

In this creative process the character of the motif is changed, and indeed this is the case in Helmer-Petersen's photographs of Kjærholm's design: the furniture loses its ties to its prosaic functions (figs. 11.2 and 11.3). Instead, we see them as abstract configurations, as easily noticed material constellations and constructions. There is no trace of a lived life as, for example, domestic props or just conventional representative distinctive marks, not even as expressive statements. From an immediate impression these images and the more flat displays seem illusion-less. They do not pretend to evoke the middle class's dream of affluence in a traditional way nor a happy nuclear family in practical and cosy physical surroundings. Nevertheless, with

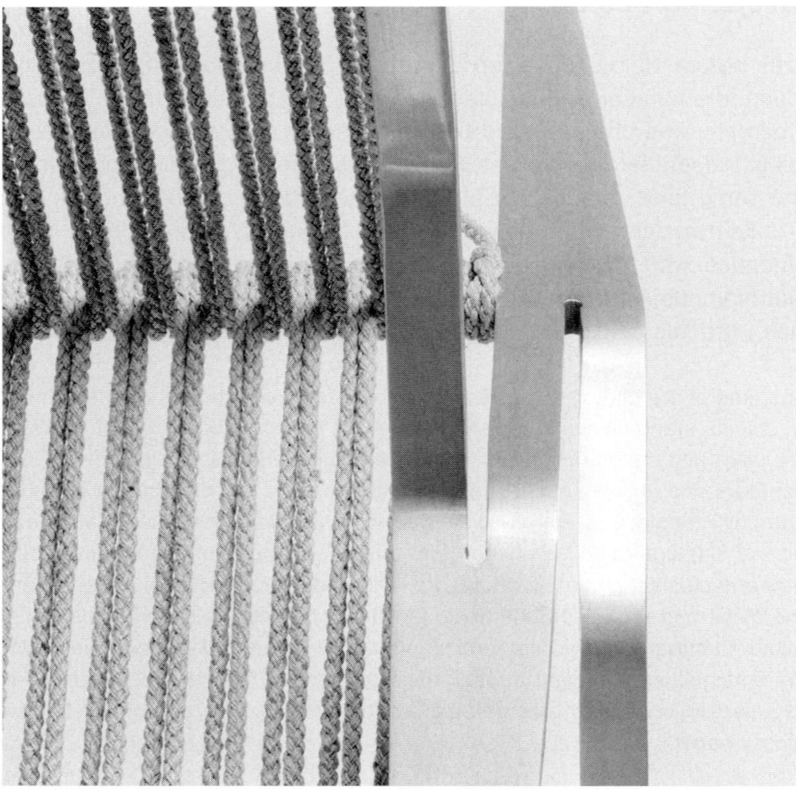

Fig. 11.2 Keld Helmer-Petersen, photo of detail of lounge chair PK25, 1951. Courtesy of Keld Helmer-Petersen.

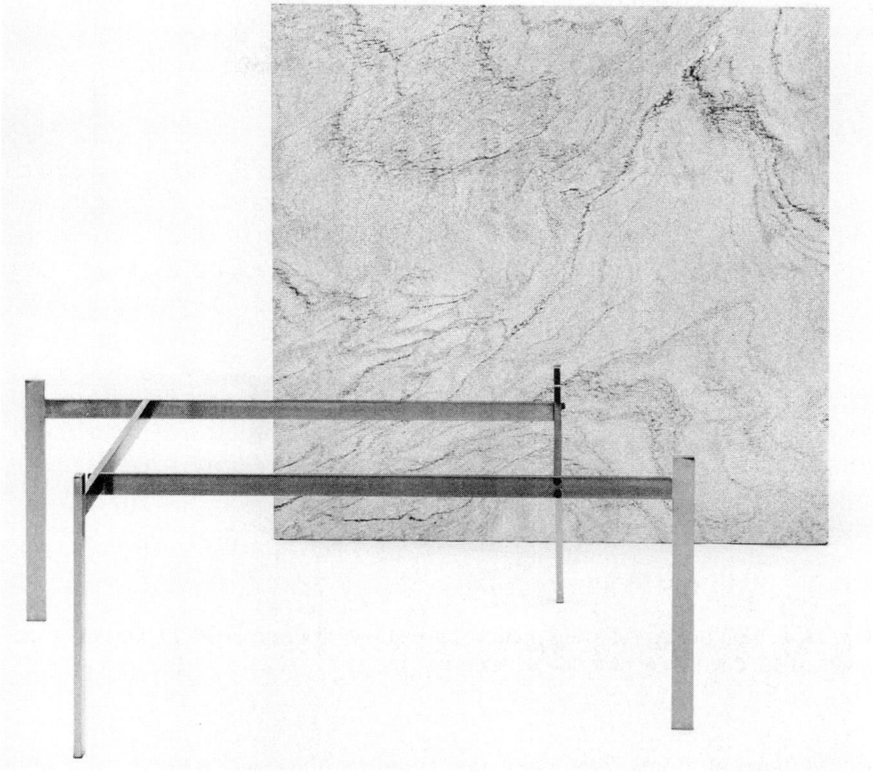

Fig. 11.3 Keld Helmer-Petersen, photo of coffee table PK61, 1955. Courtesy of Keld Helmer-Petersen.

these pictures Helmer-Petersen endowed Kjærholm's design with an intensely meaningful space, in the same way as he conveyed the meaning added to the furniture in an anything but objective photographic medium.

In accordance with Helmer-Petersen's 'photo graphics', the pictures work not just as the medium for a specific content—in this case Kjærholm's designs—but as a gestalt for meaningful space around them, which forcefully contributes to defining the furniture hermeneutically. The pictures' emptiness of anything but the essential being displayed fills it so much more by its claims to the observer of exclusion. Literally speaking, these pictures focus exactly on this—the emptiness, an untouched space that is not weighed down by the overstuffed interior decorating style of the middle class and its conventional domesticity (fig. 11.4). Helmer-Petersen thereby displays the furniture not merely as material objects which could be bought but as iconographic images of a yearning for perfection, control, discipline and exclusion. These pictures both portray and become aesthetic objects. They do not attempt to solve or cover the surrounding reality's social, economic and political conditions but

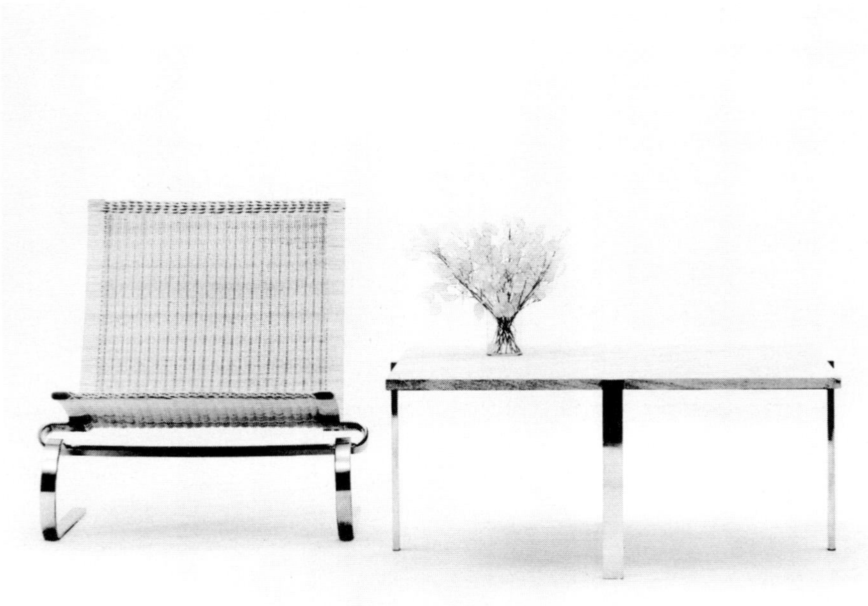

Fig. 11.4 Keld Helmer-Petersen, photo of tableau with lounge chair PK20 and coffee table PK65, 1965. Courtesy of Keld Helmer-Petersen.

rather conceal them. They 'paint over' reality's obtrusive 'images' with white and strip them bare, in a sense, dematerializing the cultural components of the physical space to make room for a mental illumination.

Thus in the darkroom and during their photo shoots, Helmer-Petersen and Kjærholm acted like iconoclasts. Through a visual and spatial minimalism, they would make room for critical reflection of a modernity in which visual and material culture abounded in obtrusive impressions and compulsive consumerism, resulting in a mental overload and blocking of quality stimulus. At the same time, through these minimalist pictures Helmer-Petersen and Kjærholm expressed what hard-core functionalists and concerned media-sociologists would call a pretense of reality, an artificial universe of photogenic and exhibitable furniture sculptures in white spaces. As such these pictures can be perceived as a suppression, or loss, of reality. Nevertheless, Helmer-Petersen's work aspired to maintain or re-establish certain aspects of the ideological values of early-twentieth-century high modernism and its promoters, who desired to keep art uncontaminated by both popular culture and the triviality of everyday life.

This conception of modernism's white cube did not materialize on a broad scale in art museums until late in the twentieth century. But ideologically and metaphorically it became a predominant figure from the 1930s, when modern architecture and design were canonized and visually mediated at MoMA. For the priests of high modernism, such as MoMA's first director, Alfred H. Barr, and the head of its department of architecture, Philip Johnson, museum spaces were considered segregated from the mass production and standardization of industrialization in order to promote the inward-looking gallery space as a last refuge from and antidote to modernity's social and psychological turbulences. Accordingly, artefacts were displayed removed from the contexts of their production, use, or social function within particular cultures, indicating that the artefacts were for the purpose of cultivating aesthetic appreciation and intellectual contemplation only. Although looking nothing like the decorated interiors of conventional homes, these modernist gallery spaces—not least for the persistent supporters of modernism—thus reconsolidated some of the defining attributes and virtues of the home, in particular in that it was not public and therefore could remain free of the gritty material concerns and ambitions that governed the realm of commerce. If order, stability and a wholly positive sense of progress were impossible to maintain in the world of lived experience, perhaps they could be established in the ideal world of an increasingly formalist artistic practice.

However, domesticity's other defining quality, as being a place for privacy, intimacy and an assertion of individual and family identity, did not move into the modernist gallery space—nor did these socio-emotional functions concern Helmer-Petersen and Kjærholm. Neither practical matters nor romanticized references to daily routines and conventional rituals in the private sphere of the home appear in their images. The furniture is placed in interior settings as spectacles to be witnessed by an audience of outsiders, rather than as comfort zones of recreation away from public life. As such, Helmer-Petersen and Kjærholm both act as modernist exhibitors displaying highly valuable gallery pieces and at the same time transforming the physical space around them into a puritan, almost monastic context of pure order and structural simplicity. To explore this further, I look at Helmer-Petersen's images of Kjærholm's design through the ideology embodied in the modernist gallery space and the myths surrounding it as characterized by the New York-based artist and art critic Brian O'Doherty.

'FROM THIS ROOM BURPS AND FARTS ARE EXILED'

Published in *Artforum* in the late 1970s and early 1980s, O'Doherty's essays evoked sympathetic attention among the conceptually oriented and formally experimental artists and art critics, especially in the United States, where a comprehensive revolt against modernism's formal language and influential institutions occurred. In these critical essays the gallery space was in retrospect construed as the White Cube: the incarnation of modernism's aesthetic discourse. The assumption was, according to O'Doherty, that the undecorated and regular illuminated space with long, stretched-out white walls without windows would not dominate the public's perception of the singular art piece. Indeed, it was assumed that the space was meaning-neutral, and this had since the 1920s become the dominating norm for the display of modern art and design. However, for O'Doherty, who mostly uses the concept of the White Cube metaphorically, it was obvious that this had to be unveiled as an illusion or rather as profoundly normative and exclusive. Displaying art in this ideal space had had its art historical rationality as a manifestation of a non-restricted room for the actions of the artist. Painting and sculpture had to be freed of literary myths, artistic and institutional dogmas and middle-class materialism. But the modern gallery space had itself, not least during the 1960s and 1970s, become a mythologizing power factor. It blocked out critical self-reflection and artistic progression, because it froze the exhibited artefacts in a position of inviolable cultish relics.

The norms and rules of the modernistic gallery space had also, in O'Doherty's presentation, come to include or at least influence the public's behaviour. It had led to or stimulated a pathos-filled aesthetic sensibility towards the exhibited objects and had reduced modern art to a matter of the individual's psychosocial alienation from society. Thus O'Doherty suggests that the intentions behind the White Cube were in part to imitate the modern human's sense of mental separation from the surroundings and in part to encourage reflection on and identification with this existential condition. The causal effects of these were not held back, he points out:

> So powerful are the perceptual fields of force within this chamber that, once outside it, art can lapse into secular status. Conversely, things become art in a space where powerful ideas about art focus on them. Indeed, the object frequently becomes the medium through which these ideas are manifested and proffered for discussion . . .
>
> . . . Works of art are mounted, hung, scattered for study. Their ungrubby surfaces are untouched by time and its vicissitudes . . . Indeed the presence of that odd piece of furniture, your own body, seems superfluous, an intrusion. The space offers the thought that while eyes and minds are welcome, space-occupying bodies are not.[8]

The use of the present tense in his language suggest that O'Doherty's historical timing of the White Cube might be a bit off. It was very much a contemporary phenomenon when he wrote his essays. The fact that this narrative modernist concept had only become acknowledged as self-evident at the time of a general intellectual and formal rupture with modernism explains why a similar exclusion mechanism dominates Helmer-Petersen's images from 1955 onwards. These are obviously not spaces which can be physically entered. They can only be observed as two-dimensional surfaces and as objectified artefacts for ideal distant perusal. As spectators, we do not need to share our visual experience with others, whose corporal presence would disturb the 'picture'. The photograph's reproduction of the constructivistic composition of the designer's forming, fashioning and styling allows the space to be untouched by human presence, including our own. As spectators of these still lifes, we are therefore not led to contemplate the more mundane qualities of the furniture as a practical stage set-up in an everyday scenography. The images mediate the furniture as aesthetic objects and their conceptual framework. They also mediate the physical forms we can observe and the consequences, which, according to the designer and the photographer, justify the choices made in respect to the form, material and production costs.

The thoughts behind this set-up mirror, in O'Doherty's interpretive scope, a central existential condition in modernity. The modern urban individual is used to interactions with the surroundings that seldom occur in a direct and immediate way. The interaction takes place through a 'filter', in this case visually mediated.

> It often feels as if we can no longer experience anything if we don't first alienate it. In fact, alienation may now be a necessary preface to experience. Anything too close to us bears the label 'Objectify and Re-ingest'. This mode of handling experience—especially art experience—is inescapably modern. But while its pathos is obvious, it is not all negative. As a mode of experience it can be called degenerate, but it is no more so than our 'space' is degenerate. It is simply the result of certain necessities pressed upon us. Much of our experience can only be brought home through mediation.[9]

Helmer-Petersen's images of Kjærholm's design evoke exactly this intellectual distance, which additionally accords with the furniture's own assertion. Without necessarily subscribing to a conception of design as something that in the same way as art can contain an intended message, it is evident that Helmer-Petersen's pictures do not create but rather accentuate an impression of a state of calmness around their motif. The pictures intensify the sense that the furniture breaks with conventional notions of domesticity and thereby contribute to Kjærholm's desire not to lull the furniture's occupants into a stuporous state of relaxation but instead keep them firmly supported and thereby alert.

STAGED SHOWPIECES

This effort to create a modern sense of comfort by virtue of two seemingly opposing psycho-emotional conditions, intimacy and control, played a vital role in Kjærholm's strategy as a designer. The same effort can be discerned also in projects where Kjærholm and Helmer-Petersen exhibited their respective work together. In these scenographic 'frameworks', carefully selected pieces of Kjærholm's design were exhibited alongside Helmer-Petersen's photographs, acting in Helmer-Petersen's optics as powerful representations of the modern interior, recognizing little difference between the private and public spheres. These images then did not only establish a cross-aesthetic dialogue between the different media of design and photography and their attributes. They also staged the interiors as still lifes giving the impression that the realm of domesticity must be seen as a highly aesthetic scene detached not only from everyday triviality but from a political agenda as well.

This ambiguity between inside and outside, private and public, was literally manifested in the showroom established in 1959 by E. Kold Christensen, the company manufacturing Kjærholm's designs, on Bredgade, a high-end street in Copenhagen dominated by art galleries, antique shops and auction houses (fig. 11.5). Taking its place in this exclusive environment, the showroom exhibited changing displays of Kjærholm's furniture staged in front of Helmer-Petersen's photostats. As an aesthetic whole, then, this collaboration was well adapted to high society, even at street level. For people strolling by, their expectations of elegance were met with a subtle distinguishing cultural expression, which was visually striking yet inaccessible. The showroom was in fact

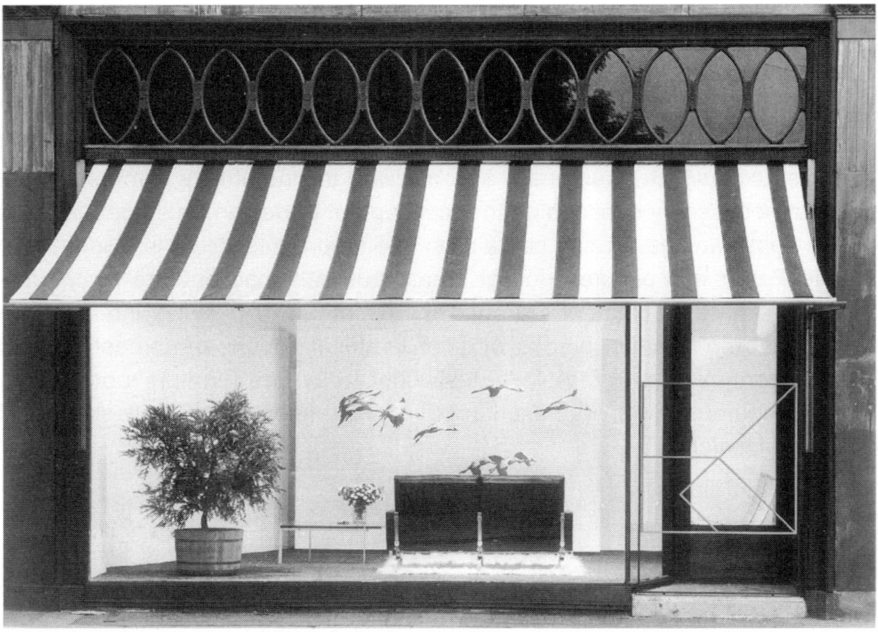

Fig. 11.5 Keld Helmer-Petersen, photo of Kold Christensen's showroom, Bredgade 27, Copenhagen, 1959. Courtesy of Keld Helmer-Petersen.

more of a showcase in that it could not be entered: the door was barred by a large grille in the shape of the company's logo—also designed by Kjærholm—making the inaccessibility literal as well as allegorical. The furniture could only be experienced by spectators as artefacts in an exhibition case.

Allowing no intrusion, this showroom's black-painted surface and grey-and-white striped awning, which graphically corresponded with the changing displays, thus staged the kind of distance required of a spectator in the contemplation of a work of art in a museum. This was even implied in the set-up of this specific tableau, where Kjærholm's sofa PK31 (1958), covered with black leather, is placed with its back facing the spectator. This was done not only to show the back's delicate craftsmanship but also to mark an undisturbed private space between the front of the sofa, where the spectator can imagine himself warming his feet on the white long-haired carpet. Observing and perhaps calmed by Helmer-Petersen's graceful photo of flying birds in a retouched white sky, the spectator is offered a visual depth in the otherwise-narrow room and a mental opening of an almost ethereal character. The square coffee table PK61 (1956), with a transparent glass top and narrow, low and light staggered legs in matted chromium-plated flat steel, is therefore placed out to the side, just like the potted tree, and on the opposite side are two perpendicularly placed lounge chairs, PK22 (1955), whose lean profile can be detected in the picture behind the door's logo.

Asked whether this tight, squared and dispersed furniture arrangement froze the space and its user, Kjærholm confidently remarked:

> No, an interior will not die when pieces are arranged at right angles; it will not stiffen. People themselves are the mobile elements in a room, after all. Naturally it is important to plan the static contact within each individual furniture group, the seated person's experience of the room that surrounds him. But movement, the experience of seeing others move around in relation to the room, and what the person himself experiences by moving around it are absolute concepts to work with. Walking over to the window, towards the light, and walking back again, from the light, for example, play a major role in the experience of a room. Even walking to and from a bookshelf.[10]

According to this conception, the showroom demonstrated, then, equivalently open and well-arranged compositions for a 'natural' and 'informal' patterned movement. Even more, it promoted a certain 'aesthetics of sitting' and 'moral of sitting' for the user of Kjærholm's design. This resembles Piet Mondrian's legendary sketches for the spatial installation 'Salon de Madame B. . . . , à Dresden' (1926) as interpreted by O'Doherty:

> In this space, the grossness of the body seems inappropriate; from this room burps and farts are exiled. Through systems of abutment and slide, rectangle and square define a space that places one inside a Cubist picture; the occupant

> is synthesized into a coefficient of order whose motion is in consonance with the rhythms enclosing him or her.[11]

In a similar way Helmer-Petersen and Kjærholm's conception of their pictures and furniture was the centre of an almost infinitely extendable spatial continuum. Their works were not supposed to manifest themselves as separate objects but together contribute to a creation of space, which was not just utilitarian and rational but formed a complete harmonic accord. In Helmer-Petersen's photographic rendering of this—which makes it possible to study it today—he created an equivalent sense of an autonomous space. Beyond a mere representation and promotion of Kjærholm's design, Helmer-Petersen's thorough understanding of the photographic medium's full potential provided the images with a status as static objects. Like artistic drawings or paintings they do not simply refer to a pre-existing object; they produce the object, or rather they construct how we should conceive it. The photographs thus become extraordinarily powerful mediators of the furniture.

As such Helmer-Petersen and Kjærholm took part in a cultural aestheticization process, which would become pronounced in the following years, when the visual expression enjoyed a privileged status as a broadly appealing and dominating communication form. However, it was only when postmodernists declared war on modernism, proclaiming the death of its grand narrative, that Helmer-Petersen and Kjærholm both metaphorically and literally kept to the aesthetics of the White Cube. It was not the public's desire for conspicuous consumption that they tried to ignite but rather their aesthetic sensibility and intellectual contemplation. As cultural mediators of new expressive forms and taste, they contributed hereby, also in their own self-understanding, to an aestheticization of everyday life. Especially in the second half of the twentieth century, this aestheticization became a prevalent feature of Western consumer societies, epitomized by the world of advertisement.[12] But Helmer-Petersen and Kjærholm practiced this in an idiom that rejected the predilection for easily available goods and profits they saw in popular culture.

This aspiration for both a physical-material and a metaphysical order was displayed in numerous ways in the showroom in Bredgade, since the palette here was kept almost identical to Helmer-Petersen's black-and-white reproduction. As such it did not hide the furniture's own idiom, but rather it materialized the design vocabulary's equivalent ideal context. It accentuated the intention of its subordinate and structuring role in respect to the space's compositional unity. The furniture—seldom more than 70 centimetres high—always looked delicate and unpretentious against both the three-winged white gallery space and the exclusive urban scenery in the foreground. The literally closed showroom, and especially the mediation of it as photographic images, tends towards a reduction of the furniture's three-dimensionality and thereby its qualities as a sculptural object. The furniture was supposed to present itself equally well from all sides. However, the photograph takes over or dictates with its optical elements our perceptual conception of the furniture.[13] They change the furniture from artefacts we can touch and sense the propositions of to surfaces seen in varied perspectives. However, this always occurs according to an artistic principle of composition based on ideal patterns of eye movement and aesthetic order.

MODERN STILL LIFE

Repeatedly emphasized in the literature about Kjærholm's design is the coexistence of material and immaterial elements, carried out by an exquisite monochrome palette and graphic contrasts, fine choices of materials and manufacturing and a perfectly adjusted scale. The presentation of Kjærholm's work has, as with so many other 'grand' designer personalities, been mostly hagiographical: no dissonance is found in his design nor in Helmer-Petersen's photographs of it. It is all presented as a flawless harmony, so exactly drawn up and brilliantly carried out that it ought only to be the furniture's high manufacturing costs and selling prices that prevent the demand for and acquisition of the furniture.

This praise has probably also led to and influenced the dedication to Kjærholm's design from leading art museums like MoMA and Louisiana outside Copenhagen. Here the furniture is included in the interior setting and has been displayed separately as design-historical 'masterpieces' and canonized 'oeuvre'. The approval of Kjærholm by these sacrosanct art institutions has therefore contributed to the distinguishing function and the meanings constructed around his design. Yet it is noteworthy that this aspect has not been subjected to reflection in exhibition designs or catalogue texts.

Even in Louisiana's latest and otherwise-excellent exhibition of Kjærholm's work, shown in 2006, this artlike mediation of his furniture—not just in Helmer-Petersen's optics but by the art museum too—as primarily semiotic objects within the conceptual frame of high modernism remains tacit.[14] This seems somewhat peculiar since the scholarly community within aesthetic and cultural studies apparently never grows weary of demonstrating critically that modernism is not an unambiguous generic and static notion, nor is it dominated by innocent and immortal conceptualizations.

In this process of 'artification', each piece of furniture is assigned added value in terms of cultural capital and a status as exhibitable artefacts. But they have, in addition, been lifted out of their prosaic functional contexts in high-end interior decorating, in which Kjærholm's designs have never gained great distribution—in many cases simply because the prototypes he developed were never put into production but only came to function as exhibition models for the gaze and admiration among design connoisseurs. Instead, the modernistic mediation has helped to make Kjærholm's furniture, not least in Denmark, become dominant icons in semipublic places like company lobbies and in exclusive lifestyle magazines. In an orthodox fashion, these spread the design writers' views and promote the furniture as a masterful testimony to 'good taste', entirely in accordance with its present manufacturer Fritz Hansen's newest visual mediation strategies. Its interest, however, is solely in the commercial aspects and not, as argued in this case study, that (1) the aesthetic framework of Kjærholm's cooperation with Helmer-Petersen is anchored in an effort to create cultural and historical awareness and to defamiliarize the symbolic values of the objects and the spaces, and (2) it was through an affinity to modern abstract painting that they came to represent an acquisition of knowledge about 'high culture' that did in fact become increasingly powerful as a mechanism for exclusion and achieving 'distinction' by integration in an idealized and desired lifestyle.

Yet it isn't certain that the visual mediation of Kjærholm's design will maintain this reception-aesthetic effect in the future. In step with changed consumption patterns and aesthetic conventions, new contextual conditions for the conception of the furniture have already been established, reshaping their 'image' as a type of negation of the cultural values attached to the home. This is in fact how they looked in Helmer-Petersen's optics: as an opposition not only to the overloaded 'tassel homes' but also to the practically oriented functionalistic ideal of a home. In this way they are manifestations of a design strategy and spatial conception that refuses to take on tradition-bound middle-class conventions.

Perhaps this is in fact how we should best comprehend these variations of mass-produced delicate steel frameworks, glass and stone tabletops, which lack both a warm organic sense and the ethos that is linked—not least in a Danish context—to wood and craftsmanship. What is missing is the comfortable padding and physical volume in favour of tight hand-sewn and plaited covers in canvas, leather, wicker or flag halyard. All the 'hard' and 'cold' parts have the simplest repertoire of shapes and colors, which are further stressed in the ascetic, some would say antiseptic, showrooms and visual mediation of them. Kjærholm hereby meshed his design in a modernistic 'spin' of cultural signs related to the modern enlightened human free from the weight of tradition yet constrained by obtrusive feelings of estrangement and unhomeliness.

Interpreted within the concept of the uncanny or *unheimlich*, this doesn't mean, however, that the furniture itself possesses uncanny properties. As Anthony Vidler has shown on the basis of a number of hermeneutic studies, one might rather interpret the uncanny as a cultural frame of reference that confronts modern human beings' desire for a cosy home and a struggle for domestic security with its apparent absence. Thus both design and images hereof

> act, historically or culturally, as representations of estrangement. If there is a single premise to be derived from the study of the uncanny in modern culture, it is that there is no such thing as an uncanny architecture, but simply architecture that, from time to time and for different purposes, is invested with uncanny qualities.[15]

The defamiliarization that was expressed through the aesthetic mediation of Kjærholm's design had the intention of fortifying the furniture with an aura of permanent value both financially and culturally. It was to transcend welfare capitalism by being good investments for a still-growing group of consumers, whose basic physical needs were met fully and who therefore should allow themselves the same luxury that had been acquired by the modern prosperous individual; to appreciate basic aesthetic qualities and challenge comfort.

–12–

The Advantages of Being Swedish: Volvo in America

Jeff Werner

No doubt about it, America is the real homeland of cars, even though evil tongues proclaim that the world's first car was made in Europe. Nowhere has the car been so admired for so long, been so much a part of everyday life and culture, or so profoundly (re)shaped the land as in the United States.

The automotive industry is an important ingredient in national pride all over the world. Few other industries are so closely intertwined with national sentiments. In the USA this is further enforced by popular culture such as movies and advertising. There is hardly an action movie without a car chase or a college movie without a make-out scene in the backseat of a car. The American dream is captured by the view through the windshield of a straight highway that stretches out into an open horizon.

This chapter is a study of the significance Volvo's Swedishness has had in the American market. American car magazines, which have constituted an important source for my study, contain careful analyses of the technical attributes of cars, but their discussions of topics like gender and ethnicity are perhaps a little naive. But with enormous circulation and good relations to the car companies, these magazines play an important role as mediators between manufacturers and consumers. They are thereby co-producers of perceptions and values about cars, which among other things touch on their ethnic identities.

In discussing Volvo's design and its reception in the USA, we need methods to analyse the relations between design, national symbols and their political, cultural and social connotations. With its identity as a Swedish car, the product of Scandinavian design, Volvo inhabits a complex network of national stereotypes, political beliefs and cultural references. This is why conservatives in the 2004 Iowa caucuses could describe the Democrats as 'tax-hiking, government-expanding, latte-drinking, sushi-eating, Volvo-driving, *New York Times*-reading, body-piercing, Hollywood-loving, left-wing freaks'.[1]

WHAT IS SO SWEDISH ABOUT VOLVO ANYWAY?

Many reports conclude that ethnic and national stereotypes profoundly affect how we behave, what we buy and what we appreciate. Producers are, of course, well aware of consumers' tendency to make choices based on prejudices. Automakers in countries with low-ranking national identities among consumers may choose to keep silent about their nationality or adjust their nationality when needed. Take the German brand Volkswagen, for example. 'Made in Germany' has become synonymous with quality. Volkswagen is a German car and therefore is trustworthy. But most Volkswagens sold in North America are actually produced in Mexico. The problem is that, even though Mexico might be regarded as a lovely place to spend a vacation, most Americans do not associate Mexico with quality manufacturing. The general assumption is that Mexicans may make good food but not good cars. Therefore, Volkswagen has chosen not to present the cars as 'made in Mexico', even though they actually are.

Research on the national origins of products has established a clear connection between where cars are manufactured and how consumers perceive their quality.[2] Consumers often assume the cars are made in the brand's homeland, and their trust sinks if they discover that's not the case.[3] One reason American consumers buy expensive cars from Volvo is that they believe they are paying for quality. 'Made in Sweden' means reliability, a long life expectancy and high resale value.

In order to further differentiate apprehensions about nationality and ethnicity in response to design, I have borrowed a few concepts from the field of economics. The abbreviation COO (country of origin) indicates the company's homeland. Often it is synonymous with COP (country of production), the country where the goods are produced. However, during recent decades COO has often been separated from COP, as in the case of Volkswagen. Country of design—COD—signifies where the design was originally done or where the designers are located. Some companies, like Apple, are meticulous about the location of their design offices, while others are not.

Since there is no classification for experienced product nationality in the contemporary discourse, I have introduced another concept: COE, or country of evocation.[4] The new term addresses the important question of what consumers believe they are looking at and buying. When the producers, designers, marketers and retailers do their jobs efficiently, COE is what actually matters.

Lately COEs have become increasingly important in differentiating products in the global market. Symbols of nationality and ethnicity have become strategic devices in the competition among products that are essentially quite similar, like cars, for example. They consist of parts produced in many different countries by a variety of subcontractors. In this way cars are truly international. Still, few other products are so closely associated with nationality. What could be more French than a Citroën? More German than a BMW? Or more Swedish than a Volvo? Moreover, we often talk about cars as if they have ethnic identities: French cars are temperamental and a little peculiar, like the French. German cars are sturdy and powerful, as are the Germans. And Swedish cars, like the Swedes, play on the safe side of the street.

The most Swedish car is, of course, Volvo—even though it has recently been sold by Ford, an American automaker, to Chinese Geely Automobile. Has the change in ownership altered Volvo's image from Swedish to American to Chinese? Volvos are assembled in Sweden, China, Belgium, Malaysia and Thailand. Previously, they have also been assembled in the Netherlands, Canada and South Africa. Volvo Cars has three design centers: one in Gothenburg, Sweden; another in Barcelona, Spain; and a third in Camarillo, California, in the USA. An Englishman, Peter Horbury, is head of design, and his staff of designers comes from all over the world and seeks inspiration from many different cultures. Despite this multinational structure, most people associate Volvo with Sweden. And Geely probably intends to keep it that way. After all, COE is what really matters.

In recent decades, Volvo has chosen to enhance the connection between the cars' design and established preconceptions of Scandinavian design—emphasizing its COE. The choice of 'Scandinavian' instead of 'Swedish' is due to its even stronger positive associations—associations that are less vulnerable to the political changes in a single country. What's more, the notion of 'Scandinavian design' has gained high currency throughout much of the world since the 1950s.

A SPORTY LITTLE SWEDE, 1955–65

Sweden's export of cars to the United States is a postwar phenomenon. The modernization of Sweden was accompanied by growth in the production of consumer goods such as cars. The USA had an extremely comprehensive automotive industry as early as the period between the World Wars, and American automakers were long the model for Swedish manufacturers. Volvos of that era borrowed both technology and design from their American big brothers. The USA was transformed by the Second World War from a net exporter to a net importer of cars. At the same time, the international trade pattern for automobiles changed from a situation in which car-producing countries exported to countries without auto industries to one in which the auto-producing nations increasingly traded with one another.

Between the wars, the Swedish automotive industry had focused on its domestic market. It exported only a few per cent of its production of cars and about a third of its trucks. After the war, exports increased quickly. In

1950 more Swedish-made buses were sold abroad than in Sweden. By 1961 the same could be said of trucks, and by 1966 it was true of cars as well.[5] It was during the first half of the 1960s that the foreign market surpassed the domestic market for Volvo. Since 1960, they have sold 20–30 per cent of their cars in the USA. At the same time, however, we must remember that Volvo is an extremely small brand: its market share in North America declined from a peak of only about 1.0 per cent during the 1980s to around 0.7 per cent in 2009.[6] Still, unlike many other brands, Volvo has survived. The history of Volvo in America is, if not a success story, at least a tale of survival.

Volvo's automobile manufacturing operation began in 1926 as a subsidiary of SKF, under the leadership of Assar Gabrielsson and Gustaf Larsson. SKF had created the Volvo company in 1915 to make track ball bearings (a complement to the spherical ball bearings and roller bearings that had made SKF a global corporation).[7] Gabrielsson had a vision of Swedish automobile manufacturing. The first cars entered the market in 1927 but were not immediately successful. In terms of technology and design they were considered old-fashioned compared to the American cars that dominated the Swedish market. The first models, ÖV4 'Jakob' (1927), PV651 (1929) and PV652 (1930), were designed by a landscape and portrait painter, the auto enthusiast Helmer MasOlle,[8] but in the 1930s the company's engineers took over the design work, and it became more influenced by examples from the USA. Many of these engineers had worked for American automakers.[9]

Under the direction of Edward Lindberg, Volvo established a design department on the model of its American predecessors in 1949–50.[10] Soon thereafter Volvo entered the North American market. In the fall of 1955 the PV444 was introduced in the USA, initially on the west coast. The Swedish car was adapted to local buyers right from the start: the export version had a stronger motor, turn signals on the fenders instead of the door posts, and differently shaped bumpers. The launch was a success, and Volvo quickly became the second-most imported car brand in the western USA. The PV444 was shown on the east coast for the first time in the spring of 1956, at the New York International Auto Show, and found success there as well.[11] The reception seems to have taken everyone by surprise (fig. 12.1):

> The most amazing success story in the imported car field—which is a pretty amazing story itself—is the one that involves the Volvo . . . There are, of course, several reasons for this sudden demonstration of popularity. One of them is the rather obvious advantage of being Swedish, since most anything coming from that country, including beauty contest entries, is highly regarded.[12]

So in its introduction, Volvo got a boost from Sweden's good reputation (or PCI: product country image)—Sweden was then known for everything from ball

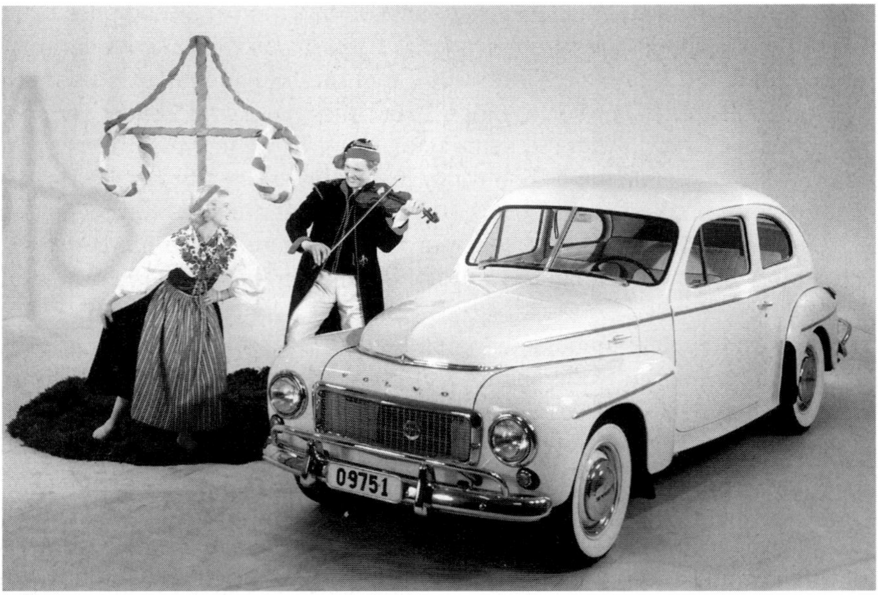

Fig. 12.1 A midsummer dream. Volvo PV444LS, 1957. Photograph courtesy of Volvo Car Corporation.

bearings and modern design to blonde girls—but Volvo's 'American' design and 'sporty' qualities were also important.

The PV444 and its follow-up, the PV544, became huge successes for Volvo in the US market, selling 160,000 cars. They were not innovative in terms of either technology or design, but they developed a reputation for being durable and reliable. The buyers who chose the unusual newcomer during those first years appear to have been mostly academics and technophiles. That may seem surprising today in light of Volvo's long-established reputation as a family car. But a look back through the rear-view mirror gives another picture. The interest in small European sports cars was strong in the USA during the 1950s, especially for Porsche and MG. Volvo responded with the introduction of the 1956–7 P1900, a convertible with the PV444's 'sport motor' and a fibreglass body. Notwithstanding the fact that only sixty-seven of them left the factory, the model strengthened Volvo's sporty image, and a couple of years later, in 1960, another sports car was introduced: the P1800.[13]

Volvo's successes in rally racing events created good opportunities to sell the PV444/544. Their marketing for the model was often clearly gender-specific, appealing often in one and the same ad both to women with the assertion that the car was spacious, could be slept in and had beautiful colors, and to men, noting the car's high resale value and sporty features.[14] This dual approach is reflected in magazines' coverage of the new Swedish car:

> Volvo's boast . . . that their machine is a 'family sports car' is no idle one. It has every attribute required for a comfortable, practical, tractable family car which the lady of the house can drive with ease. But it becomes a tiger when the competition-minded member of the family takes it out to the track.[15]

In its American marketing, Volvo constantly asserted its sporty qualities. It is clear from both the magazine reviews and the sales figures that the PV was well regarded in the USA. In spite of its antiquated design, its performance on the road was impressive. *Sports Cars Illustrated* covered the introduction of the PV444 in 1956 under the headline 'Swedish Invasion': 'It may not win any *concours d'elegance* but on all grounds other than—in some cases—esthetic ones, it can nail its competitors to the wall.'[16]

A SAINT, 1960–73

One of the few Volvo models that could have won a *concours d'élégance* might be the P1800, which was introduced at the New York Auto Show in 1960. About half of the P1800s made before 1966 were sold in the USA. Toward the end of the production cycle, the portion made for American export increased further: in 1971–3, 79 per cent of P1800s sold, which included the P1800E sedan and P1800ES station wagon, were sold in the USA.[17] It was primarily the short-lived ES model that wowed the critics of the day with its design (fig. 12.2).[18] Jan Wilsgaard had combined Pietro Frua and Pelle Petterson's original sports car with an elongated wagon back that finished with a large glass hatch. The American requirement that the bumper withstand a collision of 5 miles per hour led Volvo to cease production of all versions of the P1800 as soon as 1973.

The P1800 got a tremendous lift from the television series *The Saint* (1962–9), in which Roger Moore drove one. The Saint was originally supposed to drive a Jaguar E-type, but the British automaker was unable, or unwilling, to deliver a car in time for the filming. When the producer inquired at Volvo, they shipped a car over immediately. The public relations success was aided by the fact that Moore chose a P1800 for his own private use as well. The product placement had perhaps the most profound effect in England, but the series was quite popular in the USA as well, and it helped further strengthen Volvo's image as a sports car brand.

The combination of sporty and spacious is a niche Volvo has tried to maintain. Although the P1800ES wasn't the world's very first sport wagon—there was, for example, the MGB/GT—it was fairly successful and was later followed both by turbo-driven station wagons and by more direct formal descendants like the 480ES and the C30.[19] In the USA, Volvo has often marketed its powerful station wagons as 'sport wagons'.

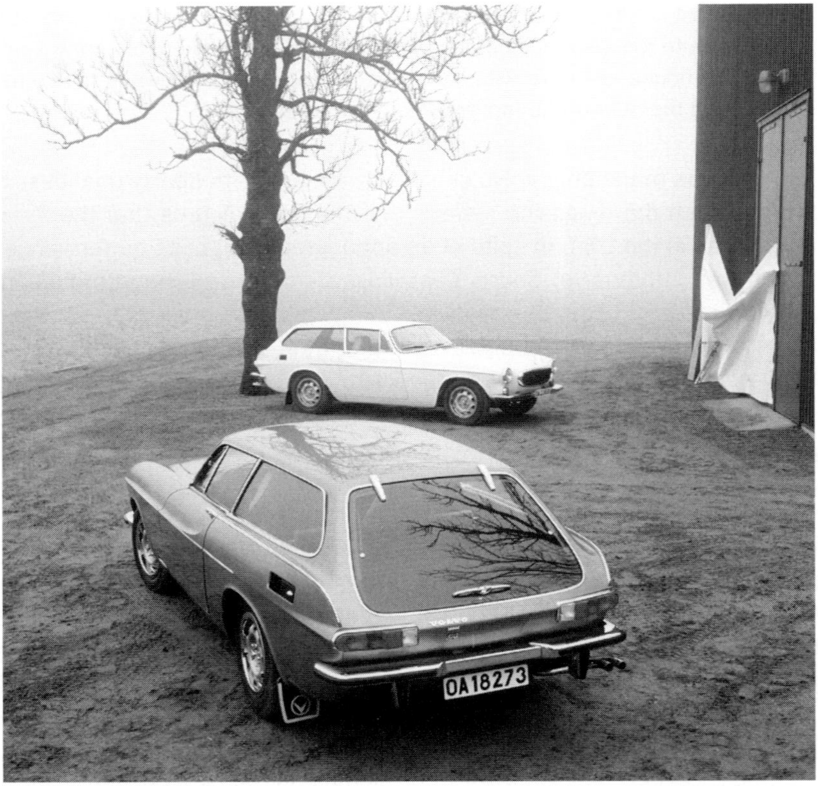

Fig. 12.2 Saint Volvo. Volvo P1800ES, 1973. Photograph courtesy of Volvo Car Corporation.

BOXY BUT GOOD, 1967–92

Alongside its sporty image, with its PV544 and Amazon/120 Volvo had already begun to build for the brand a strong, if contrasting, image of safety. This coincided with the growing interest in the automotive world for safety issues, supported by the United Nations World Forum for Harmonization of Vehicle Regulations, which was established in 1958. Laminated glass was introduced on the PV as early as 1944, and the three-point seat belt became standard in 1959. The Amazon was given a soft, padded dashboard, a steering column that folds away in the event of a crash and a three-point seat belt in the front seat, which inspired *Road & Track* to rave, 'The safety-conscious Swedes have inaugurated many features we've long advocated for cars and would like to see incorporated in all passenger vehicles.'[20]

The Volvo 140, which entered production in 1966 (the 1967 model), began a new era in which safety became increasingly visually prominent. The model was designed under the direction of Jan Wilsgaard. Its exterior was

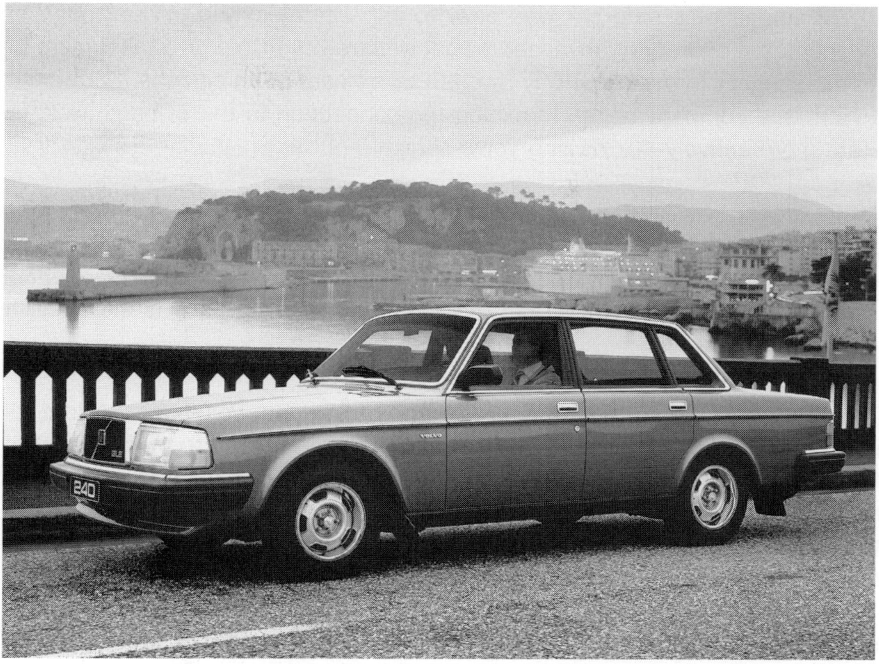

Fig. 12.3 Boxy but good. Volvo 240GLE (1983). Photograph courtesy of Volvo Car Corporation.

characterized by a generally boxy form, with the hood, roof and trunk clearly differentiated from one another. Underneath its boxy body, the 140 series had a dual-circuit triangular brake system, which was big news in 1967. Even its ability to absorb crashes and the design of the interior bore witness to the company's advanced safety program. The headrest became standard starting with the 1970 model year, and the seat belt warning light the following year.[21]

The body's visual 'safe car' signals were enhanced in 1974 with the 240 series, which had an extremely prominent bumper. Though its design was based on the 140, in the new 240 Wilsgaard and his team created a car that was demonstratively robust in its expression. More than any other Volvo model before or since, the 240 managed to unite image (safe, functional, basic) with visual identity (fig. 12.3).

Safety and security are qualities that we expect to appeal especially to families with children, and Volvo's 240 series was voted Best Family Car of 1975 by the readers of *Car and Driver*. Fully twelve years later, *Family Circle*'s readers elected the same model 'the family car of the year'. Part of Volvo's image as a family car is their investment in large station wagons. This characteristic attribute was established as early as the 1950s with the Volvo Duett. Station wagons have represented a large proportion of the company's sales in the USA—about 30 per cent for most of its history.[22]

The image of a safe car was easy to join seamlessly with the image of Sweden as a country of advanced social welfare (its PCI). Volvo takes care of its passengers in the same way Sweden takes care of its citizens. During the 1990s, the company began to exploit the connection to the Swedish welfare state more actively—or, as one Volvo designer put it:

> We at Volvo Design decided that we will enhance our Swedishness . . . use it as a guideline in the future . . . If you consider Sweden as a caring society, what would be more caring than a Volvo car with its safety? A Swedish company couldn't design and build non-safe products knowingly. So I think that reflects the Swedish society immediately.[23]

This is probably more than just a reflection of Sweden. Volvo doesn't just reiterate conceptions of Sweden as a security-obsessed country where most of life is regulated; the company also contributes to the production of this stereotype. The dominant image of Sweden forms the foundation of consumers' trust in Volvo as a safe car; at the same time Volvo strengthens this image by making the connection to Scandinavian welfare politics.[24]

With the exception of the P1800's appearance in *The Saint*, Volvo's appearances on the big and little screen have not been particularly flattering. Strikingly, the brand is often used to signal that the driver is an academic. Professor Silk in *The Human Stain* (Robert Benton, 2003) drives an old Volvo, as does the death penalty opponent Professor Gale in *The Life of David Gale* (Alan Parker, 2003) and the former head of research Jeffrey Wigand in *The Insider* (Michael Mann, 1999). True to form, television's obsessive-compulsive detective Adrian Monk, with his neurotic fear of bacteria, drove a Volvo 740.

Unlike Porsche, Jaguar and Ferrari, Volvos are usually cast as extras rather than stars. An exception is the comedy *Crazy People* (Tony Bill, 1990), in which Dudley Moore plays an ad man who has a psychotic breakdown. He drives a Volvo 740 through rush-hour traffic into Manhattan every morning. Fed up with the dishonesty, he begins to propose ad campaigns that tell the truth. On a black-and-white poster with a picture of a Volvo one reads: 'Buy Volvos. They're boxy but they're good. We know they're not sexy. This is not a smart time to be sexy anyway, with so many new diseases around. Be safe instead of sexy. Volvo. Boxy but good.' The film is itself an indication of how well established the image of Volvo as safe but boring was around 1990—especially when contrasted with the Jaguar, which, we learn from the film, is what you buy to get sex.

But for a time Volvo was also a car for the counterculture of radical students and leftists, if not to the same extent as the VW Bug. According to *Car and Driver*, 'It almost became the official car of the loons and dim-bulbs of academe and the consumer movement in the late Sixties and Seventies.'[25] There are stories that Volvo dealers, unlike their counterparts at GM and

Ford, didn't need to protect their windows during the Vietnam War.[26] Sweden had a good reputation among the radical youth who protested the war: 'Back in the antiwar days, Volvos were embraced as anti-Detroit symbols. Volvos were considered honest, forthright vehicles, anti style and anti annual model change.'[27] Volvo's Swedish roots served as a mob deterrence, even though at the time the company had yet to emphasize its origins. But whereas Volkswagen invested substantial resources to brand the Beetle as a hippie car rather than a Hitler car, the Volvo, by contrast, came across as a car meant not for life-loving hippies but rather for ascetics who see the car as a purely utilitarian product: 'Volvos . . . radiate Puritan ethics', according to *Car and Driver* in 1973.[28]

AS AMERICAN AS APPLE PIE

Most paradoxically, Volvo's conservative, traditional design has long been a key to the brand's success. Whether that conservatism is intentional or not, Volvo has always done well in a market as fundamentally conservative as that in the USA. As early as 1953, before either of the Swedish automotive brands was introduced in the USA, *Motor Trend* concluded that Volvo was 'more Americanized in design' than its Swedish cousin, Saab.[29]

It is striking that in the extremely comprehensive collection of press materials I studied, the word most commonly used to describe Volvos is 'conservative'. Also common are variations on the claim that Volvo is 'well adapted to American requirements'. From the very first reviews of the PV444, automotive critics were surprised by the antiquated design:

> Looking at the Volvo for the first time, one cannot help but be struck by the fact that the body design is of a type not built in this country since the late 'thirties. The split windshield, fat, curved rear section, squarish front end and fenders are reminiscent of such cars as the '39 Dodge (front) and '41 Ford (side and rear).[30]

In Volvo's defense we can note that the PV444 had been designed back in 1943–4. But it hadn't been innovative even then. When the first cars were delivered in Sweden in 1947, the look was even more passé, let alone when it launched in the USA in 1956. The car's appearance, however, does not seem to have negatively affected its sales. It was perceived as 'cute' and appealed to American ethnocentrism, according to auto-industry journalist Thos Bryant.[31] Others described it—admiringly—as a cross between a tank and a sports car.[32]

When production of the 544 model ceased in 1966, Volvo North America came out with an advertising campaign that mourned, 'Farewell, old friend.' With a self-deprecating smile, its antiquated appearance became an argument for the new Amazon 122S: 'A few years ago we came out with a new model. The 122 S. It does everything the 544 does . . . except it doesn't look like a '41 Ford while doing it.'[33] This does not mean that the design of the 120 series was particularly innovative: to Americans it looked like an Aero Willys (1952–4), while to Europeans it might rather have recalled the Alfa Romeo Giulietta. According to Wilsgaard, the head of design, the Amazon was inspired by the American Kaiser (fig. 12.4).[34]

Sports Cars Illustrated called the Amazon 'conservatively modern', and *Car and Driver* described the Volvo Corporation in 1962 as 'Sweden's conservative giant'.[35] If it wasn't enough that their designs looked old-fashioned the day they launched, they were also kept in production longer than most competing models. But the absence of contemporary stylistic gestures kept the resale value high and contributed to the perception of a car company that cared about the essentials rather than passing trends.

Another common theme in how Volvo has been perceived in the USA is that the designs are unusually well adapted to American demands. The PV444 'is

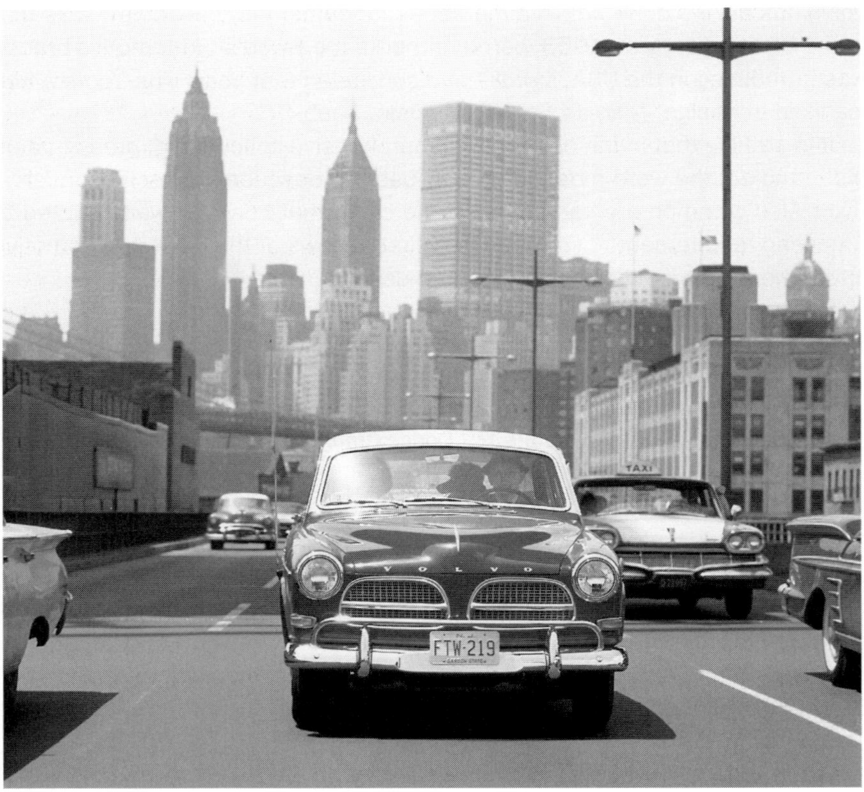

Fig. 12.4 First we take Manhattan. Volvo PV120, export version, 1958–9. Photograph courtesy of Volvo Car Corporation.

one of the extremely rare bodies in the light car field that the average U.S. motorist can enter for the first time and feel quite at home in', wrote *Sports Cars Illustrated* in 1956.[36] The same year, *Motor Life* said they couldn't find 'anything peculiarly foreign about the layout', and a year later *Sports Car Illustrated* noted that 'Volvo's policy of constant product improvement is responsible for a beefier engine, a different grille, and stronger bumpers—all more in line with American taste'.[37] This adaptation to American tastes, according to automotive journalists, included the interior and instrumentation as well: 'Unlike many foreign cars, the instruments in the Volvo are so Americanized that a person almost feels he is driving an American-built car.'[38]

The appeal of Volvos as well suited to Americans may be rooted in the fact that the models were from the beginning heavily influenced by American automotive design and in the company's more recent adaptation of those models to the tastes and demands of the North American marketplace. But the perception that a Volvo is right for American drivers and traffic conditions is also an expression of complex PCI patterns.

One reason European cars sell in the USA is that they are not American. There is status in driving a European car. They should therefore distinguish themselves from the majority but not have such odd attributes that they fail to attract a large number of buyers—as the decline of brands like Citroën, Alfa Romeo, Renault and Fiat in the US market clearly demonstrates. Volvo's success is based on just the right amount of European exoticism against the background of a perceived fundamental similarity between Sweden and the USA:

> Sweden is a country of severe climate, and hence the design of Volvos is influenced by the need for rugged, all-weather cars that will perform reliably and keep the occupants happy in all kinds of weather. Because America is also a land of extremes in weather, the Volvo is better suited to American use than are many imports.[39]

In 1967 *Car and Driver* summarized Volvo's first ten years in the American market:

> When the first Volvo PV 444 came to these shores in the middle Fifties, it was regarded as a somewhat anachronistic vehicle from a country that few Americans even suspected of having an automobile industry . . . Today, Volvo and Volvo advertising are as well known as Sweden's reputation for marvelous women (deserved) and a high suicide rate (undeserved). Hardly anybody thinks of it as an imported car anymore.[40]

During the 1970s, Volvo began an increasingly concerted effort to target a more prestigious segment of the market. The company's 164 (1969) and 264 (1976) models had already proven successful in the American market after

Japanese brands had taken over large segments of its lower end. But Volvo stuck to the middle of the road in terms of design. The first luxury model, the 164, with its English retro front grille, was judged 'a conservative sedan' with a 'dated classic look' in 1969.[41] The press panned the design, but American buyers liked it.[42]

Volvo's look grew more clearly American in the 1980s with the boxy forms of the 740 and 760 series. The squarish rear end of the sedans in particular made American automotive journalists associate it with domestic cars: 'Its styling may be American, but its soul is still Swedish.'[43] In fact, one even called the Volvo 740 as American as apple pie: 'Volvo is probably the most American car ever to come over by boat. A truly assimilated product, the Volvo is your car next door, often taken for granted, perhaps by some people even taken to be domestic apple pie.'[44]

SWEDISH LOOKS? 1991–2010

It seems a little strange that Volvo didn't try to build on the success of Scandinavian design in the 1950s. The company didn't begin to leverage its design heritage until about 1991, the year the Englishman Peter Horbury was made head of design. In all the talk of globalization in the early 1990s, it was often asserted that signs of national identity would become irrelevant as internationalization increased. But developments actually went in the opposite direction. In the global marketplace, national identifiers became effective tools for differentiating a brand.[45]

When a company undertakes a major design overhaul of its products, it must take pains to ensure that consumers still recognize its brand identity in the new models. Different brands show varying degrees of visual continuity through their histories. Since the late 1960s, Volvo's cars had been compared with cargo crates due to their predominantly rectilinear designs. This form was associated with a number of important Volvo attributes, including safety, robustness and functionality. To get rid of the distinctive box form with its overstated bumpers was therefore to take a substantial risk. Horbury notes that the trick was to redesign Volvo without losing its identity: 'We had to be very careful that we maintained the recognition of Volvo, because it stood for a lot of things, even if it didn't stand for beautiful design.'[46]

The C70 sports coupe was shown for the first time in Geneva in 1996 and began to be sold in the USA in 1998. Together with the S80, it gave Volvo a new start in terms of design. 'This is the first Volvo we've ever heard anyone call cool', wrote *AutoWeek* of the C70.[47] Such statements might very well have been catalysed by the fact that the C70 featured in Peter Noyce's 1997 movie *The Saint*—the lead role this time played by Val Kilmer—rekindling the relations between Volvo and the old fictional hero. The design transition that followed happened in stages with models like the 850, S/V40 and S/V70, from rear-wheel to front-wheel drive and from robust cargo crate to an epitome of 'Scandinavian design'. The S80 launched in 1998 with a visual look that sharply diverged from how a Volvo was expected to look. The forms had softened, and the body had taken on more dynamic curves. In particular, the way the sweep of the body extended into the shape of the taillights gave it a look that made the new model easily identifiable even from the rear (cars typically have their most distinguishing features in the front). Like most other carmakers, Volvo now stopped making projecting bumpers, integrating them instead into the form and color of the rest of the car. For Volvo this meant abandoning the feature that most clearly symbolized the safety of their models. Toni-Matti Karjalainen has interpreted the prominently thick doors on the new models as a substitute, a new sign of safety.[48] Safety indicators are important, since what really makes the car safe to drive is not visible on the surface. The S80 was the first model to receive five stars in the National Highway Transport Safety Authority's crash test.[49] At the same time, Volvo began to integrate the 'Scandinavian design tradition' into its brand identity, connecting the cars with well-known icons and heroes of Scandinavian design such as Arne Jacobsen.

Volvo's design and marketing staff like to quote the usual stereotypes of Scandinavian design: simplicity, lightness and functionality. 'In terms of purity of form', says Horbury, 'I wanted it as Swedish as possible.'[50] Next to Horbury, no one played a greater role in transforming Volvo's look than Mexican designer José de la Vega. The fact that its leading designers were an Englishman and a Mexican may well have increased the 'Scandinavianization' of Volvo, since it is often easier for an outsider to grasp a culture's characteristic attributes—or perhaps only easier to conjure up and accept a stereotypical image of it.[51] Besides, the company needed to convey its Scandinavian identity clearly to customers around the globe. One designer explained: 'To recognize and apply Scandinavian design is maybe even easier if you're not Scandinavian, because we do not apply Scandinavian design in this car to please the Scandinavians, but to please the rest of the world. So the translation has to be recognizable also by people not from Scandinavian countries.'[52]

But even if Scandinavian simplicity stands out as an essential feature of Volvo's identity among the company's designers, and perhaps also for its consumers, the most Scandinavian aspects of Volvo are the associations that are tied to the brand and its products. Since the late 1990s, Volvo has been trying to connect these associations to Scandinavian design in the mind of the consumer. Hedvig Hedqvist reported from a 1999 media presentation in Gothenburg:

> The walls of the room in which we sit are papered with examples from our proud history of design, blown up to mega format: the Hasselblad camera, a detail from an armchair of blonde wood and leather, a Jensen watch, a suggestive fashion

> photo, modern architecture. Exclusive objects that don't just encompass Scandinavian design, but also are products that are appreciated by the people Volvo sees as its target group.[53]

Thus Volvo appropriated the image of Scandinavian design that had been carefully nurtured by official representatives of the Scandinavian countries since the 1950s—a process that in its geographical and temporal loops resembles those described in several of the cases gathered in Part 2 of this book. The company's change in attitude coincided with both a renewed international interest in Scandinavian design and a marked wave of retro styling in automotive design around the world. Nissan was first with the Figaro in 1989, Volkswagen launched the new Beetle in 1998, Austin/BMW the new Mini Cooper in 2001 and Chrysler the PT Cruiser in 2001. Even if Volvo's latest models don't exactly ride the retro wave, there are clear references to older models. The V form of the S80's hood draws inspiration from the Amazon, and the curve of its midsection has a precedent in the PV544. 'The Volvo S80 has an identity that connects back to earlier Volvos without being sentimentally retro', explains Horbury.[54]

At the same time, Volvo continued to respond to American trends. Its SUVs in particular were a successful American-inspired concept during the first decade of the twenty-first century. The first was an elevated, somewhat-reinforced V70 with four-wheel drive introduced in 2001 with the name XC70. It was given prominent wheel-well extensions of plastic and a steel skid plate meant to signal toughness. The XC70 was followed by a bigger brother, the 2002 XC90, that became a sales success—well adapted to American tastes. In 2005 the XC90 was the vehicle with the most cup holders—eighteen of them for its maximum seven passengers to share. Too small, too few or too poorly located cup holders is a frequently recurring complaint from auto industry journalists in a country that eats many of its meals in the car.

During the 2000s, Volvo has continued to reference Scandinavian design. The C30, introduced in 2006, is clearly aimed at young urbanites more interested in fashion and design than in cars as such. Volvo declares its design philosophy as follows:

> Good design is not only a matter of styling the surface. It is just as important to make the product easy to understand and use. If the product is not functional, it can't be beautiful. . . . Volvo's cars possess a distinctive design, which has its roots in the heritage and the Scandinavian design tradition—with the aspiration of combining classical timelessness with human functionalism and high technology.[55]

But just how the cars are to be functional is not specified. At the same time Volvo chose to position itself as a safe, Swedish car brand epitomizing

Scandinavian design, it also reduced the trunk space. This was in part the result of the softer curves and more organic lines of its designs, clear references to Scandinavian, and especially Danish, design in the 1950s. Volvo has become less of a cargo crate. The Duett station wagon (1953–69) held more than a hundred cubic feet, more than any model that followed it. Instead, the carrying capacity has declined steadily. The 745 (1985) held about half of what the Duett had. The luggage capacity in today's Volvo V70 wagon is less than twenty cubic feet.

As we've seen, Volvo's design has always been seen as Scandinavian, even at the peak of its influence from the USA. What, then, is the advantage of being a Swedish car in America? To begin with, it is almost never a disadvantage to be Swedish: Sweden is always near the top of rankings of national reputations.[56] If you are also adaptable—which maybe Swedes aren't, but Volvo certainly has always been—your chances in foreign markets increase substantially. In 2008 it began making the S80L in China, adapting it to the Chinese market by giving it a five-and-a-half-inch-longer wheelbase. This is likely just the first step in a new phase of sensitivity to local preferences.

As noted in the introduction, there is a strong relationship between car brands and nationalities. A healthy dose of ethnic factors enhances the product's ability to attract important customer segments. Of course there are always Americans who simply refuse to drive a car associated with snobby Scandinavian design and Swedish welfare politics. But you can't win them all. After all, Volvo may be the perfect car for a 'latte-drinking, sushi-eating, *New York Times*-reading, Hollywood-loving' Democrat.

–13–

From Policies to Politics: Finnish Design on the Ideological Battlefield in the 1960s and 1970s

Pekka Korvenmaa

In the postwar Western world, design has, by its nature, belonged to the value system of culture while also to the supposedly value-neutral realm of technology, industry and commerce. In Finland, the symbiosis of these two domains functioned well after the war. Both areas supported the quite miraculous rise of Finnish design from the ashes of a lost war to international fame and panegyric publicity in the 1950s. However, cracks in the well-working machinery and hence in the image of Finnish design began to emerge in the mid-1960s. This was mainly due to contradictions between the traditional sectors of design-based production and the emergence of industrial design. But it was not until radical and soon left-wing political currents swept over the intellectual landscape of Finland in the late 1960s that the culture of design became ideologically politicized. This essay attempts to show how an initially 'neutral', instrumentalist approach to steering the development of Finnish design—design policies—resulted before long in a situation where design had become an element of a broader political conflict over ideological hegemony.

ACT I: THE RISE

The rise of Scandinavian design to international fame in the early 1950s is a story that is well known and amply documented, exhibited and told. Though not actually part of Scandinavia but one of the Nordic countries, Finland was an integral part of this burst of design on the international market. It was design that was certainly modern but at the same time a kind of domesticated avant-garde and thus highly suitable for middle-class consumption. Sweden had avoided the war, and Denmark, though occupied by Germany, had kept its system of design and production largely intact. After the war, these countries were then ready to launch new products and product categories. Norway had been occupied and was more shattered by the war than its Scandinavian neighbours. Finland, in turn, had suffered severely during the war years from late 1939 until 1945. The postwar period witnessed political unrest and the constant threat of sharing the fate of the countries that fell under communist regimes steered from Moscow. In addition, war-torn Finland had to deliver substantial war reparations to the Soviet Union until 1952. In many ways, the country had to start from scratch. Well into the 1950s, shortages of materials such as glass, steel and textiles impeded both construction and the design-intensive industries that had progressed rapidly during the economic upswing of the late 1930s. Education in design had mostly been at a standstill during the war years. Seen against this backdrop, the emergence of Finnish design that began in the late 1940s and then suddenly catapulted to international consciousness via success at the IX Triennale di Milano in 1951 was—to put it mildly—surprising (fig. 13.1). This 'Miracle of Milan' started a succession of victories not only in Milan but also at other forums, such as the major

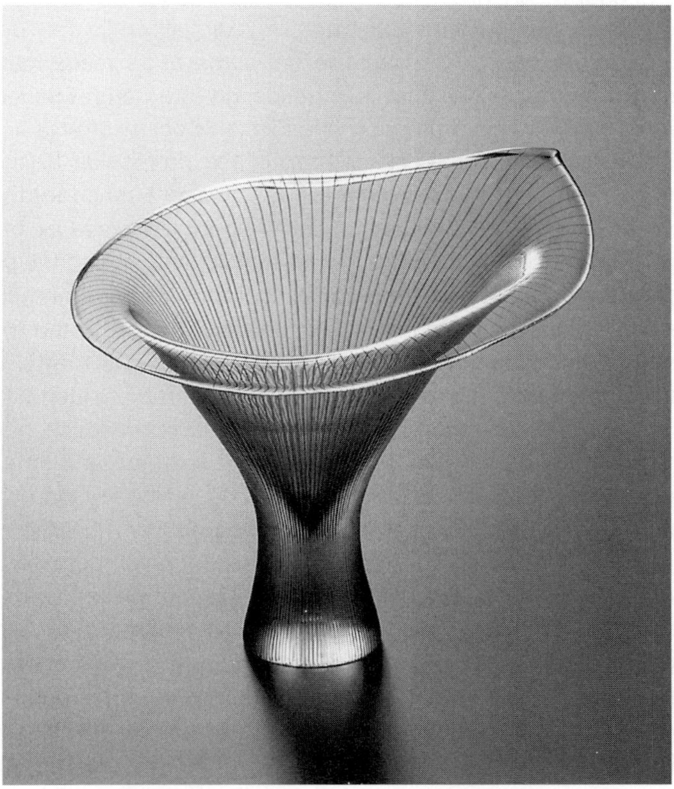

Fig. 13.1 Chanterelle vase designed by Tapio Wirkkala, Iittala Glassworks, 1946. An iconic item manifesting the rise of Finnish design from the postwar austerity. Photo: Rauno Träskelin. Courtesy of Design Museum Helsinki.

exhibition Design in Scandinavia that toured the United States and Canada in 1954–7.

The early 1950s thus saw the start of developments that were highly positive and productive for Finnish design and lasted until the late 1960s. Victories in exhibitions abroad were prominently featured in the press, and leading designers such as Tapio Wirkkala, Kaj Franck and Timo Sarpaneva were hailed as heroes in terms previously reserved for Olympic medallists. Industries, still mostly in the traditional genres of furniture, glass, ceramics and textiles, rapidly understood the value of design for both revamping their production palettes and creating publicity for products through having designers lend their aura even to everyday objects. Word of increased revenue through design spread among industrialists and entrepreneurs, leading to the constantly growing use of design expertise in the corporate sphere. Profound changes were introduced in design education, in which the country's only design school, the Central School of Arts and Crafts in Helsinki (now called Aalto University School of Art and Design), had a monopoly. Education was now brought into closer contact with industries.

In the existing 'system' of Finnish design some of its main actors dated from as early from the 1870s, that is in education (the Central School of Arts and Crafts, est. 1871) and promotion (the Finnish Society of Arts and Crafts, est. 1875), while the national organization of the profession (Ornamo, est. 1911) was somewhat later. These players now made a much stronger bond than before with industries developing rapidly under the pressure of national rebuilding. The pull from industry led to updating education, and the push from the designers led to increased employment of both in-house and consulting designers, while international promotion was skilfully orchestrated by the publicly funded but also industry-supported Society of Arts and Crafts. A kind of positive cycle came into effect, to the benefit of all stakeholders. The rising standard of living fuelled internal consumption, and the massive national rebuilding programme created new homes requiring furniture and other domestic necessities. The public sphere also boosted design-based industries—the exceptionally high birth rate just after the war meant that nurseries, schools and hospitals with their requirements of furniture and equipment were needed to serve the growing population. When business again picked up in the mid-1950s, corporate premises, shops, hotels and restaurants joined the clientele of Finnish production in design. At the same time, this production was well guarded against imported competition through high duties on foreign goods.[1]

There were, of course, similar developments in several Western countries at the same time. Finland, however, saw rapid and dramatic progress finally leading to an accelerating process of industrialization and urbanization peaking in the 1960s. By that time, the country had transformed from an agrarian nation to an urban and highly industrialized society in only a couple of decades. A milestone was the year 1966 when the pre-war standard of living and consumption of 1939 was finally achieved and then surpassed. The apparently well-functioning machinery of Finnish design involved the industries supporting it, education providing fresh and well-trained manpower and promotional efforts portraying Finland as a Western country with a refined and well-designed environment, though exhibiting a certain 'otherness', a streak of boldness and proximity to nature in comparison with its Nordic competitors. The machinery appeared to provide a cornucopia for the whole nation, but, at the same time, it came to be questioned, criticized and finally dismantled. But let us take a closer look at the mechanisms operating at the beginning of the 1960s.

DESIGN, INDUSTRY AND INSTRUMENTS OF CONTROL

International visibility and success in exhibitions were first gained via crafted objects and craft-as-art, such as unique pieces of ceramics and glass blown in limited editions along with handwoven textiles. Before long, the repertoire was enriched with serially produced furniture and printed cotton fabrics leaning more towards design in the service of industrial production. This mirrored the domestic development of traditional, industrial genres of production, such as textiles, ceramics and glass, which were becoming more design-intensive. The home was still the dominant sphere of consumption in design, and especially in the 1950s this became almost a middle-class cult, a vehicle in the competition for social status. The 'right' way to project the family habitus via design was amplified by semi-professional magazines instructing consumers skating on the thin ice of 'good taste'.

But beneath this kind of production and consumption dominating the status and visibility of design, other rapidly emerging and growing forces were at work. The industrial infrastructure of the nation was evolving from its predominantly forest-based industries towards heavy-metal industries, machinery and soon also mechanical and electromechanical consumer goods such as refrigerators, stoves, washing machines and vehicles for transportation. Electronic appliances followed before long, building on pre-war expertise in radio production. Formal, specific training in industrial design did not exist yet, and hence electric appliances represented anonymous design, usually by technicians and engineers. But now, around 1960, the expanding role of electric household products in a country with a well-developed design culture raised the issue of the role of design in both developing business-to-consumer appliances and the creation of investment goods in the business-to-business category. Furthermore, how adequate was the prevailing design education for providing design skills to serve these new product categories, and was there a need for broader, national strategies to steer this new and more complex union of design, industries and growing foreign trade?

In 1961 Finland joined EFTA, the European Free Trade Association, and education in industrial design began at the national design school. Both events belonged to the larger scheme of Finland's increasing integration in the European realm of industry and trade and the role of design in industries and national aspirations for income through exports. The new economic treaty meant heightened international competition, which called for new quality standards for Finnish products.[2] Industries with a high design profile such as furniture and glass had no doubt gained markets internationally, but their revenues as a percentage of the gross domestic product were modest. Among the design-based industries, printed cotton led exports in the early 1960s, followed by furniture. Still, in 1959 these industries accounted for only 0.9 per cent of total exports. This figure rose to 5 per cent in 1965, reaching 7 per cent in 1970. This increase was mainly due to the rise of industrial design. It was no wonder that this raised concerns over the most adequate way to manage this apparently lucrative process.[3]

The rise of industrial design caused and catalysed several already embryonic phenomena in Finnish design. Firstly, it was teamwork with other professions, mainly from engineering and commerce. It was also anonymous, and the products were sold with the label of the company or brand, not with the signature of an individual designer (fig. 13.2). The products were technologically more complex than traditional, low-tech design items such as glass, ceramics and furniture. This meant specialization and challenged the image of the traditional design titan able to master the design of the whole physical environment. In the late 1950s and early 1960s, when diversifying industries needed designers to give external form to technological products, ceramicists designed lightweight motorcycles, and graphic designers outboard motors and tractors. But after the first cohorts of industrial designers began to graduate in 1966, industrial design became professionalized. This was signified by the formation of their own professional section in 1966 within the Ornamo association, which now also changed its name from the Association of Decorative Artists to the Industrial Art Association.

Besides these changes in professional education, the field of design and the ways in which industries now utilized design expertise, other trends were active, leaning more towards the cultural and ideological aspects of design. In 1965 the highly respected designer and hailed educator Kaj Franck, one of the demiurges of the pantheon of Finnish design, published an article criticizing the prevailing custom of companies such as the glass producer Iittala of selling even everyday household items with the name and 'signature' of the designer. Franck pleaded for anonymity and for signing only one-off or small-scale artistic products. This call for anonymity was well suited to the young generation of the postwar baby boom that was now storming into the universities, very soon into professions and naturally into consumption, boosted by

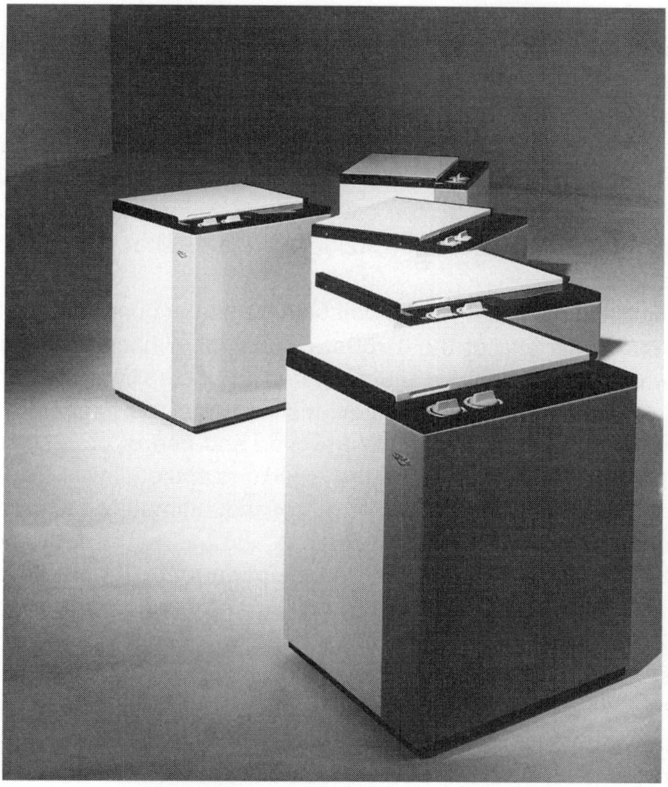

Fig. 13.2 UPO washing machine designed by Jussi Ahola, 1964. The first professionally trained class of industrial designers steps forward. Photo: Pietinen. Courtesy of Design Museum Helsinki.

the strong economic growth of the 1960s. This was particularly true of the 'angry young men' of industrial design.

A broader look at the cultural and political currents of the late 1960s is needed to understand the turbulence that shook Finnish society as a whole, and design as part of it. Rapid industrialization and urbanization, the rise of consumer culture, the influence of television and a general opening up of a closed Finnish society traumatized by war, and the clash of generations caused by the baby boomers launched a process of transformation in which earlier normative values were challenged and overthrown. Global awareness expanded towards the McLuhanian 'world village', and Third World problems, environmental issues and domestic social injustice filled the value void left by abandoning the holy triad of 'home, church and fatherland'. The continental European 'New Left' and its neo-Marxist and even Maoist trends found a throng of devoted followers. At the turn of the 1970s, this leftist radicalism evolved into a peculiarly Finnish variant of dogmatic communism, taking the Kremlin as its beacon and stifling the climate of cultural policies for years to come. This was done by a generation whose fathers had been at the front fighting this very same ideology and the nation from where it emanated, the Soviet Union. Hence, unlike in other Western countries similarly shaken by leftist radicalism, neo-Marxism in Finland was chained to pro-Soviet thinking and action. Together with the country's highly important trade contracts with its overpowering eastern neighbour, this led to what others came to call Finlandization.

Two major and apparently antagonistic forces thus operated within Finnish design towards the end of the 1960s. On the other hand, industrial design and the whole technocratic-economic paradigm increasingly sought ways to generate national strategies to steer and lubricate the cooperative mechanisms of design education and the provision and use of professional expertise. The goal here was to enhance the repertoire and quality of Finnish export goods for the benefit of the corporate realm and, ultimately, the gross domestic product. The leading strata of industries and their unions, the design professionals via their bastion Ornamo and the powerful SITRA non-governmental innovation organization (Fund of the Jubilee Year of Finnish Independence, est. 1967) all strove towards the consensus of a national design agenda, a proto design-policy programme that would anticipate the far more effective policies of the 1990s. These efforts were seemingly non-political and portrayed as neutral instruments for the good of the nation—and design.

A major concern was the upscaling and modernization of design education. By the mid-1950s, designers such as Ilmari Tapiovaara and Tapio Wirkkala had made efforts to establish education in product design that was not bound to any specific material or technique. The idea of a design education geared towards industrial production goes back at least to the Bauhaus but came to Finland in an Americanized version via extended visits by Finnish designers to schools such as Illinois Institute of Technology's Institute of Design and the Rhode Island School of Design. But, as already mentioned, it was not until 1961 that the first course in industrial design began. In 1965 the state took over the school from the Finnish Society of Arts and Crafts, and the curriculum was extended to four years. Before long, discussion began on raising vocational education to university level. This became reality in 1973 with the first independent design university in the Nordic countries. But, as we will see, it did not start as a smoothly functioning unit producing design professionals for concerted efforts to enhance design in order to serve industries. On the contrary, the school had turned into a hotbed of left-wing revolutionary ideas proclaiming anti-capitalism and the demise of the existing political order.

But before ending in political trench warfare, the late 1960s witnessed open and lively debate on the new role of design as part of culture, social activism and environmental issues. Among the main targets of the young critics were the well-established mechanisms of promoting Finnish design internationally through exhibitions. The country had been extremely successful in major foreign exhibitions, especially in the Triennale di Milano from 1951 to 1964. Extensive international media coverage following these and similar events highlighted both designers and objects lending themselves to photogenic display. Although domestic discussion on the lack of everyday objects in these exhibitions and the utmost aesthetic refinement of the displays had surfaced occasionally, now this 'tabletop aestheticism' was seen to represent values that were obsolete in an era of massive global problems. At the same time, the established, 'old' masters—now barely in their fifties—came under attack for being elitist. The peak of criticism was caused by the Finnish department at Montreal World Expo 1967, curated by Timo Sarpaneva. The themes of the Expo concerned globalization and the electronic distribution of information. The Finnish display was dominated by a few monumental panels of craft-as-art and actual abstract art.

Increased consciousness of the global realm, its problems and possibilities was augmented not only by the media and growing opportunities for travel but also by visits to Finland by new spokesmen of design. Victor Papanek visited and lectured several times in the late 1960s. Papanek, Buckminster Fuller and Christopher Alexander were guests at an eye-opening seminar organized by design students in Helsinki in 1968. Also, the ever-important Nordic collaboration was revived by the young generation, but it now centred on critical thinking and activism instead of promotional strategies linked to export industries, manifested in international exhibitions and their object-focused displays. All this was to change the 'design thinking' of the generation of new designers taking their positions around the turn of the 1970s.

Generally speaking, we can say that the Finnish design context of the late 1960s was characterized by openness, the coexistence of the traditional and radical, a tightening bond between design and industry and growing concern over the possibilities of design as part of solving social and ecological problems. The political scene was still flexible and engaged in debate. The standard of living continued to rise, fuelling the consumption of design. But there was a heated battle over the domination of the cultural capital of design. Owing to its visibility throughout the postwar decades and its role as an asset of national pride, design had become a vital part of not only consumption but also high culture. At the same time, it was vulnerable. We have to bear in mind that this was a small context, with a limited number of professionals. All of them had been educated at the same school, and they belonged to the same union. The school and the profession had close links; a handful of people were in leading professional positions and on the boards of the school and promotional organizations. When things proceeded in unison, as they had for a long while, a great deal could be achieved with a limited number of actors. But when conflicts emerged, the precarious balance, the seemingly self-evident contract, was broken, and stagnation emerged.

FROM A FULL PALETTE TO BLACK AND WHITE

Dividing the past into decades with different natures is arbitrary, and therefore we can say that the 1960s actually ended in 1973 with the international oil crisis. Both internationally and domestically, it led to an economic downturn, which in Finland deteriorated into a depression in the middle of the decade. Both this and the outmoded structures of design-based industries led to severe cutbacks in areas such as textile and ceramics production. A visible result in the manufacturing of design objects was, of course, the disappearance of plastics from furniture production because of the now much higher price of oil (fig. 3.3). But until the oil crisis, design and industry cooperated well. Turmoil, however, did not concern this base, where especially industrial design constantly found new territories, but instead the visible peak of the iceberg,

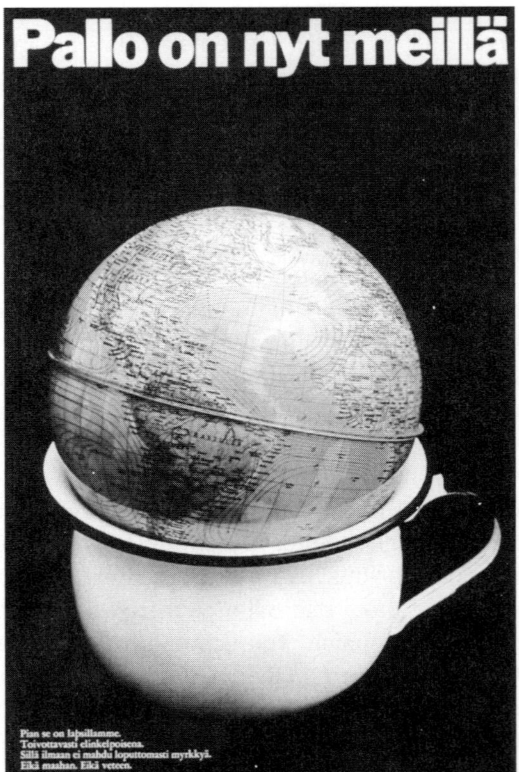

Fig. 13.3 'We have the ball now'. Anti-pollution poster by Kyösti Varis, 1970. Photo: Seppo Parkkinen. Courtesy of Design Museum Helsinki.

design as culture and the ideologies of education responsible for the mindset of the coming designers.

Owing to its continuing hegemony in design education, the national design school was a keystone for the climate and future of Finnish design. The majority of its student body and a large number of the faculty quickly moved from a general cultural radicalism to various left-wing positions, ultimately arriving at extreme Marxism-Leninism in the early 1970s. These developments mirrored a general tendency among students in Finland but in a more extreme and visible manner. Consequently, when the new design university opened its doors in 1973, its mission statement was not about cooperation with industry, technological progress or international competition—keywords of strategic plans for design since the 1960s and largely the reason why university status had been granted by the Ministry of Education. Instead, the proclaimed tasks were to promote economic and regional equality, environmentally friendly production for the good of society and the expansion of democratic thinking (fig. 13.4).

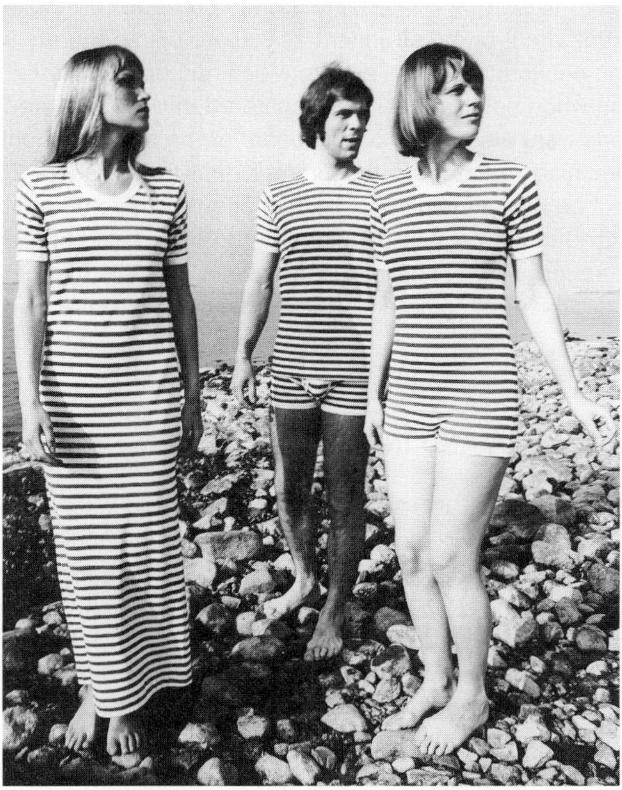

Fig. 13.4 Fashion and the politics of gender: Tasaraita unisex tricot by Annika Rimala for Marimekko from the late 1960s. Photographer unknown. Courtesy of Design Museum Helsinki.

In the years that followed, the institution was to arrive at an antagonistic position towards both the Ministry of Education, which provided the budget, and industry and its organizations.

Political turmoil hampered the development of education, which largely turned from product design to socially programmed projects such as workplace safety and the conditions of socially marginalized persons or communities. Though based on a decisively strong social and political motivation and ethos, these efforts did not spur confidence among leaders of industry. It was highly problematic to educate designers striving towards a socialist utopia in a capitalist country with a free market economy. Courses such as Anti-Capitalist Product Design were easily leading to an impasse—how to make a living in a context still driven by the evil of private ownership? During the 1970s, the much-awaited design university wound up in a position of weakness where the mistrust of the authorities and industry was complemented by the media scandalizing political upheavals within the institution.

Design education was affected not only by political polarization but also by Ornamo, the professional organization. The designer Antti Nurmesniemi, a leading figure in striving for consensus, stated in 1970 how the 'voices of political parties are growing stronger . . . you are black; you are white'.[4] Now, the close-knit network of design actors, which had been a strength, displayed its weakness when political schisms separated individuals. The fact that the same persons were also active on the board of the design school meant that politics there also radiated to the professional organization. This was not without effect on decisions on how Finnish design was to be promoted. Politically radicalized students, not in Finland but in Milan, also brought an end to the shining series of triumphs of the Triennale. The XIV Trienniale di Milano of 1968 was closed immediately after its opening because of local student revolts.[5]

CRAFT, NOSTALGIA AND INDUSTRIAL DESIGN

What had begun in the 1960s as an effort towards a design policy had thus ended in the politics of design. The neutral, instrumentalist approach was supplanted by party politics informed by ideologies, predominantly from the left but also in the mid-1970s to an increasing degree by advocates of the 'free' society inspired by figures such as Karl Popper. While the dynamism and expansion of the extreme left began to lose their appeal towards the end of the 1970s, the earlier demarcations and traumatic battles remained a frustrating factor also within the design community. But if, as said, ideological disputes mainly concerned the cultural and ideological aspects of design and its role as a national treasure, what, then, were 'non-political' alternatives for practising design?

One answer was craft, practised either individually or by small collectives as workshops, with work and ownership based on the principle of equality. This concerned mostly textiles and ceramics and to some degree glass, where investments were more significant and the demand for special skills higher. This craft movement was not completely voluntary. Both the ceramics and textile industries ended up in financial problems around the mid 1970s, and design graduates faced limited employment opportunities. Craft-workshop activities provided a certain freedom, as in the case of experimental hand-printed cotton fabrics. The same was true of ceramics, where artisans could move freely between household pottery and ceramic art in ways not possible within a streamlined corporate context. These craft workshops also showed signs of returning to the pre-capitalist modes of production of cottage industries and the conditions of governing and owning one's own work. In this way, they offered an escape from both large-scale private industry, where creativity was bound to corporate decision-making, and the ideologically frustrating agenda of aligning work to a revolutionary cause stressing obedience to a collective. The movement was also of an anti-urban character. Emptied by rapid urbanization in the previous decade, the countryside now offered affordable workspaces in abandoned cowsheds and stables. But it was also bound to broader currents in Finnish culture of the 1970s, which involved nostalgia for a lost rural way of life and a quest for alternatives to the consumer culture predominating in the cities. It was about saying 'no' to modernism, in both its capitalist and socialist guises.

In Finnish household consumption, especially furniture, references to history sneaked in around the turn of the 1970s, as analysed by Minna Sarantola-Weiss in this volume. Forbidden by the modernist agenda so vehemently guarded by the arbiters and gatekeepers of 'good design', it was welcomed particularly in the homes of newly urbanized suburban residents. But there was also a more general longing for the national past, a rural setting that been lost only recently. This pastoral past was regarded as non-political and laden with positive connotations of true Finnishness. It can be said that whereas the 1960s were all about opening up, internationalism and even cosmopolitanism, the 1970s meant turning inwards and closing windows. Neo-folklore became a trend that also led to collection of the remnants of the agrarian past, which now adorned especially upper-middle-class homes in the form of simple wooden vessels and other utensils. In actual design production, this 'roots' movement was particularly present in the motifs of knitwear, more generally in the return of clothing paraphrasing peasant culture and in pseudo-vernacular furniture in standardized suburban flats. At the same time, several leading designers such as Wirkkala and Tapiovaara were truly concerned about vanishing craft skills in the agrarian context and organized courses and workshops to keep the tradition of indigenous craft alive. But the clock could not be turned backwards, and traditional craft items became marginalized to serve tourism and decoration.

But beneath these currents of perhaps higher visibility to consumers, industrial design progressed steadily, gaining new territory and becoming a silent and anonymous yet increasingly important part of everyday life, both public and private. Design-intensiveness steadily increased among the heavy metal-working industries producing items such as ships, transportation vehicles and other business-to-business investment goods. On the other hand, industrial design, working along with other disciplines, came into use in designing workplace environments and especially their safety measures. The rapidly growing and increasingly complex sector of hospital and health care equipment also applied design. In these tasks, designers could see their work contributing to the social call of improving everyday life—and it was a way to avoid the dilemma of commercial consumer product design. Also, the contact of industrial design with other fields of knowledge—such as engineering and, most important, psychological and physiognomic studies via ergonomics—made it 'scientific' and high-tech in a way that the traditional sectors of design could not be. The rapid development of complex electronics serving information flow and surveillance in public environments like traffic, devices for measurement and soon advances in telecommunication contributed to what would become interface design. In consumer products, domestic television manufacturers in particular were quick to take advantage of design. Finally, in large public projects, such as the Helsinki metro from the late 1960s to the early 1980s, designers showed that they could contribute as equal partners in multi-professional teams. Unlike ceramicists or textile designers, industrial designers were able to advance as a professional group and also began to run their businesses through consultancies. Unlike the earlier interior design offices, which adopted the conventions of architectural offices, these firms were not named after their directors or head designers but were given corporate names.

In this way, a crisis both did and did not exist in Finnish design in the mid and late 1970s. The crisis was on the one hand political and ideological, particularly hampering education, and on the other hand economic, with a negative impact on the traditional genres of design-related production. As we have seen, however, industrial design advanced but without the traditional visibility and focus on individuals typical of the 1950s and 1960s. We can say that the policy considerations of the 1960s became a reality for industry, the public sector and their use of industrial design. Also, the tide began to turn in the late 1970s. Education and industries began to look for a dialogue, weary combatants rose from their trenches to make a new start, and a new generation came to the fore. Finnish design was preparing for the decade of hedonist consumption: the 1980s.

CONCLUDING REMARKS

This historical cross-section of Finnish design, which began its development as an institutionalized activity in the 1870s, is just one passage illustrating the entwinement of policymaking—(non)political, multilevel strategies of guidance, management and governance—and politics stemming from ideological positions and manifesting itself as parties or other groups. An illustrative case could also have been the founding period with its patriotic underpinnings and tensions between the countryside and the capital, the agrarian and the industrial; or, to take a more recent case, the final breakthrough and success of conceptualizing and implementing a national design policy in the first years of this millennium. But here we are already in a period where ideologies are supposedly dead, and the only remaining shared activity, both nationally and globally, is consumption. In this regard, the 1960s and 1970s were richer in argumentation, tensions and convictions. Alternatives were sought and found, sometimes in counterproductive ways. But as the French philosopher Jean Jaurès has said: 'Take from the altars of the past the fire—not the ashes.' Although history cannot and should not be repeated, it may inspire. Present and coming young designers might take a look at the late 1960s when trying to make design a part of the solution of pressing global problems. As was often repeated in the 1960s: if you're not part of the solution you're part of the problem.

Epilogue

Kjetil Fallan

This book has sought to offer a selection of alternative histories of Scandinavian design based on the premise that the hegemonic narratives in this field have been so persistent—particularly in its international and popular reception—as to dwarf and suppress the development and propagation of critical, complementary, unorthodox, nonconformist accounts, which in many other fields of history writing have proliferated with the demise of the *grands récits* brought about by poststructuralist theory and the so-called linguistic, or cultural, turn and more recent historiographic shifts. Clearly, the dozen case studies presented here are only a fraction of the wealth of potential alternative histories that can be told. Our alternative histories do not purport to cover any representative ground regarding which types of 'otherness' merit mention; nor do they profess to constitute a new orthodoxy in the sense that ours are more decisive or definite accounts. They do, however, make up a contribution—however modest—to the expansion and diversification of Scandinavian design history, both its subject matter and its approaches.

The case studies presented here have taken us far and wide in the landscape of Scandinavian design history: we have discussed objects as diverse as furnishing fabrics, reverse vending machines, trams, sofas and chocolate bars. We have visited early-twentieth-century working-class homes, interwar public urban arenas, postwar retail spaces and contemporary lifestyle kitchens. We have explored aspects of design culture ranging from legal protection and consumer policy via socio-technical infrastructures and ideological power to photographical representation and image construction.

Despite their heterogeneity, our accounts are intended to form a collective and have therefore been structured according to their analytical approaches. Part 1, *Networks*, highlighted the thoroughly systemic and networked character of design and how pervasive this feature is, taking design into the realms of jurisprudence, manufacturing systems, professional and educational structures, corporate strategies, marketing and retail practices and political planning. Part 2, *Appropriations*, demonstrated how design is fundamentally relational by looking at some of the many ways in which specific ideas or phenomena become elements in processes of making sense of design culture and producing meaning on many different levels or scenes: the selective appropriation of history when writing history and forming design policy; the local interpretation of and contribution to international design movements and design as cultural valuation of materials; the non-appropriation of ascetic aesthetics and modernist morality as the mirror image of the appropriation of comfortable furniture; and the transference of celebrity 'aura' and re-employment of formal vocabularies in branding new products. Part 3, *Mediations*, explored examples of how design mediates meaning and how the meaning of design is mediated: through products and advertisement; through photography; through promotional material and journalism; and through professional discourse and design policy.

These three categories of approaches, or themes, are obviously not the only valid ones—nor do they by any means cover the field in a representative manner. However, emphasizing these themes at the expense of others in the structure of the book is a way of acknowledging their perceived centrality in design history today and may, hopefully, increase this publication's relevance beyond the cohort of students of Scandinavian design history. But, as already mentioned, it is not only the book's thematic structure that is partial; so is its content. The case studies offered here are just a small part of the many alternative histories that could be told. So what remains to be done, then? With so many 'white spots' on the Scandinavian design historical map, it is difficult to make any prioritized suggestions, but it may still be worthwhile to mention a few issues that merit greater attention in future work in the field.

Regarding the need to mitigate the pervasive reductive accounts of Scandinavian design history, at least in terms of addressing a broader audience, one of the more obvious and effective ways would be to improve and expand the roster of survey books. Certainly, survey histories represent a notoriously difficult category in design history writing, and the broad strokes and quick pace they require are an effective deterrent to many scholars. Nevertheless, both Finland and Sweden have recently seen the publication of new national survey books that reflect a scholarly approach more in tune with international developments in the field: Pekka Korvenmaa's *Finnish Design* and Lasse Brunnström's *Svensk designhistoria*.[1] These books are a good start, but their equivalents in Denmark and Norway have yet to be written. Even more compelling, perhaps, in keeping with the internationalization of design culture, is the need for a pan-Scandinavian survey history. A daunting task, to be sure, but it is to be hoped that the challenge will be met. Survey histories have their limitations, especially in terms of scope, selection criteria and analytical depth, but will continue to be an essential species in the flora that is design history literature.

For the field's own development, however, there are other, more pressing concerns. Some of these are direct results of the limited impact postmodernist theory has had on Scandinavian design history. Many issues that were raised as part of the heterogenization of the humanities from the 1970s onwards remain unsatisfactorily addressed in Scandinavian design history. The most profoundly influential analytical categories to emerge in this process were probably the trinity of gender, class and race, which, combined, significantly changed the agenda of research throughout the humanities and has since become part and parcel of our scholarly consciousness. And whereas these categories—at least gender and, to a certain extent, class—have made their distinctive mark on design history internationally, such impact is harder to trace in the Scandinavian literature.

Given the strong feminist movements and the early and fast advances in women's rights in Scandinavia, one might have expected gender to be embraced by Scandinavian design history more emphatically than it has been. There is nothing to indicate that design practice has not been subject to the same gender segregations in Scandinavia as elsewhere, nor that Scandinavian objects have been less gendered than those of different origin, nor that the stereotypes and actual practice in the consumption and use of these products differs significantly from international experiences. Of course, also in Scandinavia research has been done on women designers, a genre that might in part be inspired by feminist art history—albeit in its most basic form—but even these rarely apply a critical approach to gender issues. Other, less rudimentary ways of addressing gender issues can of course be found—the notion of women entrepreneurs, for instance, as discussed by Leena Svinhufvud in this book—but this approach to design history remains under-explored in Scandinavia and clearly warrants more attention.[2]

The second category, class, which arose primarily in the form of Marxist-inspired social history, has not coloured the Scandinavian design historical map the way it has the broader field of history. As Christina Zetterlund points out in her contribution, the class aspect has been virtually absent among both reformers (beyond their 'educational' attitude to 'the masses') and historians, making it increasingly difficult to access the nuances in the material cultures of various social classes beyond the elites—a problem only worsened by the generally poor documentation of the material cultures of the lower-income strata of the population in museums and archives. Approaching this topic from another angle the sociologist Kjetil Rolness put considerable effort into ridiculing educated middle-class missionaries of modernism whilst hailing the interior decoration practices of homeowners from the lower middle class and working class less than enthused by 'good design'.[3] Minna Sarantola-Weiss in this volume moves beyond easy satire in her exposure of the limited impact of the cultural elite's tastemaking strategies, exploring instead an array of social and cultural developmental patterns in the maturation of Finnish consumer society and the accompanying empowerment of working-class consumers.

At the other end of design culture—the production sphere—where Marxist theory and social history could be appropriate approaches to exploring the class aspects of the organization of design and manufacturing processes, the potential is equally unresolved. After a marked and much-needed shift in focus from production to consumption and mediation over the recent couple of decades, design history may now be on the brink of a renewed interest in production as a result of several developments in contemporary design processes and manufacture systems: the international scope of design consultancies and industrial corporations; the globalization of manufacture and trade, with the ensuing spotlight on working conditions and labour rights (cf. the media attention to 'sweatshops'); and an increased public and political interest in sustainability. Combined, these factors may very well herald a new, critical attention to the infrastructure and ethics of the production of goods in design history—and class could become a key category, even in the allegedly 'classless' Scandinavian society of today.

As opposed to gender and class, race—or perhaps ethnicity is a more appropriate term—has not been a prominent feature in design history internationally either. When it has failed to become a major issue in design historical strongholds like Britain and the USA, both societies with a long history of multi-ethnicity, it is hardly surprising that it is not at the top of the agenda in Scandinavia either. Although relative newcomers in terms of significant non-European immigration, the Scandinavian countries have become multicultural societies—a fact that is profoundly reflected in our material culture and therefore should concern design historians. An interesting example that might point in this direction is to be found in a project at the Norwegian Museum of Cultural History (Norsk Folkemuseum): an apartment building from 1865—donated by its owner, Oslo Cooperative Housing Cooperation—was rebuilt at the museum in 1999–2001. It featured a number of flats furnished as (re)constructed homes representing different moments in time, social strata, living conditions and interior styles in Oslo from the late nineteenth century up to the present. One of these flats is a contemporary (2002) 'Pakistani home in Norway', constructed in an ethnographic manner based on acquisitions made in collaboration with a Pakistani immigrant family.[4] The exhibit shows how multicultural homes in Norway are not wholesale transpositions of immigrant customs but products of negotiations between different cultures and time periods. This project can serve as a valuable reminder that Scandinavian design history—past, present and future—is not as 'white' as it might appear in its literature. But this challenge does not extend only to the recognition of recent intercontinental migrants' design and consumption practices but equally to the region's own indigenous people—the Sami—and 'older' ethnic minorities whose material culture is just as absent from Scandinavian design history.

In addition to the insufficient implementation of these three analytical categories, there are numerous other issues that could be addressed in more detail in future work and thereby contribute to the expansion and development of the field. Some topics that have been significantly under-represented in

Scandinavian design history literature are touched upon in this volume but remain in need of further studies. Examples include the methodologically notoriously challenging sphere of consumption, probed by both Christina Zetterlund and Minna Sarantola-Weiss; the highly rewarding approach informed by business history and the history of technology, which has been little exploited by design historians but is demonstrated here by both Finn Arne Jørgensen and Stig Kvaal and Per Østby; and marginalized sectors of design practice such as graphic design and packaging, discussed by both Helena Mattsson and Kvaal and Østby. Other sectors of design practice little explored in Scandinavian design history and also not covered by this book comprise categories such as toys, sports gear, interiors, military equipment and amateur/do-it-yourself practices.

Design history in Scandinavia has suffered not only from a too narrow subject matter in term of design practices and object categories but also from a modernist bias—both synchronic and diachronic. The synchronic modernist bias is partially addressed in this book through discussions of several aspects of design culture that do not conform to modernist ideals, but the diachronic modernist bias is not mitigated correspondingly. Studies of designs from early glass works, ceramics manufacturers, and so on exist, but beyond the applied art sector very little work has been done on the premodern period (before 1850). In addition to older material, there are other, more thematic aspects that have not received much attention, such as politics and power, the incorporation of which could help bring design history closer to the domains of other, more established fields of historical scholarship.

Perhaps more pressing, and probably more plausible, in terms of future developments in the field, is the need to engage with topics like sustainability and ethics—topics that are becoming key concerns in design practice, policymaking and consumer behaviour and that therefore will command the attention of design historians as well. Among other phenomena that have and will continue to transform design culture but still await significant historical scholarship are computer-aided design and manufacture (CAD/CAM) and other digitization technologies as well as the so-called new media.[5]

Acknowledging the vast ground still to be covered and pointing out a few possible leads for future work, the accounts featured in this book and the composite they make up are nevertheless offered as a contribution to the diversification and development of Scandinavian design history in the belief that it may provide a basis for other alternative histories, be they complementary, corrective or conflicting.

Notes

INTRODUCTION

1. For a history of the concept, see Mirjam Gelfer-Jørgensen, 'Scandinavianism—a Cultural Brand', in Widar Halén and Kerstin Wickman (eds.), *Scandinavian Design beyond the Myth: Fifty Years of Design from the Nordic Countries* (Stockholm: Arvinius Förlag, 2003), pp. 17–25.
2. Viviana Narotzky, 'Selling the Nation: Identity and Design in 1980s Catalonia', *Design Issues* 25/3 (2009), p. 63.
3. Some of the issues raised here in connection with the regional and the national as analytical categories in design history are discussed in Jonathan M. Woodham, 'Local, National and Global: Redrawing the Design Historical Map', *Journal of Design History* 18/3 (2005), pp. 257–267; and Anna Calvera, 'Local, Regional, National, Global and Feedback: Several Issues to be Faced with Constructing Regional Narratives', *Journal of Design History* 18/4 (2005), pp. 371–383.
4. Jean-Francois Lyotard, *La condition postmoderne* (Paris: Minuit, 1979), p. 8.
5. See e.g. Hayden White, *The Content of the Form: Narrative Discourse and Historical Representation* (Baltimore: Johns Hopkins University Press, 1987); and Dominick LaCapra, *History and Criticism* (Ithaca, NY: Cornell University Press, 1985).
6. Fran Hannah and Tim Putnam, 'Taking Stock in Design History', *Block* 3 (1980), p. 32.
7. John A. Walker, *Design History and the History of Design* (London: Pluto Press, 1989), p. 2.
8. Nanette Salomon, 'The Art Historical Canon: Sins of Omission', in Donald Prezionsi (ed.), *The Art of Art History: A Critical Anthology* (Oxford: Oxford University Press, 1998), pp. 350–351; and Carma R. Gorman, 'Reshaping and Rethinking: Recent Feminist Scholarship on Design and Designers', *Design Issues* 17/4 (2001), p. 74.
9. Theodor Adorno, 'Valéry Proust Museum', in *Prisms* (Cambridge, MA: MIT Press, 1983), p. 175.
10. Philip Johnson, *Machine Art* (New York: MoMA/Arno Press, 1934); and Paola Antonelli, *Humble Masterpieces: Everyday Marvels of Design* (New York: Harper Collins, 2005).

11. The term 'counter-history' is often associated with Michel Foucault and can be described as 'assum[ing] a contrapuntal relationship to traditional history, whose conclusions it more rearranges than denies and whose resources it mines for its own purposes'. Thomas Flynn, 'Foucault's Mapping of History', in Gary Gutting (ed.), *The Cambridge Companion to Foucault* (Cambridge: Cambridge University Press, 1994), p. 32.
12. Hazel Conway, 'Design History Basics', in Hazel Conway (ed.), *Design History: A Student's Handbook* (London: Harper Collins, 1987), p. 9.
13. Adam Smith, 'Of the Division of Labour' [1776], in Grace Lees-Maffei and Rebecca Houze (eds.), *The Design History Reader* (Oxford: Berg, 2010), pp. 32–33.
14. Vilém Flusser, 'The Ethics of Industrial Design?' in *The Shape of Things: A Philosophy of Design* (London: Reaktion, 1999), p. 67.
15. Kjetil Fallan, 'Architecture in Action: Traveling with Actor-Network Theory in the Land of Architectural Research', *Architectural Theory Review* 13/1 (2008), pp. 80–96; and Kjetil Fallan, 'An ANT in Our Pants? A Design Historian's Reflections on Actor-Network Theory', in Fiona Hackney, Jonathan Glynne and Viv Minton (eds.), *Networks of Design: Proceedings of the 2008 Annual International Conference of the Design History Society (UK) University College Falmouth, 3–6 September* (Boca Raton, FL: Universal-Publishers, 2009), pp. 46–52.
16. Mikael Hård and Andrew Jamison, 'Conceptual Framework: Technology Debates as Appropriation Process', in Mikael Hård and Andrew Jamison (eds.), *The Intellectual Appropriation of Technology: Discourses on Modernity, 1900–1939* (Cambridge, MA: MIT Press, 1998), pp. 1–15; and Mikael Hård and Andrew Jamison, *Hubris and Hybrids: A Cultural History of Technology and Science* (London: Routledge, 2005).
17. Elizabeth E. Guffey, *Retro: The Culture of Revival* (London: Reaktion, 2006).
18. Calvera, 'Local, Regional, National, Global and Feedback', pp. 371–383.
19. Bruno Latour, *Reassembling the Social: An Introduction to Actor-Network Theory* (Oxford: Oxford University Press, 2005), p. 39.
20. Kjetil Fallan, *Design History: Understanding Theory and Method* (Oxford: Berg, 2010), pp. 18, 44.
21. Dick Hebdige, 'Object as Image: The Italian Scooter Cycle', *Block* 5 (1981), pp. 44–64.
22. Grace Lees-Maffei, 'The Production-Consumption-Mediation Paradigm', *Journal of Design History* 22/4 (2009), p. 351.
23. Viviana Narotzky, '"A Different and New Refinement": Design in Barcelona, 1960–1990', *Journal of Design History* 13/3 (2000), pp. 227–243; Michell Jones, 'Design and the Domestic Persuader: Television and the British Broadcasting Corporation's Promotion of Post-war "Good Design"', *Journal of Design History* 16/4 (2003), pp. 307–318; Jonathan

M. Woodham, 'Managing British Design Reform II: The Film *Deadly Lampshade*—An Ill-fated Episode in the Politics of "Good Taste" ', *Journal of Design History* 9/2 (1996), pp. 101–115; Kjetil Fallan, 'The Metamorphosis of a Norwegian Design Magazine: *Nye Bonytt*, 1968–1971', in Grace Lees-Maffei (ed.), *Writing Design: Words and Objects* (Oxford: Berg, 2011), pp. 47–61; Maddalena Dalla Mura, *Design e musei fra storia e nuovi approcci: Il contributo dei musei di scienza e tecnologia* [Doctoral thesis] (Venice: Università Iuav di Venezia, 2010); Gay McDonald, 'The "Advance" of American Postwar Design in Europe: MoMA and the *Design for Use, USA* Exhibition 1951–1953', *Design Issues* 24/2 (2008), pp. 15–27.

24. Peter-Paul Verbeek, *What Things Do: Philosophical Reflections on Technology, Agency, and Design* (University Park: Pennsylvania State University Press, 2005), pp. 130–132.

CHAPTER 1. A HISTORIOGRAPHY OF SCANDINAVIAN DESIGN

The research for this chapter's section on Sweden was done within the research projects Svensk design? Om Ikeas estetik på 1980-och 90-talet, export av 'svensk design' och nationella myter, funded by Riksbankens jubileumsfond, and Forms of Sustainability, funded by Vetenskapsrådet (2008–2257).

1. Arne Remlov (ed.), *Design in Scandinavia: An Exhibition of Objects for the Home from Denmark, Finland, Norway, Sweden* (Oslo: Kirstes Boktrykkeri, 1954); and Ulf Hård af Segerstad, *Design in Scandinavia: February 1968–January 1969 Denmark, Finland, Norway, Sweden* (Stockholm: Victor Pettersons Bokindustri AB, 1968).
2. Alf Bøe, *Nordisk industridesign: Hva, hvorfor, hvordan* (Oslo: Kunstindustrimuseet i Oslo, 1976), unpaged.
3. Alf Bøe, 'Scandinavian Industrial Design', in *Nordisk industridesign* (Gothenburg: Rösska Konstslöjdmuseet, 1971), pp. 23–31.
4. Ibid., pp. 23–31.
5. Stig Brøgger (ed.), *Form og funktion: Sophienholm 1980* (Lyngby: Lyngby-Taarbæk Kommune, 1980).
6. Fredrik Wildhagen, 'Samarbeid og styrke: Nordisk formgivning i tiden etter verdenskrigen', in Hermann Bongard, Rolf Himberg-Larsen and Fredrik Wildhagen (eds.), *Nordisk kunsthåndverk og design* (Oslo: Landsforbundet Norsk Brukskunst, 1981), pp. 9–40.
7. Helena Dahlbäck Lutteman and Marianne Uggla (eds.), *The Lunning Prize* (Stockholm: Nationalmuseum, 1986). The Lunning Prize has also been the subject of a doctoral study: Astrid Skjerven, *Goodwill for Scandinavian Design: Lunningprisen 1951–70* [Doctoral thesis] (Oslo: University of Oslo, 2001).

8. David R. McFadden (ed.), *Modern Scandinavian Design 1880–1980* (New York: Harry N. Abrams, 1982).
9. Jennifer H. Opie, *Scandinavia: Ceramics and Glass in the Twentieth Century* (London: Victoria & Albert Museum, 1989).
10. Widar Halén and Kerstin Wickman (eds.), *Scandinavian Design beyond the Myth* (Stockholm: Arvinius Förlag, 2003).
11. Ulf Hård af Segerstad, *Nordisk Brukskunst* (Oslo: Gyldendal Norsk Forlag, 1961); and Ulf Hård af Segerstad, *Modern Scandinavian Furniture* (Oslo: Gyldendal Norsk Forlag, 1963).
12. Erik Zahle (ed.), *A Treasury of Scandinavian Design: The Standard Authority on Scandinavian-designed Furniture, Textiles, Glass, Ceramics, and Metal* (New York: Golden Press, 1961).
13. Viggo Sten Møller, *Funktionalisme og brugskunst siden 1920erne: Danmark. Norge. Sverige* (Copenhagen: Rhodos, 1978).
14. Eileene H. Beer, *Scandinavian Design: Objects of a Life Style* (New York: Farrar, Straus and Giroux, 1975), p. 3.
15. Miriam Gelfer-Jørgensen (ed.), *Nordisk funktionalisme 1925–1950: 15 foredrag fra det nordiske seminar afholdt juni 1985 på Det danske Kunstindustrimuseum* (Copenhagen: Nordisk Forum for Formgivningshistorie, 1986); Miriam Gelfer-Jørgensen (ed.), *Kontekst og Perspektiv: 12 foredrag fra Nordisk Forum for Formgivningshistories 5. seminar på Kunstindustrimuseet i København i juni 1991* (Copenhagen: Nordisk Forum for Formgivningshistorie, 1992); and Widar Halén (guest ed., special issue on designer couples), *Kunst og Kultur* 93/2 (2010).
16. Exceptions can of course be found, such as Ingeborg Glambek, 'The Council Chambers in the UN Building in New York', *Scandinavian Journal of Design History* 15 (2005), pp. 8–39.
17. Christine Stevenson, 'Decorative Art Production in the Scandinavian Kingdoms', in Carlo Pirovano (ed.), *History of Industrial Design: 1750–1850—The Age of the Industrial Revolution* (Milan: Electa, 1990), pp. 196–211; Lars Dybdahl, 'The Scandinavian Countries: From the Viking Revival toward Functional Objectivity', in Carlo Pirovano (ed.), *History of Industrial Design: 1851–1918—The Great Emporium of the World* (Milan: Electa, 1990), pp. 228–251; and Fredrik Wildhagen, 'The Scandinavian Countries: Design for the Welfare Society', in Carlo Pirovano (ed.), *History of Industrial Design: 1919–1990—The Dominion of Design* (Milan: Electa, 1990), pp. 148–159.
18. Ingeborg Glambek, *Det nordiske i arkitektur og design: Sett utenfra* (Copenhagen and Oslo: Arkitektens Forlag and Norsk Arkitekturforlag, 1997).
19. The University of Southern Denmark ran a research project from 2006 to 2009 that was the first broader academic investigation of the complex historical character Poul Henningsen beyond his lamp designs. The results are published in the following anthologies: Carl-Erik Bay and Hans-

Christian Jensen (eds.), *Tradition og modernisme: Indfaldsvinkler til PH* (Odense: Syddansk Universitetsforlag, 2008); Jørn Guldberg and Niels Peter Skou (eds.), *Kritik og formidling: Studier i PH's kulturkritik* (Odense: Syddansk Universitetsforlag, 2008); and Anne Borup and Jørn Guldberg (eds.), *Kulturmoderniseringens paradokser: Studier i PH's kulturbegreber, kritik og praksis* (Odense: Syddansk Universitetsforlag, 2010).

20. Anders V. Munch, 'Heraus aus den Goldrahmen', in Gertrud Huidberg-Hansen and Gertrud Oelsner (eds.), *Johan Rohde 1856–1935: Ein dänisher Künstler der Moderne* (Berlin: Bröhan-Museum, 2006), pp. 68–84.
21. Viggo Sten Møller, *Dansk kunstindustri 1900–1950*, vols 1–2 (Copenhagen: Rhodos, 1970).
22. Henrik Sten Møller, *Dansk design/Danish Design* (Copenhagen: Rhodos, 1975); and Svend Erik Møller, *Danish Design* (Copenhagen: Det Danske Selskab, 1974).
23. Mirjam Gelfer-Jørgensen, *Dansk kunsthåndværk fra 1850 til vor tid* (Copenhagen: Nyt Nordisk Forlag Arnold Busck, 1982).
24. Ibid., p. 9.
25. Mirjam Gelfer-Jørgensen, *Guldalderdrømmen* (Copenhagen: Rhodos, 2002); and Mirjam Gelfer-Jørgensen, *Møbler med mening*, vols 1–2 (Copenhagen: Arkitektens Forlag, 2009).
26. Lars Dybdahl (ed.), *Dansk design 1910–1945: Art déco og funktionalisme* (Copenhagen: Danish Museum of Art and Design, 1997).
27. Lars Dybdahl, *Dansk design 1945–1975* (Copenhagen: Borgen, 2006).
28. See e.g. Lars Dybdahl (ed.), *De industrielle ikoner: Design Danmark* (Copenhagen: Danish Museum of Art and Design, 2004).
29. Also collected in one volume published as Poul Erik Tøjner (ed.), *Store danske designere* (Copenhagen: Lindhardt og Ringhof, 2008). Another example is Per H. Hansen and Birgit L. Pedersen, *Finn Juhl og hans hus* (Copenhagen: Gyldendal/Ordrupgaard, 2009).
30. Thomas Dickson, *Dansk Design* [English edition] (Copenhagen: Gyldendal, 2008); and Ida Engholm and Anders Michelsen, *Designmaskinen* (Copenhagen: Gyldendal, 1999).
31. Among the apocrypha of academia are examples of much-needed studies of this kind, e.g. Jørn Guldberg, *Tradition, modernitet og usamtidighed: Om Børge Mogensens FDB-møbler og det modernes hjemliggørelse* [Working paper] (Odense: University of Southern Denmark, 1998) and the chapter on home decoration advice literature in Hans-Christian Jensen, *Fra velfærd til designkultur: Velfærdsengagement i dansk designteori og designpraksis i det. 20. århundrede* [Doctoral thesis] (Odense: University of Southern Denmark, 2005).
32. Arne Karlsen, *Dansk møbelkunst i det 20. århundrede*, vols 1–2 (Copenhagen: Christian Ejlers, 1991).
33. Birgit Kaiser, *Den ideologiske funktionalisme* (Copenhagen: Gad, 1992). A later example more informed by material culture studies is Gertrud

Øllgaard, 'A Super-elliptical Moment in the Cultural Form of the Table: A Case Study of a Danish Table', *Journal of Design History* 12/2 (1999), pp. 143–157.

34. Kevin Davies, 'Scandinavian Furniture in Britain: Finmar and the UK Market, 1949–1952', *Journal of Design History* 10/1 (1997), pp. 39–52; and Kevin Davies, 'Markets, Marketing and Design: The Danish Furniture Industry c. 1947–65', *Scandinavian Journal of Design History* 9 (1999), pp. 56–73.
35. Per H. Hansen, *Da danske møbler blev moderne* (Copenhagen and Odense: Aschehoug and Syddansk Universitetsforlag, 2006).
36. See e.g. Tapio Periäinen, *Soul in Design: Finland as an Example* (Tampere: Kirjayhtyma, 1990).
37. Ulf Hård af Segerstad, *Finskt konsthantverk* (Stockholm: Wahlström & Widstrand, 1968).
38. Onni Okkonen, *Suomen taiteen historia* (Porvoo: WSOY, 1945); and Sixten Ringbom (ed.), *Konsten i Finland: Från medeltid till nutid* (Helsinki: Holger Schildts Förlag, 1978).
39. Salme Sarajas-Korte (ed.), *ARS: Suomen taide*, vols 1–6 (Keuruu: Weilin+Göös, 1990).
40. Päiviö Tommila, Aimo Reitala and Veikko Kallio (eds.), *Suomen kulttuurihistoria*, vols 1–3 (Porvoo: Söderström, 1979–82).
41. Laura Kolbe (ed.), *Suomen kulttuurihistoria*, vols 1–5 (Helsinki: Tammi, 2002–4).
42. Erik Kruskopf, *Suomen taideteollisuus: Suomalaisen muotoilun vaiheita* (Porvoo: WSOY, 1989). Swedish ed.: *Finlands konstindustri: Den finländska konstflitens utvecklingshistoria* (Borgå: Söderström, 1989).
43. Marianne Aav and Eeva Viljanen (eds.), *Tapio Wirkkala: Ajattelevat kädet* (Helsinki: Designmuseo, 2000); Marianne Aav, Maria Härkäpää and Eeva Viljanen (eds.), *Marimekko: Fabrics, Fashion, Architecture* (New Haven, CN: Yale University Press, 2003); and Marianne Aav et al. (eds.), *Arabia: Ceramics Art Industry* (Helsinki: Designmuseo, 2009).
44. Kaisa Koivisto, *Kolme tarinaa lasista* [Doctoral thesis] (Vammala: Suomen lasimuseo, 2001).
45. Marjo Wiberg, *The Textile Designer and the Art of Design: On the Formation of a Profession in Finland* [Doctoral thesis] (Helsinki: University of Art and Design Helsinki, 1996); and Anna Valtonen, *Redefining Industrial Design: Changes in the Design Practice in Finland* [Doctoral thesis] (Helsinki: University of Art and Design Helsinki, 2007).
46. Harri Kalha, *Muotopuolen merenneidon pauloissa: Suomen taideteollisuuden kultakausi: Mielikuvat, markkinointi, diskurssit* [Doctoral thesis] (Helsinki: Apeiron, 1997). See also his 'Myths and Mysteries of Finnish Design: Reading "Wirkkala" and the National Nature Paradigm', *Journal of Scandinavian Design History* 12 (2002), pp. 24–47.

47. Yrjö Sotamaa and Pia Strandman (eds.), *Taideteollisuuden muotoja ja murroksia: Taideteollinen korkeakoulu 130 vuotta* (Helsinki: University of Art and Design Helsinki, 1999).
48. Ilkka Huovio, *Invitation from the Future: Treatise on the Roots of the School for Arts and Crafts and its Development into a University-level School 1871–1973* [Doctoral thesis] (Tampere: University of Tampere, 1998). See also his *Bridging the Future: The General History of University of Art and Design 1973–2003* (Tampere: University of Tampere, 2009).
49. See e.g. Minna Sarantola-Weiss (ed.), *Rooms for Everyone: Perspectives on Finnish Interior Design 1949–1999* (Helsinki: Otava, 1999).
50. Kevin Davies, '"A Geographical Notion Turned into an Artistic Reality": Promoting Finland and Selling Finnish Design in Post-war Britain *c.*1953–1965', *Journal of Design History* 15/2 (2002), pp. 101–116; Kevin Davies, 'Finmar and the Furniture of the Future: The Sale of Alvar Aalto's Plywood Furniture in the UK, 1934–1939', *Journal of Design History* 11/2 (1998), pp. 145–156; Gay McDonald, 'The Modern American Home as Soft Power: Finland, MoMA and the "American Home 1953" Exhibition', *Journal of Design History* 23/4 (2010), pp. 387–408; Charlotte Ashby, 'Nation Building and Design: Finnish Textiles and the Work of the Friends of Finnish Handicrafts', *Journal of Design History* 23/4 (2010), pp. 351–365; and Asdis Olafsdottir, *Le mobilier d'Alvar Aalto dans l'espace et dans le temps: La diffusion internationale de design 1920–1940* [Doctoral thesis] (Paris: Université Paris 1, 1998).
51. Marianne Aav and Nina Stritzler-Levine (eds.), *Finnish Modern Design: Utopian Ideals and Everyday Realities 1930–1997* (New York and New Haven, CN: Bard Graduate Center and Yale University Press, 1998).
52. Leena Svinhufvud, *Moderneja ryijyjä, metritavaraa ja käsityötä: Tekstiilitaide ja nykyaikaistuva taideteollisuus Suomessa maailmansotien välisenä aikana* [Doctoral thesis, University of Helsinki] (Helsinki: Designmuseo, 2009); and Susanna Aaltonen, *Sisustaminen on kuin käsialaa: Carin Bryggman ja Lasse Ollinkari sisustusarkkitehdin ammatissa 1940-ja 1950-luvuilla* [Doctoral thesis] (Helsinki: University of Helsinki, 2010).
53. Pekka Korvenmaa, *Finnish Design: A Concise History* (Helsinki: University of Art and Design Helsinki, 2009).
54. Stephan Tschudi-Madsen, *Sources of Art Nouveau* (Oslo: Aschehoug, 1956); and Alf Bøe, *From Gothic Revival to Functional Form: A Study in Victorian Theories of Design* (Oslo: Oslo University Press, 1957). Tschudi-Madsen received his doctorate from the University of Oslo but did part of his research as a British Council scholar in London in 1952–3 under the tutelage of Nikolaus Pevsner.
55. Ingeborg Glambek, *Kunsten, nytten og moralen: Kunstindustri og husflid i Norge 1800–1900* (Oslo: Solum Forlag, 1988).

56. Thor Kielland and Eivind Engelstad, 'Kunstindustri', in Arne Nygård-Nilssen et al. (eds.), *Norsk kunstforskning i det tyvende århundre: Festskrift til Harry Fett* (Oslo: Cammermeyer, 1945), pp. 205–240.
57. See e.g. Jan-Lauritz Opstad, *Norsk emalje: Kunsthåndverk i verdenstoppen* (Oslo: Huitfeldt, 1994).
58. See e.g. Anniken Thue, *Frida Hansen: En europeer i norsk tekstilkunst omkring 1900* (Stavanger: Universitetsforlaget, 1986); Alf Bøe, *Nora Gulbrandsen på Porsgrund* (Oslo: Huitfeldt, 1994); and Karianne Bjellås Gilje (ed.), *Grete Prytz Kittelsen: Emalje—design* (Oslo: Gyldendal/The National Museum of Art, Architecture and Design, 2008).
59. Thor Kielland, 'Kunstindustrien i det 19. og 20. Aarhundrede', in Harald Aars et al., *Norsk kunsthistorie*, vol. 2 (Oslo: Gyldendal, 1927), pp. 599–630.
60. Alf Bøe, 'Kunsthåndverket 1880–1914: En nasjonal gjenstandskultur blir skapt', in Knut Berg et al. (eds.), *Norges kunsthistorie*, vol. 5 (Oslo: Gyldendal, 1981), pp. 377–467.
61. Randi Gaustad, *Foreningen Brukskunst 1918–30: Program, utstillinger og kritikk* [MPhil thesis] (Oslo: University of Oslo, 1973); Ingeborg Glambek, *Funksjonalismens gjennombrudd i Norge: Debatt og ideologisk bakgrunn* [MPhil thesis] (Oslo: University of Oslo, 1970); and Alf Bøe, 'Funkis', in Ingrid Semmingsen et al. (eds.), *Norges kulturhistorie*, vol. 6 (Oslo: Aschehoug, 1980), pp. 221–244.
62. Alf Bøe, 'Kunsthåndverk og kunstindustri 1914–1940', in Knut Berg et al. (eds.), *Norges kunsthistorie*, vol. 6 (Oslo: Gyldendal, 1983), pp. 307–338.
63. Anniken Thue, 'Kunsthåndverket 1940–1980', in Knut Berg et al. (eds.), *Norges kunsthistorie*, vol. 7 (Oslo: Gyldendal, 1983), pp. 350–420.
64. Alf Bøe, 'Kunstindustri og industridesign etter 1940', in Berg et al., *Norges kunsthistorie*, vol. 7, pp. 421–466.
65. Fredrik Wildhagen, *Norge i form: Kunsthåndverk og design under industrikulturen* (Oslo: J. M. Stenersens Forlag, 1988).
66. Michael Tucker, '[Review of] *Norge i Form. . .*', *Journal of Design History* 2/2–3 (1989), pp. 234–237.
67. Ole Rikard Høisæther, *Design på norsk: Fra Nøstetangen til Norway Says* (Oslo: Damm & Søn, 2005).
68. Frode Weium (ed.), *Plast i det moderne Norge* (Oslo: Norwegian Museum of Science and Technology, 2001).
69. Morten Bing, *Østkanthjemmene og Østkantutstillingen: Boskikk og boligidealer i mellomkrigstidens Oslo* (Oslo: Norwegian Museum of Cultural History, 2001); Morten Bing and Espen Johnsen (eds.), *Nye Hjem: Bomiljøer i mellomkrigstiden* (Oslo: Norwegian Museum of Cultural History, 1998); and Espen Johnsen, *Det moderne hjemmet 1910–1940* [Doctoral thesis] (Oslo: University of Oslo, 2002).

70. Kjetil Fallan, *Modern Transformed: The Domestication of Industrial Design Culture in Norway, ca. 1940–1970* [Doctoral thesis] (Trondheim: Norwegian University of Science and Technology, 2007). For additional references, see bibliography.
71. See, for example, Jorunn Veiteberg, *Craft in Transition* (Bergen: Bergen National Academy of the Arts, 2005).
72. Kerstin Wickman (ed.), *Formens rörelse: Svensk form genom 150 år* (Stockholm: Carlssons, 1995).
73. Nils G. Wollin, *Nutida svensk konstslöjd* (Stockholm: Natur och kultur, 1931).
74. Åke H. Huldt, Mattis Hörlén, Herbibert Seitz and Elsa Hald-Steenberg, *Konsthantverk och hemslöjd i Sverige 1930–40* (Göteborg: Förlag AB Bokförmedlingen, 1941).
75. Arthur Hald and Sven Erik Skawonius, *Nyttokonst: En bildrevy med kommentarer* (Stockholm: Nordisk Rotorgravyr, 1951), p. 13.
76. Sven Erik Skawonius, 'Konsthantverk och konstindustri i Sverige', in Erik Zahle (ed.), *Konsthantverk och konstindustri i Norden* (Stockholm: Svensk litteratur, 1961), pp. 53–72.
77. Åke Stavenow and Åke H. Huldt, *Svensk Form* (Stockholm: Gothia, 1961).
78. Per G. Råberg, *Funktionalistiskt genombrott: En analys av den svenska funktionalismens genombrott 1925–1931* [Doctoral thesis] (Stockholm: Sveriges Arkitekturmuseum, 1970); Elisabet Stavenow-Hidemark, *Villabebyggelse i Sverige 1900–1925: Inflytande från utlandet, idéer, förverkligande* [Doctoral thesis] (Stockholm: Nordiska museets handlingar, 1971); and Bengt Nyström, *Konsten till industrin! Två formgivare från sekelskiftet* [Doctoral thesis] (Stockholm: Stockholm University, 1971).
79. Dag Widman, *Konsthantverk, konstindustri, design 1895–1975* (Stockholm: AWE/Geber, 1975).
80. Hedvig Hedqvist, *1900–2000: Svensk form: Internationell design* (Stockholm: Dagens Nyheter, 2002).
81. Monica Boman (ed.), *Svenska möbler 1890–1990* (Lund: Signum, 1991); Jan Brunius (ed.), *Svenska textilier 1890–1990* (Lund: Signum, 1994); and Jan Brunius (ed.), *Svenskt glas* (Stockholm: Wahlström & Widstrand, 1991).
82. *Signums svenska konsthistoria* (Lund: Signum, 1994–2005); and Kerstin Wickman, 'Hemmet', in Claes Caldenby (ed.), *Att bygga ett land* (Stockholm: Arkitekturmuseet/Byggforskningsrådet, 1998), pp. 199–225.
83. Lennart Lindkvist, *Design in Sweden* (Stockholm: Swedish Institute, 1972); Monica Boman (ed.), *Design in Sweden* (Stockholm: Swedish Institute and Swedish Society of Crafts and Design, 1985); and Denise Hagströmer, *Swedish Design* (Stockholm: Swedish Institute, 2001).
84. Lasse Brunnström (ed.), *Svensk industridesign: En 1900-talshistoria* (Stockholm: Norstedt, 1997).

85. Lasse Brunnström, *Svensk designhistoria* (Stockholm: Raster Förlag, 2010).
86. Helena Kåberg, *Rationell arkitektur: Företagskontor för massproduktion och masskommunikation* [Doctoral thesis] (Uppsala: Uppsala University, 2003); and Johanna Rosenqvist, *Könsskillnadens estetik? Om konst och konstskapande i svensk hemslöjd 1920–1990-talet* [Doctoral thesis] (Stockholm: Nordiska museets förlag, 2007).
87. Zandra Ahl and Emma Ohlsson, *Svensk smak* (Stockholm: Ordfront, 2002).
88. Linda Rampell, *Designatlas: En resa genom designteori 1845–2002* (Stockholm: Gabor Palotai, 2003).

CHAPTER 2 'WHAT'S WORTH COPYING IS WORTH PROTECTING'

1. Today, intellectual property rights in applied art are based in copyright law as well as in design law. The latter is the successor of pattern law, which, in Denmark, originated in a law of 1905. This chapter restricts itself to copyright law, culturally and economically the more significant of the two branches of intellectual property law. In cases where a design is also an 'invention that solves a technical problem', the design may be protectable by patent law. In this volume the chapters by Fallan and Jørgensen discuss issues relating to the patenting of designs.
2. Within the legislation of many nations there is a long tradition of appointing experts to the court in copyright infringement cases. Experts are usually established members of the art and design community. Essentially, court-appointed experts function as third-party expert witnesses. On expert witnesses in Danish courts see Morten Rosenmeier, 'Lawyers and Experts in Danish Copyright Infringement Cases', in Morten Rosenmeier and Stina Teilmann (eds.), *Art and Law: The Copyright Debate* (Copenhagen: Association of Danish Economists and Lawyers (DJOEF) Publishing, 2005), pp. 75–83.
3. U.1907.619, p. 621.
4. Ibid., p. 620.
5. Some of the German coffee pots were so similar to their Royal Porcelain counterparts that they were difficult to tell apart. See Lauritz G. Dorenfeldt, *Kongeligt Porcelæn 1820–1923—Blåmalet porcelæn fra Den Kongelige Porcelainsfabrik* (Copenhagen: Nyt Nordisk Forlag Arnold Busck, 2002), pp. 51f.
6. Op. cit., note 3, p. 621.
7. Lov om Forfatterret og Kunstnerret, 19 December 1902.
8. Op. cit., note 3.

9. Widespread protests against the ruling were heard from manufacturers of 'industrial art' across Denmark. See Per Håkon Schmidt, *Teknologi og immaterialret* (Copenhagen: GAD, 1989), p. 57.
10. Lov om Forfatterret og Kunstnerret, 19 December 1902, § 24.
11. Lov om ændret Affattelse af § 24 i Lov om Forfatterret og Kunstnerret, 29 March 1904.
12. Lov om Eftergørelse af Kunstarbejder, 31 March 1864.
13. Rigsdagstidende 1907–08, Tillæg A, Sp. 2143.
14. In Sweden copyright protection of applied art was introduced in 1926. The Norwegian Copyright Act of 1930 explicitly offered protection of applied arts.
15. On this topic see Nikolaus Pevsner, *Pioneers of Modern Design: From William Morris to Walter Gropius*, 4th edn (New Haven, CN, and London: Yale University Press, 2005). See also Fiona MacCarthy, *William Morris: A Life for Our Time* (London: Faber and Faber, 1994). For a discussion of the impact of the arts and crafts movement on UK copyright law see Lord Simon in *Hensher* v *Restavile* (1976).
16. Rigsdagstidende, Tillæg A, Sp. 2144. The Berlin Revision of 1908 of the Berne Convention (1886) included applied arts for the first time but left specific definitions and legislation to each of the member states.
17. The distinction reflects the divide created by the founding, in the seventeenth and eighteenth centuries, of academies of fine art in many European countries.
18. In Germany—which had been, until the mid-twentieth century, the main influence on Danish and Nordic copyright law—Kant's ideas were adopted by the leading theorists of copyright in the nineteenth century. For more on this see Stig Strömholm, *Le droit moral de l'auteur en droit allemand, français et scandinavie avec un aperçu de l'évolution internationale*, 2 vols (Stockholm: P.A. Norstedt & Söners Förlag, 1966).
19. Immanuel Kant, 'Von der Unrechtmäßigkeit des Büchernachdrucks', *Berlinische Monatsschrift* 5 (May 1785), pp. 403–417. For discussions of this essay see Martha Woodman, *Author, Art, and the Market: Rereading the History of Aesthetics* (New York: Columbia University Press, 1996); and Stina Teilmann, 'Framing the Law: The Right of Integrity in Britain', *European Intellectual Property Review*, no. 1 (2005), pp. 19–24.
20. For contemporary scholarship on Kant and copyright law, see e.g. Kim Treiger-Bar-Am, 'Kant on Copyright: Rights of Transformative Authorship', *Cardozo Arts & Entertainment Law Journal* 25/3 (2008), pp. 1059–1103.
21. Immanuel Kant, *Critique of Judgment (1790). Including the First Introduction*, translated with an introduction by Werner S. Pluhar (Indianapolis: Hackett, 1987), § 43, pp. 170f.
22. Ibid.
23. Ibid., p. 171.

24. Ibid., p. 191.
25. Ibid., pp. 191f.
26. Ibid., pp. 174f.
27. Lov om Forfatterret og Kunstnerret, 1 April 1912, § 24. It is worth noting that by this law works of architecture—and not merely architectural drawings—were also included as the subject matter of copyright law.
28. U.1913.760, U.1924.251H, U.1930.376Ø, and U.1934.161Ø. On the first two cases, see the report *Kunstnerret: Kunsthaandværk og kunstindustri* published by Landsforeningen dansk Kunsthaandværk og Kunstindustri (Copenhagen: G.E.C. Gads Forlag, 1943).
29. U.1926.251H.
30. Ibid., p. 252.
31. This is still the procedure today: infringing copies are destroyed. The destruction usually takes place at a refuse disposal plant under the surveillance of the authorities.
32. See Morten Rosenmeier, *Værkslæren i ophavsretten* (Copenhagen: Association of Danish Economists and Lawyers (DJOEF) Publishing, 2001); and Morten Rosenmeier, 'Lawyers and Experts in Danish Copyright Infringement Cases'. Rosenmeier argues that in Danish copyright infringement cases that concern applied art, courts have, practically, handed over the power of decision to the appointed experts. Furthermore, given the small size of the Danish design community, experts and parties in copyright infringement cases will almost always know each other. And designers may also, from one case to the next, find themselves in alternating roles, either as expert witnesses or as parties to the case. Arguably, this rather incestuous state of affairs has had a considerable impact on the direction of Danish copyright law in relation to design.
33. See Schmidt, *Teknologi og immaterialret*, p. 58.
34. On this topic see Stina Teilmann-Lock, *British and French Copyright: A Historical Study of Aesthetic Implications* (Copenhagen: Association of Danish Economists and Lawyers Publishing, 2009), pp. 72ff.
35. See in particular U.1954.170Ø and U1956.237/2H. The problem is mentioned in Schmidt, *Teknologi og immaterialret*, pp. 60f. See also the discussions of the concept of *værkshøjde* (a Scandinavian version of the concept of *Werkhöhe* in German copyright law, which in itself is inspired by the notion of *Erfindungshöhe*, 'inventive step', in patent law) in Rosenmeier, *Værkslæren i ophavsretten*, pp. 127ff.; and Erling Borcher, *Produktefterligninger*, 2nd edn (Copenhagen: Thomson—GadJura, 2003), pp. 38ff. The concept of *værkshøjde* refers to 'individuality', 'originality' and 'subjective novelty' as the requirements for copyright protection of works of art and literature.

36. There were in fact three different cases that concerned the furniture of the Thonet-Mundus Factory. The one mentioned was the most important of the three, and it remains notorious in Danish legal and cultural history.
37. The models Desta SS 33, B 32, B 64, B 46 and B 37. (Some of the models have changed reference number since 1935—for example B 32 changed to S 32 and B 64 to S 64.)
38. The chairs have been a part of the New York Museum of Modern Art's collection since 1942 and are today held by museums of modern art and design all over the world.
39. RG, GRUR 1932, s. 892. Adding to the complexity of the matter, the dispute in the German court was between the company Thonet, which produced Marcel Breuer's chairs, and the businessman Anton Lorenz, who produced a similar chair designed by the Dutch designer Mart Stam. Both designers had developed a tubular steel cantilever chair. The Reichsgericht had to decide not only whether copyright could be held in such a chair but also which of the two parties was to have the right. Mart Stam was found to be the originator and hence owner of the copyright in it. For more on this see Otakar Máčel, 'Avant-garde Design and the Law: Litigation over the Cantilever Chair', *Journal of Design History* 3/2–3 (1990), pp. 125–143.
40. U.1935.695, pp. 696f.
41. Ibid., p. 698.
42. Lov om Forfatterret og Kunstnerret, 26 April 1933, § 24.
43. U.1954.170Ø.
44. U.1956.237H.
45. U.1960.483Ø. The two models are identical except that the 501 comes with a woven cane seat while the 503 has an upholstered seat.
46. U.1960.483Ø, p. 488; this expert, Professor Mogens Koch of the Royal Danish Academy of Fine Arts School of Architecture, was himself a renowned designer of furniture and a leading figure in the Danish Modern movement.
47. U.1960.483Ø, p. 488. Intriguingly, this was the opinion of the chair's manufacturer, the cabinetmaker Johannes Hansen. Hansen, in fact, had had a key role in the making of 'The Chair'. Hansen was a long-term collaborator with Wegner (from 1940 to 1966), and the decisive role of this working relationship for the realization of Wegner's chair designs is generally acknowledged.
48. U.1960.483Ø, pp. 486ff.
49. Lov om Ophavsretten til Litterære og Kunstneriske Værker, 31 May 1961, § 1. The Danish term *brugskunst* derives from the German *Gebrauchskunst*.
50. Remarks to §1 of Copyright Bill of 1959–60. Cited from *Folketingstidende 1960–61*, Tillæg B, Sp. 628.

51. 'Betænkning om lovforslag om ophavsretten til litterære og kunstneriske værker m.m', *Folketingstidende 1960–61*, Tillæg B, Sp. 628f.
52. Lov om Forfatterret og Kunstnerret, 26 April 1933, § 24.
53. In Nordic copyright law the term *værkshøjde* is often applied. This term derives from German copyright law: *Werkhöhe*.
54. Jens Schovsbo and Morten Rosenmeier, *Immaterialret*, 2nd edn (Copenhagen: Association of Danish Economists and Lawyers (DJOEF) Publishing, 2011), pp. 63ff. Paradoxically, this happened at a time when industrial designers were distancing themselves from this 'Romantic' conception of what it meant to be a 'designer.'
55. Kant, *Critique of Judgment*, p. 191.
56. U.1961.1027H, p. 1029. The set of cutlery named Langelinie was created by the designer Kaj Franck for Hackmann & Co.
57. U.1969.851H, U.1998.941SH and U.2000.212H.
58. On this see Stina Teilmann-Lock, 'Things and Words about Them: On the Legal Protection of Design', in Grace Lees-Maffei (ed.), *Writing Design: Words and Objects* (Oxford: Berg, 2011), pp. 219–229.
59. This is a truism of modern copyright law, originally uttered by Peterson J in *University of London Press* v *University Tutorial Press* [1916] 2 Ch 601.

CHAPTER 3 HANDWOVEN FABRICS BY THE YARD

1. One of the influential writings naturalizing the crafts tradition as part of modern design is Gotthard Johansson, 'Design in Scandinavia', in Arne Remlov (ed.), *Design in Scandinavia: An Exhibition of Objects for the Home from Denmark, Finland, Norway, Sweden* (Oslo: Kirstes Boktrykkeri, 1954). This article is based on my doctoral dissertation in art history: Leena Svinhufvud, *Moderneja ryijyjä, metritavaraa, käsityötä: Tekstiilitaide ja nykyaikaistuva taideteollisuus Suomessa maailmansotien välisenä aikana* (Helsinki: Designmuseo, 2009).
2. Marjo Wiberg, *The Textile Designer and the Art of Design: On the Formation of a Profession in Finland* [Doctoral thesis] (Helsinki: University of Art and Design Helsinki, 1996); Päikki Priha, *Huldasta Helenaan: Tekstiilitaiteen koulutusohjelma 80 vuotta* (Helsinki: University of Art and Design Helsinki, 2009); and Leena Svinhufvud, 'Finnish Textiles en Route to Modernity', in Marianne Aav and Nina Stritzler-Levine (eds.), *Finnish Modern Design: Utopian Ideals and Everyday Realities 1930–97* (New Haven, CN, and London: Bard Graduate Center for Studies in the Decorative Arts and Yale University Press, 1998), pp. 185–187.
3. Werner Gräff (ed.), *Innenräume: Räume und Innen-einrichtungsgegenstände aus der Werkbundausstellung 'Die Wohnung', insbesondere aus*

den Bauten der städtischen Weißenhofsiedlung in Stuttgart (Stuttgart: Wedekind/Deutscher Werkbund, 1928).

4. Leena Svinhufvud, 'Textiles in Modern Spaces: Limitations and Counter-images', in Marianne Aav and Jukka Savolainen (eds.), *Modernism: Articles on Finnish Modernism* (Helsinki: Designmuseo, 2010).
5. Alvar Aalto, Paavo Tynell, Gustaf Strengell and Harry Röneholm, *Pienasunto? Pienasuntojen rationalisoimisosaston julkaisu taideteollisuusnäyttelyssä* (Helsinki: Enso lit, 1930).
6. About the modern kitchen in Finland see for example Kirsi Saarikangas, *Asunnon muodonmuutoksia: Puhtauden estetiikka ja sukupuoli modernissa arkkitehtuurissa* (Helsinki: Suomalaisen Kirjallisuuden Seura, 2002), pp. 259–278. About Aino and Alvar Aalto, see Renja Suominen-Kokkonen, *Aino and Alvar Aalto—a Shared Journey: Interpretations of an Everyday Modernism*, Aalto Studies 1 (Jyväskylä: Alvar Aalto Foundation/Alvar Aalto Museum, 2007).
7. Märta Lagus-Waller, *Elna Kiljander: Arkitekt och formgivare* (Helsingfors: Svenska Litteratursällskapet i Finland, 2006), pp. 51–62, 95–101.
8. Ellen Key, *Skönhet för alla: Fyra uppsatser av Ellen Key* [Studentföreningen Verdandis småskrifter 77. Faksimile av 5. uppl.] (Stockholm: Bonnier, 1913 [1996]), p. 12. For an English translation and discussion, see Lucy Creagh, Helena Kåberg and Barbara Miller Lane (eds.), *Modern Swedish Design: Three Founding Texts* (New York: Museum of Modern Art, 2008), p. 39.
9. I refer here to the concept of Le Corbusier and Amédée Ozenfant that was concretized in the former's infamous pavilion at the Paris exhibition of decorative art of 1925 (L'Exposition internationale des arts décoratifs et industriels modernes).
10. Gunnar Asplund, Wolter Gahn, Sven Markelius, Gregor Paulsson, Eskil Sundahl and Uno Åhrén, *Acceptera* (Stockholm: Tidens Förlag, 1931), p. 123.
11. Ibid., pp. 129–132.
12. Gregor Paulsson, 'Möjligheten och betydelsen av samarbete mellan textilindustrin och konstnärerna', *Form* 3 (1932), pp. 85–88.
13. N.[ils]-G.[ustav] H[ahl], 'Pellavakudosten näyttely Helsingin Taidehallissa toukokuussa 1933', *Domus* 5 (1933), pp. 128–129.
14. Wiberg, *Textile Designer*, chap. 4.2; and Kirsi Niinimäki and Marjo-Riitta Saloniemi (eds.), *Kretongista printtiin: Suomalaisen painokankaan historia/From Cretonne to Print: The History of Finnish Printed Textiles* (Helsinki: Maahenki Oy, 2008); see also Camilla Pulkkinen, 'Finlayson-Forssa Oy:n Forssan tehtaiden painokangasateljee 1950-ja 1960-luvuilla', in Ilppo Aaltonen and Lauri Pohjakallio (eds.), *Lounais-Hämeen Kotiseutu ja Museoyhdistyksen vuosikirja 75* (Forssa: Lounais-Hämeen Kotiseutu ja Museoyhdistys, 2006).

15. Svinhufvud, *Moderneja ryijyjä*, pp. 104–106.
16. Wiberg, *Textile Designer*, pp. 79–100.
17. Heimer Björkqvist, 'Merenkulku ja liikenne', in Eino Jutikkala, Eirik Hornborg, Heikki Waris and Matti J. Castrén (eds.), *Helsingin kaupungin historia V, kolmas nide* (Helsinki: Helsingin kaupunki, 1967), pp. 7–136.
18. Reino Hjerppe, Riitta Hjerppe, Kauko Mannermaa, O.E. Niitamo and Kaarlo Siitari, *Suomen teollisuus ja teollinen käsityö 1900–1965*, Kasvututkimuksia 7 (Helsinki: Suomen Pankki, 1976), pp. 59–60, 73, 77.
19. Ibid., pp. 65, 67, 71. As recently as 1960, 62 per cent of the population lived outside cities; 32 per cent of the population made their living through farming.
20. Pentti Virrankoski, *Käsitöistä leivän lisää: Suomen ansiokotiteollisuus 1865–1944*, Historiallisia tutkimuksia 186 (Helsinki: Suomen Historiallinen Seura, 1994), pp. 131–151, 179–186.
21. L.[auri] Kuoppamäki, 'Norjan ja Ruotsin kotiteollisuusoloista: Vertailua nykyoloihin Suomessa', *Käsiteollisuus* 4 (1925), p. 66.
22. Märtha Gahn, 'Käsin kudotut ruotsalaiset huonekalukankaat: Käsiteollisuudelle suomennettu', *Käsiteollisuus* 1 (1925), pp. 12–14.
23. Svinhufvud, *Moderneja ryijyjä*, pp. 108–111; Kerstin Smeds, 'The Image of Finland at the World Exhibitions 1900–1992', in Peter MacKeith and Kerstin Smeds (eds.), *The Finland Pavilions: Finland at the Universal Expositions 1900–1992* (Helsinki: Kustannus Oy City, 1993), pp. 41–42.
24. Svinhufvud, *Moderneja ryijyjä*, pp. 106–108.
25. For a discussion of anonymity of crafts production see Johanna Rosenqvist, *Könsskillnadens estetik? Om konst & konstskapande i svensk hemslöjd på 1910-& 1990-talen* (Stockholm: Nordiska museets förlag, 2007), pp. 68–91.
26. Eva Anttila, 'Uusia suuntaviivoja taidetekstiilissämme', in *Ornamon vuosikirja VI* (Helsinki: Koristetaiteilijain Liitto Ornamo, 1933), pp. 58–60.
27. Svinhufvud, *Moderneja ryijyjä*, pp. 121–128, 146–149.
28. 'Vuoksenlaaksossa kukoistaa tekstiiliteollisuuskin 1937', *Ylä-Vuoksi*, 8 March 1937.
29. 'Enso-Gutzeitin pääkonttori: Arkkitehti Väinö Vähäkallio', *Arkkitehti* 2 (1937), pp. 17–21, 25–29. Obviously, Greta Skogster-Lehtinen did not weave the tapestry herself.
30. Kirsi Vainio-Korhonen, *Ruokaa, vaatteita, hoivaa: Naiset ja yrittäjyys paikallisena ja yleisenä ilmiönä 1700-luvulta nykypäivään*, Historiallisia Tutkimuksia 213 (Helsinki: Suomalaisen Kirjallisuuden Seura, 2002).
31. Elna Kiljander, 'Kodinsisustaja käy tyyppivalmistenäyttelyssä pohjoismaisilla rakennuspäivillä', *Kotiliesi* 17 (1932), pp. 654–656.
32. Minna Koljonen, *Tekstiilitaidetta postipakettina: Suomen Käsityön Ystävien tarvikepakettien postimyynti 1925–1939* [Master's thesis] (Turku: Turku University 2003); about the organization, see Päikki Priha (ed.), *Rakkaat*

Ystävät: Suomen Käsityön Ystävät 120 vuotta (Helsinki: Ajatus, 1999); Leena Svinhufvud and Anne Valkonen (eds.), *Sidos: Suomen Suomen Käsityön Ystävät 120 vuotta* (Helsinki: Taideteollisuusmuseo, 1999); and Charlotte Ashby, 'Nation Building and Design: Finnish Textiles and the Work of the Friends of Finnish Handicrafts', *Journal of Design History* 23/4 (2010), pp. 351–365.

33. The ledger 1906–10 (Pääkirja 1906–1910), the Friends of Finnish Handicraft (Suomen Käsityön Ystävät), National Archives (Kansallisarkisto), Helsinki.
34. The price book for woven products, 1919–20 (Hintakirja kutomatöille v:sta 1919, 17 January 1919–16 December 1920), Hinta-, myynti-, näyttely ja huutokauppaluetteloita 1895–1939, the Friends of Finnish Handicraft (Suomen Käsityön Ystävät), National Archives (Kansallisarkisto), Helsinki.
35. The annual report of 1931, the archives of the Friends of Finnish Handicraft Ltd, Helsinki. About the building project of the Parliament House see Liisa-Maria Hakala-Zillicus, *Suomen eduskuntatalo: Kokonaistaideteos, itsenäisyysmonumentti ja kansallisen sovinnon representaatio*, Suomalaisen Kirjallisuuden Seuran toimituksia 875 (Helsinki: Suomalaisen Kirjallisuuden Seura, 2002).
36. The inventory books 1930–6, 1937–41 (Inventariokirja 1930–6, Inventariokirja 1937–41), the Friends of Finnish Handicraft (Suomen Käsityön Ystävät), National Archives (Kansallisarkisto), Helsinki.
37. The annual report of 1930, the archives of the Friends of Finnish Handicraft Ltd, Helsinki.
38. The annual report of 1935, the archives of the Friends of Finnish Handicraft Ltd, Helsinki.
39. Finland was at war from late November 1939 to March 1940 and again from late June 1941 to 1945.
40. See also Ritva Koskennurmi-Sivonen, *Muotitaiteilija Riitta Immonen: Vaatteita naisille työhön, juhlaan, vapaa-aikaan* (Helsinki: Multikustannus, 2008), pp. 21–28.
41. *The Defence of the Sampo*, in Svinhufvud and Valkonen, *Sidos*, front inside cover.
42. Asplund et al., *Acceptera*, p. 123. By addressing a wider spectrum of consumers the Friends of Finnish Handicraft chose a different strategy compared to its Swedish sister organization, which maintained itself through the years as a workshop realizing artists' designs. See e.g. Louise Robbert (ed.), *Handarbetets vänner och konstnärerna* (Stockholm: Liljevalchs konsthall, 1991).
43. Svinhufvud, *Moderneja ryijyjä*, pp. 91–94.
44. Leena Svinhufvud, 'Ryijy, berberimatto ja modernismin toinen', in Tutta Palin (ed.) and Renja Suominen-Kokkonen (ed. in chief), *Modernia on*

moneksi: Kuvataiteen, taideteollisuuden ja arkkitehtuurin piirteitä maailmansotien välisen ajan Suomessa, Taidehistoriallisia tutkimuksia 29 (Helsinki: Taidehistorian seura, 2004); see also Leena Svinhufvud, 'The Finnish Ryijy-Rug: Living Tradition and Artistic Interpretation', in Leena Svinhufvud and Eeva Viljanen (eds.), *Ryijy! The Finnish Ryijy-Rug* (Helsinki: Designmuseo, 2009), pp. 251–261.

45. H.[arry] Röneholm, W.[erner] West and W.[alter] Wahlroos (eds.), *Applied Art in Finland* (New York: The Finnish Section of New York World's Fair, 1939), preface.
46. Rafael Blomstedt, 'Taideteollisuus', in L.[udvig] Wennervirta (ed.), *Suomen taide esihistoriallisesta ajasta meidän päiviimme* (Helsinki: Otava, 1927), pp. 617–643.
47. Kevin M. Davies, 'Marketing Ploy or Democratic Ideal: On the Mythology of Scandinavian Design', in Widar Halén and Kerstin Wickman (eds.), *Scandinavian Design beyond the Myth: Fifty Years of Design from the Nordic Countries* (Stockholm: Arvinius Förlag, 2003), pp. 101–110.
48. See also Kjetil Fallan, 'Crafting Scandinavian Design: Craft vs. Industrial Design in the Norwegian Contributions to the "Design in Scandinavia" and the "X Triennale di Milano" Exhibitions', in Javier Gimeno-Martinez and Fredie Floré (eds.), *Design and Craft: A History of Convergences and Divergences* (Brussels: Koninklijke vlaamse academie van Belgie voor Wetenschappen en kunsten, 2010), pp. 420–424 [Proceedings of the 7th Conference of the International Committee of Design History and Design Studies (ICDHS), 20–22 September 2010].
49. See e.g. Nina Stritzler-Levine (ed.), *Sheila Hicks: Weaving as Metaphor* (New York, New Haven, CN, and London: Bard Graduate Center for Studies in the Decorative Arts and Yale University Press, 2006).
50. See e.g. Jordana Pomeroy, 'Nordic Cool: Hot Women Designers', in *Nordic Cool: Hot Women Designers* (Washington: National Museum of Women in the Arts, 2004), pp. 19–24. About women designers in Finland, see Marianne Aav, Jukka Savolainen, Leena Svinhufvud and Eeva Viljanen (eds.), *Naisen muoto* (Helsinki: Designmuseo, 2006).
51. Hjerppe et al., *Suomen teollisuus ja teollinen käsityö 1900–1965*.
52. Marita Mellais, 'Taistelu olemassaolosta: taideteollisuus ja lama Strindbergin taidesalongissa', in Erkki Anttonen (ed.), *Salon Strindberg: Helsinkiläisen taidegallerian vaiheita*, Kuvataiteen keskusarkisto 10 (Helsinki: Valtion taidemuseo/Kuvataiteen keskusarkisto, 2004), pp. 76–85.
53. Minna Sarantola-Weiss, *Kalusteita kaikille: Suomalaisen puusepänteollisuuden historia* (Helsinki: Puusepänteollisuuden liitto, 1995), pp. 85–125; and Helena Leppänen, 'A Voyage of Discovery into Tableware Decoration at the Arabia Factory', in Eeva Viljanen (ed.) and Marianne Aav (ed. in chief), *Arabia: Ceramic—Art—Industry* (Helsinki: Designmuseo, 2006), pp. 78–126.

54. See, for example, Harri Kalha, *Marita Lybeck 1906–1990* (Helsinki: Galleria Septaria, 1996).

CHAPTER 4 DESIGNING THE 'CONSUMER IN INFINITY'

1. Mårten Blomkvist, 'Decenniet som inte klippte sig' ('The decade that never cut its hair') [film review], *Elle* [Swedish edition], November 2010.
2. Douglas B. Holt, *How Brands Become Icons: The Principle of Cultural Branding* (Boston: Harvard Business School of Publishing Corporation, 2004).
3. Lasse Brunnström, *Svensk designhistoria* (Stockholm: Raster Förlag, 2010), pp. 142–145.
4. Reyner Banham, *Theory and Design in the First Machine Age* (Oxford: Architectural Press, 1960).
5. 'Expendable aesthetics' was a concept formulated by Reyner Banham in his many articles in the 1950s. See Helena Mattsson, *Arkitektur och konsumtion: Reyner Banham och utbytbarhetens estetik* (Stockholm and Stehag: Symposion, 2004).
6. Richard Hamilton, 'Persuading Images', *Design* 134 (1960), pp. 131–136.
7. Roy Sheldon and Egmont Arens, *Consumer Engineering* (New York: Harpers and Brothers, 1932).
8. 'Persuading Images: A Symposium', *Design* 134 (1960), p. 137.
9. Gunnar Asplund, Wolter Gahn, Sven Markelius, Gregor Paulsson, Eskil Sundahl and Uno Åhrén, *Acceptera* (Stockholm: Tidens Förlag, 1931). Eng. trans. David Jones, in Lucy Creagh, Helena Kåberg and Barbara Miller Lane (eds.), *Modern Swedish Design: Three Founding Texts* (New York: Museum of Modern Art, 2008).
10. Stewart Brand (ed.), *Whole Earth Catalog*, Fall 1968.
11. On Mah-Jong, see Salka Hallström Bornold, *Det är rätt att göra uppror: Mah-Jong 1966–1976* (Stockholm: Modernista, 2003). On the history of the Moderna Museet, see Anna Tellgren, Martin Sundberg and John Rosell (eds.), *The History Book* (Stockholm: Moderna Museet, 2008). On Swedish design, art and handicraft in the 1960s, see Cilla Robach, *Formens frigörelse: Konsthantverk och design under debatt i 1960-talets Sverige* (Stockholm: Arvinius Förlag, 2010).
12. Sam Binkley, *Getting Loose: Lifestyle Consumption in the 1970s* (Durham, NC: Duke University Press, 2007).
13. I want to thank Orsi Husz for important discussions on Swedish consumer policy in the 1970s.
14. Gunnar Inghe and Maj-Britt Inghe, *Den ofärdiga välfärden* (Stockholm: Tiden/Folksam, 1967), and Låginkomstutredningen, published as *Preliminär rapport om låginkomstutredningens arbete* ('Preliminary report on the

work done by the low-income investigation' (Stockholm: Inrikesdepartementet, 1968).

15. Lisa Brunnström, *Det svenska folkhemsbygget: Om Kooperativa Förbundets arkitektkontor* (Stockholm: Arkitektur Förlag AB, 2004).
16. *Utan Gränser* ('Without borders'), exhibition catalogue (Stockholm: Kooperativa Förbundet, 1957). On the exhibition, see Helena Mattsson, 'Designing the Reasonable Consumer: Standardization and Personalization in Swedish Functionalism', in Helena Mattsson and Sven-Olov Wallenstein (eds.), *Swedish Modernism: Architecture, Consumption, and the Welfare State* (London: Black Dog, 2010), pp. 86–97.
17. Unfortunately, a lot of early archive material from Svea (from before 1958) has been thrown away, but it still has extensive and yet uncovered material.
18. Walter Lippman, *Public Opinion* (New York: Brace and Company, 1922).
19. 'Expressendebatten: Var finns de äkta folkrörelserna?' *Kooperativ Information*, no. 2 (1975).
20. 'Nytt KF-märke', manuscript, 18 November 1964, p. 1, Box F1a: vol. 3, KF Bibliotek och arkiv.
21. Ibid., p. 13.
22. 'Kronologisk sammanställning av symbol-data', 31 May 1967, p. 17, Box F1a: vol. 1, KF Bibliotek och arkiv.
23. Personalizing an imagined consumer and giving her or him a name, as well as certain needs and desires, is something Coop picks up from the USA, and Mrs Petersen seems to be a model.
24. '10 punkter om KF-symbolen', Box F1a: vol. 3, 1964–1968, KF Bibliotek och arkiv.
25. Ibid.
26. 'Lundströms 10 punkter', Box F1a: vol. 3, 1964–1968, KF Bibliotek och arkiv.
27. *Göteborgs-Posten*, 12 May 1967.
28. *Metallarbetaren*, no. 17 (1967).
29. Bosse Bergman, *Handelsplats, shopping, stadsliv* (Stockholm and Stehag: Symposion, 2003), p. 170.
30. Olle Eksell, 'Miljö och mygel', *Aftonbladet*, 17 May 1967, and 'Estetisk marknadsstrategi', *Aftonbladet*, 18 June 1967.
31. The idea of honest advertisement is developed in a lecture by Björn Petersson, 'Ärlig reklam', 25 August 1969, Box F1a: vol. 6, KF Bibliotek och arkiv.
32. Ibid., p. 4.
33. 'Vision—konkreta förslag', manuscript for a film clip, 21 January 1969, Box Möbiusbandet råmaterial, KF Bibliotek och arkiv.
34. Petersson, 'Ärlig reklam'.

35. Lars Berg, 'När skall vilka sända vad till vem och med vilka medel?' *Kooperativ Information*, no. 3 (1970), p. 10.
36. 'Svea 75', Ove Lind, 1972, KF Bibliotek och arkiv.
37. Leif Nylén, 'Konsums klotterplank', *Aftonbladet*, 23 April 1969, 4.
38. Berg, 'När skall vilka sända vad?' p. 10.
39. Jean Baudrillard, *Simulations*, trans. P. Foss, P. Pattman and P. Beitchman (New York: Semiotext(e), 1983).
40. Berg, 'När skall vilka sända vad?' p. 10.
41. 'Manuskript till Symbolbildbandet på engelska', p. 9, Box F1: vol. 3, KF Bibliotek och arkiv.
42. Ibid., p. 18.
43. Ibid., p. 19.
44. Björn Lövin, *Konsument i oändlighet* ('Consumer in infinity'), exhibition catalogue (Stockholm: Moderna Museet, 1971), p. 11.
45. Torsten Bergmark, 'Herr P:s peningar och konsument i oändligheten', *Dagens Nyheter*, 3 March 1971.
46. *Konsumentkongressen 1971: Ett angeläget experiment* (Stockholm: Presstjänsten KF, 1971).
47. 'Svea 75', Ove Lind, 1972, KF Bibliotek och arkiv.
48. Millie McNaughton was the chief designer for the basic wardrobe. Strongly influenced by British utility furniture and the French brand Carrefour, Hedvig Hedqvist and Inez Svensson introduced the concept of basic commodities in 1967, which was implemented some years later.
49. For more on Coop's generic products in an international perspective, see Anders Petersson and Hans Venneman, *Namnlösa varor: En studie av KF:s blå-vita varor i ett internationellt perspektiv* (Lund: Företagsekonomiska institutionen Lunds Universitet, 1980).

CHAPTER 5 DESIGNING A HOLE IN THE WALL

1. Nelly Oudshoorn and Trevor Pinch, *How Users Matter: The Co-construction of Users and Technology* (Cambridge, MA: MIT Press, 2003).
2. Barry M. Katz, 'Technology and Design: A New Agenda', *Technology and Culture* 38/2 (1997), pp. 452–466.
3. Dominique Vinck (ed.), *Everyday Engineering: An Ethnography of Design and Innovation* (Cambridge, MA: MIT Press, 2003).
4. Bruno Latour's 'sociology of a door-closer' (written under the pseudonym Jim Johnson) is perhaps the most famous discussion of how we delegate certain tasks to technologies, which in turn shape our interactions. Jim Johnson, 'Mixing Humans and Nonhumans Together: The Sociology of a Door-closer', *Social Problems* 35/3 (1988), pp. 298–310.

5. See for instance Elmer M. Jones, 'Vending Machine', US Patent no. 1,560,242, filed 13 September 1920 and issued 3 November 1925; Samuel J. Gurewitz, 'Bottle Handling Machine', US Patent no. 2,750,024, filed 19 February 1952 and issued 12 June 1956.
6. For more details on the history of the RVM, see Finn Arne Jørgensen, *Making a Green Machine: The Infrastructure of Beverage Container Recycling* (New Brunswick, NJ: Rutgers University Press, 2011).
7. The following paragraphs are primarily based on the author's interview with Aage Fremstad (Per Fremstad's son), Oslo, Norway, 1 August 2005 (digital recording), as well as documents in Fremstad's care.
8. Erik Røsrud, *Dagligvareforbundets rolle og virke mot år 2000* (Oslo: Dagligvareforbundet, 2003).
9. Called Petter Planke A/S at first, the company changed its name to Tomra A/S (short for *tomflaske returautomat*, 'empty bottle return machine') in 1973. The Planke brothers have told and retold the story of how they made the first RVM many times in slightly different versions. The version I have told here is based on Tomra's own videotaped interviews with the Planke brothers from 2000, as well as my own interviews with the Plankes in 2005.
10. Aage Fremstad and the Planke brothers, interviewed by the author.
11. Most of these machines were sold in Scandinavia. While grocery stores were the primary customers, the Swedish Wine Monopoly also was an important customer. Tomra also exported the Tomra I to a number of European countries, most importantly France.
12. Jørgensen, *Making a Green Machine*, chap. 4.
13. Petter Planke, interviewed by the author, Vollen, Norway, 2 August 2005 (digital recording).
14. 'Hjemmesløyd selger ikke', *Økonomisk Rapport*, no. 19 (1983), p. 34.
15. Rådet for industridesign (RID; Council of Industrial Design) had been founded in 1974 to support Norwegian industrial design, changing to its current name Norsk Designråd (the Norwegian Design Council) in 1985.
16. The council's predecessor, the Norwegian Design Centre, awarded the Mark of Design Excellence from 1965 to 1973. The Council of Industrial Design reinstated the award beginning in 1984. Kjetil Fallan, 'How an Excavator Got Aesthetic Pretensions—Negotiating Design in 1960s' Norway', *Journal of Design History* 20/1 (2007), p. 46.
17. 'Hjemmesløyd selger ikke', p. 33.
18. 'Roy Håvard Tandberg', *Norsk biografisk leksikon*, http://www.snl.no/Roy_Håvard_Tandberg
19. Tore Planke, interview with the author, 5 January 2011.
20. This particular laminate was developed by Norsk Hydro under the brand name Respatex in 1958 but is mostly known internationally as Formica.
21. Petter Sv. Planke, interview with the author, 7 August 2005.

22. *Smokk-smokk* can be loosely translated as 'snap-snap'. *Tomra Annual Report 1983*, p. 5. The Norwegian Language Council included *smokk-smokk* in their list of new words in *Språknytt* 12/3 (1984), p. 14.
23. *Tomra Annual Report 1983*, p. 5.
24. 'Askerbedrift hedres torsdag: Design-pris til Tomras Can-Can', *Asker og Bærums Budstikke*, 4 April 1984.
25. Tore Planke, 'Hedersbevisning for trendy kjøkkenvask', *Aftenposten*, 4 November 1987.
26. 'Tomra hedret for "God norsk design"', *Asker og Bærums Budstikke*, 10 April 1984. Note that Tore Planke also served on the jury the year Tomra received its first design award, alongside Tandberg's employer Nils Tvengsberg. Planke therefore withdrew from the jury's discussion of the Can-Can (it was also Planke who nominated his company's machine for the award).
27. The following section is based on the author's telephone interviews with Tore Planke and Roy H. Tandberg, 7 January 2011.
28. Jørgensen, *Making a Green Machine*, chap. 5.
29. 'Tomra i teten: Automat som også tar plastbokser', *Aftenposten*, 6 March 1985, evening edition.
30. *Tomra Annual Report 1984*, p. 4.
31. *Tomra Can-Can*, promotional video produced by Tomra, 1984.
32. Roy Tandberg, interviewed by the author, 5 January 2011.
33. Tore Planke, interviewed by the author, 5 January 2011.
34. Resirk, *Pante-og retursystemer på drikkevaresektoren i Norge* (Oslo: Resirk, 1990).
35. Erik Røsrud and Jarle Grytli, interviewed by the author, Oslo, Norway, 16 January 2006 (digital recording). Tomra's *Annual Report 1989* contains a model of how a deposit system works, which looks very similar to the Resirk set-up.
36. Various draft proposals for an aluminium can recycling system had circulated since 1984 but had not gained approval. The discussion on disposable containers peaked with a massive controversy in the mid-1990s, involving bottlers, the labour unions, environmentalists, the European Union and others. Tomra attempted to keep a low profile in the proposal, but Tore Planke still came to play a key role in the public debate over the new system.
37. In Sweden, having separate RVMs for different material types is much more common. This makes container returns more inconvenient.
38. Louis Bucciarelli, *Designing Engineers* (Cambridge, MA: MIT Press, 1994).
39. John Law, 'Technology and Heterogeneous Engineering: The Case of Portuguese Expansion', in Wiebe E. Bijker, Thomas P. Hughes and Trevor J. Pinch (eds.), *The Social Construction of Technological Systems: New*

Directions in the Sociology and History of Technology (Cambridge, MA: MIT Press, 1987), pp. 111–134.

40. Birgit Helene Jevnaker, 'Vita Activa: On Relationships between Design(ers) and Business', *Design Issues* 21/3 (2005), pp. 25–48.
41. Petter Planke, 'Fri ideskapning som grunnlag for industriutvikling', *Teknisk Ukeblad*, no. 48a (November 1983), p. 10.
42. Which is also a design choice—in 1997, the Norwegian Design Council gave their Mark of Design Excellence to the Norwegian Brewery Association for the new standard beer bottle, designed by Morten Throndsen and Dagheid Strømme of Strømme & Throndsen Design AS: http://www.norskdesign.no/industridesign/norsk-standard-oelflaske-0–33-l-brun-article1972-287.html

CHAPTER 6 JUST DECORATION?

The research for this article was done within the project Forms of Sustainablility funded by Vetenskapsrådet (2008–2257).

1. *Statens insatser för form och design: Slutbetänkande från Form- och designutredningen*, Statens offentliga utredningar (Government Official Report) 75 (Stockholm: Fritzes offentliga publikationer, 2000), pp. 190–191.
2. Gösta Arvidsson, *Gustavsberg: Porslinet—fabriken—konstnärerna* (Stockholm: Norstedts, 2007), p. 159.
3. Helena Dahlbäck Lutteman, 'A Background', in Monica Boman (ed.), *Design in Sweden* (Stockholm: Swedish Institute, 1985); and Denise Hagströmmer, *Swedish Design* (Stockholm: Swedish Institute, 2001).
4. Gunnela Ivanov, *Vackrare vardagsvara: Design för alla? Gregor Paulsson och Svenska slöjdföreningen 1915–1925* [Doctoral thesis] (Umeå: Umeå Universitet, 2004), pp. 118, 156.
5. Åsa Linderborg, *Socialdemokraterna skriver historia: Historieskrivning som ideologisk maktresurs 1892–2000* (Stockholm: Atlas, 2001), pp. 149–155.
6. Nils Palmgren, *Wilhelm Kåge: Konstnär och hantverkare* (Stockholm: Nordisk rotogravyr, 1953), p. 82.
7. Centralförbundet för socialt arbete (CSA), *Bostadskongressens förhandlingar i Stockholm den 21–23 september* (Stockholm: Centralförbundet för socialt arbete, 1917), p. 1.
8. Ibid., pp. 232, 247.
9. Ibid., pp. 1, 3; Shamal Kaveh, *Det villkorade tillståndet: Centralförbundet för socialt arbete och liberal politisk rationalitet 1901–1921* [Doctoral thesis] (Uppsala: Uppsala University, 2006), p. 173; and Eva Jacobsson, *Om*

bostadspolitik och bostadskooperation i Stockholm 1870–1930 [Doctoral thesis] (Stockholm: Stockholm University, 1996), pp. 124–125.

10. CSA, *Bostadskongressens förhandlingar i Stockholm*, p. 3.
11. Kaveh, *Det villkorade tillståndet*, p. 168.
12. CSA, *Utställningen i bostadsföreningen Framtidens arbetarebostadshus å enskede: Inredning till en 2 rums lägenhet utförd av Centralförbundet för socialt arbete* (Stockholm, Oskar Ekelunds boktryckeri, 1915).
13. Erik Wettergren, 'Varia', *Svenska Slöjdföreningens Tidskrift* (1914), p. 138.
14. Arvidsson, *Gustavsberg*, p. 158.
15. August Brunius, 'Carl Larsson och nationell möbelstil', *Svenska Slöjdföreningens Tidskrift* (1909); and Christina Zetterlund, 'Konstslöjdsmuseet och nationen', in Hans Henrik Brummer and Martin Olin (eds.), *Konst och nation* (Stockholm: Kungl. Vitterhets Historie och Antikvitets Akademien, forthcoming).
16. Kerstin Wickman points out that this feature was already present in the two exhibitions at the Workers' Institute in Stockholm in 1899 staged by 'Ellen Key, Carl Laurin, Richard Bergh and his wife' (Gerda Ingeborg Winkrans). This is important to note since the exhibition was part of the formation of the discourse within which the Home Exhibition could be found. Kerstin Wickman, 'Hemmet', in Claes Caldenby (ed.), *Att bygga ett land* (Stockholm: Arkitekturmuseet/Byggforskningsrådet), p. 203; and Elisabeth Stavenow-Hidemark, *Villabebyggelse i Sverige 1900–1925* [Doctoral thesis] (Stockholm: Nordiska museets Handlingar, 1971), p. 95.
17. J. S.-On (sign.), 'Vardagskönhet och hemkultur', *Morgonbris*, no. 11 (1917), p. 6.
18. Carl Westman, 'Totalomdöme', *Svenska Slöjdföreningens Tidskrift* (1917), p. 71. However, in the reviews there were disagreements as to whether the interiors and objects on display actually succeeded in expressing this Swedishness; see Nils A. Blanch, 'Om möblerna på hemutställningen', *Svenska Slöjdföreningens Tidskrift* (1917).
19. Michel Foucault, *'Society Must be Defended': Lectures at the Collège de France* (London: Allen Lane Penguin Books, 2003), p. 249; O. Sycloiv-Steffen, 'Något om arbetareklassens bostadsfråga hemma och i utlandet', *Morgonbris*, no. 6 (1911); and Sten O. Karlsson, *Arbetarfamiljen och det nya hemmet: Om bostadshygienism och klasskultur i mellankrigstidens Göteborg* [Doctoral thesis] (Linköping: Linköping University, 1993), p. 214.
20. Stavenow-Hidemark, *Villabebyggelse i Sverige 1900–1925*; Michelle Facos, 'The Ideal Swedish Home: Carl Larsson's Lilla Hyttnäs', in Christopher Reed, *Not at Home: The Suppression of Domesticity in Modern Art and Architecture* (London: Thames and Hudson, 1996); and Johan Knutsson, *I 'hemtrefnadens tid'* (Stockholm: Nordiska museet, 2010).

21. Jacobsson, *Om bostadspolitik och bostadskooperation*, p. 113; and Gustav Steffen, *Bostadsfrågan i Sverige ur sociologiska och socialpolitiska synpunkter* (Stockholm: Bostadskomissionens utredningar, 1918), p. 185.
22. Steffen, *Bostadsfrågan i Sverige*, p. 85.
23. Ibid., p. 105.
24. *Hemslöjdskommitténs betänkande* (Stockholm: Nordiska bokhandelu, 1918), pp. 35–36.
25. Vilh. Hultkrantz, 'Några ord om eugenik (rashygien)', offprint of *Social tidskrift*, no. 7–8 (1911), also referred to in K. B-na, 'Litet om rashygien', *Morgonbris*, no. 11 (1911).
26. E.G. Folcker, 'Kosta och Orrefors', *Svenska Slöjdföreningens Tidskrift* (1917), pp. 90–91; Ivanova, *Vackrare vardagsvara*, p. 194.
27. Aktiebolaget Nordiska kompaniet Stockholm, *Vinterkatalog 1918–1919* [Catalogue].
28. Rut Liedgren, *Så bodde vi: Arbetarebostaden som typ- och tidsföreteelse* (Stockholm: Nordiska museet, 1961), p. 51.
29. There are of course exceptions, for example Kjetil Fallan, ' "One Must Offer 'Something for Everyone' ": Designing Crockery for Consumer Consent in 1950s' Norway', *Journal of Design History* 22/2 (2009), pp. 133–149.
30. Carl Gernandt de Jossac, 'Ett steg frammåt. En utställning af borgliga möbler i Nordiska kompaniet', *Svenska Hem i Ord och Bilder* (1919), p. 153.
31. Gullberg, interviewed in Arthur Hald, 'Hemutställningen 1917 och dess upptakt', *Form* (1947), p. 178.
32. Mats Nilsson, *Arbetarlitteratur* (Lund: Studentlitteratur, 2006), p. 63.
33. Torsten Gårdlund, *Industrialismens samhälle* (Stockholm: Tiden, 1942), p. 381.
34. Stockholms stadsarkiv, Frida Margareta Teodora Larsson, 1917–467.
35. Stockholms stadsarkiv, Elias Magnusson, 1917–98; Gustaf Emanuel Erikson, 1917–367; and Anna Signe Andersson, 1917–360.
36. Nordiska museet frågelista NM 60, NM 81 and NM 82; and Andreas Lindblom (ed.), *Arbetaren i helg och söcken: Kulturhistoriska studier. 1 Hus och hem* (Stockholm: Tidens Förlag, 1943).
37. Several are already cited in the preceding, but see also Bo Gustafsson, *Den norrländska sågverksindustrins arbetare 1890–1913: Arbets- och levnadsförhållanden* (Stockholm: Almquist & Wiksell, 1965); Birgitta Andersson, *Idealbostad eller nödbostad* (Stockholm: Statens råd för byggnadsforskning, 1977); and Karlsson, *Arbetarfamiljen och det nya hemmet*.
38. Sven Lagerström, *Paket för miljoner: Om postorder i Sverige* (Borås: Jonito, 2006), p. 41.
39. Arvidsson, *Gustavsberg*, p. 377.
40. Åhlén och Holm AB, *Hösten–vintern 1918–1919* [Catalogue].

41. Fallan, '"One Must Offer 'Something for Everyone'"', p. 134.
42. IKEA, *Democratic Design* (Älmhult: IKEA, 1995), pp. 21, 23.
43. Another example is Volvo cars: Christina Zetterlund, *Design i informationsålder* [Doctoral thesis, Uppsala University] (Stockholm: Raster Förlag, 2002).

CHAPTER 7 GOLDFISH MEMORIES

This case study is part of the research project Alumination: Design as Aesthetic Process and Cultural Valuation, which is funded by the Research Council of Norway's Research Programme on Assigning Cultural Values (KULVER).

1. Jan Erik Vold, 'Trikken er et øye som går på skinner', Cantata in celebration of the centennial of the Oslo tramway, 3 June 1994. Later published in Jan Erik Vold, *Storytellers: En begrunnet antologi* (Oslo: Gyldendal, 1998), p. 184. Extract translated by the author.
2. Jeffrey L. Meikle, *Twentieth Century Limited: Industrial Design in America, 1925–39* (Philadelphia: Temple University Press, 1979), p. 141; and Christina Cogdell, *Eugenic Design: Streamlining America in the 1930s* (Philadelphia: University of Pennsylvania Press, 2004).
3. It was the great merit of the late Fredrik Wildhagen to first draw attention—in a design history context—to the streamlined vehicles made at Strømmens Værksted, in a paper delivered to the 1985 seminar of the Nordic Forum for Design History: Fredrik Wildhagen, 'Flodhesten, Gullfisken og Kristine Valdresdatter—Streamlining og designhistorien', in Mirjam Gelfer-Jørgensen, (ed.), *Nordisk Funktionalisme 1925–1950* (Copenhagen: Det danske Kunstindustrimuseum and Nordisk Forum for Formgivningshistorie, 1986), pp. 53–55.
4. N. N., 'Hvordan vil fremtidens bil se ut?' *Norsk Motorblad* 16/23 (December 1929), p. 1314.
5. N. N., 'Strømlinjevognen—fremtidens biltype?' *Norsk Motorblad* 17/18 (September 1930), p. 902.
6. Dipl. ing. Haase, 'Strømlinjekarosseri', *Norsk Motorblad* 19/13 (July 1932), p. 572.
7. Erling Dale, 'Et moderne eventyr', *Norsk Motorblad* 20/25 (December 1933), p. 47.
8. N. N., 'Nye amerikanske bilkonstruksjoner', *Norsk Motorblad* 19/7 (April 1932), p. 279.
9. J. Falck-Andersen, 'Nye tider—nye vogner!' *Norsk Motorblad* 21/1 (January 1934), p. 11.

10. N.N., 'Den 4. norske automobilutstilling på Frogner', *Norsk Motorblad* 21/10 (May 1934), p. 279.
11. O.L. Riegels, 'New York-automobilutstillingen', *Norsk Motorblad* 21/3 (February 1934), p. 59.
12. Erling Dale, 'Tatra Type 77', *Norsk Motorblad* 21/9 (May 1934), p. 241.
13. N.N., 'Den 4. norske automobilutstilling på Frogner', *Norsk Motorblad* 21/10 (May 1934), p. 290; and N.N., 'Den moderne vogn', *Norsk Motorblad* 21/12 (June 1934), p. 368.
14. Dale, 'Tatra Type 77', pp. 241–242.
15. N.N., 'Strømlinjeprinsippet gjennemføres nu også på båtene', *Norsk Motorblad* 22/7 (April 1935), p. 184.
16. For a discussion of transformational developments in design culture in which ideology shifts towards style, see Kjetil Fallan, *Design History: Understanding Theory and Method* (Oxford: Berg, 2010), pp. 120–121.
17. Alf Ihlen, 'Eksempler på produktutvikling ved en norsk industribedrift: A/S Strømmens Værksted', in Torleif Lindtveit (ed.), *Volund 1976* (Oslo: Norsk Teknisk Museum, 1976), p. 37.
18. Kaare Fasting, *Strømmens Værksted gjennom 100 år: 1873–1973* (Strømmen: Strømmens Værksted, 1974), pp. 12, 38.
19. Jon Gunnar Arntzen et al. (eds.), *Norsk biografisk leksikon,* vol. 5 (Oslo: Kunnskapsforlaget, 2002), p. 17.
20. Bjørn Steenstrup, *Hvem er Hvem 1964* (Oslo: Aschehoug, 1964), p. 296.
21. Arntzen et al., *Norsk biografisk leksikon*, vol. 5, p. 17.
22. Arne Brinck, *Aluminium i vognbygging: Den økonomiske betydning av vektbesparelse* (Holmestrand: Nordisk aluminiumsindustri, 1948), p. 11.
23. N.N., 'Duralumin Shapes Used in Norwegian Bus', *Automotive Industries*, 14 June 1930, p. 907.
24. Ihlen, 'Eksempler på produktutvikling', pp. 37–38.
25. Jeffrey L. Meikle, *Design in the USA* (Oxford: Oxford University Press, 2005), p. 118.
26. N.N., 'Moderne rutebilmateriell', *Norsk Motorblad* 16/4 (February 1929), p. 187.
27. N.N., 'Norsk epokegjørende konstruksjon fremstilt i legert aluminium', *Trikk og Buss* 7/5 (1935), p. 66.
28. Fredrik Wildhagen, *Norge i form: Kunsthåndverk og design under industrikulturen* (Oslo: J.M. Stenersens Forlag, 1988), p. 111.
29. It should be noted that only the first few exemplars were fitted with the tailfin and the rear-wheel covers.
30. For a discussion of the concept of inscription and construction of meaning in design, see Kjetil Fallan, 'De-scribing Design: Appropriating Script Analysis to Design History', *Design Issues* 24/4 (2008), pp. 61–75. For a case study exploring script analysis in design history, see Kjetil Fallan,

'Form, Function, Fiction: Translations of Technology and Design in Product Development', *History and Technology* 24/1 (2008), pp. 61–87.

31. Report from the newspaper *Berlingske Tidende*, reproduced in N.N., 'En sølv-omnibus på Københavns gater', *Trikk og Buss* 9/11 (1937), pp. 165–166.
32. *La Norvège à Paris 1937: Catalogue du pavillion de la Norvège à l'exposition internationale de Paris 1937* (Oslo: Blix, 1937), p. xii. A photo by Anders Beer Wilse of the bus at this exhibit is in the archives of the Norwegian Museum of Cultural History (NF.WB 47551).
33. Ihlen, 'Eksempler på produktutvikling', p. 40.
34. Bjarne Bassøe (ed.), *Ingeniørmatrikkelen: Norske sivilingeniører 1901–55* (Oslo: Teknisk ukeblad, 1961), p. 431; and O. Delphin Amundsen (ed.), *Vi fra NTH—de neste ti kull: 1920–1929* (Oslo: Dreyer, 1950), p. 148.
35. Rømcke in a lecture to the automobile group of the Norwegian Society of Engineers, 7 October 1936, cited in N.N., 'Revolusjonerende tekniske detaljer i den nye busstype til Oslo Sporveier', *Norsk Motorblad* 23/19 (October 1936), p. 1515.
36. N.N., 'Ny skinnemotorvogn på Valdresbanen', *Teknisk Ukeblad* 52/31 (August 1935), p. 319.
37. C.F. Mathiesen, 'Nye vogner på Ekebergbanen', *Teknisk Ukeblad* 50/31 (August 1933), pp. 389–390.
38. Bjørn Andersen, *Gullfiskene: Oslos strømlinjeformede aluminiumvogner* (Oslo: Lokaltrafikhistorisk Forening, 1990), pp. 6–9.
39. Ihlen, 'Eksempler på produktutvikling', p. 40.
40. Bassøe, *Ingeniørmatrikkelen*, p. 358.
41. Fallan, *Design History*, pp. 18, 98.
42. On the notion of represented users, see Johan Schot and Adri Albert de la Bruheze, 'The Mediated Design of Products, Consumption, and Consumers in the Twentieth Century', in Nelly Oudshoorn and Trevor Pinch (eds.), *How Users Matter: The Co-construction of Users and Technology* (Cambridge, MA: MIT Press, 2003), p. 235; and Madeleine Akrich, 'User Representations: Practices, Methods and Sociology', in Arie Rip, Thomas J. Misa and Johan Schot (eds.), *Managing Technology in Society: The Approach of Constructive Technology Assessment* (London: Pinter, 1995), pp. 167–184.
43. Andersen, *Gullfiskene*, p. 22.
44. In a lecture on the prospects of high-speed trains in Norway delivered to the Oslo chapter of Norske Ingeniørers Forening (Norwegian Society of Engineers), 3 April 1936, reproduced as N.N., 'Lyntog på norske baner?' *Teknisk Ukeblad* 53/16 (April 1936), p. 205.
45. N.N., 'Den tyske "skinne-zeppeliner" ', *Trikk og Buss* 2/12 (1930), p. 181.
46. N.N., 'Strømlinjeformen hos bilene', *Trikk og Buss* 5/8 (1933), p. 120.
47. N.N., 'Lyntog i Danmark', *Trikk og Buss* 5/12 (1933), pp. 180–181.

48. N. N., 'Det amerikanske lyntog', *Trikk og Buss* 6/7 (1934), p. 107.
49. N. N., 'Det flyvende tog', *Trikk og Buss* 6/1 (1934), pp. 11–12.
50. N. N., 'U.S.A.s nyeste hurtigtog', *Trikk og Buss* 6/3 (1934), pp. 43–44.
51. N. N., 'Chicago får sin første strømformede trikk', *Trikk og Buss* 6/5 (1934), p. 74.
52. Nils Carl Aspenberg, *Trikker og forstadsbaner i Oslo: Fra hestesporvei til T-bane* (Oslo: Baneforlaget, 1994), p. 46.
53. N. N., 'Chicago får sin første strømformede trikk', p. 74.
54. N. N., 'Strømlinjens seierstog', *Trikk og Buss* 7/11 (1935), p. 174.
55. H. Hjorth, 'Nye sporvogner i Milano, Kjøbenhavn, Brüssel og Bologna', *Trikk og Buss* 8/9 (1936), pp. 129–133.
56. On the notion of paradigms in design history, see Fallan, *Design History*, pp. 127–146.
57. Carl Witt, 'Våre nye sporvogner', *Trikk og Buss* 8/12 (1936), p. 178.
58. N. N., 'De nye vognene til Kjelsåsbanen', *Trikk og Buss* 9/2 (1937), p. 21.
59. The MAYA acronym was devised by Raymond Loewy, one of the most famed practitioners and promoters of American streamlining: Loewy, *Never Leave Well Enough Alone* (1951; Baltimore: Johns Hopkins University Press, 2002), p. 277.
60. Robert Friedel, 'A New Metal! Aluminum in its 19th-century Context', in Sara Nichols (ed.), *Aluminum by Design* (Pittsburgh: Carnegie Museum of Art, 2000), pp. 59–82.
61. Johan Henden, Hans Otto Frøland and Asbjørn Karlsen (eds.), *Globalisering gjennom et århundre: Norsk aluminiumindustri 1908–2008* (Bergen: Fagbokforlaget, 2008).
62. In addition to the rolling mill division, Nordisk Aluminiumsindustri included a branch making kitchen utensils under the brand name Høyang, for which the renowned goldsmith Oskar Sørensen acted as chief designer.
63. N. N., 'Aluminium: Det moderne eventyr i metallenes rike', *Trikk og Buss* 3/10 (1931), pp. 158–159.
64. Sigurd Klouman, 'Oslo Sporveiers nye busser og lettmetalls anvendelse i rullende materiell', *Trikk og Buss* 2/2 (1930), p. 22.
65. Norway's two most famous polar explorers, Fritjof Nansen and Roald Amundsen, died in 1930 and 1928, respectively, and the construction of their status as national heroes only intensified thereafter.
66. N. N., 'Aluminium—Vår tids metall', *Trikk og Buss* 7/2 (1935), pp. 26–28. This source of pride was pointed out also by Sigurd Klouman in a lecture on the aluminium industry delivered to Polyteknisk Forening (the Polytechnic Society) the same year: C. V., 'Aluminiumsindustriens utvikling særlig med henblikk på nye anvendelser av aluminium i den senere tid', *Teknisk Ukeblad* 52/8 (February 1935), p. 76.
67. N. N., 'Aluminium', *Trikk og Buss* 11/11–12 (1939), pp. 120–123.

68. 'Aluminium—for fart og fremskritt', advertisement in *Norsk Motorblad* 25/10 (May 1938), p. 238.
69. Nicholas Maffei, 'The Search for an American Design Aesthetic: From Art Deco to Streamlining', in Charlotte Benton, Tim Benton and Ghislaine Wood (eds.), *Art Deco 1900–1939* (London: V&A Publications, 2003), p. 369.
70. Judy Attfield, *Wild Things: The Material Culture of Everyday Life* (Oxford: Berg, 2000), p. 63.
71. Wildhagen, 'Flodhesten, Gullfisken og Kristine Valdresdatter', p. 53.
72. Johan Fredrik Grøgaard, 'Den gamle trikken på Bærumsbanen ruster ikke som kjærlighet', in *Elefantspråket & andre dikt* (Oslo: Gyldendal, 1971). Extract translated by the author.

CHAPTER 8 CREATURE COMFORTS

1. The Sopenkorpi company's advertising magazine *Vihje-Vakka*, no. 2 (1972).
2. Information on the design process of the Tower sofa group is based on an interview with Markku Hakovirta, former managing director of the Sopenkorpi company, on 10 June 1997. Sopenkorpi was established in 1945 and terminated its operations in 1994.
3. Edward P. Thompson, *The Making of the English Working Class* (Harmondsworth: Penguin, 1974).
4. On developments in Britain, see Clive D. Edwards, *Twentieth-century Furniture: Materials, Manufacture and Markets* (Manchester and New York: Manchester University Press, 1994). In Finland, see Minna Sarantola-Weiss, *Kalusteita kaikille: Suomalaisen puusepänteollisuuden historia* (Helsinki: Puusepänteollisuuden liitto, 1995).
5. Åke Daun, 'Sittandet—och sambandet mellan anatomi och kroppsspråk', *Tvärsnitt*, no. 1 (2000).
6. Maija Mäkikalli, 'Radion ja television läsnäolon strategioita 1950-ja 1960-luvun suomalaiskodeissa', in *Tekniikan vaiheita* (Espoo: Suomen teknillinen museoyhdistys, 2003), pp. 45–56.
7. Anneli Juntto, *Asuntokysymys Suomessa: Topeliuksesta tulopolitiikkaan* (Helsinki: Asuntohallitus, 1990), table 16. The kitchen counts as a room.
8. For the Finnish discourse of home magazines, see Minna Sarantola-Weiss, *Sohvaryhmän läpimurto: Kulutuskulttuurin tulo suomalaisiin olohuoneisiin 1960-ja 1970-lukujen vaihteessa* (Helsinki: Finnish Literature Society, 2003), and 'Representations of the Finnish Home in the Interior Decoration Magazines of the 1960s and 1970s', in Hanna Johansson and Kirsi Saarikangas (eds.), *Homes in Transformation: Dwelling, Moving, Belonging* (Helsinki: Finnish Literature Society, 2009), pp. 39–73. See

also Kjetil Fallan, 'The Metamorphosis of a Norwegian Design Magazine: *nye bonytt*, 1968–1971', in Grace Lees-Maffei (ed.), *Writing Design: Words and Objects* (Oxford: Berg, 2011), pp. 47–61.

9. Ulla ja Jorma Mäenpää, *Joka kodin sisustusopas* (Helsinki: Otava, 1953), p. 66.
10. Irma Ahlgren, 'Muovit ja metallit puun rinnalle', *Uusi Suomi*, 19 October 1971.
11. Anna-Liisa Ahmavaara, 'Pienet sohvat ovat hauskoja', *Uusi Suomi*, 21 October 1972.
12. Tomás Maldonado, 'The Idea of Comfort', in Victor Margolin and Richard Buchanan (eds.), *The Idea of Design: A Design Issues Reader* (Cambridge, MA: MIT Press, 1995), pp. 248–256.
13. For a more recent discussion about the interaction between humans and objects, see Tim Dant, *Materiality and Society* (Maidenhead and New York: Open University Press, 2005).
14. Mark M. Smith, *Sensory History* (Oxford and New York: Berg, 2007).
15. Irene Nierhaus, *Raum, Geschlecht, Architektur* (Vienna: Sonderzahl, 1999).
16. Sarantola-Weiss, *Sohvaryhmän läpimurto*, pp. 243–247.
17. An ethnographic study from Museokatu and Vaasankatu streets 1970, 1973 and 1974, Helsinki City Museum; an ethnographic study conducted in 1965 and 1975, Hämeenlinna City Museum.
18. Kotini [My home] collection campaign and Kotikutoista [Homemade] collection campaign in 2004, Finnish Literature Society.
19. Woman, born in 1940, Kotikutoista, pp. 441 and 748; woman, born in 1953, Kotini, p. 562.
20. Birgitta Rydberg Mitchell, *Att bo med soffa: En möbels betydelse för bostadens planering och livet i hemmet* (Lund: Lunds tekniska högskola, 2001), pp. 90–92.
21. Riitta Miestamo, *Suomalaisen huonekalun muoto ja sisältö* (Lahti: Askon säätiö, 1980), pp. 146–148; advertisement for Tower, *Apu* 39 (1977) and *Anna* 36 (1977).
22. Judy Attfield, *Wild Things: The Material Culture of Everyday Life* (Oxford and New York: Berg, 2000), chap. 4.
23. Johanna Hankonen, *Lähiöt ja tehokkuuden yhteiskunta* (Helsinki: Gaudeamus, 1994).
24. Elizabeth Guffey, *Retro: The Culture of Revival* (London: Reaktion, 2006), p. 8.
25. David Lowenthal, *The Past is a Foreign Country* (Cambridge and New York: Cambridge University Press, 1985), p. 6.
26. Jonathan M. Woodham, *Twentieth-century Design* (Oxford: Oxford University Press, 1997), chap. 9; Guffey, *Retro*, p. 9.
27. Mail-order catalogues 1970–5, Anttila Oy.

28. See e.g. Matti Peltonen and Susann Vihma, 'Muotoilun myyttejä', in Susann Vihma (ed.), *Suomalainen muotoilu 3. Kohti kestäviä valintoja* (Helsinki: Weilin+Göös, 2009), p. 284.
29. Riitta Jallinoja, *Moderni elämä: Ajankuva ja käytäntö* (Helsinki: Finnish Literature Society, 1991).
30. Irmeli Visanti, *Sisustamme kerrostaloasunnon* (Helsinki: Tammi, 1972), p. 10.
31. Ibid., p. 88.
32. Reyner Banham, 'Repro Time is Here', *New Society*, 12 February 1976, p. 341.
33. Pekka Suhonen, 'Suomalainen miljöö ennen ja nyt', in *Sata suomalaisen kulttuurin vuotta 1870-luvulta nykyaikaan* (Helsinki: WSOY, 1974).
34. Jukka Gronow, *The Sociology of Taste* (New York and London: Routledge, 1997), p. 20.
35. Karin Johannisson, *Nostalgia: En känslas historia* (Stockholm: Bonnier, 2001), pp. 69–72, 125–130.
36. Guffey, *Retro*, pp. 14–17.
37. Designer Ahti Taskinen, interviewed by the author, 12 August 1998.
38. See e.g. Visa Heinonen, Jukka Kortti and Mika Pantzar (eds.), *How Lifestyle Products Became Rooted in the Finnish Consumer Market* (Helsinki: National Consumer Research Centre, 2003).
39. Daniel Miller, *Material Culture and Mass Consumption* (Oxford: Blackwell 1987); and Colin Campbell, *The Romantic Ethic and the Spirit of Modern Consumerism* (Oxford: Blackwell, 1987).
40. Anneli Juntto and Anni Vilkko, 'Monta kotia: Suurten ikäluokkien asumishistoriat', in Antti Karisto (ed.), *Suuret ikäluokat* (Tampere: Vastapaino, 2005).
41. Orvar Löfgren, 'Nationella arenor', in Billy Ehn, Jonas Frykman and Orvar Löfgren (eds.), *Försvenskningen av Sverige: Det nationellas förvandlingar* (Stockholm: Natur och Kultur, 1993), pp. 61, 62; and Mike Featherstone, *Consumer Culture and Postmodernism* (London: Sage, 1991), chap. 5.
42. Sarantola-Weiss, *Sohvaryhmän läpimurto*, appendix 2.

CHAPTER 9 JACOB JENSEN AND THE LIFA KITCHEN

1. The notion of 'positive contamination' is developed by Russell W. Belk inspired by Claude Levi-Strauss: Belk, 'Possessions and the Extended Self', *Journal of Consumer Research* 15/2 (1988), p. 149.
2. Christian Holmsted Olesen, 'Designeren og mesterværket', in Jacob Jensen et al., *Bang & Olufsen 1960–1990: Fra dansk kvalitetsmærke til internationalt ikon* (Viborg: Hovedland, 2003), pp. 9–111; and Christian

Holmsted Olesen, *Jacob Jensen* (Copenhagen: Aschehoug/Louisiana, 2003).

3. Jacob Jensen, *Anderledes, men ikke mærkelig: En designers erindringer* (Copenhagen: Gyldendal, 1997).
4. Ida Engholm and Anders Michelsen, *Designmaskinen* (Copenhagen: Gyldendal, 1999), p. 129.
5. Belk, 'Possessions and the Extended Self'.
6. David A. Aaker, *Building Strong Brands* (London: Simon & Schuster, 2002), p. 141.
7. Grant McCracken, *Culture and Consumption II: Markets, Meaning and Brand Management* (Bloomington: Indiana University Press, 2005), pp. 97–115.
8. Ibid., p. 175.
9. Tony Fry, *Design History Australia* (Sydney: Hale & Iremonger, 1988), p. 59.
10. Grace Lees-Maffei, 'The Production-Consumption-Mediation Paradigm', *Journal of Design History* 22/4 (2009), pp. 351–376.
11. Daniel Miller, 'Appropriating the State on the Council Estate', *Man* 23/2 (1988), p. 354.
12. Guy Julier, *The Culture of Design*, 2nd edn (London: Sage, 2008), p. 62.
13. Kjetil Fallan, *Design History: Understanding Theory and Method* (Oxford: Berg, 2010), pp. 78–89.
14. Steve Woolgar, 'Configuring the User: The Case of Usability Trials', in John Law (ed.), *A Sociology of Monsters: Essays on Technology, Power and Domination* (London: Routledge, 1991), pp. 57–99.
15. Julier, *Culture of Design*, p. 62.

CHAPTER 10 SOMETHING OLD, SOMETHING NEW, SOMETHING STOLEN, SOMETHING BLUE

1. Helge Godø, *Innovasjonsledelse: Teknologiutvikling fra idé til foretningsplanlegging* (Trondheim: Tapir Akademiske Forlag, 2008), pp. 147–150.
2. Ruth Swarz Cowan, *A Social History of Technology* (New York: Oxford University Press, 1997); Donald MacKenzie and Judy Wajcman (eds.), *The Social Shaping of Technology* (Philadelphia: Open University Press, 1999); Bruno Latour, *Reassembling the Social: An Introduction to Actor-Network Theory* (Oxford: Oxford University Press, 2005); David E. Nye, *Technology Matters: Questions to Live With* (Cambridge, MA: MIT Press, 2007); and John M. Staudenmaier, *Technology's Storytellers: Reweaving the Human Fabric* (Cambridge, MA: MIT Press, 1985).
3. Nelly Oudshorn and Trevor Pinch (eds.), *How Users Matter: The Co-construction of Users and Technology* (Cambridge, MA: MIT Press, 2003); Mikael Hård and Andrew Jamison, *Hubris and Hybrids: A Cultural History*

of Technology and Science (New York: Routledge, 2005); and Merete Lie and Knut Holtan Sørensen (eds.), *Making Technology Our Own? Domesticating Technology into Everyday Life* (Oslo: Scandinavian University Press, 1996).

4. Fritz Hodne and Ola Honningdal Grytten, *Norsk økonomi 1900–1990* (Oslo: Tano, 1992), pp. 96–112.
5. S. tid., 20 February 1922, pp. 191–230.
6. Nidar, price lists, May 1922 and 2 January 1935.
7. Gunne Hammarstrøm, *En søt historie: Beretning ved Nidar bergenes 75-års jubileum 1912–1987* (Trondheim: Nidar, 1987), pp. 54–55.
8. *Chokolade Bladet*, no. 9 (July 1936), p. 6.
9. *Chokolade Bladet*, no. 9 (July 1936), p. 3.
10. Marshall Berman, *All That is Solid Melts into Air: The Experiences of Modernity* (New York: Verso, 1991).
11. 'Ballong', *Store norske leksikon*, http://snl.no/ballong (9 September 2010).
12. *Chokolade Bladet*, no. 11 (January 1937), back page.
13. The Nidar archive, Stratos advertisement from 1938.
14. *Chokolade Bladet*, no. 28 (January 1947), p. 2. The caption refers to the fact that the advertisement was used when Stratos first appeared on the market, i.e. some ten years before this volume of the magazine was published.
15. *Chokolade Bladet*, no. 17 (October 1938), back page.
16. The limited originality of design work in general is eloquently demonstrated in Jan Michl, 'On Seeing Design as Redesign: An Exploration of a Neglected Problem in Design Education', *Scandinavian Journal of Design History* 12 (2002), pp. 7–23.
17. Nidar, price list per 15 August 1952, p. 5; *Chokolade Bladet*, no. 38 (May 1952), pp. 12–16.
18. Nidar, price list per 15 August 1952, p. 5.
19. S. tid., 20 February 1922, pp. 191–230; S. tid., 21 September 1950, pp. 1976–1979.
20. Nidar, price list, 20 September 1939; price list, 5 December 1950.
21. *Norsk Ukeblad*, no. 7–8 (1953).
22. *Bergens Tidende*, 10 March 1961.
23. *Adresseavisen*, 2 February 1966.
24. http://freia.no/2010/ (14 September 2010).
25. *Sjokolade Bladet*, no. 62 (April 1971), p. 6.
26. *Adresseavisen*, 10 June 1980.
27. Nidar Bergene, *Årsberetning 1984* [annual report], p. 19.
28. Nidar Bergene, *Årsberetning 1982*, p. 4; Nidar Bergene, *Årsberetning 1984*, p. 19.
29. Nidar archive, video cavalcade of Stratos advertisements, undated.

30. Nidar Bergene, *Årsberetning 1984*, p. 19.
31. Nidar Bergene, *Årsberetning 1982*, p. 4; Nidar Bergene, *Årsberetning 1984*, p. 19; Ulf af Trolle and Svein-Erik Blom, *Markedsføring: Prinsipper, analyser, planlegging* (Oslo: Universitetsforlaget, 1984), pp. 331–332.
32. af Trolle and Blom, *Markedsføring*.
33. Ibid., p. 329.
34. Annual report from Nora Industrier A/S 1987, p. 4.
35. *Adresseavisen*, 2 April 1987; press release from Kjøtt-og næringsmiddelkontrollen i Trondheim [the Meat and Food Control Authority in Trondheim], 31 March 1987; Nidar, information circular, undated; *Adresseavisen*, 31 March 1987; *NTB*, 31 March 1987.
36. *Bergens Tidende*, 3 April 1987; *Aftenposten*, 30 December 1987.
37. *Morgenavisen Fremtiden*, 4 April 1987.
38. *Aftenposten*, 30 December 1987.
39. *Nationen*, 7 April 1987.
40. Nidar, information circular, undated.
41. *Arbeider-Avisa*, 21 May 1987.

CHAPTER 11 EXHIBITABLE FURNITURE

1. Keld Helmer-Petersen, 'Den fotografiske Udtryksform', in *Vindrosen* (Copenhagen: Gyldendal, 1954), p. 158.
2. *Life*, 28 November 1949, pp. 70–79.
3. Kjærholm's statements about his form-giving principles are found primarily in his summative 'Arbejdsprogram/Working Schedule', *Mobilia* 21/9 (1955), pp. 25–30, as well as in Axel Thygesen and Arne Karlsen's interview with Kjærholm in *Spatium* 2 (1963), pp. 24–29.
4. Interview with Poul Kjærholm by Axel Thygesen and Arne Karlsen (1963), quoted from Christopher Harlang et al., *Poul Kjærholm* (Copenhagen: Arkitektens Forlag, 1999), p. 166.
5. Walter Benjamin, 'Das Kunstwerk im Zeitalter seiner technischen Reproduzierbarkeit' [1936], in Detlev Schöttker (ed.), *Das Kunstwerk im Zeitalter seiner technischen Reproduzierbarkeit und weitere Dokumente* (Frankfurt: Suhrkamp, 2007).
6. Mary Anne Staniszewski, *The Power of Display: A History of Exhibition Installations at the Museum of Modern Art* (London: MIT Press, 1998), p. 64.
7. Helmer-Petersen, 'Den fotografiske Udtryksform', p. 160.
8. Brian O'Doherty, *Inside the White Cube: The Ideology of the Gallery Space* (London: University of California Press, 1999), pp. 14–15.
9. Ibid., p. 52.

10. Harlang et al., *Poul Kjærholm*, p. 164.
11. O'Doherty, *Inside the White Cube*, p. 85.
12. Mike Featherstone, 'Postmodernism and the Aesthetization of Everyday Life', in S. Lash and J. Friedman (eds.), *Modernity and Identity* (Cambridge, MA: Blackwell, 1992), pp. 265–290.
13. This point is developed in Poul Erik Tøjner, *Poul Kjærholm* (Copenhagen: Aschehoug and Louisiana Museum of Modern Art, 2003), p. 46. Tøjner's complete interpretation of Kjærholm's design is built on the premise that thinking about furniture as abstract pictures was an integrated part of Kjærholm's design and promotion strategy.
14. Michael Sheridan et al., *Poul Kjærholm: Møbelarkitekt* (Humlebæk: Louisiana Museum of Modern Art, 2006).
15. Anthony Vidler, *The Architectural Uncanny: Essays in the Modern Unhomely* (London: MIT Press, 1992), p. 12.

CHAPTER 12 THE ADVANTAGES OF BEING SWEDISH

1. *Famous Club for Growth of PAC TV Ad about Howard Dean*, 17 November 2010, http://www.youtube.com/watch?v=K4-vEwD_7Hk.
2. Jean-Claude Usunier, *Marketing across Culture* (London: Prentice Hall, 1996).
3. S. Saimee, 'Customer Evaluation of Products in a Global Market', *Journal of International Business Studies* 25/3 (1994), pp. 579–605.
4. Jeff Werner, *Medelvägens estetik*, vols 1–2 (Möklinta: Gidlunds, 2008).
5. Björn Elsässer, *Svensk bilindustri: En framgångshistoria* (Stockholm: SNS, 1995), p. 67.
6. *Financial and Operating Statistics* 1994/95, p. 34 [Volvo, unlisted Royal Library Stockholm].
7. Björn-Eric Lindh, *Volvo: Personvagnarna från 20-tal till 90-tal* (Malmö: Förlagshuset Norden, 1988), p. 9.
8. Björn Linn, 'Svenska fordon—svensk form?' in Lasse Brunnström (ed.), *Svensk industridesign: En 1900-tals historia* (Stockholm: Prisma, 2004), pp. 346, 352.
9. Hedvig Schönbäck, 'Volvos bildesign', in Brunnström, *Svensk industridesign*, p. 356.
10. Ibid., p. 363.
11. Lindh, *Volvo*, p. 94.
12. 'A Test-Guide to Volvo', *Motor Life*, November 1957, in R. M. Clarke (ed.), *Volvo PV444 & PV544, 1945–1965* (London: Brookland Books, 2001), p. 42.
13. Lindh, *Volvo*, pp. 98–104.

14. R. M. Clarke (ed.), *Forty Years of Selling Volvo: A Portfolio of Volvo's North American Advertising* (North Branch, MN: Brookland Books, 1996).
15. Al Berger, 'Tractable Tiger', *Speed Age*, June 1959, in Clarke, *Volvo PV444 & PV544, 1945–1965*, p. 66.
16. Griff Borgeson, 'Swedish Invasion: PV 444', *Sports Cars Illustrated*, September 1956, in Clarke, *Volvo PV444 & PV544, 1945–1965*, p. 23.
17. Lindh, *Volvo*, pp. 144–151.
18. 'Road Test: Volvo 1800ES', *Road & Track*, April 1967, in *Road & Track on Volvo 1957–1974* (North Branch, MN: Brookland Books, 1991), p. 81.
19. 'Road Test: Volvo 740 Turbo Wagon', *Road & Track*, June 1985, in *Road & Track on Volvo 1977–1994* (Newport Beach, undated), p. 62.
20. 'Road Test: Volvo 122-S', *Road & Track*, September 1959, in *Road & Track on Volvo 1957–1974*, p. 11.
21. Lindh, *Volvo*, pp. 157–159.
22. Elsässer, *Svensk bilindustri*, pp. 97, 102, 190.
23. Toni-Matti Karjalainen, *Semantic Transformation in Design: Communicating Strategic Brand Identity through Product Design References* [Doctoral thesis] (Helsinki: University of Art and Design Helsinki, 2004), p. 116. Sources are anonymous in this thesis.
24. Christina Zetterlund, *Design i informationsåldern: Om strategisk design, historia och praktik* [Doctoral thesis] (Uppsala: Uppsala University, 2002), p. 73.
25. David E. Davis, Jr., 'Volvo GL', *Car and Driver*, April 1980, in R.M. Clarke (ed.), *Car and Driver: On Volvo 1955–1986* (North Branch, MN: Brookland Books, 1987), p. 76.
26. Telephone interview with Daniel Johnston, Volvo North America, 3 June 2005.
27. Rich Ceppos, 'Volvo GLT Turbo', *Car and Driver*, February 1981, in Clarke, *Car and Driver: On Volvo 1955–1986*, p. 84.
28. 'Six Car Comparison Test', *Car and Driver*, January 1973, p. 31.
29. Svend Aage Nielsen, 'Scandinavia and the Auto Age', *Motor Trend*, October 1953, p. 36.
30. 'Road Test: Volvo PV444', *Road & Track*, April 1957, in *Road & Track on Volvo 1957–1974*, p. 5.
31. Thos L. Bryant, 'Road Test: Volvo 122-S', *Road & Track*, September 1959, in *Road & Track on Volvo 1957–1974*, p. 5.
32. Jerry Titus, 'Road Test: Volvo 544 Sports', *Sports Car Graphic*, April 1962, in Clarke, *Volvo PV444 & PV544, 1945–1965*, p. 74.
33. Advertisement, probably 1966, in Clarke, *Forty Years of Selling Volvo*, p. 15.
34. Bengt Sahlström, 'Mot väst. Första Amazonen i USA', *Classic Cars*, no. 7 (2006), pp. 26–28.

35. John Christy, 'Volvo 122S: Road Test', *Sports Cars Illustrated*, August 1960, in *Car and Driver: On Volvo 1955–1986*, p. 116; and 'Road Test: Volvo 122S', *Car and Driver*, April 1962, in *Car and Driver: On Volvo 1955–1986*, p. 25.
36. Borgeson, 'Swedish Invasion: PV 444', p. 26.
37. 'Road Test . . . Sweden's Hot Volvo', *Motor Life*, October 1956, in Clarke, *Volvo PV444 & PV544, 1945–1965*, p. 23; and 'A Hotter Volvo: Road Test', *Sports Cars Illustrated*, October 1957, in *Car and Driver: On Volvo 1955–1986*, p. 13.
38. Floyd Clamer, 'Floyd Clamer Road Tests the Volvo 122S', *Auto Topics*, in R.W. Clarke (ed.), *Volvo 120 Amazon: Ultimate Portfolio* (Cobham: Brookland Books, 1991), p. 121.
39. 'Road Test: Volvo P-1800S', *Road & Track*, October 1965, in *Road & Track on Volvo 1957–1974*, p. 48.
40. 'Road Test: Volvo 144S', *Car and Driver*, April 1967, in *Car and Driver: On Volvo 1955–1986*, p. 38.
41. 'Road Test: Volvo 164', *Road & Track*, May 1969, in *Road & Track on Volvo 1957–1974*, p. 64.
42. 'Road Test: Volvo 164', *Car and Driver*, July 1969, in *Car and Driver: On Volvo 1955–1986*, pp. 45–47.
43. Dennis Simanaitis, 'Volvo 760GLE', *Road & Track*, July 1982, in *Road & Track on Volvo 1977–1994*, p. 34.
44. 'Road Test: Volvo 740 Turbo Wagon', *Road & Track*, June 1985, in *Road & Track on Volvo 1977–1994*, p. 62.
45. Hanne Niss, *Made in Denmark: Nationalitetens betydning i international markedsføring* (Aalborg: Aalborg Universitetsforlag, 1994), p. 9.
46. Karjalainen, *Semantic Transformation in Design*, p. 123.
47. 'It's Swift, Sexy, and from Volvo?' *AutoWeek*, 18 May 1998, pp. 22–23.
48. Karjalainen, *Semantic Transformation in Design*, p. 126.
49. US National Highway Transport Safety Authority, http://www.nhtsa.dot.gov/cars/testing/ncap/, accessed 21 May 2007.
50. Karjalainen, *Semantic Transformation in Design*, pp. 131, 189.
51. Ibid., p. 121.
52. Ibid., p. 189.
53. Hedvig Hedqvist, 'Volvos ränder går aldrig ur', *Svenska Dagbladet*, 9 October 1999.
54. Lasse Swärd, 'Volvo fick designpris för S80', *Svenska Dagbladet*, 11 March 1993.
55. Volvo Car Corporation, 'Design & Development' [press release], 22 February 2007, Global Newsroom website, https://www.media.volvocars.com/global/enhanced/en-gb/Media/Preview.aspx?mediaid=10700, accessed 5 October 2010.

56. See e.g. the survey 'Nation Brands Index 2010' published on the website Nation Branding by Andreas Markessinis, http://nation-branding.info/2010/10/13/nation-brands-index-2010/, accessed 13 October 2010.

CHAPTER 13 FROM POLICIES TO POLITICS

1. For a broader context for this point and the essay in general, see Pekka Korvenmaa, *Finnish Design: A Concise History* (Helsinki: University of Art and Design Helsinki, 2009). The topic of Finnish design in the 1960s and 1970s and especially the politics of design and the coming of age of industrial design is also addressed in Pekka Korvenmaa, 'Tietoisuuden tasot', in Pia Strandman (ed.), *Taideteollisuuden muotoja ja murroksia: Taideteollinen korkeakoulu 130 vuotta* (Helsinki: Taideteollinen korkeakoulu, 1999), pp. 172–200.
2. The EFTA and other measures increasing international free trade posed significant challenges to the consumer goods industry throughout Scandinavia. For a Norwegian case of revised design strategies in response to this development, see Kjetil Fallan, 'The *Realpolitik* of the Artificial: Strategic Design at Figgjo Fajanse Facing International Free Trade in the 1960s', *Enterprise and Society* 10/3 (2009), pp. 559–589.
3. Korvenmaa, 'Tietoisuuden tasot', p. 173.
4. Quoted in ibid., p. 193.
5. For more on this remarkable event, see Paola Nicolin, 'Protest by Design: Giancarlo De Carlo and the 14th Milan Triennale', in David Crowley and Jane Pavitt (eds.), *Cold War Modern: Design 1945–1970* (London: V&A Publishing, 2008), pp. 228–233.

EPILOGUE

1. Pekka Korvenmaa, *Finnish Design: A Concise History* (Helsinki: University of Art and Design Helsinki, 2009); and Lasse Brunnström, *Svensk designhistoria* (Stockholm: Raster, 2010).
2. A few examples of studies that do discuss gender issues are Harri Kalha, 'Kaj Franck & Kilta: Gendering the (Aesth)Ethics of Modernism', *Scandinavian Journal of Design History* 10 (2000), pp. 29–45; Kirsi Saarikangas, 'Displays of the Everyday: Relations between Gender and the Visibility of Domestic Work in the Modern Finnish Kitchen from the 1930s to the 1950s', *Gender, Place and Culture* 13/2 (2006), pp. 161–172; and Johanna Rosenqvist, *Könsskillnadens estetik? Om konst och konstskapande i svensk hemslöjd 1920–1990-talet* [Doctoral thesis] (Stockholm: Nordiska museets förlag, 2007).

3. Kjetil Rolness, *Med smak skal hjemmet bygges: Innredning av det moderne Norge* (Oslo: Aschehoug, 1995).
4. Morten Bing, Torgeir Kjos and Birte Sandvik, En historiebok i tre etasjer: Boskikk i byen 1865–2002 (Oslo: Cappelen Damm, 2011), pp. 245–251.
5. An early example of the emerging interest in this field can be found in Ida Engholm's bid at outlining a history of website design: Engholm, *WWW's designhistorie: Webudviklingen i et genre og stilteoretisk perspektiv* [Doctoral thesis] (Copenhagen: IT University of Copenhagen, 2003).

Select Bibliography

Aaker, D. A., *Building Strong Brands*, London: Simon & Schuster, 2002.

Aaltonen, S., *Sisustaminen on kuin käsialaa: Carin Bryggman ja Lasse Ollinkari sisustusarkkitehdin ammatissa 1940-ja 1950-luvuilla* [Doctoral thesis], Helsinki: University of Helsinki, 2010.

Aav, M., J. Savolainen, L. Svinhufvud and E. Viljanen (eds.), *Naisen muoto*, Helsinki: Designmuseo, 2006.

Aav, M., and N. Stritzler-Levine (eds.), *Finnish Modern Design: Utopian Ideals and Everyday Realities 1930–1997*, New York and New Haven, CN: Bard Graduate Center and Yale University Press, 1998.

Akrich, M., 'User Representations: Practices, Methods and Sociology', in A. Rip, T. J. Misa and J. Schot (eds.), *Managing Technology in Society: The Approach of Constructive Technology Assessment*, London: Pinter, 1995.

Ashby, C., 'Nation Building and Design: Finnish Textiles and the Work of the Friends of Finnish Handicrafts', *Journal of Design History* 23/4 (2010), pp. 351–365.

Asplund, G., W. Gahn, S. Markelius, G. Paulsson, E. Sundahl and U. Åhrén, *Acceptera*, Stockholm: Tidens Förlag, 1931.

Bay, C.-E., and H.-C. Jensen (eds.), *Tradition og modernisme: Indfaldsvinkler til PH*, Odense: Syddansk Universitetsforlag, 2008.

Belk, R. W., 'Possessions and the Extended Self', *Journal of Consumer Research* 15/2 (1988), pp. 139–168.

Bergman, B., *Handelsplats, shopping, stadsliv*, Stockholm and Stehag: Symposion, 2003.

Berman, M., *All That is Solid Melts into Air: The Experiences of Modernity*, New York: Verso, 1991.

Bing, M., *Østkanthjemmene og Østkantutstillingen: Boskikk og boligidealer i mellomkrigstidens Oslo*, Oslo: Norwegian Museum of Cultural History, 2001.

Bing, M., and E. Johnsen (eds.), *Nye Hjem: Bomiljøer i mellomkrigstiden*, Oslo: Norwegian Museum of Cultural History, 1998.

Bøe, A., *Nordisk industridesign: Hva, hvorfor, hvordan*, Oslo: Kunstindustrimuseet i Oslo, 1976.

Bøe, A., 'Kunsthåndverket 1980–1914: En nasjonal gjenstandskultur blir skapt', in K. Berg et al. (eds.), *Norges kunsthistorie*, vol. 5, Oslo: Gyldendal, 1981.

Bøe, A., 'Kunsthåndverk og kunstindustri 1914–1940', in K. Berg et al. (eds.), *Norges kunsthistorie*, vol. 6, Oslo: Gyldendal, 1983.

Bøe, A., 'Kunstindustri og industridesign etter 1940', in K. Berg et al. (eds.), *Norges kunsthistorie*, vol. 7, Oslo: Gyldendal, 1983.

Brøgger, S. (ed.), *Form og funktion: Sophienholm 1980*, Lyngby: Lyngby-Taarbæk Kommune, 1980.

Brunnström, Lasse (ed.), *Svensk industridesign: En 1900-tals historia*, Stockholm: Norstedt, 1997, and Stockholm: Prisma, 2004.

Brunnström, Lasse, *Svensk designhistoria*, Stockholm: Raster Förlag, 2010.

Brunnström, Lisa, *Det svenska folkhemsbygget: Om Kooperativa Förbundets arkitektkontor*, Stockholm: Arkitektur Förlag AB, 2004.

Bucciarelli, L., *Designing Engineers*, Cambridge, MA: MIT Press, 1994.

Calvera, A., 'Local, Regional, National, Global and Feedback: Several Issues to be Faced with Constructing Regional Narratives', *Journal of Design History* 18/4 (2005), pp. 371–383.

Centralförbundet för socialt arbete (CSA), *Bostadskongressens förhandlingar i Stockholm den 21–23 september*, Stockholm: Centralförbundet för socialt arbete, 1917.

Conway, H. (ed.), *Design History: A Student's Handbook*, London: Harper Collins, 1987.

Cowan, R. S., *A Social History of Technology*, New York: Oxford University Press, 1997.

Dorenfeldt, L. G., *Kongeligt Porcelæn 1820–1923—Blåmalet porcelæn fra Den Kongelige Porcelainsfabrik*, Copenhagen: Nyt Nordisk Forlag Arnold Busck, 2002.

Dybdahl, L., 'The Scandinavian Countries: From the Viking Revival toward Functional Objectivity', in C. Pirovano (ed.), *History of Industrial Design: 1851–1918—The Great Emporium of the World*, Milan: Electa, 1990.

Dybdahl, L. (ed.), *Dansk design 1910–1945: Art déco og funktionalisme*, Copenhagen: Danish Museum of Art and Design, 1997.

Dybdahl, L. (ed.), *De industrielle ikoner: Design Danmark*, Copenhagen: Danish Museum of Art and Design, 2004.

Dybdahl, L., *Dansk design 1945–1975*, Copenhagen: Borgen, 2006.

Elsässer, B., *Svensk bilindustri: En framgångshistoria*, Stockholm: SNS, 1995.

Fallan, K., 'How an Excavator Got Aesthetic Pretensions—Negotiating Design in 1960s' Norway', *Journal of Design History* 20/1 (2007), pp. 43–59.

Fallan, K., *Modern Transformed: The Domestication of Industrial Design Culture in Norway, ca. 1940–1970* [Doctoral thesis], Trondheim: Norwegian University of Science and Technology, 2007.

Fallan, K., 'Architecture in Action: Traveling with Actor-Network Theory in the Land of Architectural Research', *Architectural Theory Review* 13/1 (2008), pp. 80–96.

Fallan, K., 'De-scribing Design: Appropriating Script Analysis to Design History', *Design Issues* 24/4 (2008), pp. 61–75.

Fallan, K., 'Form, Function, Fiction: Translations of Technology and Design in Product Development', *History and Technology* 24/1 (2008), pp. 61–87.

Fallan, K., 'An ANT in Our Pants? A Design Historian's Reflections on Actor-Network Theory', in F. Hackney, J. Glynne and V. Minton (eds.), *Networks of Design: Proceedings of the 2008 Annual International Conference of the Design History Society (UK) University College Falmouth, 3–6 September*, Boca Raton, FL: Universal-Publishers, 2009.

Fallan, K., '"One Must Offer 'Something for Everyone'": Designing Crockery for Consumer Consent in 1950s' Norway', *Journal of Design History* 22/2 (2009), pp. 133–149.

Fallan, K., 'The *Realpolitik* of the Artificial: Strategic Design at Figgjo Fajanse Facing International Free Trade in the 1960s', *Enterprise and Society* 10/3 (2009), pp. 559–589.

Fallan, K., 'Crafting Scandinavian Design: Craft vs. Industrial Design in the Norwegian Contributions to the *Design in Scandinavia* and *X Triennale di Milano* Exhibitions', in J. Gimeno-Martinez and F. Floré (eds.), *Design and Craft: A History of Convergences and Divergences*, Brussels: Koninklijke vlaamse academie van Belgie voor Wetenschappen en kunsten, 2010, pp. 420–424. [Proceedings of the 7th Conference of the International Committee of Design History and Design Studies (ICDHS), 20–22 September 2010.]

Fallan, K., *Design History: Understanding Theory and Method*, Oxford: Berg, 2010.

Fallan, K., 'The Metamorphosis of a Norwegian Design Magazine: *nye bonytt*, 1968–1971', in G. Lees-Maffei (ed.), *Writing Design: Words and Objects*, Oxford: Berg, 2011, pp. 47–61.

Flusser, V., *The Shape of Things: A Philosophy of Design*, London: Reaktion, 1999.

Friedel, R., 'A New Metal! Aluminum in its 19th-century Context', in S. Nichols (ed.), *Aluminum by Design*, Pittsburgh: Carnegie Museum of Art, 2000.

Gelfer-Jørgensen, M., *Dansk kunsthåndværk fra 1850 til vor tid*, Copenhagen: Nyt Nordisk Forlag Arnold Busck, 1982.

Glambek, I., *Kunsten, nytten og moralen: Kunstindustri og husflid i Norge 1800–1900*, Oslo: Solum Forlag, 1988.

Glambek, I., *Det nordiske i arkitektur og design: Sett utenfra*, Copenhagen and Oslo: Arkitektens Forlag and Norsk Arkitekturforlag, 1997.

Glambek, I., 'The Council Chambers in the UN Building in New York', *Scandinavian Journal of Design History* 15 (2005), pp. 8–39.

Gronow, J., *The Sociology of Taste*, New York and London: Routledge, 1997.

Guffey, E., *Retro: The Culture of Revival*, London: Reaktion, 2006.

Halén, W., and K. Wickman (eds.), *Scandinavian Design beyond the Myth*, Stockholm: Arvinius Förlag, 2003.

Hallström Bornold, S., *Det är rätt att göra uppror: Mah-Jong 1966–1976*, Stockholm: Modernista, 2003.

Hansen, P. H., *Da danske møbler blev moderne*, Copenhagen and Odense: Aschehoug and Syddansk Universitetsforlag, 2006.

Henden, J., H. O. Frøland and A. Karlsen (eds.), *Globalisering gjennom et århundre: Norsk aluminiumindustri 1908–2008*, Bergen: Fagbokforlaget, 2008.

Holt, D. B., *How Brands Become Icons: The Principle of Cultural Branding*, Boston: Harvard Business School of Publishing Corporation, 2004.

Huovio, I., *Invitation from the Future: Treatise on the Roots of the School for Arts and Crafts and its Development into a University-level School 1871–1973* [Doctoral thesis], Tampere: University of Tampere, 1998.

Hård, M., and A. Jamison (eds.), *The Intellectual Appropriation of Technology: Discourses on Modernity, 1900–1939*, Cambridge, MA: MIT Press, 1998.

Hård, M., and A. Jamison, *Hubris and Hybrids: A Cultural History of Technology and Science*, New York: Routledge, 2005.

Hård af Segerstad, U., *Modern Scandinavian Furniture*, Oslo: Gyldendal Norsk Forlag, 1963.

Inghe, G., and M.-B. Inghe, *Den ofärdiga välfärden*, Stockholm: Tiden/Folksam, 1967.

Jensen, J., *Anderledes, men ikke mærkelig: En designers erindringer*, Copenhagen: Gyldendal, 1997.

Jevnaker, B. H., 'Vita Activa: On Relationships between Design(ers) and Business', *Design Issues* 21/3 (2005), pp. 25–48.

Johnsen, E., *Det moderne hjemmet 1910–1940* [Doctoral thesis], Oslo: University of Oslo, 2002.

Johnson, J. [Bruno Latour], 'Mixing Humans and Nonhumans Together: The Sociology of a Door-closer', *Social Problems* 35/3 (1988), pp. 298–310.

Jørgensen, F. A., *Making a Green Machine: The Infrastructure of Beverage Container Recycling*, New Brunswick, NJ: Rutgers University Press, 2011.

Julier, G., *The Culture of Design*, 2nd edn, London: Sage, 2008.

Kaiser, B., *Den ideologiske funktionalisme*, Copenhagen: Gad, 1992.

Kalha, H., *Muotopuolen merenneidon pauloissa: Suomen taideteollisuuden kultakausi: Mielikuvat, markkinointi, diskurssit* [Doctoral thesis], Helsinki: Apeiron, 1997.

Kalha, H., 'Myths and Mysteries of Finnish Design: Reading "Wirkkala" and the National Nature Paradigm', *Journal of Scandinavian Design History* 12 (2002), pp. 24–47.

Kant, I., 'Von der Unrechtmäßigkeit des Büchernachdrucks', *Berlinische Monatsschrift* 5 (May 1785), pp. 403–417.

Kant, I., *Critique of Judgment. Including the First Introduction*, translated with an introduction by W. S. Pluhar, Indianapolis: Hackett, 1987.

Karjalainen, T.-M., *Semantic Transformation in Design: Communicating Strategic Brand Identity through Product Design References* [Doctoral thesis], Helsinki: University of Art and Design Helsinki, 2004.

Karlsen, A., *Dansk møbelkunst i det 20. århundrede*, vols 1–2, Copenhagen: Christian Ejlers, 1991.

Karlsson, S. O., *Arbetarfamiljen och det nya hemmet: Om bostadshygienism och klasskultur i mellankrigstidens Göteborg* [Doctoral thesis], Linköping: Linköping University, 1993.

Katz, B. M., 'Technology and Design: A New Agenda', *Technology and Culture* 38/2 (1997), pp. 452–466.

Kaveh, S., *Det villkorade tillståndet: Centralförbundet för socialt arbete och liberal politisk rationalitet 1901–1921* [Doctoral thesis], Uppsala: Uppsala University, 2006.

Koivisto, K. *Kolme tarinaa lasista* [Doctoral thesis], Vammala: Suomen lasimuseo, 2001.

Korvenmaa, P., *Finnish Design: A Concise History*, Helsinki: University of Art and Design Helsinki, 2009.

Kruskopf, E., *Suomen taideteollisuus: Suomalaisen muotoilun vaiheita*, Porvoo: WSOY, 1989. Swedish ed.: *Finlands konstindustri: Den finländska konstflitens utvecklingshistoria*, Borgå: Söderström, 1989.

LaCapra, D., *History and Criticism*, Ithaca, NY: Cornell University Press, 1985.

Latour, B., *Reassembling the Social: An Introduction to Actor-Network Theory*, Oxford: Oxford University Press, 2005.

Law, J., 'Technology and Heterogeneous Engineering: The Case of Portuguese Expansion', in W. E. Bijker, T. P. Hughes and T. J. Pinch (eds.), *The Social Construction of Technological Systems: New Directions in the Sociology and History of Technology*, Cambridge, MA: MIT Press, 1987, pp. 111–134.

Lees-Maffei, G., 'The Production-Consumption-Mediation Paradigm', *Journal of Design History* 22/4 (2009), pp. 351–376.

Lees-Maffei, G. (ed.), *Writing Design: Words and Objects*, Oxford: Berg, 2011.

Lie, M., and K. H. Sørensen (eds.), *Making Technology Our Own? Domesticating Technology into Everyday Life*, Oslo: Scandinavian University Press, 1996.

Lindblom, A. (ed.), *Arbetaren i helg och söcken: Kulturhistoriska studier. 1. Hus och hem*, Stockholm: Tidens Förlag, 1943.

Linderborg, Å., *Socialdemokraterna skriver historia: Historieskrivning som ideologisk maktresurs 1892–2000*, Stockholm: Atlas, 2001.

Lindh, B.-E., *Volvo: Personvagnarna från 20-tal till 90-tal*, Malmö: Förlagshuset Norden, 1988.

Lowenthal, D., *The Past is a Foreign Country*, Cambridge and New York: Cambridge University Press, 1985.

Lutteman, H. D., and M. Uggla (eds.), *The Lunning Prize*, Stockholm: Nationalmuseum, 1986.

Má⊠el, O., 'Avant-garde Design and the Law: Litigation over the Cantilever Chair', *Journal of Design History* 3/2–3 (1990), pp. 125–143.

McCracken, G., *Culture and Consumption II: Markets, Meaning and Brand Management*, Bloomington: Indiana University Press, 2005.

McDonald, G., 'The Modern American Home as Soft Power: Finland, MoMA and the "American Home 1953" Exhibition', *Journal of Design History* 23/4 (2010), pp. 387–408.

McFadden, D. R. (ed.), *Modern Scandinavian Design 1880–1980*, New York: Harry N. Abrams, 1982.

MacKenzie, D., and J. Wajcman (eds.), *The Social Shaping of Technology*, Philadelphia: Open University Press, 1999.

Maldonado, T., 'The Idea of Comfort', in Victor Margolin and Richard Buchanan (eds.), *The Idea of Design: A Design Issues Reader*, Cambridge, MA: MIT Press, 1995, pp. 248–256.

Mattsson, H., *Arkitektur och konsumtion: Reyner Banham och utbytbarhetens estetik*, Stockholm and Stehag: Symposion, 2004.

Mattsson, H., and S.-O. Wallenstein (eds.), *Swedish Modernism: Architecture, Consumption, and the Welfare State*, London: Black Dog, 2010.

Meikle, J. L., *Twentieth Century Limited: Industrial Design in America, 1925–39*, Philadelphia: Temple University Press, 1979.

Michl, J., 'On Seeing Design as Redesign: An Exploration of a Neglected Problem in Design Education', *Scandinavian Journal of Design History* 12 (2002), pp. 7–23.

Miller, D., 'Appropriating the State on the Council Estate', *Man* 23/2 (1988), pp. 353–372.

Møller, V. S., *Funktionalisme og brugskunst siden 1920erne: Danmark. Norge. Sverige*, Copenhagen: Rhodos, 1978.

Møller, V. S., *Dansk kunstindustri 1900–1950*, vols 1–2, Copenhagen: Rhodos, 1970.

Niinimäki, K., and M.-R. Saloniemi (eds.), *Kretongista printtiin: Suomalaisen painokankaan historia/From Cretonne to Print: The History of Finnish Printed Textiles*, Helsinki: Maahenki Oy, 2008.

Niss, H., *Made in Denmark: Nationalitetens betydning i international markedsføring*, Aalborg: Aalborg Universitetsforlag, 1994.

Nye, D. E., *Technology Matters: Questions to Live With*, Cambridge, MA: MIT Press, 2007.

O'Doherty, B., *Inside the White Cube: The Ideology of the Gallery Space*, London: University of California Press, 1999.

Olafsdottir, A. *Le mobilier d'Alvar Aalto dans l'espace et dans le temps: La diffusion internationale de design 1920–1940* [Doctoral thesis], Paris: Université Paris 1, 1998.

Olesen, C. H., 'Designeren og mesterværket', in J. Jensen et al., *Bang & Olufsen 1960–1990: Fra dansk kvalitetsmærke til internationalt ikon*, Viborg: Hovedland, 2003, pp. 9–111.

Opie, J. H., *Scandinavia: Ceramics and Glass in the Twentieth Century*, London: Victoria & Albert Museum, 1989.

Opstad, J.-L., *Norsk emalje: Kunsthåndverk i verdenstoppen*, Oslo: Huitfeldt, 1994.

Oudshoorn, N., and T. Pinch, *How Users Matter: The Co-construction of Users and Technology*, Cambridge, MA: MIT Press, 2003.

Priha, P. (ed.), *Rakkaat Ystävät: Suomen Käsityön Ystävät 120 vuotta*, Helsinki: Ajatus, 1999.

Remlov, A. (ed.), *Design in Scandinavia: An Exhibition of Objects for the Home from Denmark, Finland, Norway, Sweden*, Oslo: Kirstes Boktrykkeri, 1954.

Resirk, *Pante-og retursystemer på drikkevaresektoren i Norge*, Oslo: Resirk, 1990.

Robach, C., *Formens frigörelse: Konsthantverk och design under debatt i 1960-talets Sverige*, Stockholm: Arvinius Förlag, 2010.

Rosenmeier, M., *Værkslæren i Ophavsretten*, Copenhagen: Jurist og Økonomforbundets Forlag, 2001.

Rosenmeier, M., and S. Teilmann (eds.), *Art and Law: The Copyright Debate*, Copenhagen: Association of Danish Economists and Lawyers (DJOEF) Publishing, 2005.

Røsrud, E., *Dagligvareforbundets rolle og virke mot år 2000*, Oslo: Dagligvareforbundet, 2003.

Rydberg Mitchell, B., *Att bo med soffa: En möbels betydelse för bostadens planering och livet i hemmet*, Lund: Lunds tekniska högskola, 2001.

Sarantola-Weiss, M. (ed.), *Rooms for Everyone: Perspectives on Finnish Interior Design 1949–1999*, Helsinki: Otava, 1999.

Sarantola-Weiss, M., *Sohvaryhmän läpimurto: Kulutuskulttuurin tulo suomalaisiin olohuoneisiin 1960- ja 1970-lukujen vaihteessa*, Helsinki: Finnish Literature Society, 2003.

Sarantola-Weiss, M., 'Representations of the Finnish Home in the Interior Decoration Magazines of the 1960s and 1970s', in Hanna Johansson and Kirsi Saarikangas (eds.), *Homes in Transformation: Dwelling, Moving, Belonging*, Helsinki: Finnish Literature Society, 2009, pp. 39–73.

Schot, J., and A. Albert de la Bruheze, 'The Mediated Design of Products, Consumption, and Consumers in the Twentieth Century', in N. Oudshoorn and T. Pinch (eds.), *How Users Matter: The Co-construction of Users and Technology*, Cambridge, MA: MIT Press, 2003.

Sheridan, M., et al., *Poul Kjærholm: Møbelarkitekt*, Humlebæk: Louisiana Museum of Modern Art, 2006.

Smith, M. M., *Sensory History*, Oxford and New York: Berg, 2007.

Sotamaa, Y., and P. Strandman (eds.), *Taideteollisuuden muotoja ja murroksia: Taideteollinen korkeakoulu 130 vuotta*, Helsinki: University of Art and Design Helsinki, 1999.

Staniszewski, M. A., *The Power of Display: A History of Exhibition Installations at the Museum of Modern Art*, London: MIT Press, 1998.

Staudenmaier, J. M., *Technology's Storytellers, Reweaving the Human Fabric*, Cambridge, MA: MIT Press, 1985.

Steffen, G., *Bostadsfrågan i Sverige ur sociologiska och socialpolitiska synpunkter*, Stockholm: Bostadskomissionens utredningar, 1918.

Stevenson, C. 'Decorative Art Production in the Scandinavian Kingdoms', in C. Pirovano (ed.), *History of Industrial Design: 1750–1850—The Age of the Industrial Revolution*, Milan: Electa, 1990.

Svinhufvud, L., 'Finnish Textiles en Route to Modernity', in M. Aav and N. Stritzler-Levine (eds.), *Finnish Modern Design: Utopian Ideals and Everyday Realities 1930–97*, New Haven, CN, and London: Bard Graduate Center for Studies in the Decorative Arts and Yale University Press, 1998, pp. 181–207.

Svinhufvud, L., 'Ryijy, berberimatto ja modernismin toinen', in T. Palin (ed.) and R. Suominen-Kokkonen (ed. in chief), *Modernia on moneksi: Kuvataiteen, taideteollisuuden ja arkkitehtuurin piirteitä maailmansotien välisen ajan Suomessa*, Taidehistoriallisia tutkimuksia 29, Helsinki: Taidehistorian seura, 2004, pp. 38–53.

Svinhufvud, L., *Moderneja ryijyjä, metritavaraa, käsityötä: Tekstiilitaide ja nykyaikaistuva taideteollisuus Suomessa maailmansotien välisenä aikana*, Helsinki: Designmuseo, 2009.

Svinhufvud, L., 'Textiles in Modern Spaces: Limitations and Counter-images', in M. Aav and J. Savolainen (eds.), *Modernism: Articles on Finnish Modernism*, Helsinki: Designmuseo, 2010, pp. 6–37.

Svinhufvud, L., and E. Viljanen (eds.), *Ryijy! The Finnish Ryijy-Rug*, Helsinki: Designmuseo, 2009.

Teilmann, S., 'Framing the Law: The Right of Integrity in Britain', *European Intellectual Property Review*, no. 1 (2005), pp. 19–24.

Teilmann-Lock, S., *British and French Copyright: A Historical Study of Aesthetic Implications*, Copenhagen: Association of Danish Economists and Lawyers (DJOEF) Publishing, 2009.

Tøjner, P. E., *Store danske designere*, Copenhagen: Lindhardt og Ringhof, 2008.

Treiger-Bar-Am, K., 'Kant on Copyright: Rights of Transformative Authorship', *Cardozo Arts & Entertainment Law Journal* 25/3 (2008), pp. 1059–1103.

Usunier, J.-C., *Marketing across Culture*, London: Prentice Hall, 1996.

Valtonen, A., *Redefining Industrial Design: Changes in the Design Practice in Finland* [Doctoral thesis], Helsinki: University of Art and Design Helsinki, 2007.

Veiteberg, J., *Craft in Transition*, Bergen: Bergen National Academy of the Arts, 2005.

Verbeek, P., *What Things Do: Philosophical Reflections on Technology, Agency, and Design*, University Park: Pennsylvania State University Press, 2005.

Vidler, A., *The Architectural Uncanny: Essays in the Modern Unhomely*, London: MIT Press, 1992.

Vinck, D. (ed.), *Everyday Engineering: An Ethnography of Design and Innovation*, Cambridge, MA: MIT Press, 2003.

Walker, J. A., *Design History and the History of Design*, London: Pluto Press, 1989.

Weium, F. (ed.), *Plast i det moderne Norge*, Oslo: Norwegian Museum of Science and Technology, 2001.

Werner, J., *Medelvägens estetik*, vols 1–2, Möklinta: Gidlunds, 2008.

White, H., *The Content of the Form: Narrative Discourse and Historical Representation*, Baltimore: Johns Hopkins University Press, 1987.

Wiberg, M., *The Textile Designer and the Art of Design: On the Formation of a Profession in Finland* [Doctoral thesis], Helsinki: University of Art and Design Helsinki, 1996.

Wickman, K. (ed.), *Formens rörelse: Svensk form genom 150 år*, Stockholm: Carlssons, 1995.

Widman, D., *Konsthantverk, konstindustri, design 1895–1975*, Stockholm: AWE/Geber, 1975.

Wildhagen, F., *Norge i form: Kunsthåndverk og design under industrikulturen*, Oslo: J. M. Stenersens Forlag, 1988.

Wildhagen, F., 'The Scandinavian Countries: Design for the Welfare Society', in C. Pirovano (ed.), *History of Industrial Design: 1919–1990—The Dominion of Design*, Milan: Electa, 1990.

Woodham, J. M., *Twentieth-century Design*, Oxford: Oxford University Press, 1997.

Woodham, J. M., 'Local, National and Global: Redrawing the Design Historical Map', *Journal of Design History* 18/3 (2005), pp. 257–267.

Zahle, E. (ed.), *A Treasury of Scandinavian Design: The Standard Authority on Scandinavian-designed Furniture, Textiles, Glass, Ceramics, and Metal*, New York: Golden Press, 1961.

Zetterlund, C., *Design i informationsåldern: Om strategisk design, historia och praktik* [Doctoral thesis, Uppsala University] (Stockholm: Raster Förlag, 2002).

Index